LIVING IN THE END TIMES

LIVING IN THE END TIMES

SLAVOJ ŽIŽEK

VERSO

London • New York

First published by Verso 2010
© Slavoj Žižek 2010
All rights reserved

1 3 5 7 9 10 8 6 4 2

Verso
UK: 6 Meard Street, London W1F 0EG
US: 20 Jay Street, Suite 1010, Brooklyn, NY 11201
www.versobooks.com

Verso is the imprint of New Left Books

ISBN-13: 978-1-84467-598-2

British Library Cataloguing in Publication Data
A catalogue record for this book is available from the British Library

Library of Congress Cataloging-in-Publication Data
A catalog record for this book is available from the Library of Congress

Typeset in Cochin by Hewer Text UK Ltd, Edinburgh
Printed in the US by Worldcolor/Fairfield

Contents

Introduction: "The Spiritual Wickedness in the Heavens"

The twentieth anniversary of the fall of the Berlin Wall should have been a time for reflection. It has become a cliché to emphasize the "miraculous" nature of the fall of the Wall: it was like a dream come true. With the disintegration of the Communist regimes, which collapsed like a house of cards, something unimaginable happened, something one would not have considered possible even a couple of months earlier. Who in Poland could have imagined the arrival of free elections, or Lech Wałęsa as president? We should, however, note that an even greater "miracle" was to occur only a few years later: namely, the return of the ex-Communists to power through free democratic elections, and the total marginalization of Wałęsa who had become even more unpopular than the man who, a decade and a half earlier, had attempted to crush Solidarność in a military *coup*—General Wojciech Jaruzelski.

The standard explanation for this later reversal evokes the "immature" utopian expectations of the majority, whose desire was deemed contradictory, or, rather, inconsistent. The people wanted to have their cake and eat it: they wanted capitalist-democratic freedom and material abundance but without paying the full price of life in a "risk society"; that is, without losing the security and stability once (more or less) guaranteed by the Communist regimes. As sarcastic Western commentators duly noted, the noble struggle for freedom and justice turned out to be little more than a craving for bananas and pornography.

When the unavoidable sense of disappointment set in, it gave rise to three (sometimes opposed, sometimes overlapping) reactions: (1) nostalgia for the "good old" Communist era;[1] (2) right-wing nationalist

---

1 The exhaustion of twentieth-century Party-State Socialism is obvious. In a major public speech in August 2009, Raúl Castro attacked those who merely shout "Death to US imperialism! Long live the revolution!", instead of engaging in difficult and patient work. According to Castro, all the blame for the Cuban situation (a fertile land which imports 80 percent of its food) could be laid at the feet of the US embargo: there are idle people on the one side and empty tracts of land on the other. Surely the solution is just to start working the fields? While all this is obviously true, Castro nonetheless

populism; (3) a renewed and "belated" anti-Communist paranoia. The first two reactions are easy enough to comprehend. Communist nostalgia in particular should not be taken too seriously: far from expressing a genuine wish to return to the grey reality of the pre-existing regime, it was closer to a form of mourning, a process of gently relinquishing the past. The rise of rightist populism, for its part, is not an Eastern European specialty, but a feature common to all countries caught up in the vortex of globalization. More interesting then is the third reaction, the weird resurrection of anti-Communist paranoia two decades on. To the question "If capitalism is really so much better than socialism, why are our lives still miserable?" it provides a simple answer: it is because we are not yet really in capitalism, for the Communists are still ruling, only now wearing the masks of new owners and managers . . .

It is an obvious fact that, among the people protesting against the Communist regimes in Eastern Europe, a large majority of them were not demanding a capitalist society. They wanted social security, solidarity, some kind of justice; they wanted the freedom to live their own lives outside the purview of state control, to come together and talk as they please; they wanted a life liberated from primitive ideological indoctrination and the prevailing cynical hypocrisy. As many perspicuous analysts have observed, the ideals that inspired the protesters were to a large extent taken from the ruling socialist ideology itself—they aspired to what can most appropriately be designated "Socialism with a human face."

The crucial question is how we are to read the collapse of these hopes. The standard answer, as we have seen, appeals to capitalist realism, or the lack of it: the people simply did not possess a realistic image of capitalism; they were full of immature utopian expectations. The morning after the enthusiasm of the drunken days of victory, the people had to sober up and face the painful process of learning the rules of the new reality, coming to terms with the price one has to pay for political and economic freedom. It is, in effect, as if the European Left had to die twice: first as the "totalitarian" Communist Left, then as the moderate democratic Left which, over recent years, has been gradually losing ground in Italy, in France, in Germany. Up to a point, this process can be accounted for by the fact

---

forgot to include his own position in the picture he was describing: if people do not work the fields, it is obviously not because they are lazy, but because the state-run economy is not able to provide them with work. So, instead of lambasting ordinary people, he should have applied the old Stalinist motto according to which the motor of progress in Socialism is self-criticism, and subjected to radical critique the very system he and Fidel personify. Here, again, evil resides in the critical gaze which perceives evil all around . . .

that the centrist and even the conservative parties now in the ascendant have integrated many traditionally Leftist perspectives (support for some form of welfare state, tolerance towards minorities, etc.), to the extent that, were someone like Angela Merkel to present her program in the US, she would be dismissed as a radical Leftist. But this is indeed true only up to a point. In today's post-political democracy, the traditional bipolarity between a Social-Democratic Center-Left and a Conservative Center-Right is gradually being replaced by a new bipolarity between politics and post-politics: the technocratic-liberal multiculturalist-tolerant party of post-political administration and its Rightist-populist counterpart of passionate political struggle—no wonder that the old Centrist opponents (Conservatives or Christian Democrats and Social Democrats or Liberals) are often compelled to join forces against the common enemy.[2] (Freud wrote about *Unbehagen in der Kultur*, the discontent/unease in culture; today, twenty years after the fall of the Berlin Wall, we experience a kind of *Unbehagen* in liberal capitalism. The key question now is: who will articulate this discontent? Will it be left to nationalist populists to exploit? Therein resides the big task for the Left.)

Should we, then, dismiss the utopian impulse which motivated the anti-Communist protests as a sign of immaturity, or should we remain faithful to it? At this point, it is well worth noting that the resistance to Communism in Eastern Europe in fact took three successive forms: (1) the "revisionist" Marxist critique of really-existing Socialisms ("this is not true Socialism, we want a return to the authentic vision of Socialism as a free society")—here one might slyly remark that the same process went on in the early modern period in Europe, where secular opposition to the hegemonic role of religion first had to express itself in the guise of religious heresy; (2) the demand for an autonomous space of civil society freed from the constraints of Party-State control (this was the official position of Solidarity during the first years of its existence—its message to the Communist Party was: "we do not want power, we just want a free space outside your control where we can engage in critical reflection on

---

2   Two passionate explosions occurred in May 2008. In Italy, a mob burned the Roma slums in the suburbs of Rome (with the silent approval of the new Right-populist government); this scandal cannot but force us to recall the late Husserl's remark that, although the Gypsies have lived for centuries in Europe, they are not really a part of the European spiritual space—a remark all the more uncanny if one remembers that Husserl wrote this when the Nazis were already in power and he had been expelled from the university for exactly the same reasons—the Roma being effectively a kind of proxy Jewry. The other explosion took place in South Africa, when crowds attacked refugees from other countries (especially Zimbabwe), claiming that they were stealing their jobs and houses—an example of European populist racism reproducing itself among black Africans themselves.

what goes on in society"); (3) finally, the open struggle for power: "we *do* want full democratically legitimized power; which means it's time for you to go." Are the first two forms really just illusions (or rather, strategic compromises), and therefore to be discarded?

The underlying premise of the present book is a simple one: the global capitalist system is approaching an apocalyptic zero-point. Its "four riders of the apocalypse" are comprised by the ecological crisis, the consequences of the biogenetic revolution, imbalances within the system itself (problems with intellectual property; forthcoming struggles over raw materials, food and water), and the explosive growth of social divisions and exclusions.

To take up only the last point, nowhere are the new forms of apartheid more palpable than in the wealthy Middle Eastern oil states—Kuwait, Saudi Arabia, Dubai. Hidden on the outskirts of the cities, often literally behind walls, are tens of thousands of "invisible" immigrant workers doing all the dirty work, from servicing to construction, separated from their families and refused all privileges.[3] Such a situation clearly embodies an explosive potential which, while now exploited by religious fundamentalists, should have been channeled by the Left in its struggle against exploitation and corruption. A country like Saudi Arabia is literally "beyond corruption": there is no need for corruption because the ruling gang (the royal family) is already in possession of all the wealth, which it can distribute freely as it sees fit. In such countries, the only alternative to fundamentalist reaction would be a kind of social-democratic welfare state. Should this situation persist, can we even imagine the change in the Western "collective psyche" when (not *if*, but precisely *when*) some "rogue nation" or group obtains a nuclear device, or powerful biological or chemical weapon, and declares its "irrational" readiness to risk all in using it? The most basic coordinates of our awareness will have to change, insofar as, today, we live in a state of collective fetishistic disavowal: we know very well that this will happen at some point, but nevertheless cannot

---

3   See Johann Hari, "A morally bankrupt dictatorship built by slave labour," *Independent*, November 27, 2009, p. 6. Invisible to those who visit Dubai for the glitz of the consumerist high-society paradise, immigrant workers are ringed off in filthy suburbs with no air conditioning. They are brought to Dubai from Bangladesh or the Philippines, lured by the promise of high wages; once in Dubai, their passports are taken, they are informed that the wages will be much lower than promised, and then have to work for years in extremely dangerous conditions just to pay off their initial debt (incurred through the expense of bringing them to Dubai); if they protest or strike, they are simply beaten into submission by the police. This is the reality sustained by great "humanitarians" like Brad Pitt who invested heavily in Dubai.

bring ourselves to really believe that it will. The US attempt to prevent such an occurrence through continuous pre-emptive activity is a battle that has been lost in advance: the very notion that it might succeed relies on a fantasmatic vision.

A more standard form of "inclusive exclusion" are the slums—large areas outside of state governance. While generally perceived as spaces in which gangs and religious sects fight for control, slums also offer the space for radical political organizations, as is the case in India, where the Maoist movement of Naxalites is organizing a vast alternate social space. To quote an Indian state official: "The point is if you don't govern an area, it is not yours. Except on the maps, it is not part of India. At least half of India today is not being governed. It is not in your control . . . you have to create a complete society in which local people have very significant stakes. We're not doing that . . . And that is giving the Maoists space to move in."[4]

Although similar signs of the "great disorder under heaven" abound, the truth hurts, and we desperately try to avoid it. To explain how, we can turn to an unexpected guide. The Swiss-born psychologist Elisabeth Kübler-Ross proposed the famous scheme of the five stages of grief, which follow, for example, upon learning that one has a terminal illness: *denial* (one simply refuses to accept the fact: "This can't be happening, not to me"); *anger* (which explodes when we can no longer deny the fact: "How can this happen to me?"); *bargaining* (in the hope that we can somehow postpone or diminish the fact: "Just let me live to see my children graduate"); *depression* (libidinal disinvestment: "I'm going to die, so why bother with anything?"); and *acceptance* ("I can't fight it, so I may as well prepare for it"). Later, Kübler-Ross applied the same scheme to any form of catastrophic personal loss (joblessness, death of a loved one, divorce, drug addiction), emphasizing that the five stages do not necessarily come in the same order, nor are they all experienced by every patient.[5]

One can discern the same five figures in the way our social consciousness attempts to deal with the forthcoming apocalypse. The first reaction is one of ideological denial: there is no fundamental disorder; the second is exemplified by explosions of anger at the injustices of the new world order; the third involves attempts at bargaining ("if we change things here and there, life could perhaps go on as before"); when the bargaining fails, depression and withdrawal set in; finally, after passing through this zero-point, the subject no longer perceives the situation as a threat, but as the chance of a new beginning—or, as Mao Zedong put it: "There is great disorder under heaven, the situation is excellent."

The following five chapters refer to these five stances. Chapter 1—*denial*—analyzes the predominant modes of ideological obfuscation, from the latest Hollywood blockbusters up to false (displaced) apocalyptism (New Age obscurantism, and so forth). Chapter 2—*anger*—looks at violent protests against the global system, and the rise of religious fundamentalism in particular. Chapter 3—*bargaining*—focuses on the critique of political economy, with a plea for the renewal of this central ingredient of Marxist theory. Chapter 4—*depression*—considers the impact of the forthcoming collapse in its less familiar aspects, such as the rise of new forms of subjective pathology (the "post-traumatic" subject). Finally, Chapter 5—*acceptance*—discerns the signs of an emerging emancipatory subjectivity, isolating the germs of a communist culture in all its diverse forms, including in literary and other utopias (from Kafka's community of mice to the collective of freak outcasts in the TV series *Heroes*). This basic skeleton of the book is supplemented by four interludes, each of which provides a variation on the theme of the preceding chapter.

The turn towards an emancipatory enthusiasm takes place only when the traumatic truth is not only accepted in a disengaged way, but is fully lived: "Truth has to be lived, not taught. Prepare for battle!" Like Rilke's famous lines, "for there's no place that doesn't see you. You must change your life," this passage from Hermann Hesse's *The Glass Bead Game* cannot but appear as a weird non sequitur: if the Thing looks back at me from everywhere, why does this oblige me to change my life? Why not rather a depersonalized mystical experience in which I "step out of myself" and identify with the other's gaze? Likewise, if truth has to be lived, why need this involve a struggle? Why not rather a meditative inner experience? The reason is that the "spontaneous" state of our daily lives is that of a lived lie, to break out of which requires a continuous struggle. The starting point for this process is to become terrified by oneself. When, in his early "Contribution to the Critique of Hegel's *Philosophy of Right*," Marx analyzed the backwardness of Germany, he made a rarely noticed yet crucial observation about the link between *shame*, *terror* and *courage*:

> The actual burden must be made even more burdensome by creating an awareness of it. The humiliation must be increased by making it public. Each sphere of German society must be depicted as the *partie honteuse*

of that society and these petrified conditions must be made to dance by having their own tune sung to them! The people must be put in *terror* of themselves in order to give them *courage*.[6]

Such is our task today, when faced with the shameless cynicism of the existing global order.

In pursuing this task, one should not be afraid to learn from one's enemies. After meeting Nixon and Kissinger, Mao said: "I like to deal with rightists. They say what they really think—not like the leftists, who say one thing and mean another." There is a deep truth in this observation. Mao's lesson holds today even more than in his own day: one can learn much more from intelligent critical conservatives (*not* reactionaries) than one can from liberal progressives. The latter tend to obliterate the "contradictions" inherent in the existing order which the former are ready to admit as irresolvable. What Daniel Bell called the "cultural contradictions of capitalism" are at the origin of today's ideological malaise: the progress of capitalism, which necessitates a consumerist ideology, is gradually undermining the very (Protestant ethical) attitude which rendered capitalism possible—today's capitalism increasingly functions as the "institutionalization of envy."

The truth we are dealing with here is not "objective" truth, but the self-relating truth about one's own subjective position; as such, it is an engaged truth, measured not by its factual accuracy but by the way it affects the subjective position of enunciation. In his Seminar 18, on "a discourse which would not be of a semblance," Lacan provided a succinct definition of the truth of interpretation in psychoanalysis: "Interpretation is not tested by a truth that would decide by yes or no, it unleashes truth as such. It is only true inasmuch as it is truly followed." There is nothing "theological" in this precise formulation, only the insight into the properly dialectical unity of theory and practice in (not only) psychoanalytic interpretation: the "test" of the analyst's interpretation lies in the truth-effect it unleashes in the patient. This is also how one should (re)read Marx's Thesis XI: the "test" of Marxist theory is the truth-effect it unleashes in its addressees (the proletarians), in transforming them into revolutionary subjects.

The *locus communis* "You have to see it to believe it!" should always be read together with its inversion: "You have to believe in it to see it!"

---

6   Karl Marx, "A Contribution to the Critique of Hegel's *Philosophy of Right*. Introduction," in *Early Writings*, introduced by L. Colleti, Harmondsworth: Penguin 1975, p. 247.

Though one may be tempted to oppose these perspectives—the dogmatism of blind faith versus an openness towards the unexpected—one should nevertheless insist on the truth contained in the second version: truth, as opposed to knowledge, is, like a Badiouian Event, something that only an engaged gaze, the gaze of a subject who "believes in it," is able to see. Take the case of love: in love, only the lover sees in the object of love that X which is the cause of his love, the parallax-object; in this sense the structure of love is the same as that of the Badiouian Event, which also exists only for those who recognize themselves in it: there can be no Event for a non-engaged objective observer. Lacking this engaged position, mere descriptions of the state of things, no matter how accurate, fail to generate emancipatory effects—ultimately, they only render the burden of the lie still more oppressive, or, to quote Mao again, "lift up a rock only to drop it on their own feet."

When, in 1948, Sartre saw that he was likely to be maligned by both sides in the Cold War, he wrote: "if that were to happen, it would prove only one thing: either that I am very clumsy, or that I am on the right road."[7] As it happens, this is often how I also feel: I am attacked for being anti-Semitic *and* for spreading Zionist lies, for being a covert Slovene nationalist *and* an unpatriotic traitor to my nation,[8] for being a crypto-Stalinist defending terror *and* for spreading bourgeois lies about Communism . . . So maybe, just maybe, I am on the right path, the path of fidelity to freedom.[9] In the otherwise all too sentimental-humanist dialogue of Stanley Kubrick's *Spartacus*, there is an exchange between Spartacus and a pirate who offers to organize transport for the slaves across the Adriatic. The pirate asks Spartacus frankly whether he is aware that the slave rebellion is doomed, that sooner or later the rebels will be crushed by the Roman army; would he continue to fight to the end, even in the face of inevitable defeat? Spartacus's answer is, of course, affirmative: the slaves' struggle is not merely a pragmatic attempt to ameliorate their position, it is a principled rebellion on behalf of freedom, so even if they lose and are all killed, their fight will not have been in vain since they

---

7   Quoted in Ian H. Birchall, *Sartre Against Stalinism*, New York: Berghahn Books 2004, p. 3.

8   Golda Meir once said: "We can forgive Arabs for killing our children. We cannot forgive them for forcing us to kill their children." In a homologous way, I am tempted to say: I can forgive those who attack me as a bad Slovene for what they are doing to me, but I can never forgive them for forcing me to act as a representative of Slovene interests, thereby countering their primitive racism.

9   Fidelity should be strictly opposed to zealotry: a zealot's fanatical attachment to his Cause is nothing but a desperate expression of his uncertainty and doubt, of his lack of trust in the Cause. A subject truly dedicated to his Cause regulates his eternal fidelity by means of incessant betrayals.

will have asserted their unconditional commitment to freedom — in other words, their act of rebellion itself, whatever the outcome, already counts as a success, insofar as it instantiates the immortal idea of freedom (and one should give to "idea" here its full Platonic weight).

The present book is thus a book of struggle, following Paul's surprisingly relevant definition: "For our struggle is not against flesh and blood, but against leaders, against authorities, against the world rulers [*kosmokratoras*] of this darkness, against the spiritual wickedness in the heavens" (*Ephesians* 6:12). Or, translated into today's language: "Our struggle is not against actual corrupt individuals, but against those in power in general, against their authority, against the global order and the ideological mystification which sustains it." To engage in this struggle means to endorse Badiou's formula *mieux vaut un désastre qu'un désêtre*: better to take the risk and engage in fidelity to a Truth-Event, even if it ends in catastrophe, than to vegetate in the eventless utilitarian-hedonist survival of what Nietzsche called the "last men." What Badiou rejects is thus the liberal ideology of victimhood, with its reduction of politics to a program of avoiding the worst, to renouncing all positive projects and pursuing the least bad option. Not least since, as Arthur Feldmann, a Viennese Jewish writer, bitterly noted: the price we usually pay for survival is our lives.

1 Denial: The Liberal Utopia

Against the Tartar-Lovers

What is ideology? In January 2010 Jean-François Copé, the parliamentary leader of the *Union pour un Mouvement Populaire*, the ruling French party, proposed the draft of a law which bans the full-body veil from French streets and all other public places. This announcement came after an anguished six-month debate on the burqa and its Arab equivalent, the niqab, which cover the woman's face, except for a small slit for the eyes. All main political parties expressed their rejection of the burqa: the main opposition party, the *Parti Socialiste*, said it is "totally opposed to the burqa" which amounted to a "prison for women." The disagreements are of a purely tactical nature: although President Nicolas Sarkozy opposes an outright ban on the burqa as counter-productive, he called for a "debate on national identity" in October 2009, claiming that the burqa is "against French culture." The law imposes fines of up to 750 euros on anyone appearing in public "with their face entirely masked"; exemptions permit the wearing of masks on "traditional, festive occasions," such as carnivals. Stiffer punishments are proposed for men who "force" their wives or daughters to wear full-body veils. The underlying idea is that the burqa or niqab are contrary to French traditions of freedom and laws on women's rights, or, to quote Copé: "We can measure the modernity of a society by the way it treats and respects women." The new legislation is thus intended to protect the dignity and security of women — and what could be less problematic than such a struggle against an ideology (and a practice) which subjugates women to the most ruthless male domination?

Problems, however, begin with Sarkozy's statement that veils are "not welcome" because, in a secular country like France, they intimidate and alienate non-Muslims . . . one cannot but note how the allegedly universalist attack on the burqa on behalf of human rights and women's dignity ends up as a defense of the particular French way of life. It is, however, not enough to submit this law to pragmatic criticism, such as the claim that, if implemented, it will only increase the oppression of Muslim women, since they will simply not be allowed to leave home and thus be even more cut off from society, exposed to harsh treatment within forced marriages, etc. (Furthermore, the fine will exacerbate the problems of poverty and joblessness: it will punish the very women who are least likely to have control over their own money.) The problem is a more fundamental one—what makes the whole debate symptomatic is, first, the marginal status of the problem: the whole nation talks about it, while the total number of women wearing both types of full-body veil in France is around 2,000, out of a total French population of adult Muslim women of about 1,500,000. (And, incidentally, most of those women who wear full-length veils are below the age of thirty, with a substantial proportion of them being French women who have converted.) The next curious feature is the ambiguity of the critique of the burqa: it moves at two levels. First, it is presented as a defense of the dignity and freedom of oppressed Muslim women—it is unacceptable that, in a secular France, any woman has to live a hidden life secluded from public space, subordinated to brutal patriarchal authority, and so on. Secondly, however, as a rule the argument then shifts towards the anxieties of non-Muslim French people: faces covered by the burqa do not fit with the coordinates of French culture and identity, they "intimidate and alienate non-Muslims" ... Some French women have even suggested that they perceive the wearing of a burqa as *their own* humiliation, as being brutally excluded, rejected from a social link.

This brings us to the true enigma here: why does the encounter with a face covered by a burqa trigger such anxiety? Is it that a face so covered is no longer the Levinasian face: that Otherness from which the unconditional ethical call emanates? But what if the opposite is the case? From a Freudian perspective, the face is the ultimate mask that conceals the horror of the Neighbor-Thing: the face is what makes the Neighbor *le semblable*, a fellow-man with whom we can identify and empathize. (Not to mention the fact that, today, many faces are surgically modified and thus deprived of the last vestiges of natural authenticity.) This, then, is why the covered face causes such anxiety: because it confronts us directly with the abyss of the Other-Thing, with the Neighbor in its uncanny dimension. The very covering-up of the face obliterates a protective shield, so that the Other-Thing stares at us directly (recall that the burqa has a narrow slit for the eyes; we don't see the eyes, but we know there is a gaze there). Alphonse

Allais presented his own version of Salome's dance of seven veils: when Salome is completely naked, Herod shouts "Go on! On!", expecting her to take off also the veil of her skin. We should imagine something similar with the burqa: the opposite of a woman removing her burqa to reveal her face. What if we go a step further and imagine a woman "taking off" the skin of her face itself, so that what we see beneath is precisely an anonymous dark smooth burqa-like surface, with a narrow slit for the gaze? "Love thy neighbor!" means, at its most radical, precisely the impossible = real love for this de-subjectivized subject, for this monstrous dark blot cut with a slit/gaze . . . This is why, in psychoanalytic treatment, the patient does not sit face to face with the analyst: they both stare at a third point, since it is only this suspension of the face which opens up the space for the proper dimension of the Neighbor. And therein also resides the limit of the well-known critico-ideological topic of the society of total control, in which we are constantly tracked and recorded—what eludes the eye of the camera is not some intimate secret but the gaze itself, the object-gaze as the crack/stain in the Other.

This brings us to the proper base (almost in the military sense of the term) of ideology. When we read an abstract "ideological" proclamation we are well aware that "real people" do not experience it abstractly: in order to pass from abstract propositions to people's "real lives," it is necessary to add the unfathomable density of a lifeworld context. Ideology is not constituted by abstract propositions in themselves, rather, ideology is itself this very texture of the lifeworld which "schematizes" the propositions, rendering them "livable." Take military ideology for instance: it becomes "livable" only against the background of the obscene unwritten rules and rituals (marching chants, fragging, sexual innuendo . . .) in which it is embedded. Which is why, if there is an ideological experience at its purest, at its zero-level, then it occurs the moment we adopt an attitude of ironic distance, laughing at the follies in which we are ready to believe—it is at this moment of liberating laughter, when we look down on the absurdity of our faith, that we become pure subjects of ideology, that ideology exerts its strongest hold over us.[1] This is also why, if one wants to observe contemporary ideology at work, all one need do is watch a few of Michael Palin's travel programs on the BBC: their

---

1   We should here reject the underlying premise of Harry Frankfurt's critical analysis of bullshit: ideology is precisely what remains when we make the gesture of "cutting the bullshit" (no wonder that, when asked in an interview to name a politician not prone to bullshitting, Frankfurt named John McCain).

underlying attitude of adopting a benevolent ironic distance towards different customs, taking pleasure in observing local peculiarities while filtering out the really traumatic data, amounts to postmodern racism at its most essential. When we are shown scenes of starving children in Africa, with a call for us to do something to help them, the underlying *ideological* message is something like: "Don't think, don't politicize, forget about the true causes of their poverty, just act, contribute money, so that you will not have to think!" Rousseau already understood perfectly the falsity of multiculturalist admirers of foreign cultures when, in *Emile*, he warned of the "philosopher who loves Tartars in order to be dispensed from loving his neighbors."[2]

So, when we talk about "objective spirit" (the substance of mores) as the complex web of unwritten rules which determine what we can say/see/do, we should complicate further Foucault's description of a discursive *episteme*: "objective spirit" also and above all determines that which we know but about which we have to talk and act as if we do not know, and that which we do not know but about which we have to talk and act as if we do know. It determines, in short, what we have to know but have to pretend we do not know. The rise of so-called ethnic and religious fundamentalism is a rebellion against this thick network of mores which anchors our freedoms in a liberal society. What is feared is not the uncertainties of freedom and permissiveness, but, on the contrary, the oppressive web of new regulations.[3]

So where is ideology? When we are dealing with a problem which is undoubtedly real, the ideological designation-perception introduces its invisible mystification. For example, tolerance designates a real problem—when I criticize it, I am, as a rule, asked: "But how can you be in favor of intolerance towards foreigners, of misogyny, of homophobia?"

---

2   Sometimes, critique of ideology is just a matter of displacing the accent. Fox News's Glenn Beck, the infamous Groucho Marx of the populist Right, deserves his reputation for provoking laughter—but not where he intends to do so. The dramaturgy of his typical routine begins with a violently satiric presentation of his opponents and their arguments, accompanied by a grimacing worthy of Jim Carrey; this part, which is supposed to make us laugh, is then followed by a "serious" sentimental moral message. But we should simply postpone our laughter to this concluding moment: it is the stupidity of the final "serious" point which is laughable, not the acerbic satire whose vulgarity should merely embarrass any decent thinking person.

3   It would have been interesting to reread Marcel Proust against the background of this topic of unwritten customs: the problem of his *In Search of Lost Time* is "How is aristocracy possible in democratic times, once the external marks of hierarchy are abolished?", and his reply is: through the complex network of unwritten informal habits (gestures, tastes) by means of which those who are "in" recognize "their own," and identify those who just pretend to belong to the inner circle and are to be ostracized. I owe this reference to Proust to Mladen Dolar.

Therein resides the catch: of course I am not against tolerance per se; what I oppose is the (contemporary and automatic) perception of racism as a problem of intolerance. Why are so many problems today perceived as problems of intolerance, rather than as problems of inequality, exploitation, or injustice? Why is the proposed remedy tolerance, rather than emancipation, political struggle, or even armed struggle? The source of this culturalization is defeat, the failure of directly political solutions such as the social-democratic welfare state or various socialist projects: "tolerance" has become their post-political *ersatz*. (The same goes for "harassment": in today's ideological space, very real forms of harassment such as rape are intertwined with the narcissistic notion of the individual who experiences the close proximity of others as an intrusion into his or her private space.) "Ideology" is, in this precise sense, a notion which, while designating a real problem, blurs a crucial line of separation.

This is also why Lacan claims: "I am not even saying 'politics is the unconscious,' but only 'the unconscious is politics.'" The difference is crucial here. In the first case, the unconscious is elevated into the "big Other": it is posited as a substance which really dominates and regulates political activity, as in the claim that "the true driving force of our political activity is not ideology or interest, but rather unconscious libidinal motivations." In the second case, the big Other itself loses its substantial character, it is no longer "*the* Unconscious," for it transforms into a fragile inconsistent field overdetermined by political struggles. During a public debate at the New York Public Library a few years ago, Bernard-Henri Lévy made a pathetic case for liberal tolerance ("Would you not like to live in a society where you can make fun of the predominant religion without the fear of being killed for it? Where women are free to dress the way they like and choose a man they love?" and so on), while I made a similarly pathetic case for communism ("With the growing food crisis, the ecological crisis, the uncertainties about how to deal with questions such as intellectual property and biogenetics, with the erection of new walls between countries and within each country, is there not a need to find a new form of collective action which radically differs from market as well as from state administration?"). The irony of the situation was that, the case having been stated in these abstract terms, we could not but agree with each other. Lévy, a hard-line liberal anti-communist proponent of the free market, ironically remarked that, in this sense, even he was for communism . . . This sense of mutual understanding was proof that we were both knee-deep in ideology: "ideology" is precisely such a reduction to the simplified "essence" that conveniently forgets the "background noise" which provides the density of its actual meaning. Such an erasure of the "background noise" is the very core of utopian dreaming.

What this "background noise" conveys is—more often than not—the obscenity of the barbarian violence which sustains the public face of law and order. This is why Benjamin's thesis, that every monument of civilization is a monument of barbarism, has a precise impact on the very notion of being civilized: "to be civilized means to know one is potentially a barbarian."[4] Every civilization which disavows its barbarian potential has already capitulated to barbarism. This is how one should read the report about a weird confrontation in Vienna in 1938, when the SS arrived to search Freud's apartment: the aged and dignified Freud standing face to face with a young SS thug is a metaphor of what was best in the old European culture confronting the worst of the newly emerging barbarism. One should nonetheless remember that the SS perceived and legitimized themselves as the defenders of European culture and its spiritual values against the barbarism of modernity, with its focus on money and sex—a barbarism which, for the Nazis, was epitomized by the name "Freud." This suggests that we should push Benjamin's claim a step further: what if culture itself is nothing but a halt, a break, a respite, in the pursuit of barbarity? This, perhaps, is one of the ways to read Paul Celan's succinct paraphrase of Brecht:

> What times are these
> when a conversation
> is almost a crime
> because it includes
> so much [implicitly] told?[5]

Parenthetically, the continuous rumors regarding wild orgies at the top of the KGB in Stalinist Russia, and even the personal characterizations of its various leaders (Yagoda, Yezhov, Beria) as voracious sexual perverts, may or may not have been true, but even if they were correct, they clearly contain a fantasmatic core, which imagines a site of extreme debauchery as the hidden truth, the obscene Other Scene, of the official Bolshevik asceticism. One should always be aware that such hidden truth is the inherent obverse of the official ideology and, as such, no less fantasmatic.

---

4   Pascal Bruckner, *La Tyrannie de la pénitence*, Paris: Grasset 2006, p. 53.
5   *Poems of Paul Celan*, New York: Persea Books 2002, p. 319.

This brings us to the limit of liberal interpretations of Stalinism, which becomes palpable when liberal critics tackle the motivations of the Stalinist: they dismiss Stalinist ideology as a mere cynical and deceptive mask, and locate beneath it a brutal, egotistic individual who cares only about power and pleasure. In this way, the "pre-ideological" utilitarian individual is posited as the true figure beneath the ideological mask. The presupposition is here that the Stalinist subject related in a purely external-instrumental way towards his language, disposing of another code (the pre-ideological utilitarian one) which enabled him to be fully aware of his true motivations. But, what if—cynical though the Stalinists' use of official jargon was—they did not dispose of any such alternative language to articulate their truth? Is it not this properly Stalinist madness which is obliterated by the liberal critics, ensuring that we remain safely moored in the commonsense image of a human being?[6]

The gap between the official text of the Law and its obscene supplement is not limited to Western cultures; in Hindu culture, it occurs as the opposition between *vaiðika* (the Vedic corpus) and *tantrika*—tantra being the obscene (secret) supplement to the Vedas, the unwritten (or secret, non-canonic) core of the public teaching of the Vedas, a publicly disavowed but necessary element. No wonder that tantra is so popular today in the West: it offers the ultimate "spiritual logic of late capitalism"[7] uniting spirituality and earthly pleasures, transcendence and material benefits, divine experience and unlimited shopping. It propagates the permanent transgression of all rules, the violation of all taboos, instant gratification as the path to enlightenment; it overcomes old-fashioned "binary" thought, the dualism of mind and body, in claiming that the body at its most material (the site of sex and lust) *is* the royal path to spiritual awakening. Bliss comes from "saying *yes*" to all bodily needs, not from denying them: spiritual perfection comes from the insight that we *already are* divine and perfect, not that we have to achieve this through effort and discipline. The body is not something to be cultivated or crafted into an expression of spiritual truths, rather it is immediately the "temple for expressing divinity." We should note in passing here the opposition to Tarkovsky's spiritual materialism that I have often touched on elsewhere: for Tarkovsky, the very material process of *corruption* (decay, decomposition, rotting, inertia) is spiritual, while here the ethereal incorruptibility

---

6   See Igal Halfin, *Stalinist Confessions*, Pittsburgh: University of Pittsburgh Press 2009.

7   Hugh B. Urban, *Tantra: Sex, Secrecy, Politics, and Power in the Study of Religion*, Berkeley: University of California Press 2003, pp. 22, 207.

of the flesh is celebrated. This tendency reaches its apogee with cyber-space: it is no coincidence that tantra is one of the constant references of the New Age ideologists who insist on the fusion of body and spirituality, in the guise of the virtual "incorporeal spiritual body" able to experience extreme pleasures. Our biological body itself is a form of hardware that needs re-programming through tantra like a new spiritual software which can release or unblock its potential. Tantric notions are here translated into cyberspeak: phone wires become *nadis* of the virtual subtle corpus, computer terminals *chakras* (nodes of energy), the flow of vital *prajna* the infinite stream of information; we thus obtain "a cyborgasm that combines the incorruptibility of cyberspace with the most this-worldly sensual pleasure of the self"[8]:

> Real Tantric sex blows your mind completely because it takes you beyond all our conceptions of everyday reality . . . Understanding that our bodies are temples for expressing divinity we can . . . expand, celebrate and share *vibrational engorgement* in every cell of our being . . . blending sex and spirit.[9]

What we should always bear in mind is that there is nothing "sponta-neous" in such transgressive outbursts. For example, we truly enjoy smoking and drinking only in public, as part of a public "carnival," the sacred suspension of ordinary rules. The same goes for swearing and sex: neither, at its most intense, is an activity in which we "explode" in spontaneous passion against stifling public conventions—they are, on the contrary, both practiced "against the pleasure principle," for the gaze of the Other. (Personally, I like to swear only in public, never in private, where I find doing so stupid and inappropriate, even indecent.) The violation of public rules is thus not performed by the private ego, but is enjoined by the very same public rules which are in themselves redoubled. This is what distinguishes such violations from the stance of tolerant wisdom, which allows for private transgressions, for transgres-sions beyond the public gaze (as with the proverbial Catholic attitude of ignoring—even suggesting—occasional infidelities if they help maintain the marriage).[10]

How does one really become an adult? By knowing when to violate the explicit rule one is committed to. So, with regard to marriage, one

---

8   Ibid., pp. 252–4.
9   "Sexual Energy Ecstasy," quoted in ibid., p. 253.
10   I rely here on the reflections of Robert Pfaller.

can well say that one reaches adulthood when one is able to commit adultery. The only proof of reason is the occasional lapse into "irrationality" (as Hegel knew very well). The only proof of taste is that one knows how to occasionally appreciate things which do not meet the criteria of good taste—those who follow good taste too strictly only display their total lack of taste. (Likewise, someone who expresses his admiration for Beethoven's ninth symphony or some other masterpiece of Western civilization immediately bears witness to his tastelessness—true taste is displayed by praising a minor work of Beethoven as being superior to his "greatest hits.")

Perhaps one should invert the terms of Bertrand Russell's well-known barber paradox (does the barber who follows the rule of shaving all who do not shave themselves thereby shave himself?), which led him to prohibit the principle of self-inclusion, or inconsistent self-redoubling, as the only way to avoid contradiction. What if, on the contrary, it is the "consistent" adherence to rules which is truly self-contradictory, which turns into its opposite? And what if the only way to truly be reasonable or to truly display taste is to fully engage in self-redoubling, to violate the rule one follows self-reflexively?

It is as if, in today's permissive society, transgressive violations are permitted only in a "privatized" form, as a personal idiosyncrasy deprived of any public, spectacular or ritualistic dimension. We can thus publicly confess all our weird private practices, but they remain simply private idiosyncrasies. Perhaps we should also invert here the standard formula of fetishistic disavowal: "I know very well (that I should obey the rules), but nonetheless . . . (I occasionally violate them, since this too is part of the rules)." In contemporary society, the predominant stance is rather: "I believe (that repeated hedonistic transgressions are what make life worth living), but nonetheless . . . (I know very well that these transgressions are not really transgressive, but are just artificial coloring serving to re-emphasize the grayness of social reality)."

Legalists Versus Confucians

The philosopher who tried to undermine the very possibility of such unwritten obscene rules was Immanuel Kant. In his essay on "Perpetual Peace," he grounds what he calls the "transcendental formula of public law" ("All actions relating to the right of other men are unjust if their maxim is not consistent with publicity") in the obvious fact that a secret law, a law unknown to its subjects, would legitimize the arbitrary despotism of those who exercise it:

> A maxim which I cannot divulge without defeating my own purpose must be kept secret if it is to succeed; and, if I cannot publicly avow it without inevitably exciting universal opposition to my project, the necessary and universal opposition which can be foreseen a priori is due only to the injustice with which the maxim threatens everyone.[11]

Things, however, soon become ambiguous in Kant. As every Kant scholar knows apropos his prohibition of lying, one has always to be very attentive with regard to the exceptions to Kant's universal maxims. In the Second Supplement to his "Perpetual Peace" essay, Kant asks a naïve question: can the contract between states which obliges them to perpetual peace have a secret clause? Although he admits that a secret article in a contract under public law is objectively a contradiction, he allows for an exception for subjective reasons. This exception is not what one would have expected, namely a clause allowing for the sordid compromises of *Realpolitik* in order to maintain peace, such as the infamous secret clause in the Soviet–German Treaty of 1939 regarding the partition of Poland and other Eastern European states. It is, rather, something which may appear much more innocent, even ridiculous as the topic of a secret clause: "The opinions of philosophers on the conditions of the possibility of public peace shall be consulted by those states armed for war." Why should this clause remain secret? If made public, it would appear humiliating to the legislative authority of a state: how can the supreme authority, to whom "we must naturally attribute the utmost wisdom," seek instruction from its subjects? This may sound absurd, but do we not respect it even today? When Habermas was in England during the period of Blair's government, did not Tony Blair invite him to a discreet dinner which went unreported in the media? Kant was thus correct: this clause should remain secret, because it does something more terrifying than exposing the dark, cynical underside of legal power (in today's epoch, a state power can proudly admit to its dark side, advertising the fact that it is discreetly doing dirty things it is better for us not to know about). It underlines the blindness, stupidity and ignorance of power, none of which is personal but is rather institutional: in spite of input from hundreds of highly educated experts, for example, the results of the US invasion of Iraq were catastrophic.

---

11   Immanuel Kant, *Perpetual Peace*, New York: Penguin Books 2009, p. 62.

There is, however, a problem with Kant's thesis: what was unthinkable for Kant was modern "totalitarian ideology," as opposed to mere authoritarian lust for power: the will to impose on reality a theoretically developed vision of a better world. In totalitarian regimes such as Stalinism, the rulers did indeed listen too much to the advice of philosophers—and was the same not already true of Robespierre, who relied on Rousseau, so much beloved by Kant? And the story continues up to today: Brecht, Sartre, Heidegger . . . Thank God that those in power do not listen to the philosophers' advice too much! In the 1960s, when China detonated its first atomic bomb, Karl Jaspers advocated a large-scale atomic assault on China to prevent it becoming a threat to world peace. In ancient China itself, the king of Qin—who ruthlessly united the country and, in 221 BCE, proclaimed himself its First Emperor, instituting the ur-model of "totalitarian" rule—also relied so heavily on the advice of the "Legalist" philosophers that one can see this as the first case of a state regime forced on a society by a conscious, well-planned decision to break with past traditions and impose a new order originally conceived in theory:

> The king of Qin was not necessarily the brains of the outfit—his advisers, free of the strictures of courtly life, were the ones who had masterminded his rise to power. The plan to install him as the ruler of the world had commenced before he was even born, with the contention of long-dead scholars that the world required an enlightened prince. It had proceeded with . . . an alliance of scholars in search of a patron who might allow them to secure their own political ends. Ying Zheng, the king of Qin, became the First Emperor with the help of great minds.[12]

These Legalists—first among them Han Fei and the great Li Si—emerged out of the crisis of Confucianism. When, in the fifth to third centuries BCE, China went through the period of the "Warring States," Confucians saw the ultimate cause of this slow but persistent decay in the betrayal of age-old traditions and customs. Confucius was not so much a philosopher as a proto-ideologist: what interested him was not metaphysical Truths but rather a harmonious social order within which individuals could lead happy and ethical lives. He was the first to outline clearly what one is tempted to call the elementary scene of ideology, its zero-level, which consists in asserting the (nameless) authority of some substantial

---

12   Jonathan Clements, *The First Emperor of China*, Chalford: Suton Publishing 2006, p. 16.

Tradition. Reference was made to an original time when this Tradition still fully reigned (when "a king was really a king, a father really a father," etc.), in contrast to which the current period appeared as the time of decay, of the disintegration of organic social ties, of the growing gap between things and words, between individuals and their titles or social roles. No wonder Confucius represented his teachings as lessons transmitted from antiquity. And the fact that it is easy to demonstrate how he often did the exact opposite by proposing something quite new — in other words, that the tradition he appealed to was what Eric Hobsbawm has called an "invented tradition" — renders his insistence that he was simply "a transmitter and not a maker" all the more symptomatic: his reference to tradition was a necessary structural illusion.

According to Confucius, people live their lives within parameters firmly established by Heaven (which, more so than a purposeful Supreme Being, designates the higher natural order of things with its fixed cycles and patterns). Men are nonetheless responsible for their actions, especially for their treatment of others: we can do little or nothing to alter our fated span of existence, but we determine what we accomplish and what we are remembered for. Heaven rules the physical universe through *ming*, or "destiny," which is beyond human understanding and control, and it rules the moral universe, the universe of human behavior, through *T'ien ming*, or "The Mandate of Heaven." This "Mandate of Heaven" is based on the idea that Heaven is primarily concerned with the well-being of humans and human society; in order to bring this about, Heaven institutes government and authority. Heaven gives its mandate to a family or individual to rule over other human beings with justice and fairness; rulers are to make the welfare of their people their principal concern. When rulers or a dynasty fail to rule in this manner, Heaven removes its mandate and bestows it on another. Is "Heaven," then, not the Chinese name for the big Other? In this sense, is not the rule of the Communist Party legitimized by the "Mandate of Heaven," obliging the Communists to rule in a way that makes the welfare of their people their principal concern?[13]

Most troubling to Confucius was his perception that the political institutions of his day had completely broken down. He attributed this

---

13   A truly radical revolutionary subject should drop this reference to Heaven: there is no Heaven, no higher cosmic Law which would justify our acts. So when Mao Zedong said "There is great disorder under heaven, and the situation is excellent," he thereby made a point which can be precisely rendered in Lacanian terms: the inconsistency of the big Other opens up the space for the act.

collapse to the fact that those who wielded power, as well as those who occupied subordinate positions, did so by making claim to titles of which they were not worthy. When asked about the principles of good government, Confucius is reported to have replied: "Good government consists in the ruler being a ruler, the minister a minister, the father a father, and the son a son." In Europe, we call this a corporatist vision: society is like a body where each individual has to stay in his proper place and play his particular role. This is the very opposite of democracy: in democracy, nobody is constrained to stay in his or her particular place, everybody has the right to participate in universal affairs, to have her say in deliberations about the direction of society. No wonder, then, that Confucius's description of the disorder he sees in society around him—"Rulers do not rule and subjects do not serve"—provides a good description of a really democratic society, in which the united subjects rule and the nominal rulers serve them.

Confucius proposes here a kind of proto-Althusserian theory of ideological interpellation: the ideological "big Other" (Tradition), embodied in its apparatuses (rituals), interpellates individuals, and it is up to the individual to live and act in accordance with the title that makes him what he is. If I claim for myself a title and attempt to participate in the various hierarchical relationships to which I would be entitled by virtue of that title, then I should live up to the meaning of the title. Confucius's analysis of the lack of connection between things and their names and the need to correct such circumstances is usually referred to as his teaching on *zhengming*, the "rectification of names" (this name is itself a symptomatic misnomer: what needs to be rectified are the acts—which should be made to correspond to their names):

> If language is not correct, then what is said is not what is meant; if what is said is not what is meant, then what must be done remains undone; if this remains undone, morals and art will deteriorate; if justice goes astray, people will stand about in helpless confusion. Hence there must be no arbitrariness in what is said. This matters above everything.[14]

Confucius, who always calls for the respect of tradition, rituals, and politeness, here undermines the very thing he defends. Are not all good manners based on the fact that "what is said is not what is meant"? When, at a table, I ask my colleague "Can you please pass the salt?" I do not

---

14   Arthur Waley, *The Analects of Confucius*, New York: Alfred A. Knopf 2000, p. 161.

say what I mean. I ask him if he *can* do it, but what I really mean is that he simply *should* do it. If my colleague wanted to be really brutal, he would answer with "Yes, I can," and then ignore the request. So, when Confucius writes: "Look at nothing in defiance of ritual, listen to nothing in defiance of ritual, speak of nothing in defiance of ritual, never stir hand or foot in defiance of ritual,"[15] he is asking us precisely to "say what we don't mean": rituals are to be followed, not understood; when we obey them, we repeat formulae whose true meaning is always obscure to us.

What the "Legalists" did was to drop the very coordinates of such a perception of the situation: for the Confucians, the land was in chaos because ancient traditions were not being obeyed, and states such as Qin with their centralized-military organization which ignored the old customs were perceived as the embodiment of what was wrong. However, in contrast to his teacher Xunzi who regarded nations like Qin as a threat to peace, Han Fei "proposed the unthinkable, that maybe the way of the Qin government was not an anomaly to be addressed, but a practice to be emulated."[16] The solution resided in what appeared as the problem: the true cause of the troubles was not the abandonment of old traditions, but *these traditions themselves* which daily demonstrated their inability to serve as guiding principles of social life—as Hegel put it in the "Foreword" to his *Phenomenology of Spirit*, the standard by means of which we measure the situation and establish that it is problematic is itself part of the problem and should be abandoned. Han Fei applied the same logic to the fact that most men are evil by nature, not ready to act for the common Good: instead of bemoaning it, he saw human evil as an opportunity for state power, as something that a power enlightened by the right theory (a theory which describes things the way they really are, "beyond good and evil") could steer by applying to it the appropriate mechanism: "Where Xunzi saw an unfortunate observation, that men were evil by nature, Han Fei saw a challenge for the institution of stern laws to control this nature and use it to the benefit of the state."[17]

One of the great achievements of contemporary Leftist political theory (Althusser, Balibar, Negri, and so forth) has been the rehabilitation of Machiavelli, to save him from the standard "Machiavellian" reading. Since the Legalists are often presented as ur-Machiavellians, one should do the same with them, extricating a radical-emancipatory kernel from

---

15   Ibid., p. 153.
16   Clements, *The First Emperor of China*, p. 34.
17   Ibid., p. 77.

their predominant image as proto-"totalitarians." A quick glance at the three central premises of the Legalist doctrine makes this kernel clear:

"Fa": law or principle. The code of law must be clearly written and made public. All people under the ruler are equal before the law. Laws should reward those who obey them and punish accordingly those who dare to break them. The system of law runs the state, rather than the ruler. — These are unambiguous trademarks of anti-feudal egalitarianism: laws must be public, known to everyone; all are equal in the eyes of the law; the legal system stands even higher than the ruler.

"Shu": tactic or art. Special tactics and "secrets" are to be employed by the ruler to make sure others do not take over control of the state; especially important is that no one should fathom the ruler's motivations, and thus no one can know what form of behavior might help him get ahead, except for following the laws. — This "Machiavellian" point also has an egalitarian-emancipatory core: if the ruler's motivations are unknown, all that remains are the laws themselves.

"Shi": legitimacy, power or charisma. It is the position of the ruler, not the ruler himself, that holds the power. Therefore, analysis of the trends, the context, and the facts are essential for a real ruler . . . Is this not the first version of the insight, formulated by great European modern thinkers from Pascal to Marx, that people do not treat a person as a king because he is a king, but rather that this person is a king because he is treated as one? Charisma is the "performative" result of symbolic social practices, not a natural (or spiritual) property of the person who exerts it.[18]

In (theory and) practice, these three principles were, of course, given a "totalitarian" twist: a ruler had to have at his disposal an excessive number of laws which, although each of them was in itself public, clear and unambiguous, partially contradicted each other. Within such a complex framework of laws, where submission to one law readily brings one into conflict with another, a mere accusation will find almost anyone of any station in violation of something, with their innocence difficult if not impossible to prove. This enables the ruler's agents to practice "shu," the tactic or art of choosing which law to enforce in a specific situation: power is enacted not only through the prosecution of the law, but also in the selection of which law to enforce, and by the absence or cessation

18   See the Wikipedia entry for "Legalism (Chinese Philosophy)."

of enforcement due to some other contravening law. Such a selective enforcement of laws ultimately occurred at the pleasure of the ruler: in this way the mystery of the Emperor's pleasure was communicated to the masses. The lesson is totally Lacanian: it is in the inconsistency of the Other (the system of Laws), in the contingency that dwells in its very heart, that the Other's impenetrable desire, as well as its *jouissance*, are located.

One should note here a thing unthinkable for our Western tradition: the two opposed theories, Confucianism and Legalism, share a deeply materialist premise. For both of them, the truth of ideology does not matter, it is even implied that ideological myths are "beautiful lies"; what matters is how ideological myths and rituals function, their role in sustaining social order. It is also interesting to note how the Chinese Legalists, these proto-"totalitarians," already formulated a vision later propounded by liberalism, namely a vision of state power that, instead of relying on people's mores, submits them to a mechanism which makes their very vices work for the common Good. For all those who dismiss such a "totalitarian" notion of state power as a neutral mechanism for steering individuals, one could thus imagine a new version of the Kantian secret clause: "Pretend publicly to consult philosophers, but do not trust their words!"

No Castes Without Outcasts

This same materialism is also clearly discernible in *The Laws of Manu*,[19] the ancient Indian text which is one of the most exemplary ideological texts in the entire history of humanity. Firstly because, while the text encompasses the entire universe including its mythic origins, it nevertheless focuses on *everyday practices as the immediate materiality of ideology*: how (what, where, with whom, when . . .) we eat, defecate, have sex, walk, enter a building, work, make war, etc., etc. But also because the book stages a radical shift with regard to its starting point (its presupposition): the ancient code of Veda. What we find in the Veda is a brutal cosmology based on killing and eating: higher things kill and eat/consume lower ones, the stronger eat the weaker; that is, life is a zero-sum game in which one's victory is another's defeat. The "great chain of being" appears here as founded in the "food chain," the great chain of eating: gods eat mortal

---

19   *The Laws of Manu*, trans. Wendy Doniger, New Delhi: Penguin Books 2000.

humans, humans eat mammals, mammals eat lesser animals who eat plants, plants "eat" water and earth . . . such is the eternal cycle of being. So why does the Veda claim that the top social stratum consists not of warrior-kings stronger than all other humans, "eating" them all, but of the caste of priests? It is here that the code's ideological ingenuity becomes apparent: the function of the priests is to prevent the first, highest, level of cosmic eating, the eating of human mortals by gods. How? By way of performing sacrificial rituals. Gods must be appeased, their hunger for blood must be satisfied, and the trick of the priests is to offer the gods a substitute (symbolic) sacrifice: an animal or other prescribed food instead of human life. The sacrifice is needed not to secure any special favors from the gods, but to make sure that the wheel of life goes on turning. Priests perform a function which concerns the balance of the entire universe: if the gods remain hungry, the whole cycle of cosmic life is disturbed. From the very beginning, the "holistic" notion of the great chain of Being — the reality of which is the brutal chain of the strong eating the weak — is thus based on a deception: it is not a "natural" chain, but a chain based on an exception (humans who don't want to be eaten). Thus sacrifices are substitute insertions aimed at restoring the complete life cycle.

This was the first contract between ideologists (priests) and those in power (warrior-kings): the kings, who retain actual power (over the life and death of other people), will recognize the formal superiority of the priests as the highest caste, and, in exchange for this appearance of superiority, the priests will legitimize the power of the warrior-kings as part of the natural cosmic order. However, around the sixth and fifth centuries BCE, something new took place: a radical "revaluation of all values" in the guise of a universalist backlash against this cosmic food chain; the ascetic rejection of this entire infernal machine of life reproducing itself through sacrifice and eating. The circle of the food chain is now perceived as the circle of eternal suffering, and the only way to achieve peace is to exempt oneself from it. (With regard to food, this, of course, entails vegetarianism: not eating dead animals.) From perpetuating the life cycle in time, we move on to the goal of entering the timeless Void. With this reversal from a life-affirming stance to world-renunciation, comparable to the Christian rejection of the pagan universe, the highest values are no longer strength and fertility, but compassion, humility, and love. The very meaning of sacrifice changes with this reversal: we no longer sacrifice so that the infernal life cycle might go on, but in order to rid ourselves of the guilt of participating in that cycle.

What are the socio-political consequences of this reversal? How can we avoid the conclusion that the entire social hierarchy, grounded in the "great food chain" of eaters and eaten, should be suspended? It is here that the genius of *The Laws of Manu* shines through: its basic ideological operation is to *unite the hierarchy of castes and the ascetic world-renunciation by making purity itself the criterion of one's place in the caste hierarchy*: "Vegetarianism was put forward as the only way to liberate oneself from the bonds of natural violence that adversely affected one's karma. A concomitant of this new dietary practice was a social hierarchy governed to a large extent by the relative realization of the ideal of non-violence. The rank order of the social classes did not change. But the rationale for the ranking did."[20] Vegetarian priests are at the top, as close as humanly possible to purity; they are followed by the warrior-kings who control society by dominating it and killing life — they are in a way the negative of the priests, i.e., they entertain towards the Wheel of Life the same negative attitude as the priests, albeit in aggressive/interventional mode. Then come the producers who provide food and other material conditions for life; and, finally, at the bottom, are the outcasts whose main task is to deal with all kinds of excrements, the putrefying dead remainders of life (from cleaning the toilets to butchering animals and disposing of human bodies).

Since the two attitudes are ultimately incompatible, the task of their unification is an impossible one and can be achieved only by a complex panoply of tricks, displacements and compromises whose basic formula is that of universality with exceptions: in principle yes, but . . . *The Laws of Manu* demonstrates a breathtaking ingenuity in accomplishing this task, with examples often coming dangerously close to the ridiculous. For example, priests should study the Veda, not trade; in extremity, however, a priest can engage in trade, but he is not allowed to trade in certain things like sesame seed, except in certain circumstances; and if he sells sesame seed in the wrong circumstances, he will be reborn as a worm in dogshit . . . Is the structure here not exactly the same as that of the famous Jewish joke on the marriage-mediator who reinterprets every deficiency in the bride-to-be as a positive asset: "She is poor . . ." — "so she will know how to handle the family money, making the most of it!" "She is ugly . . ." — "so the husband will not have to worry that she will cheat on him!" "She stutters . . ." — "so she will keep quiet and not annoy the husband with incessant prattle!" and so on until the final "She really stinks!" — "So

---

20   Ibid., p. xxxvii (translator's Introduction).

you want her to be perfect, without any defect?" The general formula of this procedure is to "state one general rule, to which the whole of the subsequent treatise constitutes nothing but a series of increasingly specific exceptions . . . 'A specific injunction is stronger than a general one.'"[21] In other words, the great lesson of *The Laws of Manu* is that the true regulating power of the law resides not in its direct prohibitions, in the division of our acts into permitted and prohibited, but in *regulating the very violations of prohibitions*: the law silently accepts that the basic prohibitions are violated (or even discreetly solicits us to violate them), and then, once we find ourselves in this position of guilt, it tells us how to reconcile the violation with the law by violating the prohibition in a regulated way.

There is nothing "Oriental" about this procedure: the Christian church faced the same problem from the fourth century onwards, when it became the state church: how to reconcile the feudal class society where rich lords ruled over impoverished peasants with the egalitarian poverty of the collective of believers as described in the Gospels? The solution of Thomas Aquinas was that, while in principle shared property is better, this holds only for perfect humans; for the majority of us who dwell in sin, private property and difference in wealth are natural, and it is even sinful to demand egalitarianism or the abolishment of private property in our fallen societies, i.e., to demand for imperfect people what befits only the perfect. Even Buddhism often falls into this trap — say, in the guise of allowing (only) a violence perpetrated in a non-violent attitude, through inner peace and distance: "Even though the Buddha forbade the taking of life, he also taught that until all sentient beings are united together through the exercise of infinite compassion, there will never be peace. Therefore, as a means of bringing into harmony those things which are incompatible, killing and war are necessary."[22]

Is this supplementing of universality with exceptions a case of what Hegel called the "concrete universal"? Definitely not, and for a very precise reason: although both the structure of universal law with exceptions and Hegelian "concrete universality" mobilize the gap between the universal and the particular, the nature of the gap is different in each case. In the first case, it is simply the gap between the pure universal principle or law and the pragmatic consideration of particular circumstances, i.e., the (ultimately empiricist) notion of the excess of the wealth of concrete particular content over any abstract principle — in other words, here,

---

21   Ibid., p. lv.
22   Shaku Soen, quoted in Brian A. Victoria, *Zen at War*, New York: Weatherhilt 1998, p. 29.

universality precisely *remains abstract*, which is why it has to be twisted
or adapted to particular circumstances in order to become operative in
real life. In the second case, on the contrary, the tension is absolutely
immanent, inherent to universality itself: the fact that a universality actu-
alizes itself in a series of exceptions is an effect of this universality being
at war with itself, marked by an inherent deadlock or impossibility. (The
same goes for the idea of Communism: it is not enough to say that the
idea of Communism should not be applied as an abstract dogma, that,
in each case, concrete circumstances should be taken into consideration.
It is also not enough to say, apropos the fiasco of the twentieth-century
Communist countries, that this mis-application in no way disqualifies the
idea of Communism. The idea's imperfect [or, rather, catastrophic] actu-
alizations bear witness to an "inner contradiction" at the very heart of the
idea.)

Let us take a (surprising, perhaps) case of the Hegelian "concrete
universality": a wonderful Jewish story about an anti-death-penalty
Talmud specialist who, embarrassed by the fact that the death penalty is
ordained by God himself, proposed a delightfully practical solution: one
should not directly overturn the divine injunction, that would have been
blasphemous; but one should treat it as God's slip of tongue, his moment
of madness, and invent a complex network of sub-regulations and conditions which, while leaving the possibility of a death penalty intact, ensure
that this possibility will never be realized.[23] The beauty of this procedure
is that it turns around the standard trick of prohibiting something in principle (torture, for instance), but then slipping in enough qualifications
("except in specified extreme circumstances . . .") to ensure it can be done
whenever one really wants to do it. It is thus either "In principle yes, but
in practice never" or "In principle no, but when exceptional circumstances
demand it, yes." Note the asymmetry between the two cases: the prohibition is much stronger when one allows torture in principle—in this case,
the principled "yes" is *never* allowed to realize itself; while in the other
case, the principled "no" is *exceptionally* allowed to realize itself. In other
words, the only "reconciliation" between the universal and the particular
is that of the *universalized exception*: only the stance which re-casts every
particular case as an exception treats all particular cases *without exception*
in the same way. And it should be clear now why this is a case of "concrete
universality": the reason we should find a way to argue, in each particular

---

23   I owe this data to Eric Santner.

case, that the death penalty is not deserved, lies in our awareness that there is something wrong with the very idea of the death penalty, that this idea is an injustice masked as justice.

This reference to Judaism should be linked to the fact that the *Book of Job* (from the Old Testament) can be counted as the first exercise in the critique of ideology in the entire history of humanity. *The Laws of Manu* should thus be opposed to the *Book of Job* as one of the founding texts of ideology versus one of the founding texts of its critique. No wonder the British colonial administration in India elevated *The Laws of Manu* into the privileged text to be used as a reference for establishing the legal code which would render possible the most efficient domination of India—up to a point, one can even say that *The Laws of Manu* only became *the* book of the Hindu tradition retroactively, chosen to stand for the tradition by the British from among a vast choice (the same goes for its obscene obverse, "tantra," also systematized into a coherent, dark, violent, and dangerous cult by the British colonizers). In all these cases we are dealing with "invented traditions." What this also implies is that the persistence of the phenomenon and social practice of the Untouchables is not simply a remainder of tradition: their number grew throughout the nineteenth century, with the spreading of cities which lacked proper sewers, so that more outcasts were needed to deal with the resulting dirt and excrement. At a more general level, one should thus reject the idea that globalization threatens local traditions, that it flattens differences: sometimes it threatens them, more often it keeps them alive, resuscitates them or even creates them by way of ex-apting them to new conditions—in the way, say, the British and Spanish re-invented slavery in early modernity.

With the formal prohibition of discrimination against the Untouchables, their exclusion changed its status to become the obscene supplement of the official/public order: publicly disavowed, it continues in its subterranean existence. However, this subterranean existence is nonetheless formal (it concerns the subject's symbolic title/status), which is why it does not follow the same logic as the well-known Marxist opposition between formal equality and actual inequality in the capitalist system. Here, it is the inequality (the persistence of the hierarchic caste system) which is formal, while in their actual economic and legal life, individuals are in a way equal (an Untouchable can also become rich, etc.).[24] The status of the caste hierarchy is not the same as that of nobility in a

---

24   I am grateful to Shuddhabrata Sengupta, New Delhi, for drawing my attention to this crucial distinction.

bourgeois society, which is effectively irrelevant, merely a feature which may add to the subject's public glamor.

Exemplary here is the conflict between B. R. Ambedkar and Gandhi during the 1930s. Although Gandhi was the first Hindu politician to advocate the full integration of the Untouchables, and called them "the children of god," he perceived their exclusion as the result of the corruption of the original Hindu system. What Gandhi envisaged was rather a (formally) non-hierarchical order of castes within which each individual has his or her own allotted place; he emphasized the importance of scavenging and celebrated the Untouchables for performing this "sacred" mission. It is here that the Untouchables are exposed to the greatest ideological temptation: in a way which prefigures today's "identity politics," Gandhi allowed them to "fall in love with themselves" in their humiliating identity, to accept their degrading work as a noble and necessary social task, to see even the degrading nature of their work as a sign of their sacrifice, of their readiness to do a dirty job for the sake of society. Even his more "radical" injunction that everyone, Brahmins included, should clean up his or her own shit, obfuscates the true issue, which, rather than having to do with our individual attitude, is of a global social nature. (The same ideological trick is performed today when we are bombarded from all sides with injunctions to recycle personal waste, placing bottles, newspapers, etc., in the appropriate bins. In this way, guilt and responsibility are personalized—it is not the entire organization of the economy which is to blame, but our subjective attitude which needs to change.) The task is not to change our inner selves, but to abolish Untouchability as such, that is, not merely an element of the system, but the system itself which generates it. In contrast to Gandhi, Ambedkar saw this clearly when he

> underlined the futility of merely abolishing Untouchability: this evil being the product of a social hierarchy of a particular kind, it was the entire caste system that had to be eradicated: "There will be outcasts [Untouchables] as long as there are castes." . . . Gandhi responded that, on the contrary, here it was a question of the foundation of Hinduism, a civilization which, in its original form, in fact ignored hierarchy.[25]

Although Gandhi and Ambedkar respected each other and often collaborated in the struggle for the dignity of the Untouchables, their difference

25   Christophe Jaffrelot, *Dr Ambedkar and Untouchability*, New Delhi: Permanent Black 2005, pp. 68–9.

is here insurmountable: it is the difference between the "organic" solution (solving the problem by returning to the purity of the original non-corrupted system) and the truly radical solution (identifying the problem as the "symptom" of the entire system, the symptom which can only be resolved by abolishing the entire system). Ambedkar saw clearly how the structure of four castes does not unite four elements belonging to the same order: while the first three castes (priests, warrior-kings, merchant-producers) form a consistent All, an organic triad, the Untouchables are, like Marx's "Asiatic mode of production," the "part of no part," the inconsistent element within the system which holds the place of what the system as such excludes—and as such, the Untouchables stand for universality. Or, as Ambedkar put it with his ingenious wordplay: "There will be outcasts as long as there are castes." As long as there are castes, there will be an excessive excremental zero-value element which, while formally part of the system, has no proper place within it. Gandhi obfuscates this paradox, as if a harmonious caste structure were possible. The paradox of the Untouchables is that they are doubly marked by the excremental logic: they not only deal with impure excrements, their own formal status within the social body is that of excrement.

This is why the properly dialectical paradox is that, if one is to break out of the caste system, it is not enough to reverse the status of the Untouchables, elevating them into the "children of god"—the first step should rather be exactly the opposite one: to *universalize* their excremental status to the whole of humanity. Martin Luther directly proposed just such an excremental identity for man: man is like a divine shit, he fell out of God's anus—and, effectively, it is only within this Protestant logic of man's excremental identity that the true meaning of Incarnation can be formulated. In Orthodoxy, Christ ultimately loses his exceptional status: his very idealization, elevation to a noble model, reduces him to an ideal *image*, a figure to be *imitated* (all men should strive to become God) —*imitatio Christi* is more an Orthodox than a Catholic formula. In Catholicism, the predominant logic is that of a *symbolic exchange*: Catholic theologians enjoy pondering over scholastic juridical arguments about how Christ paid the price for our sins, etc. No wonder Luther reacted badly to the lowest outcome of this logic: the reduction of redemption to something that can be bought from the Church. Protestantism, finally, posits the relationship as *real*, conceiving Christ as a God who, in His act of Incarnation, freely *identified Himself with His own shit*, with the excremental real that is man—and it is only at this level that the properly Christian notion of divine love can be apprehended, as the love for the miserable excremental entity called "man." We are dealing here with what can be ironically referred to as the cosmic-theological proletarian position, whose "infinite judgment" is the identity of excess and universality: the shit of the earth is the universal subject. (This excremental status of man is signaled already by the role of sacrifice in the original Veda: by way of substituting the sacrificial victim for humans, the sacrifice bears witness to the eccentric, exceptional, role of man in the great chain of food—to paraphrase Lacan, the sacrificial object represents man for other "ordinary" members of the food chain.) Here is a quite surprising, if not outright shocking, passage from Pablo Neruda's *Memoirs*, which deals precisely with the invisible excremental space and what one might discover by way of probing into it—the event described took place when he was the Chilean consul in Sri Lanka (Ceylon):

> My solitary bungalow was far from any urban development. When I rented it, I tried to find out where the toilet was; I couldn't see it anywhere. Actually, it was nowhere near the shower, it was at the back of the house. I inspected it with curiosity. It was a wooden box with a hole in the middle, very much like the artifact I had known as a child in the Chilean countryside. But our toilets were set over a deep well or over running water. Here the receptacle was a simple metal pail under the round hole.
>
> The pail was clean every morning, but I had no idea how its contents disappeared. One morning I rose earlier than usual, and I was amazed when I saw what had been happening.
>
> Into the back of the house, walking like a dusky statue, came the most beautiful woman I had yet seen in Ceylon, a Tamil of the pariah caste. She was wearing a red-and-gold sari of the cheapest kind of cloth. She had heavy bangles on her bare ankles. Two tiny red dots glittered on either side of her nose. They must have been ordinary glass, but on her they were rubies.
>
> She walked solemnly toward the latrine, without so much as a side glance at me, not bothering to acknowledge my existence, and vanished with the disgusting receptacle on her head, moving away with the steps of a goddess.
>
> She was so lovely that, regardless of her humble job, I couldn't get her off my mind. Like a shy jungle animal she belonged to another kind of existence, a different world. I called to her, but it was no use. After that, I sometimes put a gift in her path, a piece of silk or some fruit. She would go past without hearing or looking. The ignoble routine had been transformed by her dark beauty into the dutiful ceremony of an indifferent queen.

One morning, I decided to go all the way. I got a strong grip on her wrist and stared into her eyes. There was no language I could talk with her. Unsmiling, she let herself be led away, and was soon naked in my bed. Her waist, so very slim, her full hips, the brimming cups of her breasts made her like one of the thousand-year-old sculptures from the south of India. It was the coming together of a man and a statue. She kept her eyes wide open all the while, completely unresponsive. She was right to despise me. The experience was never repeated.[26]

Neruda then simply passes to other things. This passage is remarkable not only for obvious reasons: a shameless story of a rape, with the dirty details discreetly passed over ("she let herself be led away, and was soon naked in my bed"—how did she come to be naked? Obviously, she didn't do it herself), the mystification of the victim's passivity into a divine indifference, the lack of elementary decency and shame on the part of the narrator (if he was attracted to the girl, wasn't he embarrassed by the awareness that she was smelling, seeing, and dealing with his shit every morning?). Its most remarkable feature is the divinization of the excrement: a sublime goddess appears at the very site where excrements are hidden. One should take this equation very seriously: elevating the exotic Other into an indifferent divinity is strictly equal to treating it like shit.

Legal Luck, or, the Loop of the Act

What, then, is the dimension of the law that the law cannot admit to publicly? The best way to discern it is through a logical paradox deployed by Jean-Pierre Dupuy in his admirable text on Hitchcock's *Vertigo*:

> An object possesses a property x until the time t; after t, it is not only that the object no longer has the property x; it is that it is not true that it possessed x at any time. The truth-value of the proposition "the object O has the property x at the moment t" therefore depends on the moment when this proposition is enunciated.[27]

---

26   Pablo Neruda, *Memoirs*, New York: Farrar, Strauss and Giroux 2001, pp. 99–100. I owe this reference to S. Anand, New Delhi.
27   Jean-Pierre Dupuy, "Quand je mourrai, rien de notre amour n'aura jamais existé," unpublished manuscript of an intervention at the colloquium *Vertigo et la philosophie*, Ecole Normale Supérieure, Paris, October 14, 2005.

One should note here the precise formulation: it is not that the truth-value of the proposition "the object O has the property x" depends on the time to which this proposition refers—*even when this time is specified, the truth-value depends on the time at which the proposition itself is enounced*. Or, to quote the title of Dupuy's text, "When I Die, Nothing of Our Love Will Ever Have Existed." Think about marriage and divorce: the most intelligent argument for the right to divorce (proposed, among others, by none other than the young Marx) does not refer to commonplaces such as "like all things, love affairs are not eternal, they change over the course of time," and so on; rather it concedes that indissolvability is inherent in the very notion of marriage. The conclusion is that divorce always has a retroactive scope: it does not mean only that a marriage is now annulled, but something much more radical—a marriage should be annulled because *it never was a true marriage*. And the same holds for Soviet Communism: it is clearly insufficient to say that, during the years of the Brezhnev "stagnation," it "exhausted its potential," it "was no longer adapted to new times"; what its miserable end demonstrates is that it was caught in a historical deadlock *from the very beginning*.

Perhaps this paradox provides a clue to the twists and turns of the Hegelian dialectical process. Let us take Hegel's critique of the Jacobin Revolutionary Terror as an exercise in the abstract negativity of absolute freedom which cannot stabilize itself in a concrete social order of freedom and thus has to end in the fury of self-destruction. One should bear in mind, however, that, insofar as we are dealing here with a historical choice (between the "French" way of remaining within Catholicism and thus being obliged to engage in self-destructive Revolutionary Terror, and the "German" path of the Reformation), it involves exactly the same elementary dialectical paradox as does that other choice, also from *The Phenomenology of Spirit*, between the two readings of "the Spirit is a bone" which Hegel illustrates by way of the phallic metaphor (the phallus as organ of insemination or as the organ of urination). Hegel's point is *not* that, in contrast to the vulgar empiricist mind which sees only urination, the proper speculative attitude has to choose insemination. The paradox is that making the direct choice of insemination is the infallible way to miss the point: it is not possible directly to choose the "true meaning," for one *has* to begin by making the "wrong" choice (of urination)—the true speculative meaning emerges only through the repeated reading, as the after-effect (or by-product) of the first, "wrong," reading. And the same goes for social life in which the direct choice of the "concrete universality" of a particular ethical lifeworld can end only in a regression to a pre-modern organic society that denies the infinite right of subjectivity as the fundamental feature of modernity. Since the subject-citizen of a modern state can no longer accept immersion in some particular social role that would confer on him a determinate place within the organic social Whole, the construction of the rational totality of the modern state leads to Revolutionary Terror: one should ruthlessly tear up the constraints of the pre-modern organic "concrete universality," and fully assert the infinite right of subjectivity in its abstract negativity. In other words, the point of Hegel's analysis of the Revolutionary Terror is not the rather obvious insight into how the revolutionary project involved the unilateral and direct assertion of abstract universal reason, and as such was doomed to perish in self-destructive fury since it was unable to channel the transposition of its revolutionary energy into a concrete, stable and differentiated social order; Hegel's point turns rather on the enigma of why, in spite of the fact that the Revolutionary Terror was a historical deadlock, we have to pass through it in order to arrive at the modern rational state.[28]

This is why Hegelian dialectics is not a vulgar evolutionism claiming that while a phenomenon may be justified in its own time, it deserves to disappear when its time passes: the "eternity" of dialectics means that the de-legitimization is always retroactive, what disappears "in itself" always deserves to disappear. Recall also the paradox of the process of apologizing: if I hurt someone with a rude remark, the proper thing for me to do is to offer a sincere apology, and the proper thing for the other party to do is to say something like "Thanks, I appreciate it, but I wasn't offended, I knew you didn't mean it, so you really owe me no apology!" The point is, of course, that although the final result is that no apology is needed, one has to go through the elaborate process of offering it — "you owe me no apology" can only be said once I have actually offered an apology, so that, although formally "nothing happens," and the offer of apology is proclaimed unnecessary, there is still a gain at the end of the process (perhaps, even, the friendship is saved).[29]

---

28   See Slavoj Žižek, *In Defense of Lost Causes*, London and New York: Verso 2008, pp. 208–9.
29   A scene in Ernst Lubitch's wonderful *To Be or Not To Be*, a short dialogue between the two famous Polish theater actors, Maria Tura and her self-centered husband Josef, playfully subverts this logic. Josef tells his wife: "I gave orders that, in the posters announcing the new play we're starring in, your name will be at the top, ahead of mine—you deserve it, darling!" She kindly replies: "Thanks, but you really didn't have to do it, it wasn't necessary!" His answer is: "I knew you would say that, so I already cancelled the order and put my name back on top . . .").
There is a well-known joke about cooking which relies on the same logic: "How anyone can make a good soup in one hour: prepare all the ingredients, cut the vegetables, etc., boil the water, put the ingredients into it, cook them at a simmer for half an hour, occasionally stirring; when, after three quarters of an hour, you discover that the soup is tasteless and unpalatable, throw it away, open up a good can of soup and quickly warm it up in a microwave oven. This is how we, humans, make soup."

Is it not that, here also, one has to do something (offer an apology, choose terror) in order to see how superfluous it is? This paradox is sustained by the distinction between the "constative" and the "performative," between the "subject of the enunciated" and the "subject of the enunciation": at the level of the enunciated content, the whole operation is meaningless (why do it—offer an apology, choose terror—when it is superfluous?); but what this commonsensical insight overlooks is that it was only the "wrong" superfluous gesture which created the subjective conditions that made it possible for the subject to really see *why* this gesture was indeed superfluous. The dialectical process is thus more refined than it may appear; the standard notion is that one can only arrive at the final truth at the end of a series of errors, so that these errors are not simply discarded, but are "sublated" in the final truth, preserved therein as moments within it. What this standard notion misses, however, is how the previous moments are preserved *precisely as superfluous*.

This is why the obvious response "But is this idea of retroactively canceling the contingent historical conditions, of transforming contingency into Fate, not ideology at its formally purest, the very form of ideology?" misses the point, namely that this retroactivity is inscribed into reality itself: what is truly "ideological" is the idea that, freed from "ideological illusions," one can pass from moment A to moment B directly, without retroactivity—as if, for instance, in an ideal and authentic society, I could apologize and the other party could respond "I was hurt, an apology was required, and I accept it" without breaking any implicit rules. Or as if we could reach the modern rational state without having to pass through the "superfluous" detour of the Terror.

How is this circle of changing the past possible without recourse to time travel? The solution was already proposed by Henri Bergson: of course one cannot change the past reality/actuality, but what one can change is the virtual dimension of the past—when something radically New emerges it retroactively creates its own possibility, its own causes or conditions.[30] A potentiality can be inserted into (or withdrawn from) past reality. Falling in love changes the past: it is as if I *always already* loved you, our love was destined to be, is the "answer of the real." My present love causes the past which gave birth to it. The same goes for *legal power*: here too, synchrony precedes diachrony. In the same way that, once I contingently fall in love, this love becomes my necessary Fate, once a

---

30   For a more detailed elaboration of this line of thought of Bergson, see Chapter 9 of Žižek, *In Defense of Lost Causes*.

legal order is installed, its contingent origins are erased. Once it *is* here, it was *always already* here, every story about its origin is now a myth, just like Swift's story of the origins of language in *Gulliver's Travels*: the result is already presupposed.

In *Vertigo*, it is the opposite that occurs: the past is changed so that it loses the *objet a*. What Scottie first experiences in *Vertigo* is the *loss* of Madeleine, his fatal love; when he recreates Madeleine in Judy and then discovers that the Madeleine he knew was actually Judy already pretending to be Madeleine, what he discovers is not simply that Judy was a fake (he knew that she was not the true Madeleine, since he had used her to recreate a copy of Madeleine), but that, *because she was* not *a fake — she* is *Madeleine — Madeleine herself was already a fake* — the *objet a* disintegrates, the very loss is lost, and we have a "negation of negation." His discovery *changes the past*, deprives the lost object of the *objet a*.

Are, then, today's ethico-legal neoconservatives not a little bit like Scottie in Hitchcock's *Vertigo*? In wanting to recreate the lost order, to make a new distinguished Madeleine out of today's promiscuous and vulgar Judy, they will sooner or later be forced to admit not that it is impossible to restore Madeleine (the old traditional mores) to life, but that Madeleine *was* already Judy: the corruption they are fighting in the modern permissive, secular, egotistic, etc., society was present from the very beginning. One can compare this with Zen Buddhism: those who criticize the Westernized New Age image and practice of Zen — its reduction to a "relaxation technique" — as a betrayal of authentic Japanese Zen, forget the fact that the features they deplore in Westernized Zen were already there in "true" Japanese Zen: after World War II, Japanese Zen Buddhists immediately started to organize Zen courses for business managers, whilst during the war the majority supported Japanese militarism, and so on.

In the case of true love, after discovering the truth, Scottie would have accepted Judy as "more Madeleine than Madeleine herself" (he does in fact do that just before the rise of the mother superior . . .): here Dupuy should be corrected. Dupuy's perspective is that Scottie should have left Madeleine to her past — true, but what should he have done upon discovering that Judy was in fact Madeleine? The Madeleine of the past was an imaginary lure, pretending to be what she was not (Judy was playing Madeleine). What Judy was doing in playing Madeleine was *true love*. In *Vertigo*, Scottie does *not* love Madeleine — the proof is that he tries to recreate her in Judy, changing Judy's properties to make her resemble

Madeleine. Similarly, the idea of cloning a dead child for bereaved parents is an abomination: if the parents are satisfied by this, it is proof that their love was not genuine—love is not love for the properties of the object, but for the abyssal X, the *je ne sais quoi*, in the object.

In his *Wissen und Gewissen*, Viktor Frankl reports on one of his post-World War II patients, a concentration camp survivor who had been reunited with his wife after the war, only for her to die soon afterwards due to an illness contracted in the camp. The patient fell into total despair, and all Frankl's attempts to drag him out of depression failed, till, one day, he told the patient: "Imagine that God gave me the power to create a woman who would have all the features of your dead wife, so that she would be indistinguishable from her—would you ask me to create her?" The patient was silent for a short time, then stood up, said "No, thanks, doctor!" and, shaking his hand, left to set out on a new and normal life.[31] The patient in this case did what Scottie, who did indeed try to recreate the same woman, was not able to do: he became aware that, while one may be able to find the same woman with regard to all positive features, one cannot recreate the unfathomable *objet a* in her.

There is a science-fiction story, set a couple of hundred years in the future, when time travel is assumed to be possible, about an art critic who becomes so fascinated by the works of a New York painter from our era that he travels back in time to meet him. The painter, however, turns out to be a worthless drunk who steals the time machine from him and escapes into the future; alone in the world of today, the art critic paints all the paintings that fascinated him in the future and had made him travel into the past. Surprisingly, none other than Henry James had already used the same plot: *The Sense of the Past*, an unfinished manuscript found among James's papers and published posthumously in 1917, tells a similar story which also uncannily resembles *Vertigo*, and stimulated penetrating interpretations by both Stephen Spender and Borges. (Dupuy notes that James was a friend of H. G. Wells—*The Sense of the Past* is his version of Wells's *Time Machine*.[32]) After James's death, the novel was adapted as a very successful play, *Berkeley Square*, which was made into a movie in 1933 with Leslie Howard as Ralph Pendrel, a young New Yorker who, upon inheriting an eighteenth-century house in London, finds in it a portrait of a remote ancestor, also named Ralph Pendrel. Fascinated by the portrait,

---

31   Viktor Frankl, *Wissen und Gewissen*, Frankfurt: Suhrkamp 1966.
32   James was more interested in the contrast of mores between the near past and the present: the mechanics of time travel were foreign to him, which is why he wisely left the novel unfinished.

he steps across a mysterious threshold and finds himself back in the eighteenth century. Among the people he meets there is a painter who was
the author of the portrait that had captivated him—it is, of course, a self-
portrait. In his commentary, Borges provided a succinct formulation of the
paradox: "*The cause is posterior to the effect, the motif of the voyage is one of the
consequences of this voyage.*"[33] James added a love aspect to the trip into the
past: back in the eighteenth century, Ralph falls in love with Nan, a sister
of his (eighteenth-century) fiancée Molly. Nan eventually realizes that
Ralph is a time-traveler from the future, and she sacrifices her own happiness to help him return to his own time and to Aurora Coyne, a woman
who had previously rejected Ralph but would now accept him.

James's story thus psychotically (in the real) mystifies the circle of
the symbolic economy, in which effect precedes cause, i.e., retroactively
creates it—and exactly the same holds for the legal status of the rebellion
against a (legal) power in Kant: the proposition "what the rebels are doing
is a crime which deserves to be punished" is true if pronounced while the
rebellion is taking place; however, once the rebellion has succeeded and a
new legal order is established, this statement concerning the legal status
of the same past act no longer holds. Here is Kant's answer to the question "Is rebellion a legitimate means for a people to employ in throwing
off the yoke of an alleged tyrant?":

> The rights of the people are injured; no injustice befalls the tyrant when he
> is deposed. There can be no doubt on this point. Nevertheless, it is in the
> highest degree illegitimate for the subjects to seek their rights in this way.
> If they fail in the struggle and are then subjected to severest punishment,
> they cannot complain about injustice any more than the tyrant could if
> they had succeeded . . . If the revolt of the people succeeds, what has been
> said is still quite compatible with the fact that the chief, on retiring to the
> status of a subject, cannot begin a revolt for his restoration but need not
> fear being made to account for his earlier administration of the state.[34]

Does Kant not offer here his own version of what Bernard Williams has
called "moral luck" (or, better, "legal luck")? The (not ethical, but legal)
status of rebellion is decided retroactively: if a rebellion succeeds and
establishes a new legal order, then it brings about its own *circulus vitiosus*,
i.e., it pushes its own illegal origins into the ontological void, it enacts the

---

33   Quoted in Dupuy, "Quand je mourrai . . ."
34   Kant, *Perpetual Peace*, Appendix II, pp. 62–3.

paradox of retroactively grounding itself. Kant states this paradox even more clearly a couple of pages earlier:

> If a violent revolution, engendered by a bad constitution, introduces by illegal means a more legal constitution, to lead the people back to the earlier constitution would not be permitted; but, while the revolution lasted, each person who openly or covertly shared in it would have justly incurred the punishment due to those who rebel.[35]

He could not have been clearer: the legal status of the same act changes with time. What is, while the rebellion goes on, a punishable crime, becomes, after the new legal order is established, the opposite — more precisely, it simply disappears, as a vanishing mediator which retroactively cancels/erases itself in its result. The same holds for the very beginning, for the emergence of the legal order out of the violent "state of nature" — Kant is fully aware that there is no historical moment of the "social contract": the unity and law of a civil society is imposed onto the people by an act of violence whose agent is not motivated by any moral considerations:

> since a uniting cause must supervene upon the variety of particular volitions in order to produce a common will from them, establishing this whole is something no one individual in the group can perform; hence in the practical execution of this idea we can count on nothing but force to establish the juridical condition, on the compulsion of which public law will later be established. We can scarcely hope to find in the legislator a moral intention sufficient to induce him to commit to the general will the establishment of a legal constitution after he has formed the nation from a horde of savages.[36]

What Kant is struggling with here is nothing other than the paradoxical nature of the political *act*. Recall, from the history of Marxism, how Lenin saved his most acerbic irony for those who engage in the endless search for some kind of "guarantee" for the revolution. This guarantee assumes two main forms: either the reified notion of social necessity (one should not risk the revolution too early; one has to wait for the right moment, when the situation is "mature" with regard to the laws of historical development: "it is too early for the Socialist revolution, the working class is not yet mature"), or the conception of normative ("democratic")

---

35   Ibid., Appendix I.
36   Ibid.

legitimacy ("the majority of the population is not on our side, so the revolution would not really be democratic") — as a Lacanian Lenin might have put it, it is as if, before a revolutionary agent risks the seizure of power, it should obtain permission from some figure of the big Other — by, say, organizing a referendum to ascertain whether the majority does in fact support the revolution.[37] With Lenin, as with Lacan, the point is that a revolution *ne s'autorise que d'elle-même*: one should take responsibility for the revolutionary *act* not covered by the big Other. The fear of taking power "prematurely," the search for the guarantee, is the fear of the abyss of the act and is nicely rendered in the anecdote about the exchange between Lenin and Trotsky just prior to the October Revolution: Lenin is said to have asked: "What will happen to us if we fail?" To which Trotsky supposedly replied: "And what will happen if we succeed?" *Se non e vero e ben trovato* . . . What is unimaginable within the positivist vision of history as an "objective" process which determines in advance the possible coordinates of political interventions is precisely a radical political intervention which changes these very "objective" coordinates and thus, in a way, creates the conditions for its own success. An act proper is not just a strategic intervention into a situation, bound by its conditions — it retroactively creates its conditions.

We can see where Kant's weakness resides: there is no need to evoke "radical Evil" in the guise of some dark primordial crime — all these obscure fantasies have to be evoked to obfuscate the act itself. The paradox is clear: Kant himself, who put such an accent on the ethical act as autonomous, non-pathological, irreducible to its conditions, is unable to recognize it where it happens, misreading it as its opposite, as unthinkable "diabolical Evil." Kant is here one in a series of many conservative (and not only conservative) political thinkers, including Pascal and Joseph de Maistre, who elaborated on the notion of the illegitimate origins of power, of a "founding crime" on which state power is based; to obfuscate these origins, one must offer the people "noble lies," heroic narratives of the origins. One cannot but respect the brutal honesty of the first-generation founders of the State of Israel who in no way obliterated the "founding crime" involved in establishing the new state: they openly admitted

---

37   Even some Lacanians praise democracy as the "institutionalization of the lack in the Other": the premise of democracy is that no political agent is a priori legitimized to hold power, that the place of power is empty, open to competition. However, by institutionalizing the lack, democracy neutralizes — normalizes — it, so that the big Other is again here in the guise of the democratic legitimization of our acts — in a democracy, my acts are "covered" as the legitimate acts which carry out the will of the majority.

they had no right to the land of Palestine, it was just a matter of their force against the force of the Palestinians. On April 29, 1956, a group of Palestinians from Gaza crossed the border to plunder the harvest in the Nahal Oz kibbutz's fields; Roi, a young Jewish member of the kibbutz who patrolled the fields galloped towards them on his horse brandishing a stick to chase them away; he was seized by the Palestinians and carried back to the Gaza Strip. When the UN returned his body to the Israelis, his eyes had been gouged out. Moshe Dayan, the then Israeli Chief of Staff, delivered the eulogy at his funeral the following day:

> Let us not cast blame on the murderers today. What claim do we have against their mortal hatred of us? They have lived in the refugee camps of Gaza for the past eight years, while right before their eyes we have transformed the land and villages where they and their ancestors once lived into our own inheritance.
>
> It is not among the Arabs of Gaza but in our own midst that we must seek Roi's blood. How have we shut our eyes and refused to look squarely at our fate and see the destiny of our generation in all its brutality? Have we forgotten that this group of young people living in Nahal Oz bears the burden of Gaza's gates on its shoulders?[38]

Apart from the parallel between Roi and the blinded Samson (which plays a key role in the later mythology of the Israeli Defense Force), what cannot but strike one is the apparent non sequitur, the gap, between the first and the second paragraph: in the first paragraph, Dayan openly admits that the Palestinians have every right to hate the Israeli Jews, since they had taken their land; his conclusion, however, is not the obvious admission of guilt, but rather the need for a full acceptance of "the destiny of our generation in all its brutality," or in other words, the assumption of the burden—not of guilt, but of the war in which might is right, in which the stronger force wins. The war was not about principles or justice, it was an exercise in "mythic violence"—an insight totally obliterated by recent Israeli self-legitimization. As in the case of feminism, which taught us to discover the traces of violence in what appears, in a patriarchal culture, as a natural authority (of the father), we should remember the grounding violence obliterated by today's Zionism—Zionists should simply read Dayan and Ben Gurion.

---

38   Quoted from Udi Aloni's outstanding analysis of this case, "Samson the Non-European" (unpublished manuscript).

This brings us to the contemporary liberal idea of global justice, whose aim is not only to characterize all past injustices as collective crimes, for it also involves the politically correct utopia of "restituting" the past collective violence (towards blacks, Native Americans, Chinese immigrants . . .) by payment or legal measures. *This* is the true utopia, the idea that a legal order can make recompense for its founding crimes, thereby retroactively cleansing itself of its guilt and regaining its innocence. What lies at the end of this road is the ecological utopia of humanity in its entirety repaying its debt to Nature for all its past exploitation. In effect, is not the idea of "recycling" part of the same pattern as that of restitution for past injustices? The underlying utopian notion is the same: the system which emerged through violence should repay its debt in order to regain an ethico-ecological balance. The ideal of "recycling" involves the utopia of a self-enclosed circle in which all waste, all useless remainder, is sublated: nothing gets lost, all trash is re-used. It is at this level that one should make the shift from the circle to the ellipse: already in nature itself, there is no circle of total recycling, there is un-usable waste. Recall the methodical madness of Jeremy Bentham's "Panopticon" in which everything, up to and including the prisoners' excrement and urine, should be put to further use. Regarding urine, Bentham proposed the following ingenious solution: the external walls of the cells should not be fully vertical, but lightly curved inside, so that, when the prisoners urinated on the wall, the liquid would drip downwards, keeping the cells warm in winter . . . This is why the properly aesthetic attitude of a radical ecologist is not that of admiring or longing for a pristine nature of virgin forests and clear sky, but rather that of accepting waste as such, of discovering the aesthetic potential of waste, of decay, of the inertia of rotten material which serves no purpose.

The Utopia for a Race of Devils

This, finally, brings us to the core of the liberal utopia. For liberalism, at least in its radical form, the wish to submit people to an ethical ideal held to be universal is "the crime which contains all crimes," the mother of all crimes — it amounts to the brutal imposition of one's own view onto others, the cause of civil disorder. Which is why, if one wants to establish civil peace and tolerance, the first condition is to get rid of "*moral temptation*": politics should be thoroughly purged of moral ideals and rendered "realistic," taking people as they are, counting on their true nature, not on moral exhortations. Here the market is exemplary: human nature is egotistic, there is no way to change it—what is needed is a mechanism that makes private vices work for the common good (the "Cunning of Reason"). In his "Perpetual Peace" essay, Kant provided a precise formulation of this key feature:

> many say a republic would have to be a nation of angels, because men with their selfish inclinations are not capable of a constitution of such sublime form. But precisely with these inclinations nature comes to the aid of the general will established on reason, which is revered even though impotent in practice. Thus it is only a question of a good organization of the state (which does lie in man's power), whereby the powers of each selfish inclination are so arranged in opposition that one moderates or destroys the ruinous effect of the other. The consequence for reason is the same as if none of them existed, and man is forced to be a good citizen even if not a morally good person.
>
> The problem of organizing a state, however hard it may seem, can be solved even for a race of devils, if only they are intelligent. The problem is: "Given a multitude of rational beings requiring universal laws for their preservation, but each of whom is secretly inclined to exempt himself from them, to establish a constitution in such a way that, although their private intentions conflict, they check each other, with the result that their public conduct is the same as if they had no such intentions." A problem like this must be capable of solution; it does not require that we know how to attain the moral improvement of men but only that we should know the mechanism of nature in order to use it on men, organizing the conflict of the hostile intentions present in a people in such a way that they must compel themselves to submit to coercive laws. Thus a state of peace is established in which laws have force.[39]

One should pursue this line of argument to its conclusion: a fully self-conscious liberal should intentionally limit his altruistic readiness to sacrifice his own good for the good of others, aware that the most effective way to act for the common good is to follow one's private egotism. The inevitable obverse of the Cunning of Reason motto "private vices, common good" is "private goods, common disaster." There is in liberalism, from its very inception, a tension between individual freedom and objective mechanisms which regulate the behavior of a crowd—early on, Benjamin Constant clearly formulated this tension: everything is moral in individuals,

---

39   Kant, *Perpetual Peace*, p. 36.

but everything is physical in crowds; everybody is free as individual, but merely a cog in a machine when part of a crowd. Nowhere is the legacy of religion clearer: this, exactly, is the paradox of Predestination, of the unfathomable mechanism of Grace embodied, among other places, in market success. The mechanisms which will bring about social peace are independent of the will of individuals as well as of their merits.

The tension internal to this project is discernible in the two aspects of liberalism, market liberalism and political liberalism. Jean-Claude Michéa perspicuously links this to two meanings of the term "right": the political Right insists on the market economy, the politically correct culturalized Left insists on the defense of human rights—often its sole remaining *raison d'être*. Although the tension between these two aspects of liberalism is irreducible, they are nonetheless inextricably linked, like the two sides of the same coin.

Today, the meaning of "liberalism" moves between two opposed poles: economic liberalism (free market individualism, opposition to strong state regulation, etc.) and political liberalism (with an accent on equality, social solidarity, permissiveness, etc.). In the US, Republicans are more liberal in the first sense and Democrats in the second. The point, of course, is that while one cannot decide through closer analysis which is the "true" liberalism, one also cannot resolve the deadlock by proposing a kind of "higher" dialectical synthesis, or "avoid the confusion" by making a clear distinction between the two senses of the term. The tension between the two meanings is inherent to the very content that "liberalism" endeavors to designate, it is constitutive of the notion itself, so that this ambiguity, far from signaling a limitation of our knowledge, signals the innermost "truth" of the notion of liberalism.

Traditionally, each basic form of liberalism necessarily appears as the opposite of the other: liberal multiculturalist advocates of tolerance as a rule resist economic liberalism and try to protect the vulnerable from unencumbered market forces, while market liberals as a rule advocate conservative family values, and so on. We thus get the double paradox of the traditionalist Rightist supporting the market economy while ferociously rejecting the culture and mores that economy engenders, and his counterpoint, the multiculturalist Leftist, resisting the market (though less and less so, it is true, as Michéa notices) while enthusiastically enforcing the ideology it engenders. (Half a century ago, the symptomatic exception was the unique Ayn Rand, who advocated both market liberalism *and* a full individualist egotism deprived of all traditional forms of morality concerning family values and sacrifice for the common good.) Today, however, we seem to be entering a new era in which it is possible for both aspects to be combined: figures such as Bill Gates, for instance, pose as market radicals *and* as multiculturalist humanitarians.

Here, we encounter the basic paradox of liberalism. An anti-ideological and anti-utopian stance is inscribed into the very core of the liberal vision: liberalism conceives itself as a "politics of the lesser evil," its ambition is to bring about the "least worst society possible," thus preventing a greater evil, since it considers any attempt to directly impose a positive good as the ultimate source of all evil. Churchill's quip about democracy being the worst of all political systems, with the exception of all the others, holds even better for liberalism. Such a view is sustained by a profound pessimism about human nature: man is a selfish and envious animal, and if one attempts to build a political system appealing to his goodness and altruism, the result will be the worst kind of terror (both the Jacobins and the Stalinists presupposed human virtue).[40] However, the liberal critique of the "tyranny of the Good" comes at a price: the more its program permeates society, the more it turns into its opposite. The claim to want nothing but the lesser evil, once asserted as the principle of the new global order, gradually replicates the very features of the enemy it claims to be fighting against. The global liberal order clearly presents itself as the best of all possible worlds; its modest rejection of utopias ends with the imposition of its own market-liberal utopia which will supposedly become reality when we subject ourselves fully to the mechanisms of the market and universal human rights. Behind all this lurks the ultimate totalitarian nightmare, the vision of a New Man who has left behind all the old ideological baggage.

As every close observer of the deadlocks arising from political correctness knows, the separation of legal justice from moral Goodness—which should be relativized and historicized—ends up in an oppressive moralism brimming with resentment. Without any "organic" social substance grounding the standards of what Orwell approvingly referred to as "common decency" (all such standards having been dismissed as subordinating individual freedoms to proto-Fascist social forms), the minimalist program of laws intended simply to prevent individuals from encroaching upon one another (annoying

---

40   The standard liberal-conservative argument against Communism is that, since it wants to impose on reality an impossible utopian dream, it necessarily ends in deadly terror. What, however, if one should nonetheless insist on taking the risk of enforcing the Impossible onto reality? Even if, in this way, we do not get what we wanted and/or expected, we nonetheless change the coordinates of what appears as "possible" and give birth to something genuinely new.

or "harassing" each other) turns into an explosion of legal and moral rules, an endless process (a "spurious infinity" in Hegel's sense) of legalization and moralization, known as "the fight against all forms of discrimination." If there are no shared mores in place to influence the law, only the basic fact of subjects "harassing" other subjects, who—in the absence of such mores—is to decide what counts as "harassment"? In France, there are associations for obese people demanding that all public campaigns against obesity and in favor of healthy eating habits be stopped, since they damage the self-esteem of obese persons. The militants of Veggie Pride condemn the "speciesism" of meat-eaters (who discriminate against animals, privileging the human animal—for them, a particularly disgusting form of "fascism") and demand that "vegeto-phobia" should be treated as a kind of xenophobia and proclaimed a crime. And we could extend the list to include those fighting for the right to incest-marriage, consensual murder, cannibalism . . .

The problem here is the obvious arbitrariness of the ever-new rules. Take child sexuality, for example: one could argue that its criminalization is an unwarranted discrimination, but one could also argue that children should be protected from sexual molestation by adults. And we could go on: the same people who advocate the legalization of soft drugs usually support the prohibition of smoking in public places; the same people who protest the patriarchal abuse of small children in our societies worry when someone condemns members of certain minority cultures for doing exactly this (say, the Roma preventing their children from attending public schools), claiming that this is a case of meddling with other "ways of life." It is thus for necessary structural reasons that the "fight against discrimination" is an endless process which interminably postpones its final point: namely a society freed of all moral prejudices which, as Michéa puts it, "would be on this very account *a society condemned to see crimes everywhere.*"[41]

The ideological coordinates of such liberal multiculturalism are determined by two features of our "postmodern" *zeitgeist*: universalized multiculturalist historicism (all values and rights are historically specific, hence any elevation of them into universal notions to be imposed onto others is cultural imperialism at its most violent)[42] and the universalized "hermeneutics of suspicion" (all "high" ethical motifs are generated and

---

41   Jean-Claude Michéa, *L'Empire du moindre mal*, Paris: Climats 2007, p. 145.

42   The limit of this historicism is discernible in the way it coincides with a ruthless measurement of the past by our own standards. It is easy to imagine one and the same person, on the one hand, warning against imposing our Eurocentric values on other cultures, and, on the other, advocating that classics like Mark Twain's Tom Sawyer and Huck Finn novels should be removed from school libraries because of their racially insensitive portrayal of blacks and Native Americans.

sustained by "low" motives of resentment, envy, etc.—the call to sacrifice our life for a higher cause is either a mask for manipulation by those who need war to sustain their power and wealth, or a pathological expression of masochism—and this either/or is an inclusive *vel*, i.e., both terms can be true at the same time). Another way to formulate Badiou's insight that we live in a world-less universe would be to say that the functioning of ideology today no longer relies on mechanisms for the interpellation of individuals into subjects: what liberalism proposes is a value-neutral mechanism of rights, and so on, a mechanism "whose free play can automatically generate a desired political order, without at any point interpellating individuals into subjects."[43] The nameless *jouissance* cannot be a title of interpellation proper; it is more a kind of blind drive with no symbolic value-form attached to it—all such symbolic features are temporary and flexible, which is why the individual is constantly called upon to "re-create" himself or herself.

There is a problem with this liberal vision of which every good anthropologist, psychoanalyst, or even perspicuous social critic such as Francis Fukuyama, is aware: it cannot stand on its own, it is parasitic upon some preceding form of what is usually referred to as "socialization" which it simultaneously undermines, thereby sawing off the branch on which it is sitting. In the market—and, more generally, in the social exchange based on the market—individuals encounter each other as free rational subjects, but such subjects are the result of a complex previous process which concerns symbolic debt, authority, and, above all, trust (in the big Other which regulates exchanges). In other words, the domain of exchange is never purely symmetrical: it is an a priori condition for each of the participants to be able to give something without return so that he or she can participate in the game of give-and-take. For a market exchange to take place, there have to be subjects involved who participate in the basic symbolic pact and display an elementary *trust* in the Word. Of course, the market is a domain of egotistic cheating and lying; however, as Lacan taught us, in order for a lie to function, it has to present itself and be taken as truth, i.e., the dimension of Truth has to be already established.

Kant missed the *necessity* of unwritten, disavowed, but necessary rules for every legal structure or set of social rules—it is only such rules that provide the "substance" on which laws can thrive, or properly function.

---

43   Michéa, *L'Empire du moindre mal*, p. 69.

(One could again imagine, along these lines, yet another version of the Kantian secret clause enjoining states to always take into account the unwritten rules, without publicly admitting so.) The exemplary case of the effectiveness of such unwritten rules is "potlatch"; the key feature that opposes potlatch to direct market exchange is thus the temporal dimension. In market exchange, the two complementary acts occur simultaneously (I pay and I get what I paid for), so that the act of exchange does not lead to a permanent social bond, but merely to a momentary exchange between atomized individuals who, immediately afterwards, return to their solitude. In potlatch, on the contrary, the time elapsed between my giving a gift and the other side returning it to me creates a social link which lasts (for a time, at least): we are all linked together by bonds of debt. From this standpoint, money can be defined as the means which enables us to have contacts with others without entering into proper relations with them. (Is the function of the masochistic practice of bondage not [also] to supplement this lack of social bond proper, so that, in it, the foreclosed returns in the real—the suspended symbolic bond returns as literal bodily bondage?)[44]

This atomized society, in which we have contact with others without entering into proper relations with them, is the presupposition of liberalism. The problem of organizing a state thus cannot be solved "even for a race of devils," as Kant put it—the idea that it can be is the key moment of the liberal utopia. One should link this Kantian reference to a race of devils to another detail of his ethical thought. According to Kant, if one finds oneself alone on the sea with another survivor of a sunken ship near a floating piece of wood which can keep only one person afloat, moral considerations are no longer valid—there is no moral law preventing me from fighting to the death with the other survivor for the place on the raft; I can engage in it with moral impunity. It is here, perhaps, that one encounters the limit of Kantian ethics: what about someone prepared willingly to sacrifice himself in order to give the other person a chance of survival—and, furthermore, who is ready to do it for non-pathological reasons? If there is no moral law commanding one to do this, does this mean that such an act has no ethical status proper? Does this strange exception not demonstrate that ruthless egotism, a concern for personal survival and gain, is the silent "pathological" presupposition of Kantian ethics—that the Kantian ethical edifice can only maintain itself by silently

---

44   For a more detailed analysis of "potlatch," see Chapter 1 of Žižek, *In Defense of Lost Causes*.

presupposing the "pathological" image of man as a ruthless utilitarian egotist? In exactly the same way, the Kantian political structure, with his notion of ideal legal power, can maintain itself only by silently presupposing the "pathological" image of the subjects of this power as "a race of devils."

According to Kant, the mechanisms which will bring about social peace are independent of the will of individuals as well as of their merits: "The guarantee of perpetual peace is nothing less than that great artist, nature (*natura ∂ae∂ala rerum*). In her mechanical course we see that her aim is to produce a harmony among men, against their will and indeed through their discord." *This* is ideology at its purest. One can claim that the notion of ideology was posited "for itself" only in the liberal universe, with its founding distinction between the ordinary people immersed in their universe of Meaning—of (what appears from the properly modern perspective as) the confusion between facts and values—and the cold rational observers who are able to perceive the world the way it is, without moralistic prejudices, as a mechanism regulated by laws (of passions) like any other natural mechanism. Only in this modern universe does society appear as an object of a possible experiment, as a chaotic field to which one can (and should) apply a value-free Theory or Science (a political "geometry of passions," or economics, or racist science). It is only this modern position of the value-free scientist, approaching society the same way as a natural scientist approaches nature, that amounts to ideology proper, not the spontaneous attitude of the meaningful experience of life dismissed by the scientist as a set of superstitious prejudices—it is ideology because it imitates the form of the natural sciences without really being one. "Ideology" in a strict sense is thus always reflexive, redoubled on itself: it is a name for neutral knowledge which opposes itself to common "ideology."[45] There is thus a duality inscribed into the very notion of ideology: (1) "mere ideology" as the spontaneous self-apprehension of individuals with all their prejudices; (2) neutral, "value-free" knowledge to be applied to society to engineer its development. In other words, ideology always is (or, rather, appears) as its own species.

---

45   Even in Stalinist Marxism, which—in total opposition to Marx—uses the term "ideology" in a positive sense, ideology is opposed to science: first, Marxists analyze society in a neutral scientific way; then, in order to mobilize the masses, they translate their insights into "ideology." All one has to add here is that this "Marxist science" opposed to ideology is ideology at its purest.

Coda: Multiculturalism, the Reality of an Illusion

In a critical reading of my plenary talk at the Law and Critique Conference in 2007, Sara Ahmed challenged my claim that it is an "empirical fact" that liberal multiculturalism is hegemonic.[46] Her first step was to emphasize the distinction between the semblance of hegemony (ideological illusion) and actual hegemony:

> Hegemony is not really reducible to facts as it involves semblance, fantasy and illusion, being a question of how things appear and the gap between appearance and how bodies are distributed. To read hegemony we have to distrust how things appear. Indeed, what is striking about Žižek's retort is how much his reading of "political correctness" and "liberal multiculturalism" involved a certain literalism, as if the prohibition of speech acts that are not based on respecting the other's difference are "really" what is prohibited, or as if the prohibition is simply real by virtue of being articulated within public culture. So the speech act, "we must support the other's difference," is read as hegemonic, is taken literally as a sign not only that it is compulsory to support the other's difference, but that we are not allowed to refuse this support. The speech act is read as doing what it says. In order to re-consider the effects of such injunctions and prohibitions, I have introduced a new class of what I call non-performatives: speech acts that do not do what they say, that do not bring into effect that which they name. Could the speech work to create an illusion that we do support the other's difference, which might work by not bringing such support into existence?

My point is double here. First, I agree with the category of the "non-performatives," but with a twist: they are performatives, even very effective ones, but *different from what they claim to be*. There are other theoretical notions we can use to describe this duality, such as the "pragmatic paradox," the gap between the "subject of the enunciated" and the "subject of the enunciation," the "double bind"; there are nonetheless differences between these notions. The "double bind" implies an unbearable subjective tension (the proverbial mother who explicitly enjoins her son to leave home and start an autonomous life, but whose message between the lines is a desperate call for him to stay; the father who tells his son to act autonomously, but if the son effectively does so, he thereby asserts his

---

46   Sara Ahmed, "'Liberal Multiculturalism Is the Hegemony—It's an Empirical Fact'—A response to Slavoj Žižek" (unpublished manuscript).

subordination to his mother, since he is following her injunction), while the "non-performative" works smoothly, enabling you, as it were, to both have your cake and eat it, in other words to assert your superiority over the Other in/through the very gesture of guaranteeing their equality and your respect for their difference.

When I claim that multiculturalism is hegemonic, I claim only that it is hegemonic as ideology, not that it describes the reality of the predominant form of social relations—which is why I criticize it so ferociously. So when Ahmed writes that "multiculturalism is a fantasy which conceals forms of racism, violence and inequality," I can only add that this goes for every hegemonic ideology. I do not confuse ideological fantasy and fact—they are confused in reality: the reality of what Ahmed calls "civil racism" can only function through (in the guise of) the illusion of anti-racist multiculturalism. And, furthermore, an illusion is never simply an illusion: it is not enough to make the old Marxist point about the gap between the ideological appearance of the universal legal form and the particular interests that really sustain it—as is so common amongst politically correct critics on the Left. The counter-argument that the form is never a "mere" form, but involves a dynamic of its own which leaves traces in the materiality of social life, made by Claude Lefort and Jacques Rancière, is fully valid. After all, the "formal freedom" of the bourgeois sets in motion processes of altogether "material" political demands and practices, from trade unions to feminism.

Rancière rightly emphasizes the radical *ambiguity* of the Marxist notion of the gap between formal democracy, with its discourse of the rights of man and political freedom, and the economic reality of exploitation and domination. This gap between the "appearance" of equality-freedom and the social reality of economic and cultural differences can be interpreted in the standard symptomatic way, namely that the form of universal rights, equality, freedom, and democracy is just a necessary, but illusory expression of its concrete social content, the universe of exploitation and class domination. Or it can be interpreted in the much more subversive sense of a tension in which the "appearance" of *égaliberté* is precisely *not* a "mere appearance," but has a power of its own. This power allows it to set in motion the process of the re-articulation of actual socio-economic relations by way of their progressive "politicization": why shouldn't women also vote? Why shouldn't conditions at the workplace also be of public political concern? And on we could go. If bourgeois freedom is merely formal and does not disturb the true relations of power, why, then, did the

Stalinist regime not permit it? What was it so afraid of? In the opposition between form and content, the form possesses an autonomy of its own — one could almost say: a content of its own.

To return to Ahmed: how, then, does multiculturalism as fantasy function?

> In such a fantasy, racism is "officially prohibited." This is true. We are "supposed" to be for racial equality, tolerance and diversity, and we are not "allowed" to express hatred towards others, or to incite racist hatred. I would argue that this prohibition against racism is imaginary, and that it conceals everyday forms of racism, and involves a certain desire for racism. Take Big Brother and the Jade Goody story. You could argue that Big Brother's exposure of racism functions as evidence that political correctness is hegemonic: you are not allowed to be racist towards others. But that would be a misreading. What was at stake was the desire to locate racism in the body of Jade Goody, who comes to stand for the ignorance of the white working classes, as a way of showing that "we" (Channel 4 and its well-meaning liberal viewers) are not racist like that. When anti-racism becomes an ego ideal you know you are in trouble.
>
> The prohibition of racist speech should not then be taken literally: rather, it is a way of imagining "us" as beyond racism, as being good multicultural subjects who are not like that. By saying racism is over there — "Look, there it is! in the located body of the racist" — other forms of racism remain unnamed, what we could call civil racism. We might even say that the desire for racism is an articulation of a wider unnamed racism that accumulates force by not being named, or by operating under the sign of civility.

The best example one can imagine of this was the presidential election in France in 2002, when Jean-Marie Le Pen made it into the second round: reacting to this racist and chauvinist threat, the entirety of "democratic France" closed ranks behind Jacques Chirac, who was re-elected with an overwhelming majority of 80 percent. No wonder everyone felt good after this display of French anti-racism, no wonder people "loved to hate" Le Pen; by way of clearly locating racism in him and his party, general "civil racism" was rendered invisible.

Similarly, in Slovenia recently, a big problem arose with a Roma family who were camping close to a small town. When a man was killed in the camp, the townspeople started to protest, demanding that the Roma be moved from the camp (which they had occupied illegally) to another location, organizing vigilante groups, etc. Predictably, Slovenian liberals condemned them as racists, locating racism in this isolated small town, though the liberals, living comfortably in the big cities, had no contact with the Roma other than meeting their representatives in front of the TV cameras. When the TV reporters interviewed the "racists" from the town, it became clear they were a group of people frightened by the constant fighting and shooting in the Roma camp, by the theft of animals from their farms, and by other forms of minor harassment. It is all too easy to say (as did the liberals) that the Roma way of life is (also) a consequence of centuries of exclusion and mistreatment, that the townspeople should be more receptive to the Roma, and so on and so forth. What nobody was prepared to do vis-à-vis the local "racists" was offer concrete solutions for the very real problems the Roma camp evidently posed for them.

One of the most irritating liberal-tolerant strategies is that of distinguishing between Islam as a great religion of spiritual peace and compassion and its fundamentalist-terrorist abuse—whenever Bush or Netanyahu or Sharon announced a new phase in the War on Terror, they never forgot to include this mantra. (One is almost tempted to counter it by claiming that, as with all religions, Islam is, in itself, a rather stupid and inconsistent construction, and that what makes it truly great are its possible political uses.) This is liberal-tolerant racism at its purest: this kind of "respect" for the Other is the very form of the appearance of its opposite, of patronizing disrespect. The very term "tolerance" is here indicative: one "tolerates" something one does not approve of, but cannot abolish, either because one is not strong enough to do so or because one is benevolent enough to allow the Other to retain its illusions—in this way, a secular liberal "tolerates" religion, a permissive parent "tolerates" his children's excesses, and so on.

Where I disagree with Ahmed is in her supposition that the underlying injunction of liberal tolerance is monocultural—"Be like us, become British!" On the contrary, I claim that the injunction is one of cultural apartheid: others should not come too close to us, we should protect our "way of life." The demand "Become like us!" is a superego demand, a demand which counts on the other's inability to really become like us, so that we can then gleefully "deplore" their failure. (Recall how, in apartheid South Africa, the official regime's ideology was multiculturalist: apartheid was needed so that all the diverse African tribes would not get drowned in white civilization.) The *truly* unbearable fact for a multiculturalist liberal is an Other who *really does* become like us, while retaining their own specific features.[47]

Furthermore, Ahmed passes too easily between forms of racism which should be distinguished. In a kind of spectral analysis, one can identify at least three different modes of contemporary racism. First, there is the old-fashioned unabashed rejection of the Other (despotic, barbarian, orthodox, Muslim, corrupt, oriental . . .) on behalf of authentic values (Western, civilized, democratic, Christian . . .). Then there is the "reflexive" politically correct racism: the multiculturalist perception of, for example, the Balkans as the terrain of ethnic horror and intolerance, of primitive irrational bellicose passions, as opposed to the post-national liberal-democratic process of solving conflicts through rational negotiation, compromise, and mutual respect. Here racism is, as it were, elevated to the second power: it is attributed to the Other, while we occupy the convenient position of a neutral benevolent observer, righteously dismayed at the horrors going on down there. Finally, there is reversed racism, which celebrates the exotic authenticity of the Balkan Other, as in the notion of the Serbs who, in contrast to the inhibited, anemic Western Europeans, still exhibit a prodigious lust for life.

Ahmed further claims that racists themselves present themselves as a "threatened minority" whose free speech must be protected:

[They] use the prohibition as evidence that racism is a minority position which has to be defended against the multicultural hegemony. Racism can then be articulated as a minority position, a refusal of orthodoxy. In this perverse logic, racism can then be embraced as a form of free speech. We have articulated a new discourse of freedom: as the freedom to be offensive, in which racism becomes an offense that restores our freedom: the story goes, we have worried too much about offending the other, we must get beyond this restriction, which sustains the fantasy that "that" was the worry in the first place. Note here that the other, especially the Muslim subject who is represented as easily offended, becomes the one who causes injury, insofar as it is the Muslim other's "offendability" that is read as restricting our free speech. The offendable subject "gets in the way" of our freedom. So rather than saying racism is prohibited by the liberal multicultural consensus, under the banner of respect for difference, I would

---

47   Furthermore, the liberal-multiculturalist's opposition to direct racism is not a mere illusion whose truth is the protection of racism: there is a class-coded dimension to it, of which Ahmed is aware, directed against (white) working-class fundamentalism/racism/anti-feminism.

argue that racism is what is protected under the banner of free speech through the appearance of being prohibited.

We should here supplement Ahmed's presentation with different examples which render visible the perhaps unexpected implications of her theoretical propositions. Consider the paradox of Chomsky, when he wrote the preface to a book by Robert Faurisson, a Holocaust denier, defending the author's right to publish the book. Chomsky makes it clear that he is personally disgusted by Faurisson's reasoning; but the problem, as he goes on to say, is that once we start to prohibit certain opinions, who will be next in line? The question is thus: how to counteract the fake liberal prohibition on racism? In the Chomsky mode, or by replacing it with a "true" prohibition?

Another unexpected example: according to Jean-Claude Milner, a unified Europe could only constitute itself on the basis of a progressive erasure of all divisive historical traditions and legitimizations; consequently, a unified Europe will be based on the erasure of history, of historical memory. Recent phenomena such as Holocaust revisionism, or the moral equation of all victims of World War II (Germans suffered under aerial bombardments no less than did the Russians or the British; the fate of Nazi collaborators liquidated by the Russians after the war was comparable to that of victims of the Nazi genocide, etc.), are the logical outcome of this tendency: all specified limits are potentially erased on behalf of abstract suffering and victimization. And this Europe—and this is what Milner is aiming at all along—in its very advocacy of unlimited openness and multicultural tolerance, again needs the figure of the "Jew" as a structural obstacle to this drive to unlimited unification. Contemporary anti-Semitism, however, no longer takes the same form as the old ethnic anti-Semitism; its focus has been displaced from Jews as an ethnic group onto the State of Israel: "in the program of the Europe of the twenty-first century, the State of Israel occupies exactly the position that the name 'Jew' occupied in the Europe before the rupture of 39–45."[48] In this way, the anti-Semitism of today can present itself as anti-anti-Semitism, full of solidarity with the victims of the Holocaust; the reproach is just that, in our era of the gradual dissolution of all limits, of the fluidification of all traditions, the Jews wanted to build their own clearly delimited nation-state. Here are the very last lines of Milner's book:

---

48   Jean-Claude Milner, *Les Penchants criminels de l'Europe démocratique*, Paris: Editions Verdier 2003, p. 97.

If modernity is defined by the belief in an unlimited realization of dreams, our future is fully outlined. It leads through absolute theoretical and practical anti-Judaism. To follow Lacan beyond what he explicitly stated, the foundations of a new religion are thus posited: anti-Judaism will be the natural religion of the humanity-to-come.[49]

Is Milner, a passionate pro-Zionist, not relying here on the same logic as used by Ahmed? In his view, are Jews not caught in the same paradoxical predicament as, say, British Muslims: they were offered civil rights, the chance to integrate into UK society, but, ungrateful as they are, they persisted in their separate way of life? Plus, again similarly to Muslims, they are perceived as being excessively sensitive, seeing "anti-Semitism" everywhere. Milner's point is thus that the official anti-anti-Semitism, which issues prohibitions (recall the case of David Irving), is but the form of appearance of a secret anti-Semitism.

Returning to Ahmed's line of argumentation: the hegemony of multiculturalism is thus not a direct form of hegemony, but a reflexive one:

the hegemonic position is that liberal multiculturalism is the hegemony. This is why the current monocultural political agenda functions as a kind of retrospective defense against multiculturalism. The explicit argument of New Labour is that multiculturalism went "too far": we gave the other "too much" respect, we celebrated difference "too much," such that multiculturalism is read as the cause of segregation, riots and even terrorism.

I totally agree with the general principle that "hegemonies are often presented as minority positions, as defenses against what are perceived to be hegemonic positions." Today's celebration of "minorities" and "marginals" *is* the predominant majority position. But we could add a series of other examples, such as the neocons who complain about the terrors of liberal political correctness, presenting themselves as protectors of an endangered minority. Or take those critics of patriarchy who attack it as if it were still a hegemonic position, ignoring what Marx and Engels wrote more than 150 years ago, in the first chapter of *The Communist Manifesto*: "The bourgeoisie, wherever it has got the upper hand, has put an end to all feudal, *patriarchal*, idyllic relations." Such an insight is still ignored by those leftist cultural theorists who focus their critique on patriarchal ideology and practice. Is it not time to start wondering about the fact that

---

49   Ibid., p. 126.

the critique of patriarchal "phallogocentrism" and so forth was elevated into the main question at the very historical moment — ours — when patriarchy definitively lost its hegemonic role, when it was progressively swept away by the market individualism of rights? What becomes of patriarchal family values when a child can sue his parents for neglect and abuse, or when the family and parenthood itself are *de jure* reduced to a temporary and dissolvable contract between independent individuals? (And, incidentally, Freud was no less aware of this: for him, the decline of the Oedipal mode of socialization was the historical condition of the rise of psychoanalysis.[50]) In other words, *the critical claim that patriarchal ideology continues to be the hegemonic ideology* is the form of *the hegemonic ideology of our times* — its function is to enable us to evade the deadlock of the hedonistic permissiveness which is actually hegemonic.

On February 7, 2008, the Archbishop of Canterbury told BBC Radio 4's World at One that the adoption of certain aspects of Sharia law in the UK "seems unavoidable": the UK has to "face up to the fact" that some of its citizens do not relate to the British legal system, so that adopting parts of Islamic Sharia law would help maintain social cohesion. He stressed that "nobody in their right mind would want to see in this country the kind of inhumanity that's sometimes been associated with the practice of the law in some Islamic states; the extreme punishments, the attitudes to women as well"; however, an approach to law which simply said "there's one law for everybody and that's all there is to be said, and anything else that commands your loyalty or allegiance is completely irrelevant in the processes of the courts — I think that's a bit of a danger." Muslims should not have to choose between "the stark alternatives of cultural

---

50   One feminist strategy (especially in France and Italy) is to admit that the paternal authority is disintegrating, and that late capitalism is approaching a globalized perverse society of "pathological narcissists" caught up in the superego call to enjoy, but to claim that, to counter this lack, a new figure of authority is emerging "from below," unnoticed by the media — the symbolic authority of the mother which has nothing to do with the traditional patriarchal figure of the Mother; the new mother here does not fit into the existing ideological coordinates. The problem with this solution is that as a rule it amounts to descriptions and generalizations of actual cases of (single and other) mothers who have to take care of children — in short, it reads as a (sometimes almost Catholic-sentimental) description of the heroic and compassionate single parent who keeps the family together when the father is absent. Such an approach does not really confront the key question, that of the Name-of-the-Father. That is to say, the Name-of-the-Father plays a key role in structuring the symbolic space, sustaining prohibitions which constitute and stabilize desires — what happens to this role with the rise of maternal authority? Also, for Lacan, the Name-of-the-Father only functions when recognized — referred to — by the mother; that is, for him, the Name-of-the-Father is a structuring principle for the entire field of sexual difference. Thus one can well imagine a lesbian couple raising children where, although there is no father, the Name-of-the-Father is fully operative. So what happens to sexual difference, as well as to the symbolic function of the father, with the rise of maternal authority?

loyalty or state loyalty." The issue of whether Catholic adoption agencies should be forced to accept gay parents under equality laws already showed the potential for legal confusion: "The principle that there is only one law for everybody is an important pillar of our social identity as a Western democracy. But I think it is a misunderstanding to suppose this means people don't have other affiliations, other loyalties which shape and dictate how they behave in society and that the law needs to take some account of that." People may legally devise their own way to settle a dispute in front of a designated third party as long as both sides agree to the process. Muslim Sharia courts and the Jewish Beth Din come into this category: the country's main Beth Din at Finchley in north London oversees a wide range of cases including divorce settlements, contractual rows between traders, and tenancy disputes; in a similar way, Muslims should be allowed to choose to have marital disputes or financial matters dealt with in a Sharia court.[51]

However, notwithstanding all my sympathies for Rowan Williams, I think the devil hides in the details of his proposal, where the old dilemma of group rights versus individual rights explodes with a vengeance. Williams is careful enough to emphasize two limitations of his proposal: (1) individual Muslims should retain a choice: they should not be forced to obey the Sharia, just permitted to choose it; (2) the Sharia should be implemented only in certain areas, applying norms which are not in conflict with the general law (marital disputes, not amputations of hands for theft . . .). But if we really follow these two principles, then nothing radical really happens: if some group of people wants to regulate its affairs in a way which adds new rules without infringing upon the existing legal order, so what? Things become problematic the moment we move a step further and concede to one particular ethnic-religious community a more substantial role as the untranscendable foundation of one's existence.

This is what makes the issue of universal compulsory education so controversial: liberals insist that children should be given the right to remain part of their particular community, but on condition that they are given a choice. But for, say, Amish children to really have a free choice of which way of life to choose, either their parents' life or that of the "English," they would have to be properly informed on all the options, educated in them, and the only way to do that would be to extract them

---

51   It is interesting to note that the Evo Morales government in Bolivia is pursuing a similar goal: it set itself the task of exploring the possibilities of combining the legal order of a modern state with older indigenous practices of resolving conflictual situations.

from their embeddedness in the Amish community, in other words, to effectively render them "English." This also clearly demonstrates the limitations of the standard liberal attitude towards Muslim women wearing a veil: it is deemed acceptable if it is their free choice and not an option imposed on them by their husbands or family. However, the moment a woman wears a veil as the result of her free individual choice, the meaning of her act changes completely: it is no longer a sign of her direct substantial belongingness to the Muslim community, but an expression of her idiosyncratic individuality, of her spiritual quest and her protest against the vulgarity of the commodification of sexuality, or else a political gesture of protest against the West. A choice is always a meta-choice, a choice of the modality of the choice itself: it is one thing to wear a veil because of one's immediate immersion in a tradition; it is quite another to refuse to wear a veil; and yet another to wear one not out of a sense of belonging, but as an ethico-political choice. This is why, in our secular societies based on "choice," people who maintain a substantial religious belonging are in a subordinate position: even if they are allowed to practice their beliefs, these beliefs are "tolerated" as their idiosyncratic personal choice or opinion; the moment they present them publicly as what they really are for them, they are accused of "funda-mentalism." What this means is that the "subject of free choice" (in the Western "tolerant" multicultural sense) can only emerge as the result of an extremely *violent* process of being torn away from one's particular lifeworld, of being cut off from one's roots.

Western secular law not only promotes laws that are different from those of religious legal systems, it also relies on a different *formal* mode of how subjects relate to legal regulations. This is what is missed in the simple reduction of the gap that separates liberal universalism from particular substantial ethnic identities to a gap between two particularities ("liberal universalism is an illusion, a mask concealing its own particularity which it imposes onto others as universal"): the universalism of a Western liberal society does not reside in the fact that its values (human rights, etc.) are universal in the sense of holding for *all* cultures, but in a much more radical sense, for individuals relate to *themselves* as "universal," they participate in the universal dimension directly, by-passing their particular social position. The problem with particular laws for particular ethnic or religious groups is that not all people experience themselves as belonging to a particular ethnic or religious community—so that aside from people belonging to such groups, there should be "universal" individuals who just belong to the realm of state law. Apart from apples, pears, and grapes, there should be a place for fruit as such.

The catch here is that of the freedom of choice given to you if you make the right choice: others should be tolerated only if they accept our society. As Ahmed explains:

> this involves a reading of the other as abusing our multicultural love: as if to say, we gave our love to you, and you abused our love by living apart from us, so now you must become British. There is a threat implied here: become us, become like us (and support democracy and give up the burqa, so we can see your face and communicate with you like the ordinary people we are) or go away . . . Migrants enter the national consciousness as ungrateful. Ironically then racism becomes attributed to the failure of migrants to receive our love. The monocultural hegemony involves the fantasy that multiculturalism is the hegemony. The best description of today's hegemony is "liberal monoculturalism" in which common values are read as under threat by the support for the other's difference, as a form of support that supports the fantasy of the nation as being respectful at the same time as it allows the withdrawal of this so-called respect. The speech act that declares liberal multiculturalism as hegemonic is thus the hegemonic position.

If we formulate the problem in these terms, the alternative appears as follows: either "true" multiculturalism, or else drop the universal claim as such. Both solutions are wrong, for the simple reason that they are not different at all, but ultimately coincide: "true" multiculturalism would be the utopia of a neutral universal legal frame enabling each particular culture to assert its identity. The thing to do is to change the entire field, introducing a totally different Universal, that of an antagonistic struggle which, rather than taking place between particular communities, splits each community from within, so that the "trans-cultural" link between communities is one of a shared struggle.

Interlude 1. Hollywood Today:
Report from an Ideological Battlefield

Let us begin, quite arbitrarily, with Michael Apted's *Enigma* (2001, screen-play by Tom Stoppard, based on the novel by Robert Harris), which takes place in 1943, among the cryptanalysts at Bletchley Park working day and night to crack the German "Enigma" code. They are rejoined by Tom Jericho, a troubled working-class mathematical genius who is back after a period of recuperation brought on by overwork and an unhappy love affair with Claire, the easy-going *femme fatale*, which led to his psychic breakdown. Jericho immediately tries to see Claire again and finds that she has mysteriously disappeared. He enlists the help of Claire's house-mate Hester to follow the trail of clues and learn what has happened to her; the two repeatedly break both the rules of the Bletchley Park estab-lishment and the law as their hunt gets more intense. Jericho is closely watched by Wigram, an upper-class MI5 agent, who plays cat and mouse with him throughout the film. Jericho is tolerated at the Park, despite his transgressions, because of the brilliant plan he invents for uncovering the new key. Tom and Hester at the same time uncover a British government plot to bury the intelligence information on the Katyn massacre, for fear it might weaken American willingness to remain in the war on the same side as the Soviet Union. This, in turn, leads to their discovery that a Polish cryptanalyst, Jozef Pukowski, was so incensed on learning of the massacre that he is prepared to betray Bletchley's secrets to the Nazis in order to take revenge on Stalin. The fate of Claire remains unclear to the end: was she killed or did she just disappear? All we learn is that she was in reality also an MI5 agent under Wigram's control.

The film was criticized for its manipulation of historical facts: apart from a minor series of changes (for example, the only known traitor at Bletchley Park was John Cairncross, who worked for the Soviet Union), the film's biggest alteration concerns the character of Jericho, who is obviously a sanitized version of the legendary Alan Turing, a key figure at the real Bletchley Park in both the cracking of the Enigma code and the development of the digital computer; in the 1950s, Turing was prosecuted for homosexual acts, lost his security clearance, and was subjected to brutal chemical treatment, which resulted in his suicide in 1954. In the film, a firmly heterosexual Turing-Jericho finally gets over his traumatic crush on Claire—in the final scene, we see him in 1946, meeting Hester, pregnant with their child, in front of the National Gallery in London.[1]

However, such an analysis moves at the level of what one is tempted to call constituted ideology, following the distinction proposed by Alain Badiou between two types (or rather levels) of corruption in democracy: *de facto* empirical corruption, and the corruption that pertains to the very *form* of democracy with its reduction of politics to the negotiation of private interests. In a homologous way, one should distinguish between constituted ideology—empirical manipulations and distortions at the level of content—and constitutive ideology—the ideological form which provides the coordinates of the very space within which the content is located.[2]

To discern the contours of the "constitutive ideology" of *Enigma*, one should focus on how the film rather obviously plays upon the register of two enigmas: the enigma of the German secret code and the enigma of the Woman. No matter how complex the military codes are, they can be cracked—the true enigma which cannot ever be cracked is the Woman. (The split between Claire and Hester is crucial here: the only way for

---

1   We all know of Alan Turing's famous "imitation game," designed to test whether a machine can think: we communicate with two computer interfaces, asking them any imaginable question; behind one of the interfaces, there is a human person typing the answers, while behind the other, there is a machine. If, based on the answers we get, we cannot tell the intelligent machine from the intelligent human, then, according to Turing, our failure proves that machines can think. What is less known is that, in its first formulation, the test was not to distinguish the human from the machine, but man from woman. Why this strange displacement from sexual difference to the difference between human and machine? Was it a result of Turing's simple eccentricity due to his homosexuality? According to some interpreters, the point is to oppose the two experiments: the successful imitation of a woman's responses by a man (or vice versa) *would not prove anything*, because gender identity does not depend on sequences of symbols, while the successful imitation of a human by a machine would prove that this machine can think, because "thinking" is ultimately the proper way of sequencing symbols. What if, however, the solution to this enigma is much more simple and radical? What if sexual difference is not simply a biological fact, but the Real of an antagonism that *defines humanity*, so that once sexual difference is abolished, a human being effectively becomes indistinguishable from a machine?

2   In the same way, apropos the ongoing healthcare debate in the US, one should distinguish between the "constituted" level of empirical falsifications (like the absurd charge that Obama's healthcare reform will lead to the establishment of "death committees"), and the "constitutive" level of the threat to freedom of choice which informs the entire field of the attacks on Obama. Not to mention the Benjaminian distinction between constituted violence (empirical acts of violence within society) and constitutive violence (the violence inscribed into the very institutional frame of a society).

a man to normalize the sexual relationship is to erase the enigmatic Woman and accept the ordinary woman as a partner.) By re-framing the story of the effort to break the German "enigma" code into a story about the enigma of woman, what the film adds to the narrative is ideological surplus-enjoyment: it is this re-framing which sustains our pleasure in the otherwise narratively rather dull work of cracking secret codes. This feature is also what makes the film part of the Hollywood ideological universe: if a movie on the same topic (military decoding) had been made in, say, the Soviet Union, there would have been no erotic re-framing of the "enigma" (which is why the film would also have been much more boring. . .).

What Does the Joker Want?

Today, this fundamental level of constitutive ideology assumes the guise of its very opposite: *non-ideology*.

David Grossman stands for the Jewish attitude at its purest, as rendered in a nice personal anecdote: when, just prior to the 1967 Israeli–Arab war, he heard on the radio about the Arab threats to throw the Jews into the sea, his reaction was to take swimming lessons—a paradigmatic Jewish reaction if there ever was one, in the spirit of the long talk between Josef K. and the priest (the prison chaplain) that follows the parable on the door of the law in Kafka's *Trial*. Grossman's work is marked by a strange line of separation. His non-fiction texts deal almost exclusively with what the Israelis refer to as *hamatzav*, "The Situation," a neutral-sounding word that encompasses everything from the Intifada to the security fence and the withdrawal from Gaza. (Its equivalent in Cuba would be the "special period," a code-word for the economic catastrophe that followed the disintegration of the Soviet bloc.) "The Situation" is not a specific event but rather every event; it bleeds into every part of life. In stark contrast, his fiction withdraws into the claustrophobic space of private passions and obsessions. However, even when he writes of marriage and desire, jealousy and motherhood, loyalty and betrayal, he is mapping an entire country's anxieties and longings. Rather than explicitly reporting the facts on the ground, Grossman constructs his own alternate reality that evokes "The Situation" as their absent Real-Cause.

The central character of "Frenzy," the first novella of Grossman's *Her Body Knows*, is Shaul, an official in the Ministry of Education, who has convinced himself that his wife, Elisheva, is having an affair. Consumed with jealousy, he conjures up every detail of the lovers' time together. When Elisheva goes off for a few days alone, Shaul insists on following her. Because his leg has been fractured in a mysterious accident, he enlists the help of his brother's wife, Esti, who agrees to drive him to where Elisheva is staying. On this hallucinatory journey, the normally reticent Shaul finds himself telling Esti the elaborate story of Elisheva's affair. Is the affair real or just a fantasy? Is it rooted in Elisheva's actual emotions or in Shaul's obsessive jealousy? Somewhere along the way, that distinction stops mattering: Shaul blurs into the figure of his wife's lover and the Elisheva of his imagination blurs into the Elisheva of real life. Esti is transformed as well: as their journey stretches deeper into the night, Shaul's story stirs Esti's own longing for a past love.

The second novella, "Her Body Knows," is also about jealousy and betrayal; at its center are two women: a yoga teacher named Nili who is dying of cancer, and her estranged daughter Rotem, a writer living in London who has returned to Israel to read her mother a story she's been working on, about a yoga teacher named Nili. In the story, which takes place during her own childhood, Nili is asked by the father of a shy teen-age boy to initiate the latter into the secrets of sexuality and thus "make him a man." It is easy to recognize here the logic of fantasy at its purest: inventing a scenario which touches on the mystery of the parents' sexual lives.

What both novellas are really about is the transformative power of storytelling, the need to construct alternate fictional realities: what actually happened is beside the point, both Shaul and Rotem refashion reality to create a story they need to tell. Rewriting the past is an act of generosity which enables the subject to change her future. Even if the fictional realities they construct are not pretty (there are no happy marriages in these fantasies, no idyllic childhoods), even if it appears that one pain is merely "replaced with another in a widening, an opening up, of the past," there is a secret "pathological" profit in this shift, a "surplus-enjoyment" is generated.

And it is here that ideology enters: such retreats into intimate real-ity take place against the background of *hamatzav*, "The Situation." No wonder that, in recent years, this same desire for an alternate reality has become part of Israel's national psyche: dealing with "The Situation" generates an atmosphere of anxiety, a deep sense of claustrophobia, a retreat into the relative safety of the indoors. Though an Israeli writer need not directly address the political atmosphere that surrounds him, these concerns seep in, quietly and evocatively. The properly ideological function of this retreat is thus clear — its underlying message is: "we are just ordinary people who want only peace and normal life." A similar attitude forms part of the mythology of the IDF: the Israeli media love to dwell on the imperfections and psychic traumas of Israeli soldiers, presenting them not as perfect military machines, but as ordinary people who, caught into the vicissitudes of history and warfare, are just as likely as anyone else to make mistakes or lose their way.

This ideological operation accounts for the success of two recent Israeli films about the 1982 Lebanon war: Ari Folman's animated documentary *Waltz with Bashir* and Samuel Maoz's *Lebanon*. *Lebanon* draws on Maoz's own memories as a young soldier, rendering the war's fear and claustrophobia by shooting most of the action from inside a tank. The movie follows four inexperienced soldiers dispatched in the tank to "mop up" enemies in a Lebanese town that has already been bombarded by the Israeli Air Force. Interviewed at the 2009 Venice festival, Yoav Donat, the actor who plays the director as a soldier a quarter of a century ago, said: "This is not a movie that makes you think 'I've just been to a movie'. This is a movie that makes you feel like you've been to war." In a similar way, *Waltz with Bashir* renders the horrors of the 1982 conflict from the point of view of Israeli soldiers. Maoz said his film is not a condemnation of Israel's policies, but a personal account of what he went through: "The mistake I made is to call the film 'Lebanon' because the Lebanon war is no different in its essence from any other war and for me any attempt to be political would have flattened the film."[3] This is ideology at its purest: the focus on the perpetrator's traumatic experience enables us to obliterate the entire ethico-political background of the conflict, involving questions such as what was the Israeli army doing deep in Lebanon? (In *Lebanon*, the spatial limitation to the inside of a tank quite literally enacts such an erasure.) Such a "humanization" thus serves to obfuscate the key question: the need for the ruthless political analysis of what is being done in terms of political-military activity. Our politico-military struggles are precisely not an opaque History which brutally disrupts our intimate lives — they are a field in which we are always already engaged, even if it is in a mode of ignorance.

Should we be surprised to find the same ideological mechanism in Leonardo Padura's Mario Conde police procedurals set in today's Havana? On a first approach, these novels provide such a critical view of the Cuban

---

3   Silvia Aloisi, "Israeli film relives Lebanon war from inside tank," Reuters, September 8, 2009.

situation (poverty, corruption, cynical disbelief.) that one cannot but be shocked to learn not only that Padura lives in Havana, but that he is an establishment figure who has received major state prizes. His heroes — although disappointed, depressed, seeking refuge in alcohol and dreams of alternate historical realities, mourning their missed chances, and, of course, depoliticized, completely ignoring the official socialist ideology — nonetheless fundamentally accept their situation. The novels' underlying message is thus that one should heroically accept the situation the way it is, rather than attempt to escape to the false paradise of Miami. This acceptance forms the backdrop to all the critical remarks and dark descriptions: although totally disillusioned, the characters are from *here* and are *here to stay*, this misery is their world, and they struggle to find a meaningful life within its framework rather than resisting it in any radical way. Back in the Cold War era, Leftist critics often pointed out the ambiguity of John le Carré's stance towards his own society: his critical portrayal of opportunist cynicism, ruthless maneuvering and moral betrayal nonetheless presupposes a basically positive stance — the very moral complexity of secret service life is proof that one lives in an "open" society which allows the expression of such complexities. *Mutatis mutandis*, does not exactly the same hold also for Padura? The very fact that he is able to write the way he does within Cuban society only contributes to its legitimization.

There is a very thin line separating this "humanization" from a resigned coming to terms with *lying* as a social principle: what matters in such a "humanized" universe is authentic intimate experience, not the truth. At the end of Christopher Nolan's *The Dark Knight*, a film which also "humanizes" its superhero, presenting him as full of doubts and weaknesses, the new DA Harvey Dent, an obsessive vigilante against mob rule who became corrupted and committed a number of murders, dies. Batman and his police friend Gordon recognize the loss of morale the city would suffer if Dent's crimes became known. So Batman persuades Gordon to preserve Dent's image by holding Batman responsible for the murders; Gordon destroys the Bat-Signal and a manhunt for Batman ensues. This need to perpetuate a lie in order to sustain public morale is the film's final message: only a lie can redeem us. No wonder that, paradoxically, the only figure of truth in the film is the Joker, its supreme villain.[4] The aim

---

4   I rely here on Andrej Nikolaidis's outstanding "Odresujoca laz," *Ljubljanski dnevnik*, August 28, 2008 (in Slovene). Nikolaidis, a younger generation Montenegrin writer, was sued by Emir Kusturica and scandalously condemned for writing a text in which he denounced Kusturica's complicity with aggressive Serb nationalism.

of his terrorist attacks on Gotham City is made clear: the attacks will stop only when Batman takes off his mask and reveals his true identity; to prevent this disclosure and thus protect Batman, Dent tells the press that he is Batman—another lie. In order to entrap the Joker, Gordon stages his own (fake) death—yet another lie.

The logic of Batman's (or Superman's or Spiderman's) mask is given a comical twist in *The Mask* with Jim Carrey: it is the Mask itself which changes the ordinary guy into a superhero. The link between the Mask and sexuality is rendered clear in the second Superman movie: making love to a woman is incompatible with the power of the Mask, that is, the price Superman has to pay for his consummated love is to become a normal mortal human. The Mask is thus the asexual "partial object" which allows the subject to remain in (or regress to) the pre-Oedipal anal-oral universe where there is no death or guilt, just endless fun and fighting—no wonder the Jim Carrey character in *The Mask* is obsessed with cartoons: the universe of cartoons is an undead universe of infinite plasticity in which every time a character is destroyed it magically recomposes itself and the struggle recommences.

What, then, does the Joker, who wants to disclose the truth beneath the Mask, convinced that this disclosure will destroy the social order, represent? He is not a man without a mask, but, on the contrary, a man fully identified with his mask, a man who *is* his mask—there is nothing, no "ordinary guy," beneath it.[5] This is why the Joker has no back-story and lacks any clear motivation: he tells different people different stories about his scars, mocking the idea that some deep-rooted trauma drives him.[6] How, then, do Batman and the Joker relate? Is the Joker Batman's own death-drive embodied? Is Batman the Joker's destructivity put in the service of society?

A further parallel can be drawn between *The Dark Knight* and Edgar Allen Poe's "The Masque of the Red Death." In the secluded castle in which the mighty retire to survive the plague ("Red Death") ravaging the country, Prince Prospero organizes a lavish masked ball. At midnight, Prospero notices a figure in a blood-spattered, dark robe resembling a funeral shroud, with a skull-like mask depicting a victim of the Red Death. Gravely insulted, Prospero demands to know the identity of the

---

5   Let us recall a similar story about Lacan: those who got to know him personally, to observe how he behaved in private, when he was not maintaining his public image, were surprised to learn that he conducted himself in exactly the same way as in public, with all his ridiculously affected mannerisms.
6   I owe this idea to Bernard Keenan.

mysterious guest; when the figure turns to face him, the Prince falls dead at a glance. The enraged bystanders corner the stranger and remove his mask, only to find the costume empty—the figure is revealed as the person-ification of the Red Death itself which goes on to destroy all life in the castle. Like the Joker and all revolutionaries, the Red Death also wants the masks to be torn off and the truth to be disclosed to the public—one could thus also suggest that, in Russia in 1917, the Red Death penetrated the Romanov castle and caused its downfall.[7]

Does *The Dark Knight*'s extraordinary popularity not then point towards the fact that it touches a nerve in our ideologico-political constel-lation: the undesirability of truth? In this sense, the film is effectively a new version of the two classic John Ford westerns (*Fort Apache* and *The Man Who Shot Liberty Valance*) which demonstrate how, in order to civilize the Wild West, the lie had to be elevated into truth—in short, how our civilization is grounded on a lie. The question to be raised here is: why, at this precise moment, this renewed need for a lie to maintain the social system?

The Sad Lesson of Remakes

The Dark Knight is a sign of a global ideological regression for which one is almost tempted to use the title of Georg Lukács's most Stalinist work: the destruction of (emancipatory) reason. This regression reached its peak in *I Am Legend*, a recent blockbuster casting Will Smith as the last man alive. The film's only interest resides in its comparative value: one of the best ways to detect shifts in the ideological constellation is to compare consecutive remakes of the same story. There are three (or, rather, four, including the original source) versions of *I Am Legend*: Richard Matheson's novel from 1954; the first film version, *The Last Man on Earth* (Italian title: *L'Ultimo uomo della Terra*, 1964, Ubaldo Ragona and Sidney Salkow), with Vincent Price; the second version, *The Omega Man* (1971, Boris Sagal), with Charlton Heston; and the last one, *I Am Legend* (2007, Francis Lawrence), with Will Smith. The first film version, argu-ably still the best, is basically faithful to the novel. The startling premise is well known—as the publicity slogan for the 2007 remake says: "The last man . . . is not alone." The story is yet another fantasy of witnessing one's own absence: Neville, the sole survivor of a catastrophe which has

---

7   There is, effectively, an early Soviet film (Vladimir Gardin's *A Spectre Haunts Europe*, from 1922) which directly stages the October Revolution in the terms of Poe's story.

killed all humans apart from him, wanders the desolate city streets—
and soon discovers that he is not alone, that a mutated species of the
living dead (or, rather, vampires) is stalking him. There is no paradox
in the slogan: even the last man alive is not alone—what remains with
him are the living dead. In Lacan's terms, they are the *a* which adds
itself to the 1 of the last man. As the story progresses, it is revealed that
some infected people have discovered a means to hold the disease at
bay; however, the "still living" people appear no different from the true
vampires during the day, while both are immobilized in sleep. They send
a woman named Ruth to spy on Neville, and much of their interaction
focuses on Neville's internal struggle between his deep-seated paranoia
and his hope. Eventually Neville performs a blood test on her, revealing
her true nature, before she knocks him out and escapes. Months later,
the still living people attack Neville and take him alive so that he can
be executed in front of everyone in the new society. Before his execu-
tion, Ruth provides him with an envelope of pills so that he will feel no
pain. Neville finally realizes why the new society of the infected living
regards him as a monster: just as vampires were regarded as legendary
monsters that preyed on vulnerable humans in their beds, Neville has
become a mythical figure who kills both vampires and the living while
they are sleeping. He is a legend as the vampires once were. The first
film version's main difference with the novel was a shift in the ending:
the hero (here called Morgan) develops a cure for Ruth in his lab; a few
hours later, at nightfall, the still living people attack Morgan, who flees,
but is finally gunned down in the church where his wife has been buried.

The second film version, *The Omega Man*, is set in Los Angeles, where a
group of resistant albinos calling themselves "The Family" have survived
the plague, which has turned them into violent light-sensitive albino
mutants, and affected their minds with psychotic delusions of grandeur.
Although resistant, the members are slowly dying off, apparently due to
mutations of the plague. The Family is led by Matthias, formerly a popular Los Angeles television newscaster; he and his followers believe that
modern science, and not the flaws of humanity, are the cause of their
misfortune. They have reverted to a Luddite lifestyle, employing medieval imagery and technology, complete with long black robes, torches,
bows and arrows. As they see it, Neville, the last symbol of science and a
"user of the wheel," must die. The final scene shows the human survivors
departing in a Land Rover after the dying Neville gives them a flask of
blood serum, presumably to restore humanity.

In the last version, which takes place on Manhattan, the woman who appears to Neville (here called Anna, accompanied by a young boy Ethan and coming somewhere from the South—Maryland and São Paolo are mentioned) tells him that God has sent her to bring him to the colony of survivors in Vermont. Neville refuses to believe her, saying that there cannot be a God in a world afflicted by such suffering and mass death. When the Infected attack the house that night and overrun its defenses, Neville, Anna, and Ethan retreat into the basement laboratory, sealing themselves in with an infected woman on whom Neville was experimenting. Discovering that the last treatment has successfully cured the woman, Neville realizes that he has to find a way to pass it on to other survivors before they are killed. After drawing a vial of blood from the patient and giving it to Anna, he pushes her and Ethan into an old coal chute and sacrifices himself with a hand grenade, killing the attacking Infected. Anna and Ethan escape to Vermont and reach the fortified survivors' colony. In the concluding voice-over, Anna states that Neville's cure enabled humanity to survive and rebuild, establishing his status as a legend, a Christ-like figure whose sacrifice redeemed humanity.

The gradual ideological regression can be observed here at its clinically purest. The main shift (between first and second film versions) is registered in the radical change in the meaning of the title: the original paradox (the hero is now legendary for vampires, as vampires once were for humanity) gets lost, so that, in the last version, the hero is simply a legend for the surviving humans in Vermont. What gets obliterated in this change is the authentically "multicultural" experience rendered by the title's original meaning, the realization that one's own tradition is no better than what appear to us as the "eccentric" traditions of others, a realization nicely formulated by Descartes who, in his *Discourse of Method*, wrote how, in the course of his travels, he recognized that "all those whose sentiments are very contrary to ours are yet not necessarily barbarians or savages, but may be possessed of reason in as great or even a greater degree than ourselves." The irony is that this dimension disappears precisely in our era, in which multicultural tolerance has been elevated into an official ideology.[8]

---

8   In order to encourage peace and tolerance between Albanians and Serbs in Kosovo, the UN forces controlling its independence distributed posters with a photo of a dog and a cat sitting side by side in a friendly manner, accompanied by the message: "If they can live peacefully together, you can too!" If ever there was an example of multicultural racism, this is it: as we all know, in reality, dogs and cats do not tolerate each other, with the exception of circuses and other places where they are trained to do so—hence Albanians and Serbs are implicitly being treated as two different wild (animal) species who have to be properly trained to tolerate each other's proximity.

Let us follow this ideological regression step by step. The first film version is marred by its conclusion: instead of dying by being burned at stake as a legend, the hero's death reasserts his roots in his lost community (the church, the family). The powerful "multicultural" insight into the contingency of our background is thus weakened, the final message is no longer the exchange of positions (we are now legends the way vampires used to be legends for us), which renders palpable the abyss of our rootlessness, but our irreducible attachment to our roots. The second film version completes this obliteration of the topic of the legend by displacing the focus onto the survival of humanity rendered possible by the hero's invention of a cure for the plague. This displacement reinscribes the film into the standard topic of a threat to humanity and its last-minute escape. However, as a positive element, we at least get a dose of liberal anti-fundamentalism and enlightened scientism, rejecting the obscurantist hermeneutics of the search for a "deeper meaning" of the catastrophe. The latest version puts the nail in the coffin, turning things around and openly opting for religious fundamentalism. Indicative already are the geopolitical coordinates of the story: the opposition between a destitute New York and the pure eco-paradise of Vermont, a gated community protected by a wall and security guards, which, to add insult to injury, is joined by the newcomers from the fundamentalist South who have survived the passage through devastated New York. A strictly homologous shift takes place with regard to religion: the film's first ideological climax is Neville's Job-like moment of doubt (there can be no God given that such a catastrophe was possible) opposed to Anna's fundamentalist trust that she is an instrument of God who has sent her to Vermont on a mission whose meaning is not yet clear to her. In the film's final moments, just before his death, Neville changes sides and adopts her fundamentalist perspective by assuming a Christological identification: Anna was brought to him so that he could give her the serum that she will take to Vermont. His sinful doubts are thus redeemed and we are at the exact opposite of the original book's premise: Neville is again a legend, but a legend for the new humanity whose rebirth was made possible by his invention and sacrifice.

A more refined case is that of the two versions of *3:10 to Yuma*, Delmer Daves' (1957) original and James Manigold's (2007) remake. The relationship between the two is best encapsulated by the German title change: the Germans (who as a rule reinvent film titles for local release) called the first version *Zaehl bis drei und bete* [*Count to Three and Pray*], and the remake

Todeszug nach Yuma [*Death-Train to Yuma*]. *3:10 to Yuma* tells the story of a poor farmer (called Evans) who, for $200 that he badly needs in order to save his cattle from drought, accepts a job escorting a bandit (Wade) with a high price on his head from the hotel where he is held to the train that will take him to prison in Yuma. What we have, of course, is a classic story of an ethical ordeal; throughout the film, it seems that the farmer himself is the one subjected to the ordeal, exposed as he is to temptations in the style of the (undeservedly) more famous *High Noon*. All those who have promised to help abandon him when they discover that the hotel is surrounded by the gang sworn to save their boss; the imprisoned bandit himself alternately threatens the farmer and tries to bribe him, and so on. The last scene, however, retrospectively changes our perception of the film totally: close by the train, which is already leaving the station, Wade and Evans find themselves face to face with the entire gang waiting for the right moment to shoot the farmer and thus free their boss.

At this tense moment, when the situation seems hopeless for Evans, Wade suddenly turns to him and says: "Trust me! Let's jump together onto the wagon!" In short, the one really undergoing the ordeal was the bandit himself, the apparent agent of temptation: at the end, having been overcome by the farmer's integrity, he sacrifices his own freedom for him.

In James Manigold's 2007 remake, Evans's adolescent son Will accompanies his father to help him on the mission; Evans's bravery redeems him in the eyes of his son. At the last moment, when they reach the train, Wade's gang guns down Evans; Wade is freed, but he turns his gun on his own gang members and then allows Will to put him onto the train . . . The (regressive, again) shift of accent with regard to the original is here double. First, the film shifts its focus from the duel concerning the test of moral endurance between Wade and Evans to the father–son relationship: the father fears appearing weak, so his entire effort is undertaken in order to assert his paternal authority in the eyes of his son—following the Oedipal formula, the ultimate way of doing so is to die and return as the Name, a symbolic authority, thereby enabling the son to assume his real place. Far from being the figure whose ethical integrity is tested, Wade is now reduced to the role of a "vanishing mediator" in the transference of paternal authority. There is one feature which may appear to contradict this analysis: is Wade's change of heart not overemphasized in the remake—he not only helps Evans, he even turns his gun on his comrades and eliminates them? But the dimension of the ethical act pertaining to this change in the original is here nullified by its very overemphasis: what in the original is a momentary decision, an act of "something in me more than myself," now becomes a fully conscious changing of sides which no longer transforms the subjective identity of the agent involved, and thereby loses its character as an act.[9]

Les non-dupes errent

When even products of an allegedly "liberal" Hollywood display the most blatant ideological regression, is any further proof required that ideology is alive and kicking in our post-ideological world? It should not surprise us, then, to discover ideology at its purest in what may appear to be products of Hollywood at its most innocent: the big blockbuster cartoons.

"The truth has the structure of a fiction"—is there a better exemplification of this thesis than those cartoons, in which the truth about the existing social order is rendered in such a direct way that it would never be allowed in narrative cinema with "real" actors? Recall the image of society we get from violent cartoons in which animals fight: the ruthless struggle for survival, brutal traps and attacks, the exploitation of others . . . if the same story were to be told in a feature film with "real" actors, it would undoubtedly be either censored or dismissed as ridiculously negative. *Kung Fu Panda* (2008, John Stevenson and Mark Osborne), the recent Dreamworks animated hit, is ideology at its most embarrassingly pure. Here is the story: Po is a panda who works in a noodle restaurant owned by his goose father Ping, in the Valley of Peace in China. He is a kung fu fanatic with secret dreams of becoming a great master in the discipline; his weight and clumsiness, however, seem to make this goal unattainable. Ping hopes instead that Po will one day take over the restaurant, and waits for the perfect opportunity to disclose the secret ingredient of his family's noodle recipe. The tortoise Master Oogway, the spiritual leader of the Valley, has a premonition that the evil leopard warrior Tai Lung—a former student of his own protégé, the red panda Master Shifu—will escape from prison and return to threaten the Valley of Peace. Oogway orders a formal ceremony to choose the mighty Dragon Warrior who will

---

9   To add insult to injury, two further details spoil the film's last moments. When a member of Wade's gang shoots Evans to death and then throws Wade his gun, Wade takes a quick glance at the gun's handle, notices a metal relief of Christ on the cross and then changes sides, coldly and quickly killing his entire gang, as if divine intervention pushed him to betray his rescuers. Then, in the very last seconds, when the train is leaving for Yuma with Wade on board, he whistles to his horse outside the train on the station, which then starts to run after the train—a clear hint that Wade has already planned his escape, and everything will end well for him.

be capable of defeating Tai Lung. Po arrives too late and finds himself locked outside the walled palace square. In a last-ditch attempt to get in, he ties several fireworks to a chair and ignites them, which sends him crashing into the center of the arena. Inspired by this sudden appearance, to everyone's shock the old master tortoise designates Po the Dragon Warrior. Meanwhile, Tai Lung escapes from prison; upon learning of this, Po confesses to Shifu his deep self-loathing due to his obesity and his belief that he will never be a match for Tai Lung. Shifu is at a loss for a solution. The following morning, Shifu discovers that Po is capable of impressive physical feats when motivated by food. Shifu leads Po to the countryside for an intensive training regime in which Po is offered food as a reward for learning his lessons. Po excels. Shifu now decides he is ready to face the villain and gives him the sacred Dragon Scroll, which promises great power to the possessor. But when Po opens it, he finds nothing but a blank reflective surface. Both are stricken with despair at the scroll's apparent worthlessness. Wandering alone in the city, Po meets his father, who tries to cheer him up by revealing the secret ingredient of the family's noodle soup: nothing. Things become special, he explains, because people believe them to be special. Realizing that precisely this is the very point of the Dragon Scroll, Po rushes off to challenge Tai Lung. Despite Po's skill, Tai Lung temporarily stuns him and takes the Dragon Scroll, but is unable to understand its symbolism. Po counter-attacks and defeats him in an explosion of light that ripples through the valley. The villagers, including Po's father, hail Po as a hero. In the very last scene, Po rests on the floor with Shifu; after a few seconds, Po suggests that they get something to eat and Shifu agrees.

The first thing that strikes one about the film is a linguistic detail: the abundance of ironically tautological statements, from the trailer's claim that the film is about "the legend of a legendary warrior," to the father's reference to the "special ingredient of my soup with special ingredient." In the Lacanian "logic of the signifier," tautology stands for the point at which, as Lacan put it, the signifier falls into its signified. Recall the old Polish anti-Communist joke: "Socialism is the synthesis of the highest achievements of all previous historical epochs: from tribal society, it took barbarism; from antiquity, it took slavery; from feudalism, it took relations of domination; from capitalism, it took exploitation; and from socialism, it took the name. . . ." Does the same not hold for the anti-Semitic image of the Jew? From the rich bankers, it took financial speculation; from capitalists, it took exploitation; from lawyers, it took legal trickery; from corrupted journalists, it took media manipulation; from the poor, it took indifference towards personal hygiene; from sexual libertines it took promiscuity; and from the Jews it took the name . . . Or take the shark in Spielberg's *Jaws*: from the immigrants, it took their threat to small-town daily life; from natural catastrophes, it took their blind destructive rage; from big capital, it took the ravaging effects of an unknown cause on the daily lives of ordinary people; and from the shark it took its image . . . In all these cases, the "signifier falls into the signified" in the precise sense that the name is included in the object it designates.

What this means is that, to be a true anti-Semite, it is not enough to say that Jews are dirty, exploitative, manipulative, and so on: one has to add that they are dirty, exploiting, manipulative, etc., *because they are Jews*. What accounts for these visible positive properties is the mysterious *je ne sais quoi* which makes them Jews—this mysterious ingredient, "what is in a Jew more than a Jew" (or, in *Kung Fu Panda*, "what is in the soup more than the soup itself, more than its usual ingredients"), is what Lacan called the *objet petit a*, the object-cause of desire. Here, we encounter the first paradox of the *objet a*: the X beyond words is a pure effect of words. This object which is, by definition, ineffable—the *je ne sais quoi* which cannot be adequately translated into any explicit positive determinations, whose transcendence only shines through the flow of speech—is, with regard to its genesis, totally immanent to language, the product of a signifying reversal or self-relation. It emerges at the point where "the signifier falls into the signified," in other words, its transcendence is the inverted mode of appearance of its immanence. This is why its presence is indicated by tautology: the two terms in a tautology are not at the same level: the first occurrence of the term is as a signifier, and the second as a signifier *within the signified*. In the statement "A Jew is a Jew," one expects, after the first occurrence ("A Jew is . . ."), an explication of its signified, a definition of the term, an answer to the question "*What* is a Jew?"; but, when one gets the same term repeated, this signifying repetition generates the specter of an ineffable X beyond words. The paradox is thus that language reaches "beyond itself," to the reality of objects and processes in the world, when it designates these objects and proceeds by means of clear denotative/discursive meanings; but when it refers to an ineffable transcendent X "beyond words," it is caught in itself. The specter of radical Otherness is the mode of appearance of pure immanence, or, to put it in Hegelese, the truth of the relation to transcendent Otherness is self-relating.

Should we then read *Kung Fu Panda* as a somewhat naïve, but none-theless basically accurate illustration of an important aspect of Lacanian theory? When Po opens the Dragon Scroll and sees nothing, only the empty surface, does he not thereby confirm Lacan's thesis that the *objet a* is a lure, a stand-in for the void at the very heart of the symbolic order, that it has no positive ontological consistency? When Lacan proposes as the formula of fantasy $-a, does he not thereby indicate that the *objet a* is ultimately the fantasmatic object? The elementary feature of fantasy is the belief in the actual positive existence of the *objet a*, of the "special ingredient," the quintessence, the sublime "fifth element" over and above the ordinary four (earth, fire, water, air); so when Po realizes that "there is no special ingredient. It's only you. To make something special you just have to believe it's special," does he not thereby accomplish a kind of wild *traversée du fantasme*, breaking its spell?

There are indeed some surprisingly complex moments in *Kung Fu Panda*. When Po enters the forbidden hall in which the Dragon Scroll is kept, he sees a precious sacred painting and exclaims with awe: "I've only seen paintings of this painting"—an authentically Platonic moment, with its reference to the distinction between the copy and the copy of a copy. Furthermore, there is an interesting moment of psychological (and narrative) vacillation in the great confrontation between Shifu and Tai Lung: aware of his responsibility for Tai Lung's failure to become a Master, Shifu apologizes to him, confessing how, due to his love for Tai Lung, he blinded himself to the dangerous path Tai Lung was taking and thus contributed to his downfall. At this moment, Tai Lung's expression changes: taken aback, he looks at Shifu with a perplexed gaze mixed with sympathy, and we (the viewers) are led to believe that a moment of authentic existential contact has taken place, well beyond the simplistic confrontation of good and evil characters. However, the moment passes quickly and Tai Lung explodes in rage, once again ferociously attacking the paternal figure of Shifu. It is as if, at the level of the narrative logic, the offer Shifu makes to Tai Lung is: "Let us change the rules and move from this stupid cartoon confrontation to authentic drama!", an offer which is rejected by his opponent.

So, again—is the film's insight into the illusory nature of the object-cause of desire, into the primacy of the void over every object that occupies the place of the void, effectively proto-Lacanian? It is—but only if we misread Lacan's notion of "traversing the fantasy" as a new version of traditional *wisdom*. That is to say, what is wisdom at its most elementary? In the film, it is embodied in the old tortoise Oogway, whose ultimate wisdom is that there is no *objet a*, no quintessence, every object of our desire is a lure, and we have to accept the vanity of all reality. But what about the obvious opposite of wisdom, the sarcastic denunciation and unmasking of all pretense to sublimity which abounds in the film? *Kung Fu Panda* continuously oscillates between these two extremes: serene wisdom and its cynical undermining by commonsense, with reference to common needs and fears. Such undermining becomes almost a running gag throughout the film — for example, when Shifu runs to Oogway to tell him he has some bad news, Oogway replies with the standard wisdom "There is no good or bad news, there is just news." But when Shifu informs him that Tai Lung has escaped, Oogway says: "Well, this is bad news . . ." Or when, as mentioned, in the final scene of the film, Shifu and Po are laying on their backs meditating in silence, and Po, becoming agitated, says: "What about getting something to eat?", to which Shifu agrees. But are these two levels (wisdom and everyday commonsense) really opposed? Are they not the two sides of one and the same attitude of wisdom? What unites them is their rejection of the *objet a*, of the sublime object of passionate attachment — in the universe of *Kung Fu Panda*, there are only everyday objects and needs, and the void beneath, all the rest is illusion. This, incidentally, is why the universe of the film is asexual: there is no sex or sexual attraction in the film; its economy is the pre-Oedipal oral-anal one (incidentally, the very name of the hero, Po, is a common term for "ass" in German). Po is fat, clumsy, common, *and* a kung fu hero, the new Master — the excluded third in this coincidence of opposites is sexuality.[10]

In what, then, does the ideology of the film reside? Let us return to the key formula: "There is no special ingredient. It's only you. To make something special you just have to believe it is special." This formula renders the fetishistic disavowal (split) at its purest — its message is: "I *know* very well there is no special ingredient, but I nonetheless *believe* in it (and act accordingly)." Cynical denunciation (at the level of rational knowledge) is counteracted by the call of "irrational" belief — and this is the most elementary formula of how ideology functions today. (Note how, by

---

10   Perhaps one should link this asexual character of the Panda to the gradual abandonment of the "production of the couple" in mainstream Hollywood (*Quantum of Solace* as the first James Bond film in which there is no sexual act between Bond and the Bond-girl; the absence of sex in the last two Dan Brown novels [*Da Vinci Code* and *The Lost Symbol*] as well as in the film version of *Angels and Demons*).

merely "believing in himself," Po becomes the superior warrior after just a couple of training sessions, leaving behind his co-warriors who have been training for years—the magic of belief really works . . .)

This, however, is *not* the lesson of Lacanian psychoanalysis. Psychoanalysis is firmly entrenched in the Western Judeo-Christian tradition, not only against Oriental spirituality but also against Islam, one of the religions of the Book, which, like Oriental spirituality, endorses the thesis of the ultimate vanity, the illusory nature, of every object of desire. In the *Thousand and One Nights*, on the 614th night, Judar, following the orders of a Moroccan magician, had to penetrate seven doors that would lead him to a treasure. When he came to the seventh door,

> there issued forth to him his mother, saying, "I salute thee, O my son!" He asked, "What art thou?" and she answered, "O my son, I am thy mother who bore thee nine months and suckled thee and reared thee." Quoth he, "Put off thy clothes." Quoth she, "Thou art my son, how wouldst thou strip me naked?" But he said "Strip, or I will strike off thy head with this sword"; and he stretched out his hand to the brand and drew it upon her saying, "Except thou strip, I will slay thee." Then the strife became long between them and as often as he redoubled on her his threats, she put off somewhat of her clothes and he said to her, "Doff the rest," with many menaces; while she removed each article slowly and kept saying, "O my son, thou hast disappointed my fosterage of thee," till she had nothing left but her petticoat trousers. Then said she, "O my son, is thy heart stone? Wilt thou dishonor me by discovering my shame? Indeed, this is unlawful, O my son!" And he answered, "Thou sayest sooth; put not off thy trousers." At once, as he uttered these words, she cried out, "He hath made default; beat him!" Whereupon there fell upon him blows like raindrops and the servants of the treasure flocked to him and dealt him a funding which he forgot not in all his days.[11]

On the 615th night, we learn that Judar was given another chance and tried again; when he came to the seventh door,

> the semblance of his mother appeared before him, saying, "Welcome, O my son!" But he said to her, "How am I thy son, O accursed? Strip!" And she began to wheedle him and put off garment after garment, till only her trousers remained; and he said to her, "Strip, O accursed!" So she put off

---

11   Sir Richard Francis Burton, *The Arabian Nights: Tales from a Thousand and One Nights*, New York: Random House 2001, p. 441.

her trousers and became a body without a soul. Then he entered the hall
of the treasures, where he saw gold lying in heaps . . .

Fethi Benslama points out how this passage indicates that Islam knows
what our Western universe denies: the fact that incest is not forbidden,
but is inherently impossible (when one finally gets to the naked mother,
she disintegrates as a bad specter).[12] Benslama refers here to Jean-Joseph
Goux's *Œdipe philosophe*,[13] where he demonstrates how the Oedipus myth,
far from being universal, the underlying arche-myth, is an exception with
regard to other myths, a Western myth, its basic feature being precisely
that *"behind the prohibition, the impossible withdraws itself"*:[14] the very prohibition is read as an indication that incest is possible. From the standard
position of commonsensical wisdom, Oedipus is a Western aberration,
a confusion of the ontic object with the ontological void; it is a blinding
short circuit, the elevation of an ontic object into the ontological Absolute,
where the goal should be to distance them, to see the vanity of all objects.
Here, however, one should remain faithful to the Western "Oedipal"
tradition: of course every object of desire is an illusory lure; of course
the full *jouissance* of incest is not only prohibited, but is in itself impossible; however, it is here that one should fully assert Lacan's claim that
les non-dupes errent. Even if the object of desire is an illusory lure, *there is a
real in this illusion*: the object of desire in its positive nature is vain, *but not
the place it occupies*, the place of the Real, which is why there is more truth
in unconditional fidelity to one's desire than in a resigned insight into the
vanity of one's striving.

There is a parallax shift at work here: from illusion as mere illusion
to the real in illusion, from the object which is a metonym/mask of the
Void to the object which stands in for the void. This parallax shift is,
in Lacanese, the shift from desire to drive. The key distinction to be
maintained here can be exemplified with reference to the (apparent)
opposite of religion: intense sexual experience. Eroticization relies on
the inversion-into-itself of movement directed at an external goal: the
movement itself becomes its own goal. (When, instead of simply gently
shaking the hand offered to me by the beloved person, I hold onto it and
squeeze repeatedly, my activity will be automatically experienced as—
welcome or, perhaps, intrusively unwelcome—eroticization: what I do is

---

12   See Fethi Benslama, *La Psychanalyse à l'épreuve de l'Islam*, Paris: Aubier 2002.
13   See Jean-Joseph Goux, *Œdipe philosophe*, Paris: Aubier 1990.
14   Benslama, *La Psychanalyse à l'épreuve de l'Islam*, p. 259.

change the goal-oriented activity into an end-in-itself.) Therein resides the difference between the goal and the aim of a drive: say, with regard to the oral drive, its goal may be to eliminate hunger, but its aim is the satisfaction provided by the activity of eating itself (sucking, swallowing). One can imagine the two satisfactions entirely separated: when, in hospital, I am fed intravenously, my hunger is satisfied, but not my oral drive; when, on the contrary, a small child sucks rhythmically on the comforter, the only satisfaction he gets is that of the drive. This gap that separates the aim from the goal "eternalizes" the drive, transforming the simple instinctual movement which finds peace and calm when it reaches its goal (a full stomach, say) into a process which gets caught in its own loop and insists on endlessly repeating itself.

The crucial feature to take note of here is that this inversion cannot be formulated in terms of a primordial lack and a series of metonymic objects trying (and ultimately failing) to fill the void. When the eroticized body of my partner starts to function as the object around which the drive circulates, this does *not* mean that his or her ordinary ("pathological," in the Kantian sense of the term) flesh-and-blood body is "transubstantiated" into a contingent embodiment of the sublime impossible Thing, holding (filling out) its empty place. Let us take a direct and "vulgar" example: when a (heterosexual male) lover is fascinated by his partner's vagina, "can never get enough of it," is obsessed not only with penetrating it, but with exploring and caressing it in all possible ways, the point is *not* that, in a kind of deceptive short-circuit, he mistakes this bit of skin, hair and muscle for the Thing itself—his lover's vagina *is*, in all its bodily materiality, "the thing itself," not the spectral appearance of another dimension. What makes it an "infinitely" desirable object whose "mystery" cannot ever be fully penetrated is its non-identity with itself, that is, the way it is never directly "itself." The gap which "eternalizes" the drive, turning it into the endlessly repetitive circular movement around the object, is not the gap that separates the void of the Thing from its contingent embodiments, but the gap that separates the very "pathological" object *from itself*, in the same way that Christ is not the contingent material ("pathological") embodiment of the suprasensible God: his "divine" dimension is reduced to the aura of a pure *Schein*. It is this self-separation of the object that makes it sublime: wisdom cannot grasp sublimation proper.

Lacan's *les non-dupes errent* should thus be read at two levels: against the cynic who dismisses symbolic fiction on account of the real of *jouissance* being the only thing that counts; and against the sage who dismisses the real of *jouissance* as itself transient and illusory. How, then, does psychoanalysis stand with regard to enjoyment? Its great task is to break the hold over us of the superego injunction to enjoy, that is, to help us include in the freedom *to* enjoy also the freedom *not* to enjoy, the freedom *from* enjoyment.

The opposition between the Pelagians and Augustine with regard to (sexual) lust is instructive here. For the Pelagians, lust was in itself a good thing which might be put to bad use, while, for Augustine, lust was a bad thing which might, in marriage, be put to good use.[15] Did the Communist movement not face exactly the same dilemma in how to deal with "sexual liberation," oscillating between the two extremes: on the one side, the Wilhelm-Reichian "Pelagians" who emphasized the liberating potential of free sexuality; on the other, the ascetic "Augustinians" who castigated "free sexuality" as the exemplary phenomenon of bourgeois decadence, destined to confound people and divert their energy away from revolutionary objectives? Although the Pelagian view may appear more sympathetic, "progressive" and "life-affirming," there is more truth in the Augustinian position: lust (*jouissance*) is formally "evil," an "unnamable" excess threatening the stable order; the correct solution is that *jouissance* is in itself neutral, and the ethical problem is how to put it to use. What makes Augustine more true is his linking of excessive sexuality (and sexuality *is* by definition excessive) to the Fall of man: sexuality is not natural, it is the result of the denaturalization of human beings through the "original sin." This is why, in his *On Free Will*, Augustine writes:

> To approve falsehood instead of truth so as to err in spite of himself, and not to be able to refrain from the works of lust because of the pain involved in breaking away from fleshly bonds: these do not belong to the nature of man as he was created before the fall. They are the penalty of man as now condemned by original sin.[16]

Augustine here comes close to Paul's insight into the intimate link between lust (sin) and law: lust does not come "naturally," it is an obscene perverted "duty," a painful drive of which we cannot rid ourselves. The entanglement of lust (sin) and law resides not only in the fact that the prohibition of sexuality makes lust desirable; one should also add that

---

15   See Charles Freeman, *The Closing of the Western Mind: The Rise of Faith and the Fall of Reason*, New York: Vintage Books 2005, p. 395.

16   Quoted in ibid., p. 401.

the pain and guilt we feel when, against our will, we are dragged into sexual lust, are themselves sexualized. Not only do we feel pain and guilt at sexual enjoyment, we enjoy this very pain and guilt.

It is at this precise point that perversion enters. The fateful step towards masochistic perversion is accomplished when the claim that a clean body and clean clothes may nonetheless contain a dirty mind (and vice versa) is radicalized into the claim that a clean body and clean clothes as such are the proof of a dirty mind — or, as Paula, the ascetic Roman aristocrat, put it: "A clean body and clean clothes betoken an unclean mind."[17] A similar fateful step from heroism to perverse *jouissance* occurred on April 25, 1915, before the battle with the British-Australian forces on the Gallipoli peninsula, when Mustafa Kemal Atatürk told his troops: "I don't order you to fight, I order you to die. In the time it takes us to die, other troops and commanders can come and take our places." This "passion to die" is the last great example of the Thermopylae-Alamo logic of consciously sacrificing oneself so that one's forces are able to regroup for the decisive battle, the last great temptation to be resisted, the last mask in which a non-ethical attitude disguises itself as ethics itself.

The Price of Survival

Here, then, is our conclusion. Common sense tells us that the actual lives of people, of real individuals with their wealth of experience and practice, cannot be reduced to a "spontaneous" impersonation of ideology. But it is precisely this recourse to the non-ideological lifeworld that one should abandon. This is why Elfriede Jelinek's advice to theater writers is not only aesthetically correct, but has a deep ethical justification:

Characters on stage should be flat, like clothes in a fashion show: what you get should be no more than what you see. Psychological realism is repulsive, because it allows us to escape unpalatable reality by taking shelter in the "luxuriousness" of personality, losing ourselves in the depth of individual character. The writer's task is to block this manoeuvre, to chase us off to a point from which we can view the horror with a dispassionate eye.[18]

17   Quoted in ibid., p. 233.
18   Nicholas Spice, "Up from the Cellar. *London Review of Books*, June 5, 2008.

In other words, we should resist the urge to fill in the void with the rich texture of what makes us a person.[19] Two half-forgotten classic films stage such an emptying of the wealth of "personality" at its most radical, rendering a subject who survives as a shell deprived of substance. First, there is Lina Wertmüller's *Pasqualino Settebellezze* (itself a true counterpoint to Roberto Benigni's *La vita è bella*. All one has to do to see what is wrong with Benigni's film is to carry out a simple thought experiment: imagine the same film with one change—the father fails in his "noble lie," and his son dies. Or another alternative: at the end, the father learns that his son knew all the time where he was, namely in a concentration camp, and that he was pretending to believe his father's story in order to make life easier for his father.) *Pasqualino Settebellezze* is the ultimate film on survivalism. Its climax involves a unique sex scene which, apart from the one in Handke's *The Piano Teacher*, is perhaps the most painful in the history of cinema. Its perverse twist cannot but recall the weirdest moments in David Lynch's *Wild at Heart*. In order to survive the concentration camp, the hero (played superbly by Giancarlo Giannini) decides to seduce the kapo, a cold, ugly, and fat German "bitch." The horror of the act lies in making love to the maternal Thing and/or Lady in a scene of courtly love, to the absolutely capricious Mistress on whose whims one's life depends: during the act, she remains cold, unsmiling, and expresses not a moan or groan of pleasure, just yawning once—a true "netrebko."[20] After Pasqualino arouses himself through fantasizing, she sees through him, realizing that the seduction is merely an expression of this "Mediterranean worm's" pure will to survive, and contrasts this survivalist attitude to the German ethic of risking life for honor. (The nice irony is that, in the figure of Pasqualino himself, the reality of this survivalism is opposed to the pathetic and operatic Neapolitan sense of honor, which belongs to the lineage of Italian opera from Rossini through to the films of Sergio Leone with their excess of life.) After the act, she nominates him kapo of his barrack, and immediately gives him the task of selecting six prisoners to be executed—should he fail, they will all be

19   When we are pressed to do it, the only way out may be to undermine what we are forced to do with recourse to ridiculous obscenity; as with Patricia Highsmith who, when she was invited to visit an elementary school in Switzerland to give the pupils an edifying talk on how they could make a difference by helping adults, wrote down a list of ten things the children could do at home, like mixing the pills from different bottles (putting laxative pills into the tranquilizer bottles, etc.)

20   To anyone versed in Slavic languages, the irony of the family name of the voluptuously beautiful Russian soprano Anna Netrebko is fully evident: "treb" is the root of the verb "to need," and "ne" is, of course, negation, so the message is clear: she, the erotic symbol, "doesn't need it," has no need of sex—and this is what makes her a Mistress who can mercilessly manipulate men.

executed. Then, he has personally to shoot his best friend. Such is the price of his survival: he survives alone. In the film's last scene, after the war, he returns home and proposes marriage to a young prostitute, just to have as many children as possible as a guarantee of survival. When his mother exclaims with joy: "But you are alive!", he replies after a long silence: "Yes, I am alive!"—the last words of the film. Is he truly alive? Would not a true act of life have been, in the last scene in the camp, for him to shoot the kapo and other guards, before being shot himself? The standard idealist question "Is there (eternal) life after death?" should be countered by the materialist question: "Is there life before death?" This is the question Wolf Biermann asked in one of his songs—what bothers a materialist is: am I really alive here and now, or am I just vegetating, as a mere human animal bent on survival? When am I really alive? Precisely when I enact the "undead" drive in me, the "too-much-ness" of life (Eric Santner). And I reach this point when I no longer act directly, but when "it [*es*]"—which the Christians name the Holy Spirit—acts through me: at this point, I reach the Absolute.

The other film is John Frankenheimer's *Seconds* (1966), a neglected companion-piece to his cult masterpiece *The Manchurian Candidate*, shot in pure *noir* style. There is no space here to dwell on the film's many outstanding features, beginning with one of Saul Bass's best title sequences (on a par with his titles for Hitchcock's great trilogy *Vertigo*, *North-by-Northwest*, and *Psycho*), composed of anamorphically distorted fragments of a face in a disfiguring mirror. *Seconds* tells the story of Arthur Hamilton, a middle-aged man whose life has lost its purpose: he is bored by his job as a banker, and the love between him and his wife has waned. Through an unexpected phone call from Evans, a friend whom he thought had died years earlier, Hamilton is approached by a secret organization, known simply as the "Company," which offers wealthy people a second chance at life. After he signs the contract, the Company makes Hamilton appear as if he has died by faking an accident with a corpse disguised as him. Through extensive plastic surgery and psychoanalysis, Hamilton is transformed into Tony Wilson (played by Rock Hudson), with a fancy new Malibu home, a new identity as an established artist, new friends and a devoted manservant. (The details of his new existence suggest that there was indeed once a real Tony Wilson, but what became of him is a mystery.) He soon commences a relationship with Nora, a young woman whom he meets on the beach. They visit a nearby wine festival which develops into a full-scale drunken sexual orgy, and he reluctantly relaxes enough to participate in it. For a time he is happy, but soon he becomes troubled by the emotional confusion of his new identity, and by the exuberance of renewing his youth. At a dinner party he hosts for his neighbors, he drinks himself into a stupor and begins to babble about his former life as Hamilton.

It turns out that his neighbors are "reborns" like himself, sent to keep an eye on his adjustment to his new life. Nora is actually an agent of the Company, and her attention to Wilson is designed merely to ensure his cooperation. Escaping his Malibu home, Wilson visits his former wife in his new persona, and learns that his marriage failed because he was distracted by the pursuit of his career and material possessions, the very things in life that others made him believe were important. Depressed, he returns to the Company and asks them to provide him with yet another identity; the Company agrees on condition that he directs to them some rich past acquaintances who might like to be "reborn." While awaiting his reassignment, Wilson encounters Evans, who was also "reborn" but could not accept his new identity. At the film's ominous end, doctors drag Wilson to an operating room, where, strapped to the table, he learns the truth: those who, like him, fail to adjust to their new identity, are not, as promised, provided with a new one, but become cadavers used to fake new clients' deaths.

All the philosophico-ideological topics we have been dealing with reverberate in *Seconds*: the reduction of the subject to a *tabula rasa*, the emptying of all its substantial content, and its rebirth, its recreation from a zero-point. The motif of rebirth is here given a clear critico-ideological twist: transforming himself into Wilson, Hamilton realizes what he always dreamt of; but things go terribly wrong when he becomes aware that those transgressive dreams were part of the same oppressive reality from which he had tried to escape. In other words, Hamilton-Evans pays the bitter price for the fact that his negation of the past was not radical enough: his revolution failed to revolutionize its own presuppositions. Hegel had a presentiment of this necessity when he wrote: "It is a modern folly to alter a corrupt ethical system, its constitution and legislation, without changing the religion, to have a revolution without a reformation."[21] In a radical revolution, people not only "realize their old (emancipatory, etc.) dreams"; they have also to reinvent their very modes of dreaming. Is this not the exact formula of the link between the death drive and sublimation? Therein resides the necessity of the Cultural Revolution, as clearly grasped by Mao: as

---

21   G. W. F. Hegel, *Enzyklopaedie der philosophischen Wissenschaften*, Hamburg 1959, p. 436.

Herbert Marcuse put, it in another wonderfully circular formula from the same epoch, *freedom* (from ideological constraints, from the predominant mode of dreaming) *is the condition of liberation*, in other words, if we change reality only in order to realize our dreams, without changing these dreams themselves, then sooner or later we will regress to the former reality. There is a Hegelian "positing of presuppositions" at work here: the hard work of liberation retroactively forms its own presupposition.

In *Seconds*, Wilson pays the price for his "revolution without reformation": when he rejects his old life as a banker trapped in a loveless marriage, he thinks he has escaped an oppressive social reality in which others (or, rather, the ideological "big Other") define his dreams, telling him what he desires. What he discovers after his rebirth is that this very fantasmatic core of his being—his innermost dream of an authentic life which he felt was being claustrophobically oppressed—was no less determined by the existing order. Nowhere is this trap of "inherent transgression" more obvious than in the bacchic orgy scene with its wink to the hippy lifestyle (recall that the film is from 1966), a scene which was censored on the film's first release, when full frontal nudity was not yet permitted. The scene drags on painfully, its depressive inertia clearly refuting the notion of a liberating explosion of spontaneous *joie de vivre*.

The film's conclusion, in which Wilson is sacrificed as a stand-in body so that another subject can be reborn, restates the Hegelian-Christian lesson: the price of my rebirth is another's annihilated body, like Christ's.

2 Anger: The Actuality of the Theologico-Political

Thinking Backwards

Alan Weisman's book *The World Without Us* offers a vision of what would happen if humanity (and *only* humanity) were suddenly to disappear from the earth—natural diversity would bloom again, with nature gradually colonizing human artefacts. We, the humans, are here reduced to a pure disembodied gaze observing our own absence. As Lacan pointed out, this is the fundamental subjective position of fantasy: to be reduced to a gaze observing the world in the condition of the subject's non-existence—like the fantasy of witnessing the act of one's own conception, parental copulation, or the act of witnessing one's own burial, like Tom Sawyer and Huck Finn. "The world without us" is thus fantasy at its purest: witnessing the Earth itself regaining its pre-castrated state of innocence, before we humans spoiled it in our hubris. The irony is that the most obvious example is the catastrophe at Chernobyl: flourishing nature has taken over the disintegrating debris of the nearby city of Pripyat, which had to be abandoned. A good counterpoint to such fantasizing, which relies on the notion of Nature as a balanced and harmonious cycle derailed by human intervention, is the thesis of an environmental scientist that, while one cannot be sure of the ultimate result of humanity's interventions in the geosphere, one thing is certain: if humanity were to stop its immense industrial activity abruptly and let nature retake its balanced course, the result would be total breakdown, an unimaginable catastrophe. "Nature" on Earth is already "adapted" to human intervention to such an extent—human "pollution" being already deeply implicated in the shaky and fragile equilibrium of "natural" reproduction on Earth—that its cessation would cause a cataclysmic imbalance.

We find exactly the same structure at the very heart of utopia. In "Frenzy," the aforementioned novella from *Her Body Knows*, David Grossman does for jealousy in literature what Luis Buñuel did for it in cinema with his *El* — he produces a masterpiece displaying the basic fantasmatic coordinates of the notion. In jealousy, the subject *creates/ imagines a paradise* (a utopia of full *jouissance*) *from which he is excluded*. The same definition applies to what one can call political jealousy, from anti-Semitic fantasies about the excessive enjoyment of the Jews to Christian fundamentalists' fantasies about the weird sexual practices of gays and lesbians. As Klaus Theweleit has pointed out, it is all too easy to read such phenomena as mere "projections": jealousy can be quite real and well-founded, other people can and often do have a much more intense sexual life than the jealous subject — a fact which, as Lacan remarked, does not make jealousy any less pathological. And does this also not tell us something about the position of the spectator in cinema? Is she not, by definition, a *jealous subject*, excluding herself from the utopia observed on screen? We find this stance even where we would never expect it. Gérard Wajcman begins his memorable essay on "the animals that treat us badly" by recounting his experience of a trip to an African wilderness park:

A whole team of tourists traverses the savannah back and forth, arrives on the scene with an engine backfiring and a dust cloud looming to plant themselves twenty meters from three big bad lions . . . and nothing. As if we didn't exist. Such was my definitive experience with the animal world. A thorough disenchantment. An encounter of the zero type. We do not share animal space. We invade their territory or we cross over it, but we never meet them. The zoo, the circus (less and less), state parks (more and more), hunting grounds, television channels consecrated to animals, protection societies, nature museums, animal houses of every kind, we multiply the places, the occasions, and the modes of encounter. Humanity passes its time watching the animals. We've invented all kinds of devices expressly for the purpose. We never grow tired of it. No doubt they represent for us a perfect world. Something strange, different from our own, from our uncertain screwed up chaotic mess of a world. All of which makes the animal world look that much better. Sometimes it seems so foreign that we stand before their perfection and we are stupefied and stricken mute, and despite our sincere wishes, we wonder whether we could ever be like them, ever become so marvelous a society as have the ants and the penguins, where everyone has his place, where everyone is in his place, and where everyone knows and does exactly as he must so that everything can keep on in its proper place, so that society can perpetuate itself, unchanged, indefinitely the same and infinitely perfect. We've had a hard time of it, finding our places. After the disasters of the 20th century the animal societies seem to have become the ideal.[1]

The fact that the animals ignore the intruding tourists is crucial — it points towards a double movement of de-realization that characterizes utopian fantasies: the scene presented is a fantasy (even if it "really happened," as is the case here — what makes it into a fantasy is the libidinal investment that determines its meaning); we (the participants) de-realize ourselves, reducing ourselves to a pure de-substantialized gaze ignored by the objects of the gaze — as if we are not part of the reality we observe (despite disturbing the wildlife park's rhythm with our vehicles), but rather a spectral presence unseen by living beings — we are reduced to spectral entities observing "the world without us." As external observers of the paradise barred to us, we assume the same position as the unfortunate Stella Dallas in the final scene of the Hollywood melodrama of the same name: from outside the big house where the ceremony is in progress, Stella watches through the window the marriage of her daughter to her rich suitor — the paradise of a happy rich family from which she is excluded.

This utopia accounts for two further phenomena of contemporary culture: first, the popularity of Darwinist reductions of human societies to animal ones, with their explanations of human achievements in terms of evolutionary adaptation. Pop-scientific texts abound in journals and reviews reporting on how scientists have succeeded in explaining apparently crazy or useless human behavior as grounded in adaptive strategies. (Why such useless luxury? To impress the potential sexual partner with our ability to afford such excess, and so on and so forth.) In this way, the scientists suggest that

> we might yet have a chance to orient ourselves, to be led over and above our animality. If the subject has a nasty habit of fooling himself all the time, we must bear in mind that nature is never mistaken. Salvation will come in our being animal — body, genes, neurons, and all the rest of it. So whispers the cognitivist in the politicians' ears to help them find their way. Follow the body, more monkey business![2]

Such "reports" thus represent dreams of how we might counteract the growing dysfunctionalization and reflexivity of our "postmodern"

---

1   Gérard Wajcman, "The Animals that Treat Us Badly," *lacanian ink* 33, pp. 128–9.
2   Ibid., p. 130.

societies, in which relying on inherited traditions to provide models for behavior becomes increasingly untenable: animals, by contrast, do not need any coaching, they just do it . . .

Second, we can also explain why we obviously find it so pleasurable to watch endless animal documentaries on specialized channels (*Nature*, *Animal Kingdom*, *National Geographic*): they provide a glimpse into a utopian world where no language or training are needed, in other words, into a "harmonious society" (as they put it today in China) in which everyone spontaneously knows his or her role:

> Man is a denatured animal. We are animals sick with language. And how sometimes we long for a cure. But just shutting up won't do it. You can't just wish your way into animality. So it is then, as a matter of consolation, that we watch the animal channels and marvel at a world untamed by language. The animals get us to hear a voice of pure silence. Nostalgia for the fish life. Humanity seems to have been hit by the [Jacques] Cousteau syndrome.[3]

This is why the case of *National Geographic* (the journal even more than the TV channel) is so interesting: although it combines reports on both nature and human societies, its trick essentially is to treat a human society (whether a tribe in the middle of the Sahara or a small town in the USA) as an animal community in which things somehow work, where "everyone has his place, where everyone is in his place, and where everyone knows and does exactly as he must so that everything can keep on in its proper place." And, since the basic inconsistency constitutive of human being as such is the discord (the "impossibility") of the sexual relationship, no wonder that one of the key elements in our fascination with the animal kingdom is represented by its perfectly regulated mating rituals — animals do not need to worry themselves with all the complex fantasies and stimulants needed to sustain sexual lust, they are able to "have sex ahistorically," as Wajcman puts it in a wonderful phrase:

> Between men and women it's been pretty messy, the big disorder. Not necessarily unpleasant of course; it's not war, it's not some kind of permanent fuck-up, it's rather a kind of mixing up and clearing up . . . No set rule, no rhyme or reason. Not at all as it is with animals, where everybody seems to know perfectly well how to do it. How, and with whom, and

---

3   Ibid., p. 131.

when . . . The animal world has realized the human dream of sex without a back-story, sex without (hi)story precisely when we humans have gone and invented literature to tell ourselves love stories in which nothing ever happens but a (hi)story . . . We'd be happy to put down our books and get straight to the point of what exactly it is to have sex ahistorically.[4]

Examples like this indicate an approach to utopias which leaves behind the usual focus on content (on the structure of society proposed in a utopian vision). Perhaps it is time to step back from the fascination with content and reflect on the subjective position from which such content appears as utopian. On account of its temporal loop, the fantasmatic narrative always involves an *impossible gaze*, the gaze by means of which the subject is already present at the scene of its own absence. When the subject directly identifies its own gaze with the *objet a*, the paradoxical implication of this identification is that the *objet a* disappears from the field of vision. This brings us to the core of a Lacanian notion of utopia: a vision of desire functioning without an *objet a* and its twists and loops. It is utopian not only to think that one can reach full, unencumbered "incestuous" enjoyment; for it is no less utopian to think that one can renounce enjoyment without this renunciation generating its own surplus-enjoyment.

However, the way to avoid this utopian reduction of the subject to the impossible gaze witnessing an alternate reality from which it is absent is not to abandon the topos of an alternate reality as such. Recall Walter Benjamin's notion of revolution as redemption-through-repetition of the past: apropos the French Revolution, the task of a genuine Marxist historiography is not to describe the events the way they really were (and to explain how these events generated the ideological illusions that accompanied them); the task is rather to unearth the hidden potentiality (the utopian emancipatory potential) which was betrayed in the actuality of revolution and in its final outcome (the rise of utilitarian market capitalism). Marx's point is not primarily to make fun of the Jacobins' revolutionary enthusiasm, to show how their high-flown emancipatory rhetoric was just a means used by the historical "cunning of reason" to establish the vulgar reality of commercial capitalism; it is, rather, to explain how these radical-emancipatory potentials continue to "insist" as types of historical specters which haunt the revolutionary memory, demanding their enactment, such that the later proletarian revolution should also redeem (or put to rest) these ghosts of the past. These alternate versions

---

4   Ibid., pp. 132–3.

of the past persisting in a spectral form constitute the ontological "open-ness" of the historical process, as was — again — clear to Chesterton:

> The things that might have been are not even present to the imagination. If somebody says that the world would now be better if Napoleon had never fallen, but had established his Imperial dynasty, people have to adjust their minds with a jerk. The very notion is new to them. Yet it would have prevented the Prussian reaction; saved equality and enlightenment with-out a mortal quarrel with religion; unified Europeans and perhaps avoided the Parliamentary corruption and the Fascist and Bolshevist revenges. But in this age of free-thinkers, men's minds are not really free to think such a thought.
>
> What I complain of is that those who accept the verdict of fate in this way accept it without knowing why. By a quaint paradox, those who thus assume that history always took the right turning are generally the very people who do not believe there was any special providence to guide it. The very rationalists who jeer at the trial by combat, in the old feudal ordeal, do in fact accept a trial by combat as deciding all human history.[5]

Why, then, is the burgeoning genre of "What If?" histories hegemonized by conservative historians? The typical Introduction to such a volume begins with an attack on Marxists who allegedly believe in histori-cal determinism. The editors' conservative sympathies become clear as soon as one sees the contents pages of the leading What-If volumes: the favored topics oscillate between the "major premise" — how much *better* history would have been if a revolutionary or "radical" event had been avoided (if King Charles had won the civil war against Parliament; if the English Crown had won the war of independence against the American colonies; if the Confederacy had won the US civil war, aided by Great Britain; if Germany had won the Great War; if Lenin had been assassi-nated at the Finland Station . . .) — and the "minor premise" — how much *worse* history would have been if history had taken a more "progressive" twist (if Thatcher had been killed in the Brighton IRA bombing in 1984; if Gore had won instead of Bush and so had been president on 9/11, etc.). So what should the Marxist's answer be here? Definitely not to rehash the tiresome old ratiocinations of Georgi Plekhanov on the "role of the individual in history" (the logic of "even if there had been no Napoleon another individual would have played a similar role, since the deeper

5   G. K. Chesterton, "The Slavery of the Mind," in *The Collected Works of G. K. Chesterton, Volume 3*, San Francisco: Ignatius Press 1990, p. 290.

historical necessity called for a passage to Bonapartism"). One should rather question the very premise that Marxists (and Leftists in general) are dumb determinists opposed to entertaining such alternative scenarios.

The first thing to note is that the What-If histories are part of a more general ideological trend, of a perception of life that explodes the form of the linear, centered narrative and renders it as a multiform flow. Up to the domain of the "hard" sciences (quantum physics and its Multiple-Reality interpretation; neo-Darwinism, and so on), we seem to be haunted by the chanciness of life and alternate versions of reality—as Stephen Jay Gould, a Marxist biologist if ever there was one, bluntly put it: "Wind back the film of life and play it again. The history of evolution will be totally different." These views of our reality as being one possible, and often even not the most probable, outcome of an "open" situation, this notion that other possible outcomes are not simply cancelled but continue to haunt us as specters of what might have been, conferring on our "true" reality the status of extreme fragility and contingency, is by no means foreign to Marxism—indeed, it is on such perceptions that the felt *urgency* of the revolutionary act often depends.

Since the non-occurrence of the October Revolution is a favored topic among conservative What-If historians, let us look at how Lenin himself related to it: he was as far as imaginable from any kind of reliance on "historical necessity" (on the contrary, it was his Menshevik opponents who emphasized that one could not skip over the succession of stages prescribed by historical determinism: first bourgeois-democratic, then proletarian revolution . . .). When, in his "April Theses" from 1917, Lenin discerned the *Augenblick*, the unique chance for revolution, his proposals were met with stupor or contempt by a large majority of his own party colleagues. Within the Bolshevik Party, no prominent leader supported his call for revolution, and *Pravda* took the extraordinary step of dissociating the party, and the editorial board as a whole, from Lenin's "Theses"—far from being an opportunist flattering and exploiting the prevailing mood in the party, Lenin's views were highly idiosyncratic. Bogdanov characterized the "April Theses" as "the delirium of a madman," and Nadezhda Krupskaya herself concluded: "I am afraid it looks as if Lenin has gone crazy." Lenin immediately perceived the revolutionary chance which was the result of unique contingent circumstances: if the moment was not seized, the chance for the revolution would be forfeited, perhaps for decades. So we have here Lenin himself entertaining an alternative scenario: "*What if* we do not act now?"—and it was precisely his awareness of the catastrophic consequences of not acting that pushed him to act.

But there is a much deeper commitment to alternative histories in a radical Marxist view: it brings the What-If logic to its self-reflexive reversal. For a radical Marxist, *the actual history that we live is itself a kind of realized alternative history*, the reality we have to live in because, in the past, we failed to seize the moment and act. Military historians have demonstrated that the Confederacy lost the battle at Gettysburg because General Lee made a series of mistakes that were totally uncharacteristic: "Gettysburg was the one battle, fought by Lee, that reads like fiction. In other words, if ever there was a battle where Lee did not behave like Lee, it was there in southern Pennsylvania."[6] For each of the wrong moves, one can play the game of "What would Lee have done in that situation?"—in other words, it was as if, in the battle of Gettysburg, the alternate history actualized itself. In his less well-known *Everlasting Man*, Chesterton makes a wonderful mental experiment along these lines, in imagining the monster that man might have seemed at first to the merely natural animals around him:

The simplest truth about man is that he is a very strange being; almost in the sense of being a stranger on the earth. In all sobriety, he has much more of the external appearance of one bringing alien habits from another land than of a mere growth of this one. He has an unfair advantage and an unfair disadvantage. He cannot sleep in his own skin; he cannot trust his own instincts. He is at once a creator moving miraculous hands and fingers and a kind of cripple. He is wrapped in artificial bandages called clothes; he is propped on artificial crutches called furniture. His mind has the same doubtful liberties and the same wild limitations. Alone among the animals, he is shaken with the beautiful madness called laughter; as if he had caught sight of some secret in the very shape of the universe hidden from the universe itself. Alone among the animals he feels the need of averting his thought from the root realities of his own bodily being; of hiding them as in the presence of some higher possibility which creates the mystery of shame. Whether we praise these things as natural to man or abuse them as artificial in nature, they remain in the same sense unique.[7]

This is what Chesterton called "thinking backwards": we have to leap back in time, before the fateful decisions were made or before the accidents

---

6   Bill Fawcett, *How to Lose a Battle*, New York: Harper 2006, p. 148.

7   G. K. Chesterton, "The Everlasting Man," in *The Collected Works of G. K. Chesterton*, San Francisco: Ignatius Press 1986, p. 168.

occurred that generated the state which now seems normal to us, and the way to do so, to render palpable this open moment of decision, is to imagine how, at that point, history might have taken a different turn.

However, this does not mean that, in a historical repetition in the radical Benjaminian sense, we simply go back in time to the moment of decision and, this time, make the right choice. The lesson of repetition is rather that our first choice was necessarily the wrong one, and for a very precise reason: the "right choice" is only possible the second time, after the wrong one; that is, it is only the first wrong choice which literally creates the conditions for the right choice. The idea that we might already have made the right choice the first time, and that we just accidentally blew the chance, is a retroactive illusion. To clarify this point, let us take an example from recent historiography.

Bryan Ward-Perkins's *The Fall of Rome* describes the gradual disintegration of the Roman empire from the fourth to seventh centuries CE, emphasizing the economic and civilizatory regression, catastrophe even, that this disintegration brought about: in a short period, the majority of imperial lands fell into a state even worse than they were prior to the Roman occupation.[8] The book's explicit polemical targets are recent "revisionist" attempts to portray late Antiquity not as a traumatic regression to the early medieval "Dark Ages," but as a (mostly peaceful) gradual transformation of the united Roman empire into multiple new states, a process in which ethnic groups, freed from brutal Roman domination, matured into tolerant coexistence. Instead of collapse, one could even say that progress was taking place ... Against this new doxa, Ward-Perkins convincingly demonstrates the breathtaking decline of economic and social complexity (the decline in literacy, the virtual disappearance of the complex network of trade routes and thus of the large-scale production of everyday objects, etc.). His emphasis on the economy and daily life is a welcome correction to Foucauldian analyses focusing on spiritual shifts in late Antiquity, describing the rise of new forms of subjectivity. Ward-Perkins's book confirms two old insights: first, that all history is a history of the present; second, that our understanding of actual history always implies a (hidden or not) reference to alternate history—what "really happened" is perceived against the background of what *might have* happened, and this alternate possibility is offered as the path we should follow today. The two insights are thus closely linked—as we have said,

---

8   See Bryan Ward-Perkins, *The Fall of Rome*, Oxford: Oxford University Press 2005.

Walter Benjamin had already conceptualized social revolution in this way (it will redeem the past by repeating past revolutionary efforts, finally actualizing their missed potentials). Here, however, we get a more conservative case. The "lesson for today" is directly spelled out in the book's last paragraph:

> there is a real danger for the present day in a vision of the past that explicitly sets out to eliminate all crisis and all decline. The end of the Roman West witnessed horrors and dislocation of a kind I sincerely hope never to have to live through; and it destroyed a complex civilization, throwing the inhabitants of the West back to a standard of living typical of prehistoric times. Romans before the fall were as certain as we are today that their world would continue for ever substantially unchanged. They were wrong. We would be wise not to repeat their complacency.[9]

Echoes of the notion of a developed secular West threatened by new fundamentalisms are unmistakable here—let us not repeat the Roman mistake and minimize the mortal danger the new barbarians pose, otherwise we will find ourselves in a new Dark Ages . . . But what is even more interesting for a critico-ideological analysis is the alternate history that sustains this vision: it is the possibility that the Ostrogoths, who ruled Rome from the mid-fifth to the mid-sixth century, might have remained in power, defeating the invading Byzantine army:

> if events had fallen out differently, it is even possible to envisage a resurgent western empire under a successful Germanic dynasty. Theodoric the Ostrogoth ruled Italy and adjacent parts of the Danubian provinces and Balkans from 493; from 511 he also effectively controlled the Visigothic kingdom in Spain and many of the former Visigothic territories in Southern Gaul, where he reinstated the traditional Roman office of "Praetorian Prefect for the Gauls" based in Arles. This looks like the beginnings of a revived western empire, under Germanic kings. As things turned out, all this was brought to an end by Justinian's invasion of Italy in 535. But, given better luck, later Ostrogothic kings might have been able to expand on this early success; and—who knows?—might have revived the imperial title in the West centuries before Charlemagne in 800.[10]

---

9   Ibid., p. 183.
10   Ibid., p. 58.

Among historians, Peter Heather has developed this hypothesis most forcefully.[11] There is also an alternate history novel—*Lest Darkness Fall* (1941) by L. Sprague de Camp—which imagines this version: a modern archaeologist is transported through time to Ostrogothic Italy, helps to stabilize it after Theodoric's death, and averts its conquest by Justinian. The underlying vision here is one of the productive synthesis of Roman civilization and Gothic strength and vitality: the Goths, who saw themselves as protectors of Roman civilization, would have been able to pull the dying empire out of its inertia and invest it with new vigor. In this way, there would have been no Dark Ages, and we would have passed directly from the Roman empire to Charlemagne, and so to a strong and civilized Europe.

But there are dark ideological investments at work here, investments which found expression in Felix Dahn's novel *Struggle for Rome*, from 1876. (Returning to Germany, Robert Siodmak made a big historical spectacle out of this novel in 1968, with Orson Welles as Justinian—it was Siodmak's last film.)[12] Dahn was a honorary member of the "Germania" association, a nationalistic and anti-Semitic organization, and his works contributed to the ideological foundation of National Socialism. His story begins with the death of Theodoric the Great, when his successors try to maintain his legacy: an independent Ostrogothic kingdom. They are opposed by the Byzantine empire, ruled by the mighty emperor Justinian who tries to restore the Roman empire to its former greatness by capturing the Italian peninsula. Witiges, Totila, and Teia, who—in that order—succeed Theodoric as kings, endeavor to defend their kingdom with the help of Theodoric's faithful armorer Hildebrand. Meanwhile, Cethegus, a (fictional) Roman prefect who represents the majority of Rome's population, has his own agenda to rebuild the empire: he too tries to get rid of the Goths but is at the same time determined to keep the Byzantines out of Italy. In the end, the Byzantines win and reclaim Italy, while Cethegus dies in a duel with the last Gothic king Teia. The struggle for Rome ends at a battle near Mount Vesuvius where the Ostrogoths make their last stand defending a narrow pass (a scene reminiscent of Thermopylae); once defeated, they withdraw to the island of Thule where their roots lay ... The main motif of the book is stated in the poem which comments on the departing Ostrogoths: "Make way, you people, for our stride. / We are the last of the Goths. / We do not carry a crown with us, / We carry but a corpse." This corpse belongs to

---

11   See Peter Heather, *The Goths*, Oxford: Oxford University Press 1996.
12   See Felix Dahn, *Struggle for Rome*, Twickenham: Athena Press 2005.

Teia, a dark, dejected man, who envisions the demise of the kingdom; even though he knows this demise to be predestined, he adopts the Germanic stance of confronting fate with courage in order to be well remembered (it is impossible to miss the echoes of darkly brooding Hagen from *Nibelungs* in the figure of Teia).

Although Ward-Perkins is far from peddling any such morbid heroic-fatalistic fascination, he nonetheless presents a series of theses which (even if historically accurate, as they mostly are) sustain the contemporary vision of the need to defend the secular and civilized West against the barbarian Third World onslaught, and warns against harboring any illusions about their peaceful integration. For example, one cannot but be struck by Ward-Perkins's repeated insistence that the Roman West fell for strictly external reasons (the barbarian invasions), not because of its inherent antagonisms and weaknesses—a thesis which can be given many versions, from a Nietzschean blaming of Christianity as degenerate to the Marxist emphasis on how the gradual decline of free farmer-soldiers and their replacement by mercenary armies in the long term destabilized the empire (the Gracchus brothers, Marx's personal heroes, can thus be seen as the last defenders of the true strength of Rome). The recent shift in the popular appreciation of Rome in the space of only two decades has resulted from similar contemporary reverberations: while in the 1990s, with the end of the Cold War and the emergence of the United States as the sole global superpower, Rome was celebrated as a mighty empire with a strong army, the passage to a more multi-centric world (to which President Bush's catastrophic foreign policy gave no small aid) has since generated an obsession with the Roman empire in decline.

The topic of late Antiquity is full of similar ideological traps, like the naïve celebration of Aristotelian secular-empirical reasoning, violently suppressed in the Dark Ages when faith treated intellectual curiosity as dangerous, but which then returns, although still formally subordinated to religion, with Thomas Aquinas.[13] Aristotelian Reason, however, is organic-teleological, in clear contrast to the radical contingency which characterizes the modern scientific view. No wonder today's Catholic Church attacks Darwinism as "irrational" on behalf of the Aristotelian notion of Reason: the "reason" of which the Pope speaks is a Reason for which Darwin's theory of evolution (and, indeed, modern science itself,

---

13   See Charles Freeman, *The Closing of the Western Mind: The Rise of Faith and the Fall of Reason*, New York: Vintage Books 2005.

within which the assertion of the ultimate contingency of the universe, marking its break with Aristotelian teleology, is a constitutive axiom) is "irrational." The "reason" of which the Pope speaks is a pre-modern teleological Reason, the view of the universe as a harmonious Whole in which everything serves a higher purpose. Which is why, paradoxically, the Pope's remarks obfuscate the key role of Christian theology in the birth of modern science: what paved the way for modern science was precisely the "voluntarist" idea—elaborated by, among others, Duns Scotus and Descartes—that God is not bound by any eternal rational truths. While the view of scientific discourse as involving a pure description of facticity is illusory, the paradox resides in the coincidence of bare facticity and radical voluntarism: facticity can be sustained as meaningless, as something that "just is as it is," only if it is secretly sustained by an arbitrary divine will. This is why Descartes is the founding figure of modern science, precisely when he makes even the most elementary mathematical facts like $2 + 2 = 4$ dependent on arbitrary divine will: two plus two is four because God willed it so, with no hidden or obscure chain of reasons behind it. Even in mathematics, this unconditional voluntarism is discernible in its axiomatic character: one begins by arbitrarily positing a series of axioms, out of which everything else is then supposed to follow. The paradox is thus that it was the Christian Dark Ages which created the conditions for the specific rationality of modern science as opposed to the science of the Ancients. The lesson is thus clear: the utopia of a direct passage from late Rome to the "high" Middle Ages is a false one, ignoring the necessity of the Fall into the early "dark" Middle Ages which alone created the conditions for modern rationality.

Does this fact, however, justify the Dark Ages? In theological terms, we stumble here upon the deadlock central to religion: how to deal with the Fall? Why does the Fall have to precede Salvation? The most radical and consistently perverse answer was provided by Nicolas Malebranche, the great Cartesian Catholic, who was excommunicated after his death and whose books were destroyed on account of his very excessive orthodoxy—Lacan probably had figures like Malebranche in his mind when he claimed that theologians are the only true atheists. In the best Pascalian tradition, Malebranche laid his cards on the table and "revealed the secret" (the perverse core) of Christianity; his Christology is based on an original proto-Hegelian answer to the question "Why did God create the world?"—so that He could bask in the glory of being celebrated by His creation. God wanted recognition, and He knew that, in order to gain that recognition, He would need another subject to recognize Him; so He created the world out of pure selfish vanity. Consequently, it was not that Christ came down to Earth in order to deliver people from sin, from the legacy of Adam's Fall; on the contrary, *Adam had to fall in order to enable Christ to come down to earth and dispense salvation*. Here Malebranche applies to God Himself the "psychological" insight according to which the saintly figure who sacrifices himself for the benefit of others, to deliver them from their misery, secretly *wants* these others to suffer *so that he will be able to help them* — like the proverbial husband who works all day to support his poor crippled wife, yet would probably abandon her were she to regain her health and become a successful career woman. It is much more satisfying to sacrifice oneself for the poor victim than to enable the other to overcome their victim status and perhaps become even more successful than ourselves.

Malebranche pushes this parallel to its conclusion, to the horror of the Jesuits who organized his excommunication: in the same way that the saintly person uses the suffering of others to bring about his own narcissistic satisfaction, God also ultimately *loves only Himself*, and merely uses man to promulgate His own glory. From this reversal, Malebranche drew a consequence worthy of Lacan's reversal of Dostoevsky ("*If God doesn't exist, then nothing is permitted.*"): it is not true that, if Christ had not come to earth to deliver humanity, everyone would have been lost — quite the contrary, *nobody* would have been lost, that is, *every* human being had to fall so that Christ could come and deliver *some* of them. Malebranche's conclusion is here shattering: since the death of Christ is a key step in realizing the goal of creation, at no time was God (the Father) happier than when He was observing His son suffering and dying on the Cross.

The only way to truly avoid this perversion, not just to obfuscate it, is to fully accept the Fall as the starting point which creates the conditions of Salvation: there is no state previous to the Fall from which we fell, the Fall itself creates that from which it is a Fall — or, in theological terms, God is not the Beginning. If this sounds like yet another typical Hegelian dialectical tangle, then we should disentangle it by drawing a line of separation between the true Hegelian dialectical process and its caricature. In the caricature, we have God (or an inner Essence) externalizing itself in the domain of contingent appearances, and then gradually re-appropriating its alienated content, recognizing itself in its Otherness — "we must first lose God in order to find Him," we must fall in order to be saved. Such a position opens up the space for the justification of Evil:

if, as agents of historical Reason, we know that Evil is just a necessary detour on the path towards the final triumph of the Good, then, of course, we are justified in engaging in Evil as the means to achieve the Good. In true Hegelian spirit, however, we should insist that such a justification is always and a priori retroactive: there is no Reason in History whose divine plan can justify Evil; the Good that may come out of Evil is its contingent by-product. We may say that the ultimate result of Nazi Germany and its defeat was the institution of much higher ethical standards of human rights and international justice; but to claim that this result in any sense "justifies" Nazism would be an obscenity. Only in this way can we truly avoid the perverse consequences of religious fundamentalism. Let us take a look at such fundamentalism at its darkest: the strange case of Doctor Radovan Karadžić.

"Nothing is forbidden in my faith"

To put it in Heideggerian terms, what is the exact meaning of "is" when we read on the publicity posters for a blockbuster film statements such as "Sean Connery IS James Bond in . . ." or "Matt Damon IS Bourne in . . ."? It is not simply a close identification of the actor with the screen hero, such that "we cannot even imagine anyone else playing him." The first thing to note is that such identity claims always refer to a serial character, so that, in order to grasp the identification at stake here, we need to introduce a third term apart from the actor and the hero: namely, the screen image of the actor (John Wayne as tough Western guy, and so on) — it is *this* image, not the real actor, who is identified with the screen hero.

What about in the case of a single (non-serial) role which becomes conflated with a particular actor, as in a publicity slogan we will certainly never see: "Anthony Perkins IS Norman Bates"? As expected, it ruined the actor's career . . . When Radovan Karadžić, the leader of the Bosnian Serbs accused of organizing ethnic cleansing, was arrested, it was discovered that in his last years as a fugitive he had been "hiding in plain sight" as a spiritual healer, taking part in forums and lectures attended by several hundred people, and contributing articles to the *Zdrav Život* (Healthy Life) magazine. Can we then also say that "Radovan Karadžić IS Dragan Dabić"; the latter being not merely a mask of the former, but his "inner truth"? In other words, the relationship between the two is that of a genuine *parallax*. His editor at *Zdrav Život*, Goran Kojić, said:

"He offered me an article that speaks about similarities and differences between meditation and *tihovanje* [quietude]. I thought the text was really good and published it in several parts in our magazine." Here is a passage from the text:

> It is not only about the time you spend in prayer, or the exact position you adopt, but about a series of moments where you dive into yourself (which we could describe as pulling yourself together), where you calm down the passionate and obsessive re-living of everyday life. For each and every housewife, it is that solitary early morning coffee, when the household has still not woken up.

"Dragan Dabić" is not merely a mask, a fiction constructed to obfuscate Karadžić's true identity. Of course "Dragan Dabić" is a fiction, a fake persona, but it is here that Lacan's thesis "truth has the structure of a fiction" acquires all its weight: the fictive person "Dabić" provides the ideological key to the "real" war criminal Karadžić. Here is a saying from Dabić, whose treatments aimed at setting free the patient's "human quantum energy" which links every person to the cosmos (we are here firmly in the waters of the Jungian libido): "The basis of every religion is the idea of life as being sacred (which sets religion apart from sects)." Again, we are here immediately thrown into the pagan (pre-Christian) universe of cosmic Life and its sanctity—and, as experience teaches us (and as Walter Benjamin already warned us), whenever the sanctity of life is proclaimed, the smell of real blood being spilled is never far away.

Plato's reputation suffers from his claim that poets should be thrown out of the city—but it now appears rather sensible advice, at least judging from the post-Yugoslav experience, where ethnic cleansing was prepared for by the poets' dangerous dreams. True, Milošević "manipulated" nationalist passions—but it was the poets who delivered him the material which lent itself to manipulation. They—the sincere poets, not the corrupted politicians—were at the origin of it all, when, back in the 1970s and early '80s, they started to sow the seeds of aggressive nationalism not only in Serbia, but also in other ex-Yugoslav republics. Instead of the industrial-military complex, we in post-Yugoslavia had the *poetico-military complex*, personified in the twin figures of Radovan Karadžić and Ratko Mladić. Karadžić, a psychiatrist by profession, was not only a ruthless political and military leader, but also a poet. His poetry should not be dismissed as ridiculous—it deserves a close reading, since it provides a key to how ethnic cleansing functions. Among ancient Chinese proverbs selected personally by "Dr. Dabic," there is the following: "He who cannot agree with his enemies is controlled by them." It fits perfectly Karadžic's relation with the Bosnian Muslims. Here are the first lines of the untitled poem identified by a dedication "For Izet Sarajlić":

> Convert to my new faith crowd
> I offer you what no one has had before
> I offer you inclemency and wine
> The one who won't have bread will be fed by the light of my sun
> People nothing is forbidden in my faith
> There is loving and drinking
> And looking at the Sun for as long as you want
> And this godhead forbids you nothing
> Oh obey my call brethren people crowd[14]

The superego suspension of moral prohibitions is the crucial feature of today's "postmodern" nationalism. The cliché according to which passionate ethnic identification restores a firm set of values and beliefs in face of the confusing insecurity of a modern secular global society, is here to be turned around: nationalist "fundamentalism" rather serves as the operator of a secret, barely concealed *You may!* Without full recognition of this perverse pseudo-liberating effect of contemporary nationalism, of how the obscenely permissive superego supplements the explicit texture of the social symbolic law, we condemn ourselves to misunderstanding its true dynamic.

In his *Phenomenology of Spirit*, Hegel mentions the "silent weaving of the spirit": the underground work of changing the ideological coordinates, mostly invisible to the public eye, which then suddenly explodes into view, taking everyone by surprise. This is what was going on in ex-Yugoslavia in the 1970s and '80s, so that when things exploded in the late '80s, it was already too late: the old ideological consensus had become thoroughly putrid and collapsed in on itself.

To avoid the illusion that the poetico-military complex is a Balkan specialty, one should mention Hassan Ngeze, the Karadžić of Rwanda who, in his journal *Kangura*, systematically spread anti-Tutsi hatred and called for their genocide. It is all too easy to dismiss Karadžić and company as bad poets: other ex-Yugoslav nations (and Serbia itself) had poets

---

14   Translation available online at http://autonom.motpol.nu.

and writers recognized as "great" and "authentic" who were also fully engaged in nationalist projects. What about the Austrian Peter Handke, a great figure of contemporary European literature, who demonstratively attended the funeral of Slobodan Milošević? Almost a century ago, referring to the rise of Nazism in Germany, Karl Kraus quipped that Germany, a country of *Dichter und Denker* (poets and thinkers), had become a country of *Richter und Henker* (judges and executioners) — perhaps such a reversal should not surprise us too much . . .

But why this rise of religiously (or ethnically) justified violence today? Because we live in an era which perceives itself as post-ideological. Since great public causes can no longer be mobilized, since our hegemonic ideology calls on us to enjoy life and to fulfill ourselves, it is difficult for the majority of humans to overcome their revulsion at torturing and killing other human beings. Since the majority are spontaneously "moral" in this way, a larger, "sacred" Cause is needed, which will make individual concerns about killing seem trivial. Religious or ethnic belonging fit this role perfectly. Of course, there are cases of pathological atheists who are able to commit mass murder for pleasure, just for the sake of it, but they are rare exceptions. The majority needs to be 'anaesthetized' against its elementary sensitivity to the suffering of others. Religious ideologists usually claim that, whether true or not, religion can make otherwise bad people to do good things; from recent experience, we should rather stick to Steve Weinberg's claim that while without religion good people would do good things and bad people bad things, only religion can make good people do bad things.

"I did not come to bring peace, but a sword"

This, however, is only one side of the story — religion being, by definition, a multifarious phenomenon which offers itself for different uses. Recently, in the UK, an atheist group displayed posters with the message: "There is no God, so don't worry and enjoy life!" In response, representatives of the Russian Orthodox Church started a counter-campaign with posters saying: "There is a God, so don't worry and enjoy life!" The interesting feature is how both propositions seem to be in some way convincing: if there is no God, we are free to do what we want, so let us enjoy life; if there is a God, he will take care of things in his benevolent omnipotence, so we don't have to worry and can enjoy life. This complementarity demonstrates that there is something wrong with both statements: they both share the same secret premise: "We can act as if there is no God and be happy, because we can trust the good God (or fate, or . . .) to watch over us and protect us!" The obvious counter-proposition to both statements and their underlying premise is: "Whether there is a God or not, life is shit, so one cannot really enjoy it!" This is why we can easily imagine the following (no less convincing) alternative propositions: "There is no God, so everything depends on us and we should worry all the time!" and "There is a God who watches what we are doing all the time, so we should be anxious and worry continuously!"

The question we confront here is how, precisely, to distinguish the fundamentalist conflation of theology and politics from its emancipatory version? Both enact a unity of love and violence, justifying violence with love: killing can be done out of love. Perhaps, we should take love as our starting point—not intimate-erotic love, but that political love whose Christian name is *agape*. "If all else perished, and he remained, I should still continue to be; and if all else remained, and he were annihilated, the universe would turn to a mighty stranger: I should not seem a part of it." This is how, in *Wuthering Heights*, Cathy characterizes her relation to Heathcliff—and provides a succinct ontological definition of unconditional erotic love. There is an unmistakable dimension of terror at work here—think of the ecstatic trance of Tristan and Isolde, ready to obliterate their entire social reality in their immersion into the Night of deadly *jouissance*. Which is why the proper dialectic of erotic love consists in the tension between contraction and expansion, between erotic self-immersion and the slow work of creating a social space marked by the couple's love (children, common projects, etc.). *Agape* functions in a wholly different way—how? It may appear that, in contrast to *eros*, with its violent subtraction from collective space, the love for a collective succeeds in doing away with the excess of terrorizing violence: does *agape* not imply an emphatic *yes* to the beloved collective and ultimately to all humanity, or even—as in Buddhism—to the entire domain of (suffering) life? The object here is loved unconditionally, not on account of a selection of its qualities but in all its imperfections and weaknesses.

A first counter-argument goes by way of the reply to a simple question: which political regimes in the twentieth century legitimized their power by invoking the people's love for their leader? The so-called "totalitarian" ones. Today, it is only and precisely the North Korean regime which continually invokes the infinite love of the Korean people for Kim Il Sung and Kim Yong Il and, *vice versa*, the radiating love of the Leader for his people, expressed in continuous acts of grace. Kim Yong Il wrote a short poem along these lines: "In the same way that a sunflower can only thrive if it is turned towards the sun, the Korean people can only thrive if their eyes are turned upwards towards their Leader"—i.e., himself . . . Terror and mercy are thus closely linked; they are effectively the front and the back of the same power structure: only a power which asserts its full terroristic right and capacity to destroy anything and anyone it wants can symmetrically universalize mercy—since this power could have destroyed everyone, those who survive do so thanks to the mercy of those in power. In other words, the very fact that we, the subjects of power, are alive is proof of the power's infinite mercy. This is why the more "terroristic" a regime is, the more its leaders are praised for their infinite love, goodness, and mercy. Adorno was right to emphasize that, in politics, love is invoked precisely when another (democratic) legitimization is lacking: loving a leader means you love him for what he is, not for what he does.

So how about the next candidate for love as a political category— Oriental spirituality (Buddhism) with its more "gentle," balanced, holistic, ecological approach. Over the 150 years of Japan's rapid industrialization and militarization, with its ethics of discipline and self-sacrifice, the process was supported by the majority of Zen thinkers (who, today, knows that D. T. Suzuki himself, the high guru of Zen in the America of the 1960s, supported in his youth the spirit of total discipline and militaristic expansion in the Japan of the 1930s?). There is no contradiction here, no manipulative perversion of authentic compassionate insight: the attitude of total immersion into the self-less "now" of instant enlightenment—in which all reflexive distance is lost and "I am what I do," as C. S. Lewis put it; in which absolute discipline coincides with total spontaneity—perfectly legitimizes one's subordination to the militaristic social machine.

What this means is that the all-encompassing compassion of Buddhism (or Hinduism, for that matter) has to be opposed to Christianity's intolerant, violent love. The Buddhist stance is ultimately that of Indifference, the quenching of all passions which strive to establish differences, while Christian love is a violent passion to introduce difference, a gap in the order of being, in order to privilege and elevate some object at the expense of an other. Love is violence not (only) in the vulgar sense of the Balkan proverb: "If he doesn't beat me, he doesn't love me!"; violence is already the love choice as such, which tears its object out of its context, elevating it to the Thing. In Montenegrin folklore, the origin of Evil is a beautiful woman: she causes the men around her to lose their balance, she literally destabilizes the universe, colors all things with a tone of partiality.

In order to properly grasp the triangle of love, hatred, and indifference, one has to rely on the logic of the universal and its constitutive exception which introduces existence. The truth of the universal proposition "Man is mortal" does not imply the existence of even one man, while the "less strong" proposition "There is at least one man who exists (i.e., some men exist)" implies their existence. Lacan draws from this the conclusion that we pass from a universal proposition (which defines the content of a notion) to existence only through a proposition stating the existence, not of the singular element of the universal genus which exists, but of at least one which is an *exception* to the universality in question. What this means with regard to love is that the universal proposition "I love you all" acquires the level of actual existence only if "There is at least one whom I hate"—a thesis abundantly confirmed by the fact that universal love for humanity has always led to brutal hatred of the (actually existing) exception, of the enemies of humanity. This hatred of the exception is the "truth" of universal love, in contrast to true love which can only emerge against the background *not* of universal hatred, but of universal indifference: I am indifferent towards All, the totality of the universe, and as such, I actually love *you*, the unique individual who stands out against this indifferent background. Love and hatred are thus not symmetrical: love emerges out of universal indifference, while hatred emerges out of universal love. In short, we are dealing here again with the formulae of sexuation: "I do not love you all" is the only foundation of "There is nobody that I do not love," while "I love you all" necessarily relies on "I really hate some of you." "But I love you all!"—this is how Erich Mielke, the Secret Police boss of the GDR, defended himself; his universal love was obviously grounded in its constitutive exception, the hatred of the enemies of socialism . . .

But, again, how to distinguish *this* violence from the violence implied by authentic Christian love, the tremendous violence which dwells at the very heart of the Christian notion of love for one's neighbour, the violence which finds direct expression in a number of Christ's most disturbing statements? Here are the main versions:

Do not think that I came to bring peace on earth; I did not come to bring peace, but a sword. For I came to set a man against his father, and a daughter against her mother, and a daughter-in-law against her mother-in-law;

and a man's enemies will be the members of his household. He who loves
father or mother more than Me is not worthy of Me; and he who loves
son or daughter more than Me is not worthy of Me. And he who does
not take his cross and follow after Me is not worthy of Me. He who has
found his life will lose it, and he who has lost his life for My sake will find
it. (Matthew 10:34–9)

I have come to cast fire upon the earth; and how I wish it were already
kindled! But I have a baptism to undergo, and how distressed I am until
it is accomplished! Do you suppose that I came to grant peace on earth?
I tell you, no, but rather division; for from now on five members in one
household will be divided, three against two and two against three. They
will be divided, father against son and son against father, mother against
daughter and daughter against mother, mother-in-law against daughter-
in-law and daughter-in-law against mother-in-law. (Luke 12:49–53)

If anyone comes to me, and does not hate his own father and mother and
wife and children and brothers and sisters, yes, and even his own life, he
cannot be my disciple. (Luke 14:26)

Perhaps people think that I have come to cast peace upon the world. They
do not know that I have come to cast conflicts upon the earth: fire, sword,
war. For there will be five in a house: there'll be three against two and two
against three, father against son and son against father, and they will stand
alone. (Thomas 16, non-canonical)

How not to recognize "divine violence" here, where it is openly proclaimed,
in Jesus' "I bring not peace, but a sword"? How are we to read these
statements? Christian ideology resorts to five strategies to deal with them,
rather than heroically accepting the message imposed by a literal reading
and claiming that Christ himself advocates violence to crush his enemies.
The first two readings are outright denials of the problem: one gets rid of it
by disputing the standard translation, suggesting either a modest correction
(changing "those who do not *hate* their father, etc." into "those who do not
prefer me to their father," so that we get just a graduation of love enjoined
by a jealous god—love your father, but love me more . . .), or a more radical
correction, as in the Book of Kells, the Celtic illuminated manuscript copy
of the Gospels, which erroneously uses the word "gaudium" ("joy") rather
than "gladium" ("sword"), rendering the verse in translation: "I came not
[only] to bring peace, but joy." (One is tempted to read this mistranslation
together with the correct translation and thus compose the full message as:

"I come not to bring peace, but the joy of the sword, of struggle.") What then follows are three more sophisticated strategies, the first (arguably the most disgusting and politically dangerous) claiming that Christ's message "I bring a sword" has to be read together with its apparent opposite, the "pacifist" warning, "all those who take up the sword shall perish by the sword" (Matthew 26:52): the sword Christ is talking about when he announces that he "brings a sword" is the *second* sword in "those who take up the sword shall perish by the sword"—in other words, it is others who first use the sword, or attack Christians, and Christians have the full right to defend themselves, by the sword, if necessary. This is also how the passage from Luke 22:38 ("if you don't have a sword, better sell your clothes and buy one") should be read: buy a sword to finish off those who first used one. The problem with this reading, of course, is that it courts the danger of sanctioning the most brutal violence as a defense against those who attack us, even giving it the force of fulfilling the divine prophecy-injunction ("those who take up the sword shall perish by the sword"). Hitler all the time claimed exactly the same—he was only using the sword to destroy those who had already taken up the sword against Germany . . .

The next strategy is to read Christ's words not as an injunction or threat, but as a simple prediction and warning to his followers: "I bring a sword" means "When you spread my message, you should be ready for the hatred of those who will ferociously oppose it and use a sword against you"—a prediction fully confirmed by the many massacres of Christians in the Roman empire. It is in this sense that Christ is turning husband against wife, and so on: when a wife accepts Christianity before her husband, this can of course engender his animosity towards her. The problem with this reading is that it fails to account for the much stronger injunction to (actively) hate your father, and so forth, not merely to be prepared to (passively) endure their hatred: when Christ enjoins his followers to hate their parents, there is no qualification that they should do so only if their parents oppose their faith in Christ—the injunction clearly calls for a hatred which, as it were, makes the first move, and is not just a reaction to the hatred of others.

As might be expected, the final strategy involves a *metaphoric* reading: the "sword" in question is not the literal weapon used to hurt others but *the word of God itself which divides truth from error*, so that the violence it enacts is that of spiritual cleansing. Nice as this sounds, ambiguities and dangers lurk here.

In *The Divided Heaven*, Christa Wolf's classic GDR novel from 1963, about the subjective impact of the divided Germany, Manfred (who has chosen the West) says to Rita, his love, when they meet for the last time: "But even if our land is divided, we still share the same heaven." Rita (who has chosen to remain in the East) replies bitterly: "No, they first divided Heaven." Apologetic for the East as the novel is, it offers a correct insight into how our "earthly" divisions and struggles are ultimately always grounded in a "divided heaven," in a much more radical and exclusive division of the very (symbolic) universe in which we dwell. The bearer and instrument of this "division of heaven" is language as the "house of being," as the medium which sustains our entire worldview, the way we experience reality: language, not primitive egotistic interest, is the first and greatest divider, and it is because of language that we and our neighbors (can) "live in different worlds" even when we live on the same street. What this means is that verbal violence is not a secondary distortion, but the ultimate resort of every form of specifically human violence.

So, back to Christ: even if his divisive sword is spiritual, its "division of heaven" is ontologically more violent than any "ontic" violence, which it can easily ground and justify. In order to account for Christ's "problematic" endorsement of violence, we must confront it with traditional pagan wisdom. Although the rise of democracy and philosophy in Ancient Greece announced a different world, the traditional wisdom is still fully asserted there, exemplarily in the ethico-political poem on *eunomia* — the beautiful order — by Solon, the founder of Athenian democracy:

> These things my spirit bids me
> teach the men of Athens:
> that Dysnomia
> brings countless evils for the city,
> but Eunomia brings order
> and makes everything proper,
> by enfolding the unjust in fetters,
> smoothing those things that are rough,
> stopping greed,
> sentencing hubris to obscurity,
> making the flowers of mischief to wither,
> and straightening crooked judgments.
> It calms the deeds of arrogance
> and stops the bilious anger of harsh strife.
> Under its control, all things are proper
> and prudence reigns over human affairs.[15]

---

15   Elizabeth Irwin, *Solon and Early Greek Poetry: The Politics of Exhortation*, New York: Cambridge University Press 2005, p. 184.

No wonder that the same principle is asserted in the famous chorus on the uncanny/demonic dimension of man from Sophocles' *Antigone*:

> If he honors the laws of the land, and reveres the Gods of the State, proudly his city shall stand; but a cityless outcast I rate who so bold in his pride from the path of right does depart; never may I sit by his side, or share the thoughts of his heart.[16]

(Some, such as A. Oksenberg Rorty, even propose a much more radical translation of the last line: "a person without a city, beyond human boundary, a horror, a pollution to be avoided.") One should recall here that the chorus reacts to the news that someone (at this point we do not yet know who) has violated Creon's prohibition and performed funeral rites on Polynices' body—it is Antigone herself who is implicitly castigated as the "cityless outcast" engaged in excessive demonic acts which disturb the *eunomia* of the state, fully reasserted in the last lines of the play:

> The most important part of happiness
> is therefore wisdom—not to act impiously
> towards the gods, for boasts of arrogant men
> bring on great blows of punishment
> so in old age men can discover wisdom.[17]

From the standpoint of *eunomia*, Antigone is definitely demonic and uncanny: her defiant act expresses a stance of excessive insistence which disturbs the "beautiful order" of the city; her unconditional ethics violates the harmony of the *polis* and is as such "beyond human boundary." The irony is that, while Antigone presents herself as the guardian of the immemorial laws which sustain the human order, she acts as a freakish and ruthless abomination—there definitely is something cold and monstrous about her, as is made clear by the contrast between her and her warm and humane sister Ismene. This uncanny dimension is signaled by the ambiguity in the name "Antigone": it can be read as "unbending," coming from "anti-" and "-gon / -gony" (corner, bend, angle), but also as "opposed to motherhood" or "in place of a mother" from the root *gone*, "that which generates" (*gonos*, "-gony," as in "theogony"). It is difficult to resist the temptation of positing a link between the two meanings: is being-a-mother

---

16   Sophocles, "Antigone," in *The Oedipus Trilogy*, Charleston: Biblio Bazaar 2007, p. 201.
17   Ibid.

not the basic form of a woman's "bending," her subordination, so that Antigone's uncompromising attitude has to entail the rejection of mother-hood? Ironically, in the original myth (reported by Hyginus in his *Fabulae* 72), Antigone *was* a mother: when she was caught in the act of performing funeral rites for her brother Polynices, Creon handed her over for execu-tion to his son Haemon, to whom she had been betrothed. But Haemon, while he pretended to put her to death, smuggled her away, married her, and had a son by her. In time, having grown up, the son came to Thebes, where Creon detected him by the bodily mark which all descendants of the Sparti or Dragon-men bore on their bodies. Creon showed no mercy; so Haemon killed himself and his wife Antigone. There are indications that Hyginus here followed Euripides, who also wrote a tragedy *Antigone*, of which a few fragments survived, among them this one: "Man's best possession is a sympathetic wife"—definitely not Sophocles' Antigone.[18]

Those interpreters who see Antigone as a proto-Christian figure are right: in her unconditional commitment, she follows a different ethics that points forward towards Christianity (and can only be adequately read "anachronistically" from the later Christian standpoint)—why? Christianity introduces into the global balanced order of *eunomia* a prin-ciple totally foreign to it, a principle that, measured by the standards of the pagan cosmology, cannot but appear as a monstrous distortion: the principle according to which each individual has an immediate access to universality (of the Holy Spirit, or, today, of human rights and freedoms)—I can participate in this universal dimension directly, irre-spective of my special place within the global social order. And do Christ's "scandalous" words, quoted from Luke, not point in the same direction? Of course, we are *not* dealing here with a simple brutal hatred demanded by a cruel and jealous God: family relations stand metaphorically for the entire socio-symbolic network, for any particular ethnic "substance" that determines our place in the global order of things. The "hatred" enjoined by Christ is therefore not a kind of pseudo-dialectical opposite to love,

---

18   One is thus tempted to rewrite *Antigone* along the lines of Brecht's three versions of the same story (*Jasager, Neinsager, Jasager 2*). The first version follows Sophocles' denouement. In the second version, Antigone wins, convincing Creon to allow the proper burial of Polynices; however, the patri-otic and populist crowd insists on revenge against the traitor rebels, there is a renewed civil war, Creon is lynched by the mob, there is chaos in the city, and, in the last scene, Antigone walks in a trance among the ruins, fire all around her, crying "But I was created for love, not for war." In the third, "Aeschylized" version, the chorus is no longer the purveyor of stupid commonsensical wisdoms, but becomes an active agent: it castigates both Antigone and Creon for their struggle which threatens the city—Creon is deposed, they are both arrested, and the chorus takes over as a collective organ, imposing a new Law, introducing people's democracy in Thebes.

but a direct expression of what St. Paul, in I *Corinthians* 13, described as *agape*, the key intermediary term between faith and hope: it is love itself that enjoins us to "unplug" from the organic community into which we were born, or, as Paul put it: for a Christian, there are neither men nor women, neither Jews nor Greeks. No wonder that, for those fully identified with the Jewish "national substance," as well as for the Greek philosophers and the proponents of the global Roman empire, the appearance of Christ was perceived as a ridiculous and/or traumatic scandal.

So, when Paul writes (in I *Corinthians* 25): "The wisdom of the world is foolishness to God," his target is the most fundamental feature of pagan wisdom. This is why one should rehabilitate even Tertullian's (in)famous *credo quia absurdum* ("I believe because it is absurd"), which is a misquotation of the key passage from his *On the Flesh of Christ*: "The Son of God was crucified: I am not ashamed—because it is shameful. The Son of God died: it is immediately credible—because it is silly. He was buried, and rose again: it is certain—because it is impossible."[19] The first thing to bear in mind here is that Tertullian was not an opponent of reason: in his *On Repentance* (I, 2–3) he emphasizes that all things are to be understood by reason:

> Reason, in fact, is a thing of God, inasmuch as there is nothing which God the Maker of all has not provided, disposed, ordained by reason—nothing which He has willed should not be handled and understood by reason. All, therefore, who are ignorant of God, must necessarily be ignorant also of a thing which is His, because no treasure-house at all is accessible to strangers. And thus, voyaging all the universal course of life without the rudder of reason, they know not how to shun the hurricane which is impending over the world.[20]

No wonder, then, that Tertullian shows a deep respect for the great pagan philosophers ("Of course we shall not deny that philosophers have sometimes thought the same things as ourselves") and even calls Seneca "*saepe noster* / almost one of us."[21] One should therefore reject the popular reading according to which Tertullian advocated a crazy and irrational belief

---

19   A. Cleveland Coxe, "On the Flesh of Christ" of *Tertullian*, Part II, Chapter 5 in *The Ante-Nicene Fathers, Translation of The Writings of the Fathers Down to A.D. 325: Volume III*, New York: Charles Scribner's Sons 1903, p. 525: *Crucifixus est dei filius; non pudet, quia pudendum est. / Et mortuus est dei filius; credibile prorsus est, quia ineptum est. / Et sepultus resurrexit; certum est, quia impossibile.*
20   Coxe, "On Repentance" of *Tertullian*, ibid. Part III, Chapter 1, p. 657.
21   Tertullian, *A Treatise on the Soul*, Whitefish: Kessinger Publishing 2004, p. 7.

in something patently absurd, something that runs counter to reason and the evidence of our senses. The passage quoted above from *On the Flesh of Christ* is part of a polemic against Marcion who, dismissing as absurd the notion that God could be embodied in human flesh, reduced Christ's incarnation to a mere phantasm — Christ did not have a real body, he did not really suffer. The measure which makes the belief in full reincarnation appear absurd is thus not logic but custom and convention, not reason as such but common "wisdom," the space of what is conventionally acceptable — it is when measured by this standard that the death and resurrection of Christ appear "impossible." "Impossibility" is here meant rather in the sense of: "Impossible! How can you do a horrible thing like this! Aren't you ashamed!" The idea that God Himself could die in pain on a cross, humiliated and punished as a common criminal, is "impossible" — dangerous, shameful, absurd; it violates the conventional expectation of what befits a god.

However, is not Christ's resurrection "impossible" in a much stronger sense: while not logically impossible, it nonetheless clearly breaks the basic laws of what we perceive as our (material) reality? Here, one has to insist on the gap that separates the universe of modern science from our everyday understanding of reality; this gap reaches its apogee in quantum physics whose picture of reality simply does not make sense within the horizon of our commonsense perception. This is why a voluntarist/decisionist anti-Aristotelian view finds it much easier to accept the paradoxical results of modern physics than does our everyday understanding: scientific reason and "absurd" Christian theology end up on the same side against (Aristotelian) commonsense. Recall that Einstein provided his own scientific version of Tertullian's *certum est, quia impossibile*: "If at first an idea does not sound absurd, then there is no hope for it." Hope of what? That it will be proven true scientifically!

Lacan's notion of the Real as impossible can be of help here — to render Tertullian's *certum est, quia impossibile* much clearer, it suffices to replace "impossible" with "real": "It is certain — because it is real." The impossibility of the Real refers to the failure of its symbolization: the Real is the virtual hard core around which symbolizations fluctuate; these symbolizations are always and by definition provisory and unstable, the only "certainty" is that of the void of the Real which they (presup)pose.

Guevara as a Reader of Rousseau

It is against this Christian background that one should read Che Guevara's well-known statements on revolutionary love:

> At the risk of seeming ridiculous, let me say that the true revolutionary is guided by great feelings of love. It is impossible to think of a genuine revolutionary lacking this quality. Perhaps it is one of the great dramas of the leader that he or she must combine a passionate spirit with a cold intelligence and make painful decisions without flinching. Our vanguard revolutionaries must idealize this love of the people, of the most sacred causes, and make it one and indivisible. They cannot descend, with small doses of daily affection, to the level where ordinary people put their love into practice.
>
> The leaders of the revolution have children just beginning to talk, who are not learning to say "daddy"; their wives, too, must be part of the general sacrifice of their lives in order to take the revolution to its destiny. The circle of their friends is limited strictly to the circle of comrades in the revolution. There is no life outside of it.
>
> In these circumstances one must have a large dose of humanity, a large dose of a sense of justice and truth in order to avoid dogmatic extremes, cold scholasticism, or an isolation from the masses. We must strive every day so that this love of living humanity is transformed into actual deeds, into acts that serve as examples, as a moving force.[22]

Guevara is struggling here precisely with the relationship between *eros* (personal love) and *agape* (political love): he posits their mutual exclusion—revolutionaries "cannot descend, with small doses of daily affection, to the level where ordinary people put their love into practice," in other words their love must remain "one and indivisible," love of the people, to the exclusion of all "pathological" attachments. While this may appear to be the very formula for a "totalitarian" catastrophe (a revolutionary killing real individuals on behalf of the abstraction: "the people"), there is another, much more refined, way to read Guevara's position. One should start with the paradox that singular erotic love, taken precisely as the absolute, should not be posited as a direct goal—it should retain the status of a by-product, of something we receive as a form of undeserved grace. The point is not that "there are more important things than love"—an authentic amorous encounter remains an absolute point of reference

---

22   Ernesto Che Guevara, *Socialism and Man in Cuba*, New York: Ocean Press 1965.

in one's life (to put it in traditional terms, it is "what makes one's life meaningful"). But the hard lesson to be learned is that, precisely as such, love (the amorous relationship) should not be the direct goal of one's life—when one confronts the choice between love and duty, duty should prevail. True love is modest, like that of a couple in a Marguerite Duras novel: while the two lovers hold hands, they do not look into each other's eyes; they look together outwards, to some third point, their common Cause. Perhaps there is no greater love than that of a revolutionary couple, where each of the two lovers is ready to abandon the other at any moment should the revolution demand it. They do not love each other less than the amorous couple bent on suspending all their terrestrial links and obligations in order to burn out in a night of unconditional passion—if anything, they love each other more.

The question is thus: how does an emancipatory-revolutionary collective which embodies the "general will" affect intense erotic passion? Not surprisingly, we find an answer in Rousseau, the theoretician of the general will. His *Julie, or the New Heloise* delivers a similar message. Since (in an unfortunate sign of our contemporary barbarism) Rousseau's extraordinary novel no longer has the status of a well-known classic, here is the brief outline of the story. Set principally by Lake Geneva, the novel centers on a young tutor, Saint-Preux, and Julie, his female pupil, who fall in love. But he is a commoner, and Julie's noble father will not hear of their relationship. Forced to keep their passion a guilty secret, the couple succumb and become lovers. Julie hopes to force her father to consent by becoming pregnant, but she has a miscarriage. At this point, Lord Eduard Bomston, an immensely rich English peer and a friend of Julie's father, appears. He takes a great liking to Saint-Preux, but the latter suspects him of having designs on Julie. In a jealous rage he challenges Lord Eduard to a duel. This disaster is finally averted and Lord Eduard's generosity is proven by his efforts to persuade Baron d'Etange to permit the marriage. But Eduard also fails: Julie's father demands that she renounce Saint-Preux and accept the husband of his choice, his own companion, the older Wolmar.

At this point of despair, another character intervenes to resolve the deadlock: Claire, Julie's level-headed cousin who eventually has everyone's confidence and who acts as a sort of one-woman chorus throughout, observing, predicting, and lamenting. To save Julie's reputation, Claire sends the tutor away; his friend Lord Eduard takes him to Paris. While they are gone, Julie's mother discovers their correspondence and is very upset, and soon after she falls ill and dies. Even though the two events are unrelated, Julie feels guilty and thinks that she is to blame for her mother's death. In this state of mind, she consents to renounce her lover and to marry Wolmar. During the wedding, she undergoes a profound inner change, a conversion to virtue. She now feels ready to accept her duties as a wife and mother. In her pursuit of virtue, she is at every step helped by her extraordinary husband, a man as wise as he is good. Although she cannot bring herself to tell him of her relationship with Saint-Preux, he nevertheless knows and forgives her everything. In return, Julie embraces her new state, breaking entirely with her lover who eventually flees Europe.

But the story continues, or, rather, begins again: ten years later, Saint-Preux returns and is made welcome by Wolmar and his wife. Julie now has two children and her life is wholly devoted to them and to running a model estate at Clarens with Wolmar. The rest of the book describes these efforts, Julie's virtue, Wolmar's wisdom, the beauty of their English garden, and the prosperity of their estate.[23] Julie's only sorrow appears to be that Wolmar is an atheist. He never speaks of it, and always attends church for the sake of appearances, but he is a convinced unbeliever. This disturbs Julie, although Wolmar never tries to alter her faith. The more beneficent Wolmar is, and the more he does to cure Saint-Preux of his old infatuation, the more religious and miserable his wife becomes. But why? As was clear to Rousseau, the excess of religious commitment is a displaced return of the repressed sexual passion: the true factor of de-sexualization is not religious spirituality but the atheistic Enlightenment which dissolves passion with cold utilitarian understanding, reducing it to a pathological excess to be properly cured. No wonder that, in these conditions, sexual passion can only return in a religious guise, as the "irrational" awareness of misery and sin.

In the end, once it seems certain that Saint-Preux will marry Claire and settle down at Clarens to become tutor to the Wolmar children, Julie tells him of her profound malaise and boredom. The novel ends with an unexpected accident which nonetheless reveals a deeper deadlock: having plunged into the lake to save her younger son from drowning, Julie catches cold, falls ill, and dies an exemplary death. She was never really "cured" of her love for her former lover, and the only way out of

---

23   Is this ten-year gap not like the gap that separates the first and second parts of the Freudian dream of Irma's injection? In both cases, the same reversal occurs from tragedy to comedy: we inexplicably change the terrain, the utter despair of the separated lovers is replaced by the ridiculous happiness of the well-organized collective life at Clarens.

her predicament is death. Julie is thus very happy to die, because she is now perfectly aware that all her virtue has not helped her to forget Saint-Preux: she loves him as much as ever. As she dies, she gives an account of her tolerant and loving religious beliefs, but her greatest hope is to be reunited in heaven with Saint-Preux.[24]

While the novel's subtitle draws the parallel with the medieval story of Abelard and Heloise, a young girl and her tutor who also succumbed to passion, one should focus on the difference between the two stories. Rousseau depicts the era of the Enlightenment, where the punishment which follows the sexual transgression is no longer castration for the man and the nunnery for the woman: the new Heloise virtuously takes up her duties as wife, mother, and, together with Wolmar, the beneficent parent to everyone on their model estate; while, rather than suffering the cruelty of castration, the tutor is invited by the understanding husband into the ideal family in order to be cured of his pathological infatuation. The message could not be clearer: marriage is the contemporary form of sexual renunciation. In a first approach, the inner movement of *Julie* effectively appears as "a kind of two-stage negation" in which "the passionate rejection of false and conventional desires" is "followed by the virtuous or rational rejection of the unconventional passions themselves":[25] *Julie* is "the story of two lovers . . . whose passionate love first rejects the falsity of existing conventions but who then—through their membership in a community formed by Julie's husband, Wolmar—undergo a second development in which they virtuously abstain from those passions themselves."[26]

The problem is how to read the return of passion at the novel's end, when Julie confesses her inability to compromise her desire and opts for (a thinly disguised) suicide as the only way out—is this disturbing supplement a sign of the failure of the Hegelian "negation of negation" which forms the novel's basic frame, or is it its inherent fulfillment? In other words, is the gap between the "official" Hegelian reading of *Julie* (the "sublation" of passionate love in the new virtuous community which cures us of it) and the implicit lesson of the story itself (the failure of this "sublation," the deadly return of love) to be read as a prescient critique of Hegel, as an indication of the limit of *Aufhebung*, as the persistence of

---

24   See Judith N. Shklar, *Men and Citizens: A Study of Rousseau's Social Theory*, Cambridge: Cambridge University Press 1969.
25   Allen Speight, *Hegel, Literature and the Problem of Agency*, Cambridge: Cambridge University Press 2001, p. 92.
26   Ibid., p. 91.

the real of the obscene "undead" passion whose singularity eludes the grasp of notional universalization? One is tempted to agree with such a reading: is what characterizes the post-Hegelian break not precisely the rise of a repetition which cannot be "sublated," of a drive which persists beyond (or, rather, beneath) the movement of idealization? The memorable phrases in Julie's final letter to her lover before her death (Sixth Part, Letter VIII) certainly seem to point in this direction. It is not so much that satisfaction (well-being, happiness) are out of reach for her—they are actual, and this very fact, "ce dégoût du bien-être," is what she finds unbearably suffocating: "je suis trop heureuse: le bonheur m'ennuie."[27] When a contemporary Swiss reviewer of *Julie* wrote that "after reading this book, one has to die of pleasure . . . or, better: one has to live in order to read it again and again"[28]—is this overlapping of death and the repetitive excess of life not the most succinct description of the Freudian death drive, a dimension which eludes the Hegelian dialectical mediation.

What, however, if this perspective is turned around? What if it is only after we pass through the painful "sublation" destined to cure us of the passion of love that this passion emerges "as such," in its pure form, shorn of the naïve and heroic mask of opposing traditional and oppressive paternal morality which characterizes its first appearance? In Hegelese, if the first negation (passion against social oppression) is an "abstract negation," the second is "concrete," actual negation. Only here—when the order is no longer oppressive, but has become the order of happiness and well-being—can it be properly negated. The "negation of negation" is thus necessarily followed by an additional "turn of the screw": the absolute/undead passion is what the "negation of negation" produces, what it brings from its In-itself to its For-itself. Julie's final passionate outburst is thus uncannily similar to Sygne's "no" from Claudel's *L'Otage*: the remainder which follows the double movement of *Versagung*, the excess generated by the self-negated sacrifice; once you have sacrificed everything (all social content) for passion, you have to renounce passion itself—and yet, *eppur si muove*, the passion persists.

There is another point to add here: the way *not* to read the ending of *Julie* is to see in it the assertion of an "ontological" gap between desire and the constraints of (social) reality, as the necessary failure of an impossible utopia, along the lines of "desire can never be fully satisfied, and it is best

27   Jean-Jacques Rousseau, *Julie ou la Nouvelle Heloise*, Paris: Le Livre de Poche 2002, p. 757.
28   Quoted from Robert Darnton, *The Great Cat Massacre and Other Episodes in French Cultural History*, New York: Basic Books 1999, p. 286.

that it should not be." We should, rather, risk a somewhat naïve historicist-Marxist solution to the final deadlock of *Julie*: what if the Clarens cure/sublation fails not because of some ontological incompatibility between love and virtuous social order, but because the social order at Clarens is in fact a proto-totalitarian hierarchical-pedagogic nightmare, the realization of a fantasy proper to the despotic pre-revolutionary Enlightenment? Clarens is carefully constructed and tightly ordered, self-complete and unchanging, an Enlightenment utopia in a new intimate version: to achieve complete happiness, all must be committed to the collective good. The institutional manipulation of the workers (who happily endorse their own exploitation, with no need for overt repression), as well as the weird "cure" for Saint-Preux's amorous illness, seem to come straight out of a Foucauldian universe of biopolitical control and regulation: the oppression of the prohibitive power is replaced by benevolent administration. This new mode of the exercise of power is personified by Wolmar, who, although imposed on Julie by her own father, is not a figure of paternal authority, but a decidedly post-patriarchal authority, a good-hearted regulator/coordinator who rules with total transparency, deprived of any mystique of power, and who expects the same openness from his subjects. And the fact that he is intimately an atheist who partakes only externally in religious rites is crucial: he needs no higher transcendence to sustain his power. In Lacanese, the passage from Julie's father to Wolmar is the passage from the Master's discourse to the University discourse: deprived of the authority of the Master-Signifier, Wolmar is knowledge embodied — he knows it all, all the intimate secrets of those around him, and the only subjective stance that can sustain this excess of knowledge is that of serene forgiveness: he knows all about Julie's affair and aborted pregnancy, but there is no envy or jealousy in his reaction to it, he accepts it all. The obverse of this unconditional munificence is, of course, a form of control and domination which is much stronger than the standard oppressive exercise of power: the latter remains an external pressure, thereby allowing the subject to resist it from within; but Wolmar's power is a power which caringly accepts this inner core of resistance, neither accusing nor blaming the subject for it, but merely proposing a cure by way of re-education, with the subject's full cooperation.

This is why the community of Clarens, presided over by Wolmar and the reborn Julie, is not the truly self-transparent community it pretends to be: its "transparency" is false, an illusion obfuscating utter manipulation. The "general will" that appears to emerge in Clarens deprives the subjects of the very core of their subjectivity—and Julie's "irrational" resistance is the proof, a desperate attempt to reassert the infinite right of her subjectivity. This is why it is too easy to see Claire as superior to Julie (as some feminist interpreters are tempted to do): to oppose Julie, still caught in the split between duty and passion that characterizes traditional feminine identity, to Claire, a free and independent woman who was able to rise above traditional sex roles, cherishing liberty and friendship. Claire is here presented like a wise character from a Jane Austen novel, as opposed to Julie whose unquenchable passion prefigures the Brontë universe. Claire may well rise above the traditional feminine role—but precisely as such, she is the ultimate guarantee of the Clarens order and its stability, a behind-the-scenes fixer who wisely intervenes to manipulate excessive outbursts of passion so that social harmony is maintained. As such, Claire fits in perfectly with the existing order, in contrast to the unrest and negativity embodied in Julie.

But does the fact that Clarens is a pre-revolutionary organic community not allow for the possibility of another form of collectivity, something like an emancipatory-revolutionary collective embodying the "general will" much more authentically? The question again is: how does such a collective affect intense erotic passion? From what we know about love among the Bolshevik revolutionaries, something unique took place there, a new form of amorous couple emerged: a couple living in a permanent state of emergency, totally dedicated to the revolutionary Cause, ready to sacrifice all personal sexual fulfillment to it, even ready to abandon and betray each other if the Revolution demanded it, but simultaneously totally dedicated to each other, enjoying rare moments of extreme intensity together. The lovers' passion was tolerated, even silently respected, but ignored in the public discourse as something of no concern to others. (There are traces of this even in what we know of Lenin's affair with Inessa Armand.) In all three previous forms of managing the amorous relationship depicted in *Julie*, we have a violent attempt at *Gleichschaltung*, at enforcing the unity between intimate passion and social life (Julie's father wants her to suppress her feelings; in their affair, Julie and her tutor want to obliterate social reality; Wolmar again wants to cure the lovers of their disease and integrate them fully into the new social space), while here, the radical *disjunction* between sexual passion and social-revolutionary activity is fully recognized. The two dimensions are accepted as being totally heterogeneous, each irreducible to the other; there is no harmony between the two, but it is this very recognition of the gap which makes their relationship non-antagonistic.

There is, however, a further step to be made here: Guevara's claim that "the true revolutionary is guided by a great feeling of love" should be read together with his much more "problematic" statement on revolutionaries as "killing machines":

> Hatred is an element of struggle; relentless hatred of the enemy that impels us over and beyond the natural limitations of man and transforms us into effective, violent, selective, and cold killing machines. Our soldiers must be thus; a people without hatred cannot vanquish a brutal enemy.[29]

This is why we should go to the end here and apply Christ's words, "those who do not hate their father are not my followers," *to himself*, to his own stance at the Cross: at the moment of his dying, Christ "hates his father out of love." Elie Wiesel wrote of a rabbi in Auschwitz who, even in the camp, went on fasting on Yom Kippur, although he knew this would mean his certain death (because of the fasting, he grew weak, failed to pass the next "selection" and so was gassed). The rabbi explained that he was fasting "not out of obedience, but out of defiance": "Before the war, some Jews rebelled against the divine will by going to restaurants on the Day of Atonement; here, it is by observing the fast that we can make our indignation heard. Yes, my disciple and teacher, know that I fasted. Not for the love of God, but against God."[30] Asked why he was doing it if he was no longer a believer, the rabbi replied: "You do not see the heart of the matter. Here and now, the only way to accuse him is by praising him."[31] From the Christian standpoint, praising Christ *is* the act of accusing God-the-Father.

One should therefore reject the standard reading of Christ's "scandalous" words which interprets them as a simple call for moderation, in a movement which resembles a fake copy of the Hegelian "negation of negation": once we have rejected all worldly attachments for the sake of our unconditional love for God, we are allowed to return to the world—we can once again love our spouse, parents, and so on, but now in moderation, since only God should be loved unconditionally. But such a reading is a blasphemy which totally misses the point of Christianity: when Christ says

---

29   Guevara, "Socialism and Man in Cuba."
30   Elie Wiesel, *Legends of Our Time*, New York: Schocken Books 1982, p. 37.
31   Ibid., p. 38.

that wherever there is love between two of his disciples, he will be there, one should take this literally—Christ is not (only) loved, he *is* love, our love for our neighbors. This is why the "hatred" he speaks of is not a hatred of "lesser" humans which is supposed to somehow prove that we "really" love only God, but is rather a hatred of neighbors *on behalf of* our love for them.

Toni Morrison's *Beloved*, which brings this paradox to its painful climax, should here be opposed to Evelyn Waugh's *Brideshead Revisited*. Recall the latter novel's final twist: Julia refuses to marry Ryder (although they have both recently got divorced for that very reason) as part of what she ironically refers to as her "private deal" with God—despite her being corrupt and promiscuous, there may still be a chance for her if she sacrifices what matters most to her: her love for Ryder. As Julia makes clear in her final speech, she is fully aware that, once she drops Ryder, she will have numerous insignificant affairs; these, however, will not really count, since they will not condemn her irrevocably in the eyes of God. What would condemn her is if she were to privilege her only true love over her dedication to God, since there should be no competition between supreme goods. This is not *agape*, but its blasphemous perversion.

In his "The Intellectual Beast Is Dangerous," Brecht claims that "A beast is something strong, terrible, devastating; the word emits a barbarous sound." Surprisingly, he then writes: "The key question, in fact, is this: how can we become *beasts*, beasts in such a sense that the fascists will fear for their domination?" It is thus clear that, for Brecht, this question designates a positive task, not the usual lament about how Germans, such a highly cultured nation, could have turned into Nazi beasts: "We have to understand that goodness must also be able to injure—to injure savagely."[32] It is only against this background that we can formulate the gap separating Oriental wisdom from Christian emancipatory logic. Oriental wisdom accepts the primordial Void or Chaos as the ultimate reality, and, paradoxically, for this very reason prefers organic social order with each element in its proper place. At the very core of Christianity there is a radically different project: that of a destructive negativity which ends not in a chaotic Void, but reverts (organizes itself) into a new Order, imposing itself on reality. For this reason, Christianity is anti-Wisdom: wisdom tells us that all our efforts are vain, that everything ends in chaos, while Christianity madly insists on the impossible. Love, especially in its Christian form, is definitely not wise. This is why Paul said: "I will

---

32   Quoted in Jean-Michel Palmier, *Weimar in Exile*, London: Verso Books 2006, p. iii.

destroy the wisdom of the wise" (*sapientiam sapientum perdam*, as his saying is usually known in Latin.) We should take the term "wisdom" literally here: it is wisdom (in the sense of a "realistic" acceptance of the way things are) that Paul is challenging, not knowledge as such.

With regard to the social order, this means that the authentic Christian apocalyptic tradition rejects the wisdom according to which some kind of hierarchical order is our fate, such that any attempt to challenge it and create an alternative egalitarian order will necessarily end in destructive horror. *Agape* as political love means that an unconditional egalitarian love for the Neighbor *can* serve as the foundation for a new Order. The form of appearance of this love is so-called apocalyptic millenarianism, or the Idea of Communism: the urge to realize an egalitarian social order of solidarity. Love is the force of this universal link which, in an emancipatory collective, connects people directly, in their singularity, by-passing their particular hierarchical determinations. Terror is terror out of love for the universal-singular others and against the particular. This terror names exactly the same thing as the work of love. Our reproach to the fundamentalist terrorists, whether Islamist or Christian, should thus be precisely that they are not terroristic in the right way, that they shirk from authentic terror as the work of love. Indeed, Dostoevsky was right when he wrote: "The socialist who is a Christian is more to be dreaded than a socialist who is an atheist"—yes, dreaded by the enemy.

Among the alternatives to this terror is charity, one of the names (and practices) of *non-love* today. When, confronted with the starving child, we are told: "For the price of a couple of cappuccinos, you can save her life!", the true message is: "For the price of a couple of cappuccinos, you can continue in your ignorant and pleasurable life, not only not feeling any guilt, but even feeling good for having participated in the struggle against suffering!" Brecht's lines from his *Badener Lehrstück vom Einverständnis* are today more relevant than ever:

> When there is no longer any violence, there is no need for help
> Therefore you should not demand help, but abolish violence.
> Help and violence form a whole
> And the whole has to be changed.[33]

Did Oscar Wilde not say the same when, in the opening lines of his "The Soul of Man Under Socialism," he pointed out that "it is much more

33   Bertolt Brecht, *Gesammelte Werke* 2, Suhrkamp 1967, p. 599.

easy to have sympathy with suffering than it is to have sympathy with thought"?

> [People] find themselves surrounded by hideous poverty, by hideous ugliness, by hideous starvation. It is inevitable that they should be strongly moved by all this ... Accordingly, with admirable, though misdirected intentions, they very seriously and very sentimentally set themselves to the task of remedying the evils that they see. But their remedies do not cure the disease: they merely prolong it. Indeed, their remedies are part of the disease. They try to solve the problem of poverty, for instance, by keeping the poor alive; or, in the case of a very advanced school, by amusing the poor. But this is not a solution: it is an aggravation of the difficulty. The proper aim is to try and reconstruct society on such a basis that poverty will be impossible. And the altruistic virtues have really prevented the carrying out of this aim ... The worst slave-owners were those who were kind to their slaves, and so prevented the horror of the system being realized by those who suffered from it, and understood by those who contemplated it ... Charity degrades and demoralizes ... It is immoral to use private property in order to alleviate the horrible evils that result from the institution of private property.[34]

But are we not here confusing atheistic materialism with a radical-apocalyptic Christian stance, thereby confirming the oft-repeated claim that atheism cannot stand on its own two feet, that it can only vegetate in the shadow of Christian monotheism? In other words, how to answer the obvious reproach that "Christian materialism" amounts to a "barred" belief: not being courageous enough to make the necessary "leap of faith," I retain the Christian form of religious engagement without acknowledging its content? The reply is that this "emptying the form of its content" already takes place within Christianity itself, at its very core—the name for this emptying is *kenosis*: God dies and is resurrected as the Holy Ghost, as the *form* of collective belief. It is a fetishistic mistake to search for the material support of this form (the resurrected Christ)—the Holy Ghost is the very collective of believers, what they search for outside is already here in the guise of the love that binds them.

Contemporary (post)political thought is caught up in the space determined by two poles: ethics and jurisprudence. On the one hand, politics—in its liberal-tolerant as well as its "fundamentalist" version— is conceived of as the realization of ethical positions (on human rights,

---

34   Oscar Wilde, *The Soul of Man Under Socialism*, New York: Max N. Maisel 1915, pp. 4, 3.

abortion, freedom . . .) which pre-exist politics; on the other hand (and in a complementary way), it is formulated in the language of jurispru-dence (how to find the proper balance between the rights of individuals and of communities, etc.).[35] It is here that the reference to religion can play a positive role in resuscitating the proper dimension of the political, of re-politicizing politics: it can enable political agents to break out of the current ethico-legal entanglement. The old syntagm, the "theologico-political," acquires new relevance here: it is not only that every politics is grounded in a "theological" view of reality, it is also that every theo-logy is inherently political, an ideology of a new collective space (like the communities of believers in early Christianity, or the *umma* in early Islam). Paraphrasing Kierkegaard, one can say that what we need today is a *theologico-political* suspension of the ethico-legal.

Slap Thy Neighbor!

How does this suspension affect the way we relate to our neighbor? As Robert Pippin shows in his perspicuous reading of John Ford's *The Searchers*, this shift in relation to the neighbor occurs in the crucial scene towards the end of the film, when Ethan (played by John Wayne), having finally found Debbie (who has spent several years as an Indian captive), chases after her as she tries to run away. Ethan's explicit intent throughout the film has been not to save her, but to kill her; in other words he was motivated by the racist idea that a white girl taken captive by the Indians deserves only to die. However, once he has Debbie at his mercy, he picks her up, embraces her, and decides to take her home. What is the reason for this sudden change? The standard explanation is that, at the last moment, Ethan's innate goodness took over. Pippin, however, rejects this reading, focusing instead on the strange shot of Ethan's face just before he takes hold of Debbie, as he sees her running

---

35   "The duplicity of politics in respect to morality, in using first one branch of it and then the other for its purposes, furthers these sophistic maxims. These branches are philanthropy and respect for the rights of men; and both are duty. The former is a conditional duty, while the latter is an uncon-ditional and absolutely mandatory duty. One who wishes to give himself up to the sweet feeling of benevolence must make sure that he has not transgressed this absolute duty. Politics readily agrees with morality in its first branch (as ethics) in order to surrender the rights of men to their superiors. But with morality in the second branch (as a science of right), to which it must bend its knee, politics finds it advisable not to have any dealings, and rather denies it all reality, preferring to reduce all duties to mere benevolence" (Immanuel Kant, *Perpetual Peace*, New York: Penguin Books 2009, p. 66). These lines are today more pertinent than ever: we live in an era in which philanthropy (humani-tarianism, concern for suffering, etc.) is systematically used as an excuse to forego the rights of man.

away. His gaze does not express some reawakened human warmth and sympathy, rather:

> the primary expression here is puzzlement, some indication that Ethan does not know his own mind and suddenly realizes he does not know his own mind . . . What we need to discover here is that he did not know his own mind well, that he avowed principles that were partly confabulations and fantasy. We (and he) find out the depth and extent of his actual commitments only when he finally must act.[36]

One can thus say that, in the moment captured by this shot of his perplexed face, Ethan discovered himself as a neighbor, in the impenetrable abyss of his subjectivity. When Ethan finally found himself in the position to act, he confronted the undecidable enigma of his personality, undermining his identity as "Ethan" onto which he (and we, the film's spectators) had hitherto been fixed: a man obsessed by the murderous project of redeeming Debbie by killing her. (It is easy for Pippin, as a Hegelian, to detect this feature: how we discover our true intention only when we have to act upon it is the great motif of Hegel's dialectic of the act.) It is after Ethan's conversion into an inhuman "neighbor" that he literally becomes invisible for the "human" community around him. In the film's final scene, when he returns Debbie to her family, the community "does not *reject* Ethan. They rather ceremoniously *ignore* him. They pretend he does not exist; no one speaks to him, says goodbye, tells him he can or cannot come in. He is instantly forgotten, as if literally invisible."[37] This can be confirmed in a surprisingly direct way: everything that takes place in the last minute of the film — all the characters' moves and words — would function in a normal meaningful way even if we were digitally to erase John Wayne from the scene.

The community's response is a desperate strategy to avoid the neighbor's intrusive over-proximity; this can be further illustrated by way of a recent incident which took place when I was visiting US campuses to give a series of talks together with Mladen Dolar. The incident — a strange event for the two of us, at least — happened at a dinner following our presentations. The professor informally chairing the event proposed that each person at the table (a dozen or so individuals) briefly introduce him- or herself, stating professional position, field of research, and sexual

---

36   Robert Pippin, "What Is a Western? Politics and Self-Knowledge in John Ford's *The Searchers*," *Critical Inquiry*, Vol. 35, No. 2 (Winter 2009), pp. 240–1.
37   Ibid., p. 245.

orientation. Our American colleagues duly complied, as if this were the most natural thing in the world, while Dolar and I simply sidestepped on the last issue. I was tempted to respond in one of two ways, though of course did neither: either to give a vulgar and provocative answer, such as: "Well, I like to penetrate boys under five years old and then drink their blood" (though in such a PC atmosphere one can never know how this would have gone down), or to propose adding another feature to our self-presentations: namely, that each of us specify how much we earn per year and how much wealth we possess (I am sure my US friends would have found this much more intrusive than the question of sexual orientation). In his own wonderful comment on this incident, Dolar contrasts it with two other events: an elegant display of discretion by Gore Vidal, and an incident on a Slovene beach involving his American guests:

> One feels very European when confronted with numerous instances where the Americans speak with great ease and without reserve or inhibition about their very private experiences in front of complete strangers, as if lacking the sense of reticence and discretion, thus unwittingly causing embarrassment in European listeners. It seems that the Americans keep coming out in all directions. One would be hard put to define where the line lies, but there is a line, and one feels it ultimately as a physiological reaction, often as a surge of shame, when it is crossed.
>
> As an aside, I cannot refrain from relating another anecdote, which is told of Gore Vidal. In a TV interview he was asked: "Was your first sexual experience with a man or with a woman?" To which he replied: "I was too polite to ask." It's a wonderful rebuke, reminding the interviewer, by the simplest of means, that there is a code of discretion to be observed in public speech (and in private, for that matter, but there it has a different ramification), which has nothing to do with bashfulness and concealment. The thin line is not a European privilege.
>
> Let me give another example. Some years ago, when some American friends were visiting Slovenia in summer, I took them to a beach on the Adriatic coast. It was a public and very crowded beach, and my friends were rather perplexed when they saw that the women, in large part, freely took their bras off, as is commonly done in this part of the world, wandering around with bare breasts, while nobody made anything of it. My friends said this would never happen on a public beach in America (I have never been to one, so I take their word for it), they were rather embarrassed, despite their leftist liberal persuasions, feeling discomfort at what they saw as a deliberate public display and sexual provocation—as a European lack of reticence and discretion. It was almost like invoking

a caricature ghost of Puritanism in the midst of this age of permissiveness. This gave rise to some musings about the question of the neighbor, that strange creature next to us whom we are supposed to love, but who causes embarrassment and mortification the moment s/he comes too close, intruding upon our private space, crossing the bar of discretion, exposing us, as it were, by exposing him/herself, exposing his or her intrusive privacy which thus cannot be kept at a proper distance.[38]

Far from being opposed or incompatible, these two features — declaring one's sexual orientation and keeping one's body covered up — supplement each other within the universe of US Puritanism which is, as we can see, still very much alive. To account for such paradoxes we must bear in mind how the very act of indiscretion, of surprising openness, can function as a tool of discretion, of withdrawal: if, when a man attempts to seduce a woman, she offers herself up directly for the sexual act, this as a rule implies a withdrawal, a rejection of any deeper personal contact — the message is: "You want it? OK, let's do it fast and get it over with, it means nothing to me, I'm not really into it!" In this sense, the whole of modern hardcore pornography is marked by a profound discretion: the stupidity of the narrative clearly signals that there is no deep subjective engagement in what goes on, even though we see people performing the most intimate acts.

Until recently, hardcore pornography respected certain prohibitions: although it showed "everything," including real sex, the narrative providing the frame for these sexual encounters was, as a rule, ridiculously non-realistic, stereotypical, stupidly comical, staging a kind of return to the eighteenth-century *commedia del'arte* in which the actors do not play "real" individuals, but one-dimensional types — the Miser, the Cuckolded Husband, the Promiscuous Wife. Is not this strange compulsion to make the narrative ridiculous a kind of negative gesture of respect: yes, we show everything, but precisely for that reason we want to make it clear that it is all a great joke, that the actors are not really engaged? Although there has been a trend, more recently, to undermine this prohibition with serious pornography, that is, pornography combined with (what tries to be) an engaging story — for example in the work of Catherine Breillat in France — the censorship reasserted itself with the simultaneous rise of so-called gonzo pornography. Gonzo occurs when the author cannot — or does not want to — remove himself from the subject he is investigating: the

---

38   Mladen Dolar, "The Art of the Unsaid" (unpublished paper).

reporter becomes part of the event taking place. In some cases—such as tornado chasing, where most documenting is done by the person driving the car and holding the camera—the gonzo element is inherent; however, in gonzo pornography, it is a deliberate and voluntary choice—gonzo pornography is embedded hardcore, the pornographic equivalent of embedded journalism. It is characterized by a filming style that attempts to place the viewer directly in the scene: gonzo pornography puts the camera right into the action, often with one or more of the participants both filming and performing sexual acts, thus suspending the usual separation characteristic of conventional porn and cinema. Influenced by amateur pornography, gonzo porn tends to use far fewer full-body/wide shots, and more close-ups. What is more important, however, is that the actors themselves constantly address the camera, wink, comment on what they are doing, all in an easy-going ironic and self-mocking style. In this way, gonzo's highly reflexive realism signals a higher level of repression: while, in classic hardcore, the stupidity of the conversation was constrained by the fictional narrative, in gonzo, the narrative fiction is undermined, we are all the time reminded that what we are watching is a staged performance—as if to protect us from the danger of getting too involved in what we see.[39]

Why are we so traumatized by the neighbor's over-proximity? Habit and custom are the predominant ways in which we maintain a distance towards the "inhuman" neighbor's intrusive proximity, and we are today effectively witnessing a decline of habits: in our culture of self-exposure and "sincerity," they no longer provide a screen ensuring our distance from the neighbor. (Political correctness itself is a tell-tale sign of this failure, with its attempt to directly regulate, even legislate for, what should

---

39   A similar problem of avoiding the over-proximity of a Neighbor occurs in torture. According to Lacan, those who practice torture, "whatever may be their good reasons, do it because their *jouis-sance* is wrapped up in it. Independent of the best reasons—that it is for the good, the beautiful, the true—in practice, sadists try to wrest from the subject his *fides*, the pact of speech, based on which he has entered into a certain number of relationships." The ultimate aim of torture is thus never just the needed information; its presupposition is that the tortured subject is bound by another (secret) symbolic pact, and the aim is to make him reveal this pact—"You claim to be a good Bolshevik, but you are really a Trotskyite!" Torture aims at the very basic dimension of the relationship of the subject to the symbolic order, at the pact which links him to a community and makes him what he is, accounts for his identity. In torture, the subject is not pushed to reveal only what he knows, but also what he is. This is why, in Ancient Rome, the confession of a slave had no legal validity unless it was obtained under torture—for us a weird counter-intuitive idiosyncrasy (is it not true that, under torture, one is ready to admit anything, which should render worthless any confession obtained in this way?). One can understand this rule as an expression of the notion that a slave, although a speaking being, is not a person subjected to the social link of language, ready to stand at his/her word, aware of the honor and dignity of the "word given."

have been a matter of "spontaneous" habit.) Is the non-universalizable neighbor, however, the ultimate horizon of our ethico-political activity? Is the highest norm the injunction to respect the neighbor's Otherness? No wonder Levinas is so popular today among multiculturalist left-liberals who endlessly vary the motif of impossible universality—every universality is exclusive, it imposes a particular standard as universal . . .

The question is whether every ethical universality is necessarily based on the exclusion of the abyss of the neighbor, or whether, to the contrary, there might be a universality which does *not* exclude the neighbor. Our answer affirms the latter: namely, the universality grounded in the "part-of-no-part," the singular universality exemplified in those who lack a determined place in the social totality, who are "out of place" in it and as such directly stand for the universal dimension. This identification with the excluded is to be strictly opposed to the liberal sympathy for, and understanding of, their plight, and to the ensuing efforts to include them in the social structure. The crowds in the slums constitute a huge reservoir for political mobilization: if the Left does not act there, who will? Religious fundamentalists? Or will the slum-dwellers remain indefinitely outside civil space, as a politically unarticulated threat of violence?[40] In the summer of 1846, Thoreau was arrested for refusing to pay taxes (raised to finance the Mexican war). When Emerson visited him in jail and asked "What are you doing in here?" Thoreau answered: "What are you doing out there?"[41] This is the proper radical answer to the liberal's sympathetic concern for the excluded: "How come that they are out there, excluded from public space?"—"How come that you are in here, included in it?"

The distinction between those who are included in the legal order and *homo sacer* is not simply horizontal, a distinction between two groups of people, but is increasingly also a "vertical" distinction between two (superimposed) ways in which *the same* people can be treated. Put simply: at the level of Law, we are treated as citizens, legal subjects; but at the level of its obscene superego supplement, of this empty unconditional law, we are treated as *homo sacer*. The true problem is not so much the fragile status of the excluded, but rather the fact that, at the most elementary

---

40   No wonder the excluded domains are becoming tourist targets: we already have slum-tourism (organized visits to *favelas* in Brazil), eco-catastrophe-tourism (trips to the reactor in Chernobyl, with measuring machines buzzing as a proof that we really are in the zone; visits to fields outside Murmansk where the pollution by mineral waste generated freakish outgrowths . . .).

41   Quoted in Howard Zinn, *A People's History of the United States*, New York: HarperCollins 2001, p. 156.

level, we are *all* "excluded" in the sense that our most elementary, "zero" position is that of being an object of biopolitics, so much so that political and citizenship rights are granted us only as a secondary gesture, in accordance with strategic biopolitical considerations—*this* is the ultimate consequence of the notion of "post-politics." This is why, for Agamben, the implication of his analysis of *homo sacer* is not that we should fight for the inclusion of the excluded, but that *homo sacer* is the "truth" of all of us, that it stands for the zero-level position in which we are all placed. This is why this "part-of-no-part," the universal singularity of *homo sacer*, is not the exception constitutive of universality: it is not that, by excluding *homo sacer* from the public space of citizenship, this space constitutes itself as universal. In religious-ethical terms, exclusive universality (i.e. universality which excludes the neighbor) is the legal universality of *lex talionis*, of universal equal rights and reciprocity, while Christian non-exclusive universality is that of "turning the other cheek":

> You have heard that it was said, "An eye for an eye and a tooth for a tooth." But I tell you not to resist evil. Whoever slaps you on your right cheek, turn the other to him also. If anyone wants to sue you and take away your tunic, let him have your cloak also. And whoever compels you to go one mile, go with him two. Give to him who asks you, and from him who wants to borrow from you do not turn away. (Matthew 5:38–40)

This exceeding of symmetrical reciprocity represents a move from "abstract universality" (equality) to "concrete universality," from the utilitarian calculus of reciprocal gain to an unconditional ethical engagement: it is the excessive engagement that turns the agent into a singular universality. No wonder that, to paraphrase the opening line of *The Communist Manifesto*, the entire history of Christianity is the history of "class struggle," a series of desperate efforts to domesticate the scandalous character of the quoted lines by way of historicist contextualization. Which is not to say that one cannot learn a lot from the historical analysis of such "excessive" passages:

> We normally associate these verses with pacifism but there is a little more to it than that. These verses were spoken in a culture where honor and shame were culturally significant. A slap in the face was viewed as degrading and was an effort to lower someone's status as they were publicly shamed. What does this have to do with the right cheek and then the left cheek? For the answer we have to turn to the Mishnah, which is a

collection of legal regulations from 3rd century AD rabbinic Judaism. In the Mishnah penalties and compensation are prescribed that are due as punishments for various infractions. There was a difference in slapping someone with the back of the hand versus the palm of the hand. When Jesus says, "If someone strikes you on the right cheek," he is talking about a slap with the back of the hand as most people are right-handed. The Mishnah lays out compensation for those who experience such a shaming action: a slap with the palm of the hand carried a penalty twice as much as a slap with the back of the hand. Why would it contain a higher fine? Because to be struck on the right cheek, with the back of the hand, would be more degrading and shameful than to be struck on the left cheek with the palm of the hand. In effect, Jesus is saying, if someone degrades or shames you greatly by a backhanded slap on the right cheek, turn your left cheek to him and see if he is willing to say you are closer to his equal than the initial slap indicated. Of course, this also would inflict more compensatory damage to the one doing the slapping. This verse does not say as much about pacifism as it has to say about the culture of honor and shame that they lived in. They heard these words totally different than we hear them today.[42]

Behind the mask of submissive non-resistance, the gesture of "turning the other cheek" thus defiantly provokes the other to treat me as equal, an equal who, as equal, has the right to defend himself and strike back.

In Hell (with Jean-Claude van Damme), a bleak story set in a corrupt post-Soviet Russian prison, contains a surprisingly accurate Christological moment. Van Damme plays an American working in Moscow who, sentenced to prison long-term for killing the murderer of his wife, has to fight brutal to-the-death duels with other prisoners to satisfy the guards who put high bets on the fights. Unable to finish off his beaten opponent, van Damme refuses to fight and is cruelly punished, chained to a high mast where he hangs for days without food and water, until he will once again agree to fight. One of the prisoners, observing from the cell window, complains to his mates: "Why does he refuse to fight? He will not only lose and die, but also bring trouble to all of us!" A wiser colleague replies: "No! Can't you see he is now fighting for all of us!" And he is of course right: van Damme's refusal to fight is in itself a more dangerous fight to change the whole life of the prison, so that prisoners will no longer be forced to stage cruel combats for the obscene amusement of their jailers.

---

42   Matt Dabbs, "What Does It Mean to Turn the Other Cheek"; see http://mattdabbs.wordpress. com.

This is a paradigmatic case of Jesus' line from Matthew: "Whoever slaps you on your right cheek, turn the other to him also." Sometimes, a refusal to fight amounts to a much more violent gesture of refusing the entire field that has determined the conditions of the fight; likewise, sometimes, directly striking back is the surest sign of compromise.

It is thus crucial to read the above-quoted passage *together* with the — no less embarrassing and equally "excessive" — passage about Christ bringing a sword, not peace. Finding oneself a recipient of the "excessive" ethical act in which aggression is returned with kindness can be a quite traumatic experience, as is clearly shown in Hugo's *Les Misérables*: the difference between Jean Valjean and Javert is precisely that between the two ways a human being can react to the traumatic gesture of grace, of "turning the other cheek." At the novel's beginning in Digne, the benevolent Bishop Myriel takes Valjean in and gives him shelter. In the middle of the night, Valjean steals the bishop's silverware and runs away. He is caught and brought back, but the bishop saves him by claiming that the silverware was a gift; he then gives Valjean two silver candlesticks as well, chastising him in front of the police for leaving in such a rush that he forgot these most valuable pieces. The bishop then "reminds" Valjean of his promise, which he has no recollection of making, to use the silver to make an honest man of himself. Totally shattered by this excessive act of repaying evil with kindness, Valjean starts out on the long path of ethical recovery, pursued doggedly by Javert, a policeman obsessed with bringing the fugitive Valjean to justice. Later in the novel, in the midst of the revolutionary turmoil of 1832, Valjean saves Javert when he is unmasked by the revolutionaries as a police spy and condemned to death: he volunteers to execute Javert himself, takes him out of sight, and then shoots into the air while letting him go. When Valjean runs into him later, Javert realizes that he is caught between his belief in the law and the mercy Valjean has shown him. He feels he can no longer give Valjean up to the authorities, and lets him go. Unable to cope with this split between his commitment to the law and his conscience, Javert commits suicide, throwing himself into the Seine. The crucial point here is that it is Valjean, the criminal hardened by long years in jail, who accepts grace and undergoes a moral recovery, while Javert, the personification of pure law, cannot endure goodness, and is drawn to suicide when exposed to it — the ultimate proof that, far from being opposed to crime, law is the universalized crime, crime elevated to the level of an unconditional principle.

The Subject Supposed Not *to Know*

We should not be afraid to draw all the consequences from this assertion of the theologico-political, even if it means ruthlessly slaughtering many liberal sacred cows. Along these lines, Badiou recently proposed a rehabilitation of the Communist-revolutionary "cult of personality":[43] the real of a Truth-Event is inscribed into the space of symbolic fiction through a proper name (of a leader) — Lenin, Stalin, Mao, Che Guevara. Far from signaling the corruption of a revolutionary process, the celebration of the leader's name is immanent to that process. To put it in other terms: without the mobilizing role of a proper name, the political movement remains caught within the positive order of Being, rendered by conceptual categories — only through the intervention of a proper name do we accede to the dimension of "demanding the impossible," of changing the very contours of what appears as possible. It is in these terms that one should read the "eccentric" fact that Hugo Chávez first tried to gain power by a military coup — only after the coup failed (and the anniversary of this attempt is today not hushed up, but celebrated as a holiday in Venezuela) did he submit to elections as a second-best choice, and won. Thus in contrast to the standard scenario of the ambitious politician who, after losing the democratic election, tries to grab power through a coup, for Chávez, elections were a substitute for the coup.

Aristotle's answer to the reproach that by criticizing Plato's philosophy he was betraying his good friend is well known: "I am a friend of Plato, but an even greater friend of truth." Of course, "truth" is here understood as "factual truth", or the *adequatio* of words (statements) to things (that they designate), but in relation to a radical emancipatory politics we should shamelessly turn Aristotle's reply around, to say: "A friend of truth, but an even greater friend of [insert leader's name here — Lenin, Trotsky, Mao, etc.]." This, of course, does not mean that in the name of blind submission to the Leader one should deny the obvious facts — but it does mean that fidelity to Truth in Badiou's sense (as opposed to factual knowledge) is signaled by a reference to the *Name* (of the Leader): it is this Name which pushes us towards an engagement that goes beyond the limits of a pragmatic-strategic "politics of the possible."

In the middle of the fourth century CE, when Christianity succeeded in imposing itself as the state religion in imperial Rome, Hilary, the bishop

---

43   At his intervention at the conference "On the Idea of Communism," organized by the School of Law, Birkbeck College, London, March 13–15, 2009.

of Poitiers, warned his fellow bishops: "[the emperor] does not bring you liberty by casting you in prison, but treats you with respect within his palace and thus makes you his slave."[44] A warning which remains fully relevant today, when "radical" thinkers are often cast in the role of *Scarlet Guards*. When, during the Cultural Revolution, the Red Guards took the call for popular self-organization outside the Party-State framework seriously, the Communist Party reacted by organizing Scarlet Guards, who pretended to be "even redder than the Red Guards," though, of course, in the service of the Party. This is how, when threatened with instability, established power reacts to the threat: by creating its own pseudo-"subversive" wing[45]—such, in effect, were the *nouveaux philosophes* in France during the 1970s: a Scarlet Guard set against the Maoist "Red Guards" who had formed the radical core of 1968.

Among contemporary theologians, it was John Howard Yoder who, in his *The Politics of Jesus* (1972), condemned this fourth-century compromise of the Church with the Emperor Constantine as a fateful shift away from the New Testament pattern of pacifism and suspicion of wealth, towards a "responsible" ethic suitable for the dominant classes who did not recognize Jesus as Lord. Yoder dubbed this arrangement whereby State and Church support each other's goals "Constantinianism," and regarded it as a dangerous and constant temptation. But Yoder did not reject Constantinianism on behalf of an ascetic withdrawal of believers from social life: aware of the limitations of democracy, he understood "being Christian" as involving a non-reconciled *political* standpoint. The primary responsibility of Christians is not to take over society and impose their convictions and values on people who do not share their faith, but to "be the church." By refusing to repay evil with evil, by living in peace and sharing goods, the church bears witness to the fact that there is an alternative to a society based on violence or the threat of violence.[46]

---

44   Quoted by Freeman, *The Closing of the Western Mind*, p. 202.

45   I owe this information to Alessandro Russo.

46   The attitude of the early Christians towards slavery was thoroughly ambiguous: on the one hand, it emphasized how we are all equal in the eyes of God (to Paul's list "no Jews or Greeks, no men or women," one can easily add "no slaves, no free citizens"), and the consequences of this equality reach from a Stoic injunction to treat slaves in a humane way up to a more radical demand for the abolition of slavery; on the other hand, human slavery echoes our basic predicament—we are all slaves of Christ, so actual slaves should be obedient and work hard for their master, because by doing so they are fulfilling the will of God. The ambiguity is sustained by the difference in the logical status of our supreme slavery to God: is this highest slavery immanent to the social structure, its supreme structural principle, so that slavery should spread down from it, permeating the entire edifice, or is it its constitutive exception and as such the guarantee of our freedom in social reality ("I am a slave only to God, and this obedience gives me freedom with regard to all other earthly authorities")? This

The point here is not to oppose the theologico-political to secular atheism; on the contrary, it is from this theologico-political perspective that we can discern the hidden theological core of secular atheism. The standard ideologico-critical view of religious faith, that today it has more to do with capitalist business (the organized selling of faith), should also be turned around: not only is religious faith part of capitalism, capitalism is itself also a religion, and it too relies on faith (in the institution of money, amongst other things).[47] This point is crucial to understanding the cynical functioning of ideology: in contrast to the period when religious-ideological sentimentality covered up the brutal economic reality, today, it is ideological cynicism which obscures the religious core of capitalist beliefs.

A strange thing happened in Brazil in August 1945: when the surrender of Japan became known, a secret Japanese organization, called Shindo Renmei, was founded in São Paolo. For its members, the reports of Japan's surrender were a fraud, a propaganda coup staged by the Western powers in order to break the Japanese spirit. How could Japan have been defeated when, in its entire 2,600-year-long history, it had never lost a war? Within a couple of months, the entire community of Japanese immigrants in Brazil (altogether about 200,000 people) was divided into *kachigumi*, the "victoryists" of Shindo Renmei, and *makegumi*, the "defeatists" who acknowledged the Japanese surrender. A full civil war exploded between the two groups, once the *tokkotai*, the killers of Shindo Renmei, started to ruthlessly exterminate the leading "defeatists" as traitors to their nation. The war was brought to an end only when, after thousands had been killed, the state directly intervened, deporting the leading "victoryists" to Japan. What made this affair truly weird were the measures taken by Shindo Renmei to maintain the illusion of Japanese victory: they even went so far as to produce fake issues of *Life* magazine, with reports and photos of the surrender of US forces to Japan, including General MacArthur bowing to the Japanese officers, and so on.[48] What

difference is *not* the difference between the feminine and the masculine logics of sexuation, since both versions rely on a "singular universality" which totalizes the entire field—the difference is that, in the first case, the exemplary mode of being a slave to Christ is inherent to the totality, the summit of universal slavery, while, in the second case, being a slave to Christ is the exception which grounds our freedom in worldly affairs—and this passage from the first to the second case fits perfectly the passage from Catholicism to Protestantism.

47   See Thomas Assheuer, "Der Wahnsinn des Kapitalismus" (a review of Paul Anderson's *There Will Be Blood*), *Die Zeit* 7, 2008, p. 38.

48   See Fernando Morais, *Corações sujos. A história de Shindo Renmei*, São Paulo: Compañía das Letras 2001. I am grateful to Nuno Ramos de Almeida, Lisbon, for drawing my attention to this book.

we have here is fetishistic denial taken to an extreme: the perpetrators of the fake stuck to it fanatically, were ready to sacrifice their lives for it. They *knew* that their denial of Japan's surrender was false, but they nonetheless refused to *believe* in Japanese surrender.

The first lesson to be drawn from this paradox is that we must avoid the confusion between individual convictions and beliefs inscribed into the very logic of the system in which we participate. When, in his Christmas message of 2008, the Pope announced that if humanity did not learn to overcome its egotism, then human history would end in self-destruction, he not only stated a moralistic platitude, but also uttered a clear falsity. Let us accept that the two principal dangers today are unbridled capitalism and religious fundamentalism—nonetheless, as an even superficial analysis of "fundamentalist" subjectivity makes clear, fundamentalists are not egotists but, on the contrary, are ruthlessly dedicated to a transcendental goal, for the sake of which they are ready to sacrifice everything, their lives included. As for capitalism, one could also show that its ever-expanding circulation cannot be reduced to the egotistic striving of capitalists for more and more profit.

A parallel with Dawkins's notion of "memes" may be of some help here. A "meme" spreads neither because of its actual beneficial effects for its bearers (those who adopt a certain idea, say, become more successful in life and thus gain an upper hand in the struggle for survival), nor because of characteristics which make it subjectively attractive to its bearers (one would naturally tend to privilege an idea which promises happiness over an idea which promises nothing but misery and sacrifice). Rather, like a computer virus, a meme proliferates simply by programming its own retransmission. Recall the classic example of two missionaries working in a politically stable and wealthy country: one says, "The end is near—repent or you will suffer greatly," while the other's message is just to enjoy a happy life. Although the second message is much more attractive and beneficent, it is the first that will win out. Why? Because, if you really believe that the end is near, you will make a tremendous effort to convert as many people as possible, whereas the second belief requires no such extreme commitment to proselytizing.

What is so unsettling about this notion is that we, as humans endowed with minds, wills, and an experience of meaning, are nonetheless unwitting vehicles of a "thought contagion" which operates blindly, spreading itself like a virus. No wonder that, when talking about memes, Dawkins regularly resorts to the same metaphors Lacan uses apropos language:

in both cases, we are dealing with a parasite which penetrates and occupies the human individual, using it for its own purposes. And indeed, does "memetics" not (re)discover the notion of a specific symbolic level, which operates outside (and which consequently cannot be reduced to) the standard duo of objective biological facts (the "real" beneficial effects) and subjective experience (the attraction of the meaning of a meme)? In a liminal case, an idea can spread even if in the long term it brings only destruction to its bearers and is experienced as unattractive.

So where is the parallel with capital here? In the same way that memes, misperceived by subjects as means of communication, effectively run the show (they use *us* to reproduce and multiply themselves), the productive forces which appear to us merely as means to satisfy our needs and desires also effectively run things: the true aim of the process, its end-in-itself, is the development of the productive forces, and the satisfaction of our needs and desires is just a means towards that development. Consequently, we should not say that capitalism is sustained by the selfish greed of individual capitalists, since that greed is itself subordinated to the impersonal striving of capital to reproduce and expand. One is thus almost tempted to say that what we really need is more, not less, enlightened egotism. Take the ecological threat: no pseudo-animistic love for nature is needed here, just a calculation of long-term egotistic interest. In Lacanian terms, one can determine the distinction between individual greed and the striving of capital itself as the difference between desire and drive. Apropos the financial breakdown, Krugman made a perspicuous observation: "If we could spin a time machine back to 2004, so that people could ask themselves whether to exercise caution or to follow the herd, most of them would still follow the herd, in spite of knowing that there will be a breakdown."[49] This is how capitalism works, this is the material efficiency of capitalist ideology: even when we know how things are, we continue to act upon our false beliefs. It is here that Deleuze went wrong when he made fun of the standard psychoanalytic reply to the obvious reproach concerning "penis-envy" ("But who really believes that his mother had a penis and was castrated?"): of course no one directly believes it, for it is our unconscious which does the believing.

The last decade of President Tito's life in the former Yugoslavia bears witness to the potentially catastrophic consequences of holding on to such disavowed beliefs. As some archives and memoirs show, already in the

---

49   Paul Krugman, "The True Risk Is the Repetition of the Japanese Lost Decade" (interview, in Slovene), *Delo*, September 19, 2009.

mid-1970s, the leading figures around Tito were aware of Yugoslavia's dire economic situation; however, since Tito was nearing death, they made a collective decision to postpone the inevitable crisis until after his death—the price they paid was the reckless accumulation of external debt in the last years of Tito's life, when Yugoslavia was, in effect, and to quote the rich bank client from Hitchcock's *Psycho*, buying off its unhappiness. When, in 1980, Tito finally died, the economic crisis struck with a vengeance, leading to a 40 percent fall in standards of living, ethnic tensions, and, finally, a civil and ethnic war that destroyed the country—all because the moment for confronting the crisis successfully had been missed. One can thus say that what put the last nail in the coffin of Yugoslavia was the attempt by its leading circle to protect their Leader's ignorance, to ensure his outlook remained rosy.[50]

Is this not, ultimately, what culture is? One of the most elementary cultural skills is to know when (and how) to pretend *not* to know (or notice), how to go on and act as if something which has happened did not in fact happen. If a person close by involuntarily farts or burps, the proper thing to do is to ignore it, not to reassure him: "I know it was an accident, don't worry, it doesn't really matter!" When parents with a young child have blazing arguments or illicit affairs, as a rule (assuming they wish to retain a minimum of decency) they try to prevent the child from noticing, well aware that such knowledge could have a devastating effect on him. (Of course, in many cases, the child knows very well, and merely pretends not to notice anything wrong, aware that in this way his parents' life is made a little bit easier.) Or, on a less vulgar level, a parent might be in a difficult predicament (dying of cancer, in financial difficulties), but trying to keep this secret from his nearest and dearest.[51] Today, the ultimate figure of the subject supposed *not* to know is the small child, which is why, as Gérard Wajcman has perspicuously observed, in our permissive era which prides itself on having thrown off every sexual

---

50   A less cataclysmic example occurred in Portugal, in the last years of the dictator Salazar who ruled the country for decades. He was senile, unable to sustain a meaningful conversation, but the council of ministers nonetheless regularly met with him, going through the motions of government debates and decisions, making Salazar think that he was still running the state; after Salazar left, the ministers got down to business and took the real decisions. The reason for this ritual was that the entire ruling clique around Salazar feared the moment when the public would become aware that the dictator was no longer running the state, the moment which might—as it effectively did—open up a period of uncertainty and the search for political alternatives.

51   This is also why culture is opposed to science: science is sustained by a ruthless drive to knowledge, while culture is an attitude of feigning not to know/notice. The entity whose ignorance should be maintained is the big Other as the agency of innocent appearance.

taboo and repression, thereby rendering psychoanalysis obsolete, Freud's fundamental insight into child sexuality is strangely ignored. In order for us to indulge in our shameless orgies, the child has to remain innocent:

> The sole remaining prohibition, the one sacred value in our society that seems to remain, is to do with children. It is forbidden to touch a hair on their little blond heads, as if children had rediscovered that angelic purity on which Freud managed to cast some doubt. And it is undoubtedly the diabolical figure of Freud that we condemn today, seeing him as the one who, by uncovering the relationship of childhood to sexuality, quite simply depraved our virginal childhoods. In an age when sexuality is exhibited on every street corner, the image of the innocent child has, strangely, returned with a vengeance.[52]

Paradoxically, the fall of this big Other who is supposed not to know is not the same as the disappearance of belief—in a way, it opens up the space of an authentic belief which sustains an *act*, a belief which is no longer transposed onto, sustained, or covered by some figure of the big Other. In taking the risk of an act, I fully assume the belief in myself, accepting that there is no Other to believe for me, in my place. This is the properly Christian belief, the message of God's death: the Christian community of believers is alone with its belief, freely assuming full responsibility for it, no longer relying on a transcendental authority that would guarantee it. In his "learning play," *Der Ozeanflug*, Brecht not only offers nice examples of prosopopoeia (the pilot is addressed by mist, snowstorm, and sleep; and even the City of New York talks—"here speaks the City of New York"), he also offers a statement of "practicing materialism" to be opposed to the "practicing idealism" of our daily ideology, turning around the ideological "I know very well, but . . ." in which *I act as if I believe even if I do not believe*:

> Whatever I am and whichever stupidities I believe
> When I fly, I am
> An actual atheist.[53]

---

52   Gérard Wajcman, "Intimate Extorted, Intimate Exposed," *Umbr(a)* 2007, p. 47.
53   Brecht, *Gesammelte Werke* 2, p. 176. Peter Sloterdijk points in the same direction in *Du mußt dein Leben ändern!*, where he provides elements for a materialist theory of religion, conceiving religion as an effect of material practices of self-training and self-change—one can even claim that he thereby contributes to a Communist theory of culture.

Interlude 2.   Reverberations of the Crisis in a Multi-Centric World

"The Jew is within you, but you, you are in the Jew"

The fantasmatic status of anti-Semitism is clearly revealed by a statement attributed to Hitler: "We have to kill the Jew within us." A. B. Yehoshua commented appositely:

> This devastating portrayal of the Jew as a kind of amorphous entity that can invade the identity of a non-Jew without his being able to detect or control it stems from the feeling that Jewish identity is extremely flexible, precisely because it is structured like a sort of atom whose core is surrounded by virtual electrons in a changing orbit.[1]

In this sense, Jews are effectively the *objet petit a* of the Gentiles: what is "in Gentiles more than Gentiles themselves," not another subject who I encounter in front of me but a foreign intruder *within* me, what Lacan called *lamella*, the amorphous intruder of infinite plasticity, an undead "alien" monster who can never be pinned down to a determinate form. In this sense, Hitler's statement tells us more than it wants to say: against his intentions, it confirms that the Gentiles need the anti-Semitic figure of the "Jew" in order to maintain their own identity.[2] It is thus not only

---

1   A. B. Yehoshua, "An Attempt to Identify the Root Cause of Antisemitism," *Azure*, 32, Spring 2008; available online at www.azure.org.il

2   A taboo question should be raised: what does the fixation of Arab countries and Muslim communities worldwide on the State of Israel mean? It cannot be accounted for in the terms of any real threat to the Arab nations (after all, Israel occupies a tiny piece of land), so its role is obviously symptomatic—when forces as different as the utterly corrupt Saudi monarchy and anti-establishment Arab populist movements focus on the same enemy, an external intruder, does this not bear witness to a strategy of avoiding the true internal antagonism? In effect, the Jews function as the symptom of the Arabs (i.e., as the embodiment of their refusal to confront the immanent deadlock of their own societies, their corruption, their failure to deal with the shock of modernity). As for the Israelis, their situation is ultimately that of colonizers—there is nothing exceptional about their predicament in Palestine.

that "the Jew is within us" — what Hitler fatefully forgot to add is that *he, the anti-Semite, in his identity, is also in the Jew*.[3] What does this paradoxical entwinement mean for the destiny of anti-Semitism?

A disturbing sign of the failure of certain elements of the radical Left is their uneasiness when it comes to unambiguously condemning anti-Semitism, as if by doing so one would be playing into Zionist hands. There should be no compromise here: anti-Semitism is not just one among ideologies; it is ideology as such, *kat'exohen*. It embodies the zero-level (or the pure form) of ideology, providing its elementary coordinates: social antagonism ("class struggle") is mystified/displaced so that its cause is projected onto the external intruder. Lacan's formula "1 + 1 + a" is best exemplified by class struggle: the two classes plus the excess of the "Jew," the *objet a*, the supplement to the antagonistic couple. The function of this supplementary element is double: it is a fetishistic disavowal of class antagonism, yet, precisely as such, it stands for this antagonism, forever preventing "class peace." In other words, if we had only the two classes, 1 + 1 without the supplement, then we would get not "pure" class antagonism but, on the contrary, class peace: the two classes complementing each other in a harmonious Whole. The paradox is thus that it is the very element which blurs or displaces the "purity" of the class struggle which serves as its motivating force. Critics of Marxism who point out that there are never just two classes opposed in social life thus miss the point: *it is precisely because there are never only two opposed classes that there is class struggle.* This complication accounts for the paradox of class struggle serving as its own obfuscation. Walter Benn Michaels has noted with brutal clarity that

> the answer to the question "Why do American liberals carry on about racism and sexism when they should be carrying on about capitalism?" is pretty obvious: they carry on about racism and sexism in order to avoid doing so about capitalism. Either because they genuinely do think that inequality is fine as long as it is not a function of discrimination (in which case they are neoliberals of the right). Or because they think that fighting against racial and sexual inequality is as least a step in the direction of real equality (in which case, they are neoliberals of the left). Given these options, perhaps the neoliberals of the right are in a stronger position — the economic history of the last thirty years suggests that diversified elites do even better than undiversified ones.[4]

---

3   I am, of course, here paraphrasing Lacan's famous statement: "The picture is in my eye, but me, I am in the picture."

4   Walter Benn Michaels, "Against Diversity," *New Left Review* 52, July–August 2008, p. 36.

A partisan of discourse-theory who emphasizes radical contingency would surely raise a number of questions here: "Is not the difference between the 'proper' meaning of anti-racism and its ideological twist problematic? Is it not that every notion of anti-racist struggle involves some twist as the outcome of the struggle for hegemony? In the case of anti-racism, to claim that the focus should be on legal rights and economic justice is no more 'true' than privileging tolerance — the difference in focus merely reflects the different contexts of ideological struggles . . ." The answer is that there is an inherent falsity in focusing the anti-racist struggle on tolerance — not because it does not fit some pre-existing objective state of things, but *because, in its very discursive structure, it involves the "repression" of a different discourse to which it continues to refer*. So, when we are told today that the problems we face, at least in the developed world, are no longer socio-economic, but predominantly cultural-ethical (the right to abortion, gay marriage, etc.), one should bear in mind that this is in itself a result of ideological struggle, of the post-political repression of the socio-economic dimension.

The price that some on the Left pay for ignoring this "complication" of class struggle is, among other things, an all-too-easy and uncritical acceptance of anti-American and anti-Western Muslim groups as representing "progressive" forms of struggle, as automatic allies: groups like Hamas and Hezbollah all of a sudden appear as revolutionary agents, even though their ideology is explicitly anti-modern, rejecting the entire egalitarian legacy of the French Revolution. (Things have gone so far here that some on the contemporary Left consider even an emphasis on atheism as a Western colonialist plot.) Against this temptation, we should insist on the unconditional right to a conduct a public critical analysis of all religions, Islam included — and the saddest thing is that one should even have to mention this. While many a Leftist would concede this point, he or she would be quick to add that any such critique must be carried out in a respectful way, in order to avoid a patronizing cultural imperialism — which *de facto* means that every real critique is to be abandoned, since a genuine critique of religion will by definition be "disrespectful" of the latter's sacred character and truth claims.

Throughout 2009, the gay community in the Netherlands increasingly began turning towards the anti-immigrant nationalist parties. The reason was simple: the Muslim community locally, as the strongest and most organized immigrant group, had become more and more vociferous in its homophobia, including even occasional recourse to violent acts.

How should we to react to this tension? Who should we support? The pure liberal-multiculturalist line of tolerance gives a clear answer: we should support tolerance and symmetry. It is unfair to demand of the gay community that they work hard to convince the Muslims of their acceptability—they are what they are, and nobody should be made to have to justify what he or she is. The first move should thus be made by the Muslim immigrants: it is they who have to accept a multiplicity of (religious, sexual, etc.) ways of life, accept that the properly political struggle should not concern particular ways of life. There is also an obvious asymmetry: when, in November 2009, the Swiss decided in a referendum to prohibit the construction of minarets, Turkey (along with other Muslim countries) vigorously protested—calls were heard for the boycott of Swiss banks, etc. But what about the fact that in Turkey itself, a country which sees itself as modern and wants to join European Union, the construction of all sacred objects with the exception of mosques is prohibited? How about a new Catholic church or a synagogue in Istanbul, or—even better—a center for atheist studies in Riyadh?

What nonetheless complicates the simplicity of this position is the underlying gap in economic and political power: the tension is ultimately between the upper-middle-class Dutch gays and the poor exploited Muslim immigrants. In other words, what effectively fuels the Muslims' animosity is their perception of gays as part of a privileged elite which exploits them and treats them like outcasts. Our question to the gays should thus be: what did you do to help the immigrants socially? Why not go there, act like a Communist, organize a struggle with them, work together? The solution of the tension is thus not to be found in multicultural tolerance and understanding but in a shared struggle on behalf of a universality which cuts diagonally across both communities, dividing each of them against itself, but uniting the marginalized in both camps. Something along these lines occurred during 2009 in the West Bank village of Bilin, where a Jewish lesbian group, complete with pierced lips, tattoos, etc., came each week to demonstrate against the village's partition and demolition, joining ranks with conservative Palestinian women, each group developing a respect for the other. It is through such events, rare as they are, that the conflict between fundamentalists and gays is exposed for what it is: a pseudo-struggle, a false conflict obfuscating the true issue.

The real gay struggle is fought not in the Netherlands, but in Arab and other countries where homophobia is explicitly a part of the hegemonic ideology; it is linked to the struggle against the oppression of women, "honor killings," and so on. It is a struggle to be fought by the people who live there, not by Western liberals. The European Muslim community is confronted with a difficult choice which encapsulates its paradoxical position: the only political force which does not reduce them to second-class citizens, and which allows them the space to deploy their religious identity, is that of "godless" liberals, members of sexual minorities, etc., while those who come closest to their own religious social practice, namely, their Christian rivals, are their greatest political enemies.

Zionist Anti-Semitism

One of the supreme ironies of the history of anti-Semitism is how the Jews are made to stand for both poles of an opposition: they are stigmatized both as upper class (rich merchants) and as lower class (filthy), as overly intellectual and as too earthly (as sexual predators), as lazy and as workaholics. Sometimes they stand for a stubborn attachment to a particular lifestyle which prevents them from becoming full citizens of the state they live in, at other times for a "homeless" and uprooted universal cosmopolitanism indifferent towards all particular ethnic forms. The focus changes with different historical epochs. In the era of the French Revolution, the Jews were condemned as being overly particularistic: they continued to hold onto their identity, rejecting the possibility of becoming abstract citizens like everyone else. In the late nineteenth century, with the rise of imperialist patriotism, this accusation was turned around: the Jews were now considered all too "cosmopolitan," lacking all roots.

The key change in the history of Western anti-Semitism occurred with the Jews' political emancipation (the granting of civil rights) which followed the French Revolution. In early modernity, the pressure on them was to convert to Christianity, which itself created problems of trust: have they really converted, or are they secretly continuing to practice their rituals? By the later nineteenth century however, a shift occurs which will culminate in Nazi anti-Semitism: conversion is now out of the question, effectively meaningless. For the Nazis, the guilt of the Jews is directly rooted in their biological constitution: one does not have to prove that they are guilty; they are guilty solely by being Jews. The key is provided by the sudden rise, in the Western ideological imaginary, of the figure of the wandering "eternal Jew" in the age of Romanticism—precisely when, in real life, with the explosive development of capitalism, features attributed to the Jews began to permeate the whole of society (since commodity exchange became hegemonic). It was thus at the very moment when the Jews were deprived of their specific properties (which had made it easy to distinguish them from the rest of the population), and when the "Jewish question" was "resolved" at the political level by formal emancipation (by granting them the same rights as all other "normal" Christian citizens), that their "curse" was inscribed into their very being—they were no longer misers and usurers, but demonic heroes of eternal damnation, haunted by an unspecified and unspeakable guilt, condemned to wander, and longing to find redemption in death. It was, then, precisely when the specific figure of the Jew disappeared that the *absolute* Jew emerged, a transformation which conditioned the shift of anti-Semitism from theology to race: the Jews' damnation was their race, they were not guilty for what they had done (exploiting Christians, murdering their children, raping their women; ultimately, betraying and murdering Christ), but for what they *were*. Is it necessary to add that this shift laid the foundations for the Holocaust, for the physical annihilation of the Jews as the only appropriate final solution of their "problem"? Insofar as the Jews were identified by a series of properties, the goal was to convert them, to turn them into Christians; but, once Jewishness concerned their very being, only annihilation could solve "the Jewish question."

The true mystery of anti-Semitism, however, is why it is such a constant, why it persists through all its historical mutations. One is reminded of what Marx said about Homer's poetry: the true mystery to explain is not its origins, how it was rooted in early Greek society, but why it continues to exert its supreme artistic charm even today, long after the social conditions that gave birth to it disappeared. It is easy to date the original moment of European anti-Semitism: it started not in Ancient Rome, but in the eleventh and twelfth centuries as Europe began to awake from the inertia of the "dark ages" with the accelerated development of market exchange and the role of money. At that precise point, "the Jew" emerged as the enemy: the usurper, the parasitic intruder who disturbs the harmonious social edifice. Theologically, is also the moment of what Jacques Le Goff called the "birth of the Purgatorium": the idea that the choice was not only between Heaven and Hell, that there had to be a third, mediating, place, where one could make a deal, pay for one's sins (assuming they are not too great) with a determinate quantity of repentance—money again!

Asked about his anti-Semitism, the nationalist Croat rock singer Marko "Thompson" Perković once said in an interview: "I have nothing against [the Jews] and I did nothing to them. I know that Jesus Christ also did nothing against them, but still they hanged him on the cross." This is how anti-Semitism works today: it is not we who have anything against the Jews, it is just the way the Jews themselves actually are. Moreover, we are witnessing the last version of anti-Semitism which has reached the extreme point of self-relating. As I have put it elsewhere:

> The privileged role of Jews in the establishment of the sphere of the "public use of reason" hinges on their subtraction from every state power—this position of the "part of no-part" of every organic nation-state community, not the abstract-universal nature of their monotheism, makes them the immediate embodiment of universality. No wonder, then, that, with the establishment of the Jewish nation-state, a new figure of the Jew emerged: a Jew resisting identification with the State of Israel, refusing to accept the State of Israel as his true home, a Jew who "subtracts" himself from this state, and who includes the State of Israel among the states towards which he insists on maintaining a distance, living in their interstices and it is this uncanny Jew who is the object of what one cannot but designate as "Zionist anti-Semitism," a foreign excess disturbing the nation-state community. These Jews, the "Jews of the Jews themselves," worthy successors of Spinoza, are today the only Jews who continue to insist on the "public use of reason," refusing to submit their reasoning to the "private" domain of the nation-state.[5]

For confirmation that the term "Zionist anti-Semitism" is fully justified, one need only visit one of the most depressing websites known to me, www.masada2000.org, which contains a self-proclaimed "dirt list" of more than 7,000 SHIT (Self-Hating Israel-Threatening) Jews. Many of the names listed here are accompanied by detailed and extremely aggressive descriptions, including photos showing the person in the worst possible light, as well as email addresses (to solicit hate mail, obviously). If there was ever an inverted anti-Semitism, then this is it: the site looks like nothing so much as a Nazi list of corrupt Jewish freaks. There is clearly no need to search out Arab propaganda to find examples of brutal anti-Semitism today—fanatical Zionists are themselves doing the job perfectly adequately. They are the true Jew-haters, and what they viciously mock in their attacks on those who hold fast to the "public use of reason" is the most precious dimension of being a Jew. But what about the obvious counter-argument that the masada2000.org is simply a group of extremist

---

5   Žižek, *In Defense of Lost Causes*, p. 6.

lunatics of the kind to be found in every country, with no link to main-stream political orientations—something like an Israeli equivalent of the US survivalists who believe that Eve had sex with the Devil, producing Jews and Blacks as their offspring? Unfortunately, this easy way out does not convince: masada2000.org simply displays in extreme form the distrust of Jews critical of Israeli policies which is all too present in the US media, even more than in Israel itself.

This fact enables us also to solve another enigma: how US Christian fundamentalists—who are, as it were, by nature anti-Semitic—can now passionately support the Zionist policies of the State of Israel. There is only one solution to this enigma: Zionist anti-Semitism. That is to say, it's not that the US fundamentalists changed, it's that Zionism itself, in its hatred of Jews who do not fully identify with the politics of the State of Israel, paradoxically became anti-Semitic, and constructed the figure of the Jew who doubts the Zionist project along anti-Semitic lines.

The standard Zionist argument against the critics of Israeli policies is that, of course, like every other state, the State of Israel can and should be judged and eventually criticized, but that the critics of Israel misuse the justified critique of Israeli policy for anti-Semitic purposes. When unconditional Christian fundamentalist supporters of Israeli policies reject Leftist critiques of those policies, their implicit line of argumenta-tion is best rendered by a wonderful cartoon published in July 2008 in the Viennese daily *Die Presse*: it shows two stocky Nazi-looking Austrians, one of them holding a newspaper and commenting to his friend: "Here you can see again how totally justified anti-Semitism is being misused for a cheap critique of Israel!"

The thesis of Bernard-Henri Lévy (in his *The Left in Dark Times*) that the anti-Semitism of the twenty-first century will be "progressive," evokes Milner's thesis on the "criminal tendencies of democratic Europe": "progressive" Europe stands for the universal fluidification, the erasure, of all limits, and the Jews, with their fidelity to their way of life grounded in their Law and tradition, stand for the obstacle to this process. But is the logic of anti-Semitism not the exact opposite? Does the anti-Semitic perspective not perceive Jews precisely as agents of global fluidification, of the erasure of all particular ethnic and other forms of identity? Therein resides the irony of Milner's argumentation: it comes dangerously close to Zionist anti-Semitism, since what it effectively attacks—"universalist" fluidification—is precisely the other side of Jewish identity itself. That is to say, what Milner attacks as the "anti-Semitic" core of Europe is grounded in the Jewish contribution to European identity: "rootless" Jews were the first and most radical European universalists.[6]

This brings us to the political stakes and consequences of Zionist anti-Semitism. On August 2, 2009, after cordoning off part of the Arab neighborhood of Sheikh Jarrah in East Jerusalem, Israeli police evicted two Palestinian families (more than 50 people) from their homes, allowing Jewish settlers to immediately move into the emptied houses. Although Israeli police cited a ruling by the country's Supreme Court, the evicted Arab families had been living there for more than fifty years. This event which, rather exceptionally, did attract the attention of the world media, is part of a much larger and mostly ignored ongoing process. Five months earlier, on March 1, 2009, it was reported that the Israeli government had drafted plans to build more than 70,000 new housing units in Jewish settlements in the occupied West Bank;[7] if implemented, the plans could increase the number of settlers in the Palestinian territories by about 300,000—a move that would not only severely undermine the chances of a viable Palestinian state, but also hamper even more the everyday life of Palestinians. A government spokesman dismissed the report, arguing that the plans were of limited relevance: the actual construction of new homes in the settlements required the approval of the defense minister and prime minister. However, 15,000 planned units have already been fully approved. Moreover, almost 20,000 of the planned units lie in settlements that are far from the "green line" separating Israel from the West Bank, in other words in areas which Israel cannot expect to retain in any future peace deal with the Palestinians. The conclusion is obvious: while paying lip-service to the two-state solution, Israel is busy creating a situation on the ground which will render such a solution *de facto* impossible. The dream that underlies these policies is best rendered by the wall separating a settler's town from the Palestinian town on a nearby hill somewhere

---

6   George Steiner claimed that the purpose of the Jews is to be wanderers, eternal guardians of alienation and foreignness in the nationalistic bourgeois world, thereby therapeutically invigorating petrified values. Should we then interpret Christianity as a re-rooting of the Old Testament universe, its re-inscription into a stable hierarchical world? But what if the exact opposite is the case? What if, from a proper Christian perspective, it is the Jewish experience of being an uprooted wanderer which is not radical enough, since it maintains returning-home as its ultimate horizon ("Next year in Jerusalem!")? And what if, in order to pass from Judaism to Christianity, one has to drop this horizon of longing for a return home and accept the very situation of being a "wanderer" as primordial? In this sense, Judaism is a "negation" still caught in the horizon of what it negates, and Christianity the "negation of negation."

7   See Tobias Duck, "Israel Drafts West Bank Expansion Plans," *Financial Times*, March 2, 2009.

in the West Bank. The Israeli side of the wall is painted with an image of the countryside beyond the wall—but minus the Palestinian town, depicting just nature, grass, and trees. Is this not ethnic cleansing at its purest, imagining the outside beyond the wall as it should be, empty, virginal, waiting to be settled?

This process is sometimes presented in the guise of cultural gentrification. On October 28, 2008, the Israeli Supreme Court ruled that the Simon Wiesenthal Center could build its long-planned Center for Human Dignity–Museum of Tolerance on a contested site in the middle of Jerusalem. Who else but Frank Gehry to design the vast complex consisting of a general museum, a children's museum, a theater, conference center, library, gallery and lecture halls, cafeterias, and so on? The museum's declared mission will be to promote civility and respect among different segments of the Jewish community and between people of all faiths—the only obstacle (overruled by the Supreme Court) being that the museum site served as Jerusalem's main Muslim cemetery until 1948 (the Muslim community appealed to the Supreme Court that the construction would desecrate the cemetery, which allegedly contained the bones of Muslims killed during the Crusades of the twelfth and thirteenth centuries).[8] This dark spot wonderfully enacts the hidden truth of this multi-confessional project: it is a place celebrating tolerance, open to all but protected by the Israeli cupola which ignores the subterranean victims of intolerance—as if a little bit of intolerance is necessary in order to create the space for true tolerance.

As if this were not enough, there is another, even vaster project going on in Jerusalem:

> Israel is quietly carrying out a $100 million, multiyear development plan in the so-called "holy basin," the site of some of the most significant religious and national heritage sites just outside the walled Old City, as part of an effort to strengthen the status of Jerusalem as its capital. The plan, parts of which have been outsourced to a private group that is simultaneously buying up Palestinian property for Jewish settlement in East Jerusalem, has drawn almost no public or international scrutiny . . .
>
> As part of the plan, garbage dumps and wastelands are being cleared and turned into lush gardens and parks, now already accessible to visitors who can walk along new footpaths and take in the majestic views, along

---

8   See Tom Tugend, "Israel Supreme Court OKs Museum of Tolerance Jerusalem Project," *Observer*, October 29, 2008.

with new signs and displays that point out significant points of Jewish history . . .⁹

And, conveniently, many of the "unauthorized" Palestinian houses have to be erased to create the space for the redevelopment of the area. "The 'holy basin' is an infinitely complicated landscape dotted with shrines and still hidden treasures of the three major monotheistic religions," so the official argument is that its improvement is for everyone's benefit — Jews, Muslims and Christians — since it involves restoration that will draw more visitors to an area of exceptional global interest that has long suffered neglect. However, as Hagit Ofran of Peace Now noted, the plan aims to create "an ideological tourist park that will determine Jewish dominance in the area." Raphael Greenberg of Tel Aviv University put it even more bluntly: "The sanctity of the City of David is newly manufactured and is a crude amalgam of history, nationalism and quasi-religious pilgrimage . . . the past is used to disenfranchise and displace people in the present."¹⁰ Another great religious venue, a "public" inter-faith space under the clear domination and protective control of Israel.

What does all this mean? To get at the true dimension of the news, it is sometimes enough to read two disparate news items together — meaning emerges from their very link, like a spark exploding from an electrical short-circuit.¹¹ On the very same day as the reports about the planned new housing units in Jerusalem hit the media (March 2), Hillary Clinton criticized the rocket fire from Gaza as "cynical," claiming: "There is no doubt that any nation, including Israel, cannot stand idly by while its territory and people are subjected to rocket attacks." But should the Palestinians then stand idly while land on the West Bank is taken from them day by day? When peace-loving Israeli liberals present their conflict with Palestinians in neutral "symmetrical" terms, admitting that there are extremists on both sides who reject peace, and so on, one should ask a simple question: what happens in the Middle East when *nothing*

---

9   Ethan Bronner, Isabel Kershner, "Parks Fortify Israel's Claim to Jerusalem," *New York Times,* May 8, 2009.

10   Ibid.

11   On October 13, 2007, the Vatican's press representative Federico Lombardi confirmed that the Vatican had suspended a priest high-up in its hierarchy who, in an interview for Italian TV, had publicly admitted his homosexuality, insisting that he did not feel in any sense guilty; he was suspended because he had broken church law. The obscenity of this incident becomes clear the moment one juxtaposes it to the fact that hundreds of pedophile priests are not suspended, unlike this one homosexual priest who admitted his sexual orientation. The message is unmistakable: what matters is appearance, not reality.

happens at the direct politico-military level (when there are no attacks, negotiations, conflicts)? What happens is nothing less than the slow but incessant process of the Israelis taking land from the Palestinians on the West Bank, gradually strangling the Palestinian economy, building new settlements, pressuring Palestinian farmers to abandon their lands (crop burning, religious desecration, and even individual killings), all this supported by a Kafkaesque network of legal regulations. Saree Makdisi, in *Palestine Inside Out: An Everyday Occupation*, describes how, although the Israeli Occupation of the West Bank is ultimately enforced by the military, it is an "occupation by bureaucracy," the primary tools of which are application forms, title deeds, residency papers, and other permits.[12] It is this micro-management of daily life which does the job of securing the relentless Israeli expansion: one needs a permit in order to move around with one's family, to farm one's own land, to dig a well, to go to work, to school, to a hospital. One by one, Palestinians born in Jerusalem are thus stripped of the right to live there, prevented from earning a living, denied housing permits, etc.[13] Palestinians often use the problematic cliché describing the Gaza strip as "the largest concentration camp in the world"—but most recently this designation has come dangerously close to truth. This is the fundamental reality which makes all abstract "prayers for peace" obscene and hypocritical. The State of Israel is clearly engaged in a slow process, like that of a mole burrowing underground, invisible to and ignored by the media, such that, one day, the world will awaken and realize that there is no longer a Palestinian

---

12   See Saree Makdisi, *Palestine Inside Out: An Everyday Occupation*, New York: Norton 2008.

13   We witnessed a similar oppression without (too much) open brutality in post-1968 Czechoslovakia. In his dissident classic *Normalization*, Milan Simecka described how, after 1968, the hard-line Communists enforced the "normalization" of the Czech population, their awakening from the dream of 1968 to crude socialist reality. There was little direct pressure—most of the job was done through the gentle art of low-level everyday corruption and blackmail, in the style of: "You want your children to go to university? Then just sign a statement which will not even be published, saying that you were seduced into participating in the 1968 events and that you now see it was a mistake . . ." Is not something similar going on in our late-capitalist liberal societies: no open brutality, just small but clear signals that it will be better for your career if you do not overstep certain limits? There is nonetheless a key difference between the late-socialist corruption and our late-capitalist form, a difference which concerns the status of appearance. What mattered in the socialist regimes was maintaining appearances—recall the (deservedly) famous example of the vegetable seller from Václav Havel's "Power of the Powerless," who obediently displays in the window of his store official propaganda slogans, although neither he nor his customers take them seriously: what matters is the gesture of obedience. In liberal capitalism, however, not only does nobody care (within certain limits, of course) what slogans are put in the window, but provocative ones are even welcomed, if they help sales, for the market is the greatest ironist. Recall how big companies sometimes use ironic paraphrases of Communist topics for publicity purposes —one can hardly imagine state socialist authorities doing the same with capitalist slogans.

West Bank, that the land is Palestinian-*frei*, and that we can do nothing but accept the fact. The map of the Palestinian West Bank already looks like a fragmented archipelago.

In the last months of 2008, when attacks by illegal West Bank settlers on Palestinian farmers were becoming a daily occurrence, the State of Israel tried to contain such excesses (the Supreme Court ordered the evacuation of some settlements, and so on); but, as many observers noted, these measures cannot but appear half-hearted, counteracting as they do a policy which, at a deeper level, *is* the long-term strategy of the State of Israel in shameless violation of international treaties signed by Israel itself. The response of the illegal settlers to the Israeli authorities is: "But we are just doing the same thing as you, only more openly, so what right do you have to condemn us?" And the answer of the State is: "Be patient, don't be in too much of a hurry, we are doing what you want, just in a more moderate and acceptable manner."

The same story seems to have been repeating itself since the foundation of Israel: while Israel accepts the peace conditions proposed by the international community, it wagers that the peace plan will not work. The wild settlers sometimes sound like Brünnhilde from the last act of Wagner's *Walküre*, reproaching Wotan that, by counteracting his explicit order and protecting Siegmund, she is only realizing Wotan's own true desire which he was forced to renounce under external pressure. In the same way, the illegal settlers are only realizing the State's true desire which it was forced to renounce under pressure from the international community. While condemning the violent excesses of "illegal" settlements, the State of Israel promotes new "legal" settlements on the West Bank, continues to strangle the Palestinian economy, and so on. One look at the much-changed map of East Jerusalem, where the Palestinians are gradually encircled and their space is sliced up, tells us everything. The condemnation of non-state anti-Palestinian violence obfuscates the true problem of *state* violence; the condemnation of "illegal" settlements obfuscates the illegality of the "legal" ones. Therein resides the two-faced nature of the much-praised "honesty" of the Israeli Supreme Court: by occasionally passing a judgment in favor of the dispossessed Palestinians, now and then proclaiming their eviction illegal, it guarantees the legality of the remaining vast majority of cases.

Consequently, in the Israeli–Palestinian conflict also, *soyons réalistes, demandons l'impossible*: if there is a lesson to be learned from the endlessly protracted negotiations, it is that the main obstacle to peace is precisely what is offered as a realistic solution, namely two separate states. Although neither of the two sides really wants it (Israel would probably prefer a little bit of the West Bank, while the Palestinians consider the pre-1967 Israeli territory part of their land), it is somehow accepted by both sides as the only feasible solution. What they both exclude as an impossible dream is the simplest and most obvious solution: a bi-national secular state comprising all of Israel plus the occupied territories and Gaza. To those who dismiss the bi-national state as a utopian dream disqualified by the long history of hatred and violence, one should reply that, far from being utopian, *the bi-national state already is a fact*: the reality of Israel and the West Bank today is that it *is* one state (that is, the entire territory is *de facto* controlled by one sovereign power, the State of Israel), divided by internal borders, so that the task should rather be to abolish the current apartheid and transform it into a secular democratic state.[14]

And, to avoid any kind of misunderstanding, taking all this into account in no way implies adopting an "understanding" attitude towards terror-ist acts—on the contrary, it provides the only grounds on which one can condemn such acts without hypocrisy. Furthermore, when the Western liberal defenders of peace in the Middle East contrast the Palestinian democrats committed to compromise and peace with the radical funda-mentalists of Hamas, they fail to see that the shared origin of these two poles lies in the long and systematic endeavor by Israel and the United States to weaken the Palestinians by undermining the leading position of al Fatah—an effort which, up until a few years ago, even included financial support for Hamas. The sad result is that Palestinians are now divided between the Hamas fundamentalists and a corrupt al Fatah. The weakened al Fatah is no longer the hegemonic force truly representing the substantial longings of the Palestinians (and as such in a position to conclude peace); it is increasingly seen by the majority of Palestinians for what it is: a crippled puppet supported by the US as representative of the "democratic" Palestinians. Similarly, while the US worried about Saddam's basically secular regime in Iraq, the "Talibanization" of their ally Pakistan progressed slowly but inexorably: according to some, Taliban control has now already spread over parts of Karachi, Pakistan's largest city.

Both sides of the conflict have an interest in painting a picture of the "fundamentalists in control" in Gaza: this characterization enables Hamas

---

14   I owe this line of thought to Udi Aloni.

to monopolize the struggle, and the Israelis to gain international sympathy. Consequently, although everyone deplores the rise of fundamentalism, no one really wants secular resistance to Israel among the Palestinians. But is it really true that there is none? What if there were two secret actors in the Middle East conflict: secular Palestinians and Zionist fundamentalists—Arab fundamentalists arguing in secular terms and secular Jewish Westerners relying on theological reasoning:

> The strange thing is that it was secular Zionism that brought God to bear so much on religious ideas. In a way, the true believers in Israel are the non-religious. This is so because, for the religious life of an orthodox Jew, God is actually quite marginal. There were times when for a member of the orthodox intellectual elite it was 'uncool' to refer too much to God: a sign that he is not devoted enough to the real noble cause of the study of Talmud (the continual movement of expansion of the law and evasion of it). It was only the crude secular Zionist gaze that took God, which was a sort of alibi, so seriously. The sad thing is that now more and more orthodox Jews seem convinced that they indeed believe in God.[15]

The consequence of this unique ideological situation is the paradox of atheists defending Zionist claims in theological terms. Exemplary here is *The Arrogance of the Present*,[16] Milner's exploration of the legacy of 1968 which can also be read as a reply to Alain Badiou's *The Century*, as well as to Badiou's exploration of the politico-ideological implications of the "name of the Jew." In an implicit but for that reason all the more intense dialogue with Badiou, Milner proposes a radically different diagnosis of the twentieth century. His starting point is the same as Badiou's: "a name counts only as far as the divisions it induces go." The Master-Signifiers which matter are those which clarify their field by simplifying a complex situation into a clear division—yes or no, for or against. Milner goes on: "But here is what happened: one day, it became obvious that names believed to bear a future (glorious or sinister) no longer divide anyone; and names dismissed as thoroughly obsolete began to bring about unbridgeable divisions."[17] The names which today no longer divide, generate passionate attachment, but leave us indifferent, are those which were traditionally expected to act as the most mobilizing ("workers,"

---

15   Noam Yuran, personal communication.
16   Jean-Claude Milner, *L'Arrogance du présent. Regards sur une décennie: 1965–1975*, Paris: Grasset 2009.
17   Ibid., pp. 21–2.

"class struggle"), while those names which appeared deprived of their divisive edge have re-emerged violently in their diremptive role—today, the name "Jew" "divides most deeply speaking beings":

> Contrary to what knowledge predicted, the culminating point of the [twentieth] century did not take the form of social revolution; it took the form of an extermination. Contrary to what the Revolution promised, the extermination ignored classes and fixated on a name without any class meaning. Not even an economic one. Not a shadow of an objective meaning.[18]

Milner's conclusion is that "the only true event of the twentieth century was the return of the name Jew"[19]—and this return was an ominous surprise also for the Jews themselves. With the political emancipation of the Jews in modern Europe, a new figure of the Jew emerged: the "Jew of knowledge" (*le Juif du Savoir*) who replaced study (of the Talmud, that is, of his theological roots) with universal (scientific) knowledge. So we had Jews who excelled in the secular sciences, and this is why Marxism was so popular among Jewish intellectuals: it presented itself as "*scientific* socialism," uniting knowledge and revolution (in contrast to Jacobins who proudly said, apropos Laplace, that "the Republic does not need scientists," or millenarians who dismissed knowledge as sinful). With Marxism, inequality, injustice, and their overcoming became objects of knowledge.[20] The Enlightenment offered European Jews a chance to find a place for themselves in the universality of scientific knowledge, ignoring their name, tradition, and roots. This dream, however, was brutally ended with the Holocaust: the "Jew of knowledge" could not survive the Nazi extermination—the trauma was that knowledge had allowed it to happen, was not able to resist it, was impotent in the face of it. (Traces of this impotence are already discernible in the famous 1929 Davos debate between Ernst Cassirer and Heidegger, where Heidegger treated Cassirer very rudely, refusing to shake his hand at the end.)

How did the European Left react to this rupture? At the core of Milner's book is the close analysis of the Maoist organization *Gauche prolétarienne* (Proletarian Left), the main political organization which emerged out of May 1968. When it fell apart, some members (like Benny Lévy) opted for fidelity to the name of the Jew, others chose Christian spirituality.

---

18   Ibid., p. 214.
19   Ibid., p. 212.
20   Ibid., p. 201.

For Milner, the entire activity of the *Gauche prolétarienne* was based on a certain disavowal, on a refusal to pronounce a name. Milner proposes a nice Magrittean image: a room with a window in the middle, and a painting covering up and obstructing the view through the window; the scene on the painting exactly reproduces the exterior one would have seen through the window. Such is the function of ideological misrecognition: it obfuscates the true dimension of what we see.[21] In the case of the *Gauche prolétarienne*, this unseen dimension was the name of the Jew. That is to say, the *Gauche prolétarienne* legitimized its radical opposition to the entire French political establishment as a prolongation of the Resistance against fascist occupation: their diagnosis was that French political life was still dominated by people who stood in direct continuity with the Pétainist collaborationist regime. However, although they had identified the right enemy, they kept silent about the fact that the main target of this regime had not been the Left, but the Jews. In short, they used the event itself to obfuscate its true dimension, in a similar manner to the "Jew of knowledge" who tries to redefine his Jewishness in order to erase the real core of his being Jewish.

Benny Lévy's transformation from a Maoist to a Zionist is thus indicative of a wider tendency. The conclusion drawn by many from the "obscure disaster" of twentieth-century attempts at universal emancipation is that particular groups should no longer agree to "sublate" their own emancipation in the universal form ("we—oppressed minorities, women, etc.—can only attain our freedom through universal emancipation," that is, the Communist revolution): fidelity to the universal cause is replaced by fidelities to particular identities (being Jewish, gay, and so on), and the most we can envisage is a "strategic alliance" between particular struggles. Perhaps, however, the time has come to return to the notion of universal emancipation, and it is here that a critical analysis should begin. When Milner claims that "class struggle," and so on, are no longer divisive names, that they have been replaced by the word "Jew" as the truly divisive name, the claim is at least partially true, but what is its meaning? Could it not also be interpreted in terms of the classical Marxist theory of anti-Semitism in which the anti-Semitic figure of the "Jew" is read as the metaphoric stand-in for the class struggle? On this reading, the disappearance of class struggle and the (re)appearance of anti-Semitism are thus two sides of the same coin, since the *presence* of the figure of the "Jew" is only comprehensible

---

21   Ibid., p. 183.

against the background of the *absence* of class struggle. Walter Benjamin (to whom Milner himself refers as an authority, and who stands precisely for a Marxist Jew who remains faithful to the religious dimension of Jewishness and is thus not a "Jew of knowledge") said long ago that every rise of fascism bears witness to a failed revolution—this thesis not only still holds today, but is perhaps more pertinent than ever. Liberals like to point out similarities between Left and Right "extremisms": Hitler's terror imitated the Bolshevik terror; the Leninist party is today alive in al Qaeda. But again, even if we accept this, what exactly does it mean? It could also be read as an indication of how fascism literally replaces (takes the place of) the Leftist revolution: its rise signifies the Left's failure, but simultaneously a proof that there was indeed a revolutionary potential, a dissatisfaction, which the Left was not able to mobilize.

How are we to understand this reversal of an emancipatory force into fundamentalist populism? As I have put it elsewhere:

> It is here that the materialist-dialectic passage from the Two to the Three gains all its weight: the axiom of communist politics is not simply the dualist "class struggle," but, more precisely, the Third moment as the subtraction from the Two of hegemonic politics. That is to say, the hegemonic ideological field imposes on us a field of (ideological) visibility with its own "principal contradiction" (today, it is the opposition of market-freedom-democracy and fundamentalist-terrorist-totalitarianism—"Islamo-fascism" and so on), and the first thing we must do is to reject (to subtract ourselves from) this opposition, to perceive it as a false opposition destined to obfuscate the true line of division. Lacan's formula for this redoubling is 1 + 1 + a: the "official" antagonism (the Two) is always supplemented by an "indivisible remainder" which indicates its foreclosed dimension. In other terms, the true antagonism is always reflexive, it is the antagonism between the "official" antagonism and that which is foreclosed by it (this is why, in Lacan's mathematics, 1 + 1 = 3). Today, for example, the true antagonism is not between liberal multiculturalism and fundamentalism, but between the very field of their opposition and the excluded Third (radical emancipatory politics).[22]

Badiou has provided the contours of this passage from Two to Three in his reading of the Paulinian passage from Law to love.[23] In both

22   Žižek, *In Defense of Lost Causes*, pp. 383–4.
23   See Alain Badiou, *Saint Paul: The Foundation of Universalism*, Stanford: Stanford University Press 2003.

cases (in Law and in love), we are dealing with division, with a "divided subject"; however, the modality of the division is thoroughly different. The subject of the Law is "decentered" in the sense that it is caught in the self-destructive vicious cycle of sin and Law in which one pole engenders its opposite. Paul provided an unsurpassable description of this entanglement in Romans 7:

> We know that the law is spiritual; but I am carnal, sold into slavery to sin. What I do, I do not understand. For I do not do what I want, but I do what I hate. Now if I do what I do not want, I concur that the law is good. So now it is no longer I who do it, but sin that dwells in me. For I know that good does not dwell in me, that is, in my flesh. The willing is ready at hand, but doing the good is not. For I do not do the good I want, but I do the evil I do not want. Now if I do what I do not want, it is no longer I who do it, but sin that dwells in me. So, then, I discover the principle that when I want to do right, evil is at hand. For I take delight in the law of God, in my inner self, but I see in my members another principle at war with the law of my mind, taking me captive to the law of sin that dwells in my members. Miserable one that I am!

It is thus not that I am merely torn between the two opposites, Law and sin; the problem is that I cannot even clearly distinguish them — I want to follow the Law, and I end up in sin. This vicious cycle is not so much overcome as broken; one breaks out of it with the experience of love, more precisely, with the experience of the radical gap that separates love from the Law. Therein resides the radical difference between the couple Law/sin and the couple Law/love. The gap that separates Law and sin is not a real difference: their truth is their mutual implication or confusion — Law generates sin and feeds upon it, one can never draw a clear line of separation between the two. It is only with the couple Law/love that we attain a real difference: these two moments are radically separated, they are not "mediated," one is not the form of appearance of its opposite. In other words, the difference between the two couples (Law/sin and Law/love) is not substantial, but purely formal: we are dealing with the same content in its two modalities. In its indistinction-mediation, the couple is the one of Law/sin; in the radical distinction of the two, it is Law/love. It is therefore wrong to ask the question: "Are we then forever condemned to the split between Law and love? What about the synthesis between Law and love?" The split between Law and sin is of a radically different nature than the split between Law and love: instead of the vicious cycle of mutual reinforcement, we get a clear distinction of two different domains. Once we become fully aware of the dimension of love in its radical difference from the Law, love has, in a way, already won, since this difference is visible only when one already dwells in love, from the standpoint of love.

China, Haiti, Congo

In authentic Marxism, the totality is not an ideal, but a critical notion — to locate a phenomenon in its totality does not mean to see the hidden harmony of the Whole, but to include in a system all its "symptoms," its antagonisms and inconsistencies, as its integral parts. Let me take a contemporary example. In this sense, liberalism and fundamentalism form a "totality": the opposition of liberalism and fundamentalism is structured in exactly the same way as that between Law and sin in St. Paul, that is, liberalism itself generates its opposite. So what about the core values of liberalism: freedom, equality, and so forth? The paradox is that liberalism itself is not strong enough to save them — its own core values — against the fundamentalist onslaught. The problem with liberalism is that it cannot stand on its own: there is something missing in the liberal edifice, and liberalism is in its very notion "parasitic," relying on a presupposed network of communal values that it itself undermines with its own development. Fundamentalism is a reaction — a false, mystifying, reaction, of course — against a real flaw in liberalism, and this is why it is again and again generated by liberalism. Left to its own devices, liberalism will slowly undermine itself — the only thing capable of saving its core values is a renewed Left. Or, to put it in well-known terms from 1968, in order for its key legacy to survive, liberalism needs the fraternal aid of the radical Left.

The fragility of liberalism is made clear by what is happening in China. Instead of treating contemporary China as an oriental-despotic distortion of capitalism one should see in it the repetition of the development of capitalism in Europe itself. In early modernity, most European states were far from democratic — if they were (as was the case in Holland), they were so only for the liberal elite, not for the popular classes. The conditions for capitalism were created and sustained by a brutal state dictatorship, very much like today's China: the state legalized violent expropriations of the common people which turned them into proletarians and disciplined them in their new roles. There is thus nothing exotic about China: what is happening there merely repeats our own forgotten past. So what about the claims of some Western liberal critics that China's development would be much faster if it were combined with political democracy?

In a TV interview a couple of years ago, Ralf Dahrendorf linked the growing distrust in democracy to the fact that, after every revolutionary change, the road to new prosperity leads through a "valley of tears": after the breakdown of socialism, one cannot directly pass to the abundance of a successful market economy—the limited, but real, welfare and security provided by socialism had to be dismantled, and such first steps are necessarily painful.[24] The same goes for Western Europe, where the passage from the Welfare State to the new global economy involves painful renunciations, a reduction in security, less guaranteed social care. For Dahrendorf, the problem is best encapsulated by the simple fact that this painful passage through the "valley of tears" lasts longer than the average period between (democratic) elections, so that for politicians there is a great temptation to postpone the necessary difficult changes for short-term electoral gain. Paradigmatic is here the disappointment of many post-Communist nations with the economic results of the new democratic order: in the glorious days of 1989, they equated democracy with the abundance characteristic of Western consumerist societies, but now, ten years later, with that abundance still slow in arriving, they blame democracy itself. Unfortunately, Dahrendorf focuses much less on the opposite temptation: if the majority resists the necessary structural changes in economy, one logical conclusion would be that, for a decade or so, an enlightened elite should take power, even by non-democratic means, in order to enforce the required measures and thus to lay the foundations for a truly stable democracy. Along these lines, Fareed Zakaria points out how democracy can only "catch on" in economically developed countries: if the developing countries are "prematurely democratized," the result is a populism which ends in economic catastrophe and political despotism[25]—no wonder that some of today's economically most successful Third World countries (Taiwan, South Korea, Chile) embraced full democracy only after a period of authoritarian rule.

Is this line of reasoning not the best argument for the Chinese path to capitalism as opposed to the Russian path? After the collapse of Communism, Russia embraced "shock therapy" and threw itself headlong into democracy and the fast track to capitalism—with economic bankruptcy as the result. (There are good reasons to be modestly paranoid

---

24   See http://globetrotter.berkeley.edu.
25   See Fareed Zakaria, *The Future of Freedom*, New York: Norton 2003.

here: were the Western economic advisers to Yeltsin who proposed this path really as innocent as they appeared, or were they serving US interests by crippling Russia economically?) China, on the contrary, followed the path of Chile and South Korea, using unencumbered authoritarian state power to control the social costs of the passage to capitalism, thus avoiding chaos. In short, the weird combination of capitalism and Communist rule, far from being a ridiculous anomaly, proved a blessing (not even) in disguise; China developed so fast not in spite of authoritarian Communist rule, but because of it. So, to conclude with a Stalinist-sounding note of suspicion: what if those who worry about the lack of democracy in China are really worrying about China becoming the next global superpower, threatening Western primacy?

Switching perspectives, what are we to make of the quasi-Leninist defense of Chinese capitalist development as an expanded and prolonged case of the NEP (the New Economic Policy adopted in Soviet Russia, which emerged at the end of the Civil War in 1921, and allowed private property and market exchange, lasting roughly till 1928), with the Communist Party firmly exerting political control, able at any moment to step in and undo its concessions to the class enemy? One should push this logic to its extreme: insofar as there is a tension in capitalist democracies between the democratic-egalitarian sovereignty of the people and the class divisions of the economic sphere, and insofar as the state can in principle enforce expropriations and so forth, is not capitalism itself, in a sense, one great NEP-style detour on a path that should pass directly from feudal or slave relations of domination to Communist egalitarian justice? Insofar as modernity is generally characterized by the democratic rule of the people, one can indeed say that, in a gesture of temporary compromise, the people can permit capitalist exploitation, aware that this is the only way to bring about material progress — but that they can nonetheless maintain the right to limit or even withdraw this permission at any moment.

Is, then, today's China the ideal capitalist country in which the main task of the ruling Communist Party is to control the workers and prevent their self-organization and mobilization against exploitation, such that the Party's power is legitimized by its undercover deal with the new capitalists, taking the form: "You stay out of politics and leave power to us, and we will keep the workers under control"? There are some good reasons for holding such a view — the powers that be are so sensitive to any mention of workers' self-organization that even the official books dealing with the history of the Chinese Communist Party and workers' movement in China silently pass over the subject of trade unions and other forms of workers' resistance, even if they were supported or directly organized by the Communists, lest the evocation of this past give rise to dangerous associations with the present.

On the other hand, no matter how cynical its effective functioning, every ideology obliges to some extent, so one should not be surprised to hear stories like the one told to me by John Thornhill, a *Financial Times* journalist who, during a recent visit to China, wanted to see the poorest, least developed, place in the country. It is (according to official statistics, of course) a small town in the north, in the middle of nowhere and close to the Mongolian border. Thornhill was allowed to visit and was surprised to discover that life there was quite normal, except that the town was populated only by old people and children, the rest of its inhabitants having moved to the big cities for work, and in order to send money home to support their relatives, who could all afford TVs, DVD players, and so on. Furthermore, the local city authorities also organized the basic necessities of life: a health service, education, and the rest. When Thornhill asked a local functionary why the powers that be bothered to keep the town functioning, why they did not simply let it vegetate or fall apart, he answered: "But we cannot do that—we are Communists, we have to take care of the people!" It would be all too easy, in the traditional Marxist manner, to dismiss such attitudes as an ideological veneer masking the reality of exploitation. But precisely because the Communist authorities are not democratically legitimized they are well aware that they have to provide for the people, have to counter the most disastrous effects of rapid capitalist development with minimal social measures. This is why, paradoxically, it is important for the Chinese state to remain a strong force controlling the private sphere of wild capitalism—what the Chinese are doing is indeed, on this level, similar to how Lenin imagined the NEP: a strong Soviet state wisely using capitalism, regulating its course and counteracting its destructive effects.

Faced with China's explosive capitalist development, analysts often ask when political democracy, as the "natural" political accompaniment to capitalism, will impose itself. A closer analysis, however, quickly dispels such hopes—what if the promised democratic second stage supposed to follow the authoritarian valley of tears never in fact arrives? This, perhaps, is what is so unsettling about today's China: the suspicion that its authoritarian capitalism is not merely a reminder of our past—a repetition of the process of capitalist accumulation which took place in Europe between the sixteenth and eighteenth centuries—but a sign of the future? What if "the vicious combination of the Asian knout and the European stock market" proves to be economically more efficient than liberal capitalism? What if this signals that democracy, as we understand it, is no longer the condition and motor of economic development, but its obstacle?

The obvious counter-argument is "Why not have it both ways, a democratically elected government kept in check by social movements?" The problem is that democratic elections give such a government a legitimization which makes it much more impervious to criticism by movements: it can dismiss movements as the voice of an "extremist" minority out of sync with the majority that elected the government. A government not covered by "free elections" finds itself under much greater pressure: its acts are no longer covered by democratic legitimacy, and those in power are all of a sudden deprived of the possibility to say to those who protest against them: "Who are you to criticize us? We are an elected government, we can do what we want!" Lacking such legitimacy, they have to earn it the hard way, by their deeds. I remember the last years of Communist rule in Slovenia: there was no government so eager to earn its legitimacy and do something for the people, trying to please everyone, precisely because the Communists held power which—as everyone, including themselves, knew—was not democratically justified. Since the Communists knew their end was near, they feared being harshly judged.[26]

So where does this limitation of democracy become directly palpable? The case of Haiti over the last two decades is exemplary here—as Peter Hallward writes in *Damming the Flood*,[27] a detailed account of the "democratic containment" of Haiti's radical politics: "never have the well-worn tactics of 'democracy promotion' been applied with more devastating effect than in Haiti between 2000 and 2004."[28] One cannot miss the irony of the fact that the name of the emancipatory political movement which suffered this international pressure is *Lavalas*—"flood" in Kreol: it is the flood of the expropriated overflowing the gated communities. This is why the title of Hallward's book is so appropriate, inscribing the Haitian

---

26   Furthermore, what if, for China, a much better solution than a multi-party system would be Party rule with a strong civil society (social movements) keeping independent control over ecology, workers' conditions, etc.? In today's post-political epoch, movements which keep state power under constant pressure are often much more important than who is democratically elected to hold power.
27   Peter Hallward, *Damming the Flood*, London: Verso 2007.
28   Ibid., p. xxxiii.

events into the global tendency of new dams and walls constructed everywhere after 9/11, confronting us with the truth of "globalization," namely
the inner lines of division which sustain it.

Haiti was an exception from the very beginning, from its revolutionary fight against slavery which ended in independence in January 1804:
"Only in Haiti was the declaration of human freedom universally consistent. Only in Haiti was this declaration sustained at all costs, in direct
opposition to the social order and economic logic of the day."[29] For this
reason, "there is no single event in the whole of modern history whose
implications were more threatening to the dominant global order of
things."[30] As I have written elsewhere:

> The Haiti Revolution truly deserves the title of the *repetition* of the French
> Revolution: led by Toussaint L'Ouverture, it was clearly "ahead of its time,"
> "premature" and doomed to fail, yet, precisely as such, it was perhaps even
> more of an Event than the French Revolution itself.[31]

For this reason, the threat resided in the "mere existence of an independent Haiti,"[32] that had already been pronounced by Talleyrand as
"a horrible spectacle for all white nations."[33] Haiti thus *had* to be turned
into an exemplary case of economic failure, to dissuade other countries
from taking the same path. The price—the *literal* price—for "premature"
independence was horrible: after two decades of embargo, France, the
previous colonial master, only established trade and diplomatic relations
in 1825, and Haiti had to agree to pay 150 million francs as "compensation" for the loss of its slaves. This sum, roughly equal to the French
annual budget at the time, was later cut to 90 million, but it continued
to be a heavy burden which prevented any economic growth: at the end
of the nineteenth century, Haiti's payments to France consumed around
80 percent of the national budget, and the last installment was paid in
1947. When, in 2004, celebrating the bi-centenary of its independence,
Lavalas president Jean-Baptiste Aristide demanded that France return
this extorted sum, his claim was flatly rejected by a French commission
(whose members included Régis Debray). So while US liberals ponder
the possibility of reparations to US blacks for slavery, Haiti's demands to

29   Ibid., p. 11.
30   Ibid.
31   Žižek, *In Defense of Lost Causes*, p. 392.
32   Hallward, *Damming the Flood*, p. 11.
33   Ibid., p. 12.

be reimbursed for the tremendous amounts ex-slaves had to pay to have their freedom recognized was ignored by liberal opinion, even though the extortion here was twofold: the slaves were first exploited, and then had to pay for the recognition of their hard-won freedom.

The story continues today: what is for most of us a fond childhood memory—making mud cakes—is a desperate reality in Haiti slums like Cité Soleil. According to a recent AP report, a rise in food prices gave a new boost to a traditional Haitian remedy for hunger pangs: cookies made of dried yellow dirt. "The mud, which has long been prized by pregnant women and children as an antacid and source of calcium," is considerably cheaper than real food: dirt to make 100 cookies now costs $5. Merchants truck it from the country's central plateau to the market, where women buy it, process it into mud cookies and leave them to dry under the scorching sun; the finished cookies are carried in buckets to markets or sold on the streets.[34]

The Lavalas movement, whose periods in government over the last two decades were twice interrupted by US-sponsored military coups, is the unique combination of a political agent which won state power through free elections, but which *all the way through maintained its roots in organs of local popular democracy, of people's direct self-organization*. So, while the "free press" dominated by its enemies was never obstructed, and violent protests which continuously threatened the stability of the legal government were fully tolerated, it was clear on whose behalf the government was acting. The goal of the US and France was to impose on Haiti a "normal" democracy, a democracy which would not weaken the economic power of a narrow elite, and they were well aware that, in order to function in this way, democracy has to cut its links with direct popular self-organization.

It is interesting to note that this US–French cooperation took place soon after their public disagreement over the attack on Iraq, and was quite appropriately celebrated as a reaffirmation of their basic alliance; even Brazil's Lula, Toni Negri's hero, condoned the 2004 overthrow of Aristide. An unholy alliance was thus put together to discredit the Lavalas government as a form of mob rule which violated human rights, and President Aristide as a power-mad fundamentalist dictator—an alliance that went from illegal mercenary death-squads and US-sponsored "democratic fronts" to humanitarian NGOs and even some "radical Left" organizations which, financed by the US, denounced Aristide's

---

34   Jonathan M. Katz, "Poor Haitians Resort to Eating Dirt," AP, January 29, 2008.

"capitulation" to the IMF. Aristide himself provided a perspicuous characterization of this overlapping between radical Left and liberal Right: "somewhere, somehow, there's a little secret satisfaction, perhaps an unconscious satisfaction, in saying things that powerful white people want you to say."[35]

The struggle of Lavalas is a perfect example of principled heroism and of the limitations of what can be done today: it did not withdraw into the interstices of state power to "resist" from there, but heroically assumed power, well aware that it was doing so in the most unfavorable circumstances, when the trends not only of capitalist "modernization" and "structural readjustment," but also of the postmodern Left, were against them—where, for example, was Negri's voice, otherwise celebrating Lula's rule in Brazil, to be heard? Constrained by the measures imposed by the US and the IMF designed to enact "necessary structural readjustments," Aristide combined a politics of small and precise pragmatic measures (building schools and hospitals, creating infrastructure, raising minimum wages) with occasional acts of popular violence, reacting to military gangs. In spite of all its all too obvious flaws—as Aristide himself, the first to admit Lavalas's mistakes, put it: it is better to be wrong with the people than to be right against the people—the Lavalas regime was indeed one embodiment of what a "dictatorship of the proletariat" would look like today. While realistically engaging in all the inevitable compromises, it always remained faithful to its "base," to the crowd of ordinary dispossessed people, speaking on their behalf, not "representing" them, but directly relying on their local self-organization. Although respecting the democratic rules, Lavalas made it clear that the electoral struggle was not where things are decided: much more crucial was to supplement democracy with the direct political self-organization of the oppressed. Or, to put it in our "postmodern" terms: the struggle between Lavalas and the capitalist-military elite in Haiti is a case of antagonism which cannot be contained within the framework of parliamentary-democratic "agonistic pluralism."

What the case of Haiti makes clear is that, whenever we are tempted by the fascinating spectacle of Third World violence, we should always take a self-reflexive turn and ask ourselves how we ourselves are implicated in it. There is an old anecdote about a group of anthropologists who penetrated the heart of darkness of central New Zealand in search of a

---

35   Hallward, *Damming the Flood*, p. 338.

mysterious tribe rumored to perform a chilling death-dance with mud-and-wood masks. Late one day, they finally reached the tribe, somehow explained to them what they wanted and then went to sleep; the next morning, the members of the tribe performed a dance which met all their expectations, and so the anthropologists returned satisfied to "civilization" and wrote up a report on their discovery. Unfortunately, however, another expedition visited the same tribe a couple of years later, made a more serious effort to communicate with them, and learned the truth about the first expedition: the tribesmen had somehow grasped that their guests wanted to see a terrifying death dance, and so, in order not to disappoint them because of their sense of hospitality, they worked all night to make the masks and practice the dance invented to satisfy their guests — the anthropologists who thought they were getting a glimpse into a weird exotic ritual were actually receiving a hastily improvised staging of their own desire.

Is not something quite similar going on in contemporary Congo, which is again emerging as the African "heart of darkness"? The cover story of *Time* magazine on June 5, 2006 was headlined "The Deadliest War in the World" — a detailed documentation of how around four million people have died in Congo as the result of political violence over the last decade. None of the usual humanitarian uproar followed, just a couple of readers' letters — as if some kind of filtering mechanism had blocked this news from achieving its full impact. To put it cynically, *Time* had picked the wrong victim in the struggle for hegemony in suffering — it should have stuck to the list of usual suspects: Muslim women and their plight, oppression in Tibet, and so forth. Congo today has effectively re-emerged as a Conradean zone: no one dares to confront it head-on. The death of a West Bank Palestinian child, not to mention an Israeli or an American, is mediatically worth thousands of times more than the death of a nameless Congolese. But why this ignorance?

On October 30, 2008, AP reported that Laurent Nkunda, the rebel general besieging Congo's eastern provincial capital Goma, said that he wanted direct talks with the government about his objections to a billion-dollar deal that gives China access to the country's vast mineral riches in exchange for a railway and highways. As problematic and neo-colonialist as this transaction may be,[36] it poses a vital threat to the

---

36   To dispel any illusions about China, a quick glance at Myanmar suffices: Myanmar is effectively a Chinese (post-)colony, with China playing the standard post-colonial strategy of supporting the corrupt military regime (recall how, in the great protests led by the Buddhist monks a couple of years

interests of local warlords, since its eventual success would create the infrastructural base for the Democratic Republic of Congo to function as a united state. Back in 2001, a UN investigation into the illegal exploitation of natural resources in Congo found that the conflict in the country is mainly about access to, control of, and trade in five key mineral resources: coltan, diamonds, copper, cobalt, and gold. According to this investigation, the exploitation of Congo's natural resources by local warlords and foreign armies is "systematic and systemic," and the Ugandan and Rwandan leaders in particular (closely followed by Zimbabwe and Angola) had turned their soldiers into business armies: Rwanda's army made at least $250 million in eighteen months by selling coltan. The report concluded that the permanent civil war and disintegration of Congo "has created a 'win-win' situation for all belligerents. The only loser in this huge business venture is the Congolese people." One should bear in mind this good old "economic-reductionist" background when one reads in the media about primitive ethnic passions exploding yet again in the African jungle.

Beneath the façade of ethnic warfare, we thus discern the workings of global capitalism. After the fall of Mobutu, Congo no longer exists as a united operational state; its eastern part especially is a multiplicity of territories ruled by local warlords controlling their patch of land with an army which, as a rule, includes drugged children. Each of the warlords has business links to a foreign company or corporation exploiting the mostly mining wealth in the region. This arrangement suits both parties: the corporations get mining rights without taxes and other complications, while the warlords get rich. The irony is that many of these minerals are used in high-tech products such as laptops and cell phones—in short: forget about the savage behavior of the local population, just remove the foreign high-tech companies from the equation and the whole edifice of ethnic warfare fuelled by old passions falls apart.

A further irony here is that in among the predominant exploiters are Rwandan Tutsis, victims of the horrifying genocide over fifteen years ago. In 2008, the Rwanda government presented numerous documents which demonstrated the complicity of President Mitterrand and his administration in the genocide of the Tutsis: France had supported the Hutu plan for the takeover, to the point of arming their units, in order to regain influence in this part of Africa at the expense of the

---

ago, the military regime was saved with the discreet help of Chinese security advisers) in exchange for the freedom to exploit the vast natural resources.

Anglophone Tutsis. France's outright dismissal of the accusations as totally unfounded was, to say the least, itself somewhat flimsy. Bringing Mitterrand to The Hague Tribunal, even if posthumously, would have been a just act. The furthest the Western legal system went in this direction was with the arrest of Pinochet, who was already seen as a rogue statesman; but an indictment of Mitterrand would have crossed a fateful line, in for the first time bringing to trial a leading Western politician who had pretended to act as protector of freedom, democracy, and human rights. The lesson of such a trial would thus have been the complicity of the Western liberal powers in what the media present as the explosion of Third World barbarism.

There certainly is a great deal of darkness in the dense Congolese jungle—but its causes lie elsewhere, in the bright executive offices of our banks and high-tech companies. In order to truly awaken from the capitalist "dogmatic dream" (as Kant would have put it) and recognize this other true heart of darkness, we should re-apply to our situation Brecht's old quip from his *Beggars' Opera*: "What is the robbing of a bank compared to the founding of a bank?" What is the stealing of a couple of thousand of dollars, for which one is sent to prison, compared to the kind of financial speculation that deprives tens of millions of their homes and savings, but whose perpetrators are then rewarded with state help of sublime grandeur? What is a local Congolese warlord compared to an enlightened and ecologically sensitive Western CEO? Maybe José Saramago was right when, in a recent newspaper column, he proposed treating the big bank managers and others responsible for the global financial meltdown as perpetrators of crimes against humanity whose right place is before The Hague Tribunal. Perhaps one should not treat this proposal merely as a poetic exaggeration in the style of Jonathan Swift, but rather take it absolutely seriously.

Europe : US = Kant : Hegel?

According to postmodern wisdom, there is no objective reality: reality consists of the multiple stories we tell ourselves about ourselves. In these terms then, was not the recent war in Georgia very postmodern? There were indeed several stories in play: the story of a small heroic democratic state defending itself against the imperialist ambitions of post-Soviet Russia; of the US attempt to encircle Russia with military bases; of the struggle for the control of oil resources; and the list could go on. However, rather than get lost in this maze of competing stories, we might focus instead on that missing element whose lack triggers the ongoing profusion of political storytelling.

To know a society is not only to know its explicit rules—one needs also to know *how to apply these rules*: when to use or not use them; when to violate them; when to decline a choice which has been offered; when we are effectively obliged to do something, but have to pretend that we are doing it as a free choice. This is the paradox of the offer-meant-to-be-refused: it is customary to refuse such an offer, and anyone who accepts it commits a vulgar blunder. When I am invited to an expensive restaurant by a rich uncle, we both know that he will cover the bill, but nonetheless I have to insist a little bit that we share it—imagine my surprise if he were simply to say: "OK then, you pay it!" A similar misunderstanding happened when, during the 1980s, South Korea was hit by a series of natural disasters, and North Korea offered a large quantity of grain as humanitarian aid. Although there were no food shortages in South Korea, it accepted the offer in order not to appear to be rejecting the North's outstretched hand. The North, however, *did* lack food, and had made the offer as a "gesture to be rejected," but now had to act upon it—a country which was itself suffering from shortages thus shipped grain to a country with abundant food reserves; a nice case of politeness going astray.

The problem during the chaotic post-Soviet years of Yeltsin's rule in Russia could also be located at this level: although the legal rules were known (and were largely the same as those in the Soviet Union), what disintegrated was the complex network of implicit unwritten rules which had sustained the entire social edifice. In the former regime, if, say, you had wanted to get better hospital treatment, or a new apartment, if you had a complaint against authorities, or were summoned to a court, if you wanted your child to be accepted by a top school, or if a factory manager needed raw materials not delivered on time by the state-contractors, and so on and so forth, everyone knew what to do, who to address, who to bribe, what you could do and what you couldn't. With the collapse of Soviet power, one of the most frustrating aspects of daily existence was that these unwritten rules became blurred: people simply did not know what to do, how to react, how they were to relate to explicit legal regulations, what they could ignore, where bribery worked. (One of the functions of the rise in organized crime was to provide a kind of *ersatz*-legality: if you owned a small business and a customer owed you money, you turned to your mafia-protector who dealt with the problem, since the state legal system was inefficient.) The stabilization under Putin's reign mostly amounted to restoring the transparency of such unwritten rules: now, again, people more or less know how to act and react in the complex web of social interactions.

In international politics, we have not yet reached this stage. Back in the 1990s, a silent pact regulated the relationship between the Western powers and Russia: Western states treated Russia as a great power on condition that it did not actually behave like one. But of course, the problem arises when the one to whom the offer-to-be-rejected is made actually accepts it. What if Russia really started to act like a great power? A situation like this is properly catastrophic, since it threatens to disintegrate the entire existing framework of relations — and precisely something like this happened in Georgia. Tired of being treated only *as if* it were a superpower, Russia acted like one. How did it come to this? The "American century" is over and we are entering a period characterized by the formation of multiple centers of global capitalism: the US, Europe, China, possibly Latin America, each of them representing capitalism with a specific local twist: the US for neoliberalism; Europe for what remains of the Welfare State; China for "Eastern Values" and authoritarian capitalism; Latin America for populist capitalism. After the failure of the US to impose itself as the sole superpower ("the universal policeman"), there is now a need to establish rules of interaction between these local centers in case of conflicting interests.

This is why the present situation is potentially more dangerous than it may appear. During the Cold War, the rules of international behavior were clear, guaranteed by the MAD-ness (Mutually Assured Destruction) of the superpowers. When the Soviet Union violated these unwritten rules by invading Afghanistan, it paid dearly for the infringement — the war in Afghanistan was the beginning of the end for the regime. Today, the old and new superpowers are testing each other out, trying to impose their own versions of the global rules, experimenting with them through proxies in the form of smaller nations and states. Karl Popper once praised the scientific testing of hypotheses, remarking that, in this way, we allow our hypotheses to die instead of us. In today's political testing process, however, it is the small nations that suffer — Georgians in particular are paying the price. Although the official justifications are highly moral in tone (invoking human rights and freedom, etc.), the nature of the game is clear.

In their *The War Over Iraq*, William Kristol and Lawrence F. Kaplan write:

> The mission begins in Baghdad, but it does not end there . . . We stand at the cusp of a new historical era . . . This is a decisive moment . . . It is so clearly about more than Iraq. It is about more even than the future of the Middle East and the war on terror. It is about what sort of role the United States intends to play in the twenty-first century.[37]

One cannot but agree: it was indeed the future of the international community that was at stake—what new rules would regulate it, what the new world order would look like. And, with hindsight, we can now clearly see that the second Iraq war was a sign of US failure, of its inability to play the role of globocop. Arguably, the main reason for this came down to "bad manners": the US simply indulged in too many acts of "impoliteness" to be considered qualified for their chosen role. For example, they put pressure on other states (like Serbia) to deliver their suspected war criminals to The Hague Tribunal, while brutally rejecting the very idea that it should also cover US citizens. In many similar cases, the US tried to enforce its domination without respecting the sovereignty of others.

Justifying its intervention in Georgia, Russia deftly played on these US inconsistencies: if the US was allowed to intervene in Kosovo to enforce its independence, protected by a large US military base, why should Russia not do the same in South Ossetia, which is, after all, much closer to Russian territory than Kosovo is to the US? If the whole world was dismayed when the NATO peacekeepers in Srebrenica escaped just as the Bosnian population was threatened by the Serbs, why not allow Russia to do exactly what the West failed to do, and intervene to protect its peacekeepers and those they were guarding? When the US and other Western states condemned Russia's "excessive" response to Georgian military intervention, we could be forgiven for being reminded of the "shock and awe" bombing of Iraq which, to put it mildly, was likewise somewhat excessive.

If anything, the lesson of the Georgian conflict is that, alongside the failure of the US to act as a global policeman, we have to admit also the

---

37   Lawrence F. Kaplan and William Kristol, *The War Over Iraq*, Lanham: Encounter Books 2003, p. 5.

failure of the new network of superpowers to do the same. Not only are they unfit to keep small "rogue nations" under control, they even increasingly solicit aggressive behavior from these states in order to fight their own proxy wars. The torch of peacekeeping should be passed on to a wider circle: it is time for smaller countries around the globe to unite in their efforts to restrain the big powers and set limits to their perilous games.

One polite way to deal with the Georgian crisis would have been for Russia and Georgia to agree that while the latter has full sovereignty over its territory, it would not fully assert that sovereignty over Abkhazia and South Ossetia. It could even be claimed that *de facto* such an agreement already was implicitly in place, and that Russia saw the Georgian intervention in South Ossetia as a violation of this. The question, of course, is whether Georgia was acting entirely under its own steam. However, the puzzle as to why the Georgians decided to risk a military intervention is not really worth pursuing—what matters is that the consequences of this "excess" confronted us with the truth of the situation.

It is, clearly, time that the superpowers were taught some manners—but who is capable of doing this? Obviously, only a transnational entity could manage such a task—was it not already Kant who, more than two hundred years ago, saw the need for a trans-nation-state legal order grounded in the rise of a global society? "Since the narrower or wider community of the peoples of the earth has developed so far that a violation of rights in one place is felt throughout the world, the idea of a law of world citizenship is no high-flown or exaggerated notion."[38] This, however, brings us to what is arguably the "principal contradiction" of the New World Order: the structural impossibility of finding a global political order which might correspond to the global capitalist economy. What if, for structural reasons and not merely due to empirical limitations, a worldwide democracy or a representative world government is impossible? The structural problem (the antinomy) of global capitalism resides in the impossibility (and, simultaneously, the necessity) of a socio-political order that would match it: the global market economy cannot be directly organized as a global liberal democracy with worldwide elections, and so on. In politics, the "repressed" of the economy returns in the form of archaic fixations, particular substantial (ethnic, religious, cultural) identities. This embarrassing supplement is

---

38   Quoted from http://www.mtholyoke.edu.

the condition of both the possibility and the impossibility of the global economy, and this tension defines our predicament today: the free circulation of commodities across the globe, accompanied by growing divisions in the social sphere proper.

There are today two models for such a trans-nation-state organism: the European Union and the United States. Their duality weirdly (or not so weirdly . . .) evokes sexual difference: the "feminine" EU and the "masculine" US, or, in philosophical terms, Kant and Hegel. The opposition between Kant and Hegel gained a new relevance in the post-9/11 era, when Europe began to be perceived as representing a negotiated transstate unity which resembles Kantian perpetual peace (amongst others, Habermas, the quasi-official philosopher of the European Union, effectively refers to this Kantian idea), while the US heroically protects both itself *and* Europe by acting as a nation-state in conflict with others and dealing with its enemies. Robert Kagan describes the difference between the EU and the US in the following terms:

> Europe is turning away from power, or to put it a little differently, it is moving beyond power into a self-contained world of laws and rules and transnational negotiation and cooperation. It is entering a post-historical paradise of peace and relative prosperity, the realization of Kant's "Perpetual Peace." The United States, meanwhile, remains mired in history, exercising power in the anarchic Hobbesian world where international laws and rules are unreliable and where true security and the defense and promotion of a liberal order still depend on the possession and use of military might . . . Perhaps it is not just coincidence that the amazing progress toward European integration in recent years has been accompanied not by the emergence of a European superpower but, on the contrary, by a diminishing of European military capabilities relative to the United States. Turning Europe into a global superpower capable of balancing the power of the United States may have been one of the original selling points of the European Union—an independent European foreign and defense policy was supposed to be one of the most important by-products of European integration. But, in truth, the ambition for European "power" is something of an anachronism. It is an atavistic impulse, inconsistent with the ideals of postmodern Europe, whose very existence depends on the rejection of power politics . . . Europe's new Kantian order could flourish only under the umbrella of American power exercised according to the rules of the old Hobbesian order. American power made it possible for Europeans to believe that power was no longer important . . . Most Europeans do not see the great paradox: that their passage into post-history has depended

on the United States not making the same passage. Because Europe has neither the will nor the ability to guard its own paradise and keep it from being overrun, spiritually as well as physically, by a world that has yet to accept the rule of "moral consciousness," it has become dependent on America's willingness to use its military might to deter or defeat those around the world who still believe in power politics.[39]

Kagan here relies heavily on Robert Cooper,[40] who accounted for the post–Cold War world in terms of divisions between "pre-modern" parts of the world which lack fully functioning states, "modern" nation-states concerned with territorial sovereignty and national interests, and the "postmodern" areas, in which foreign and domestic policy are inextricably intertwined, tools of governance are shared, and security is no longer based on control over territory or the balance of power. As Kagan explains:

> If the postmodern world does not protect itself, it can be destroyed. But how does Europe protect itself without discarding the very ideals and principles that undergird its pacific system? . . . "The challenge to the postmodern world," Cooper argues, "is to get used to the idea of double standards." Among themselves, Europeans may "operate on the basis of laws and open cooperative security." But when dealing with the world outside Europe, "we need to revert to the rougher methods of an earlier era—force, pre-emptive attack, deception, whatever is necessary." . . . What this means is that although the United States has played the critical role in bringing Europe into this Kantian paradise, and still plays a key role in making that paradise possible, it cannot enter this paradise itself. It mans the walls but cannot walk through the gate. The United States, with all its vast power, remains stuck in history, left to deal with the Saddams and the ayatollahs, the Kim Jong Ils and the Jiang Zemins, leaving the happy benefits to others . . . The problem is that the United States must sometimes play by the rules of a Hobbesian world, even though in doing so it violates European norms. It must refuse to abide by certain international conventions that may constrain its ability to fight effectively in Robert Cooper's jungle . . . American power, even employed under a double standard, may be the best means of advancing human progress—and perhaps the only means. Instead, many Europeans

---

39   Robert Kagan, "Power and Weakness: Why the United States and Europe See the World Differently," *Policy Review*, June–July 2002, p. 7.
40   See Robert Cooper, *The Breaking of Nations: Order and Chaos in the Twenty-first Century*, Atlantic Books 2007.

today have come to consider the United States itself to be the outlaw, a rogue colossus.[41]

This is why, in the new global order, we no longer have wars in the old sense of a regulated conflict between sovereign states in which certain rules apply (humane treatment of prisoners, prohibition of certain weapons, etc.). What remains are "ethnic-religious conflicts" which violate the rules of universal human rights; they do not count as wars proper, and call for the "humanitarian" intervention of the Western powers — even more so in the case of direct attacks on the US or other representatives of the new global order, where, again, we do not have wars proper, but merely "unlawful combatants" criminally resisting the forces of universal order. Here, one cannot even imagine a neutral humanitarian organization like the Red Cross mediating between the warring parties, organizing the exchange of prisoners, and so on: one side in the conflict (the US-dominated global force) already assumes the role of the Red Cross — it does not perceive itself as one of the warring sides, but as a mediating agent of peace and global order crushing particular rebellions and, simultaneously, providing humanitarian aid to "local populations."

There is a moment of truth in this description — suffice it to mention the surprising correlation between European unification and its loss of global military-political power; this loss was triumphantly displayed apropos the post-Yugoslav crisis, when Europe was not able to mediate a peace in its own backyard.[42] There is thus real hypocrisy in the European attitude of sticking to high moral principles while silently counting on the US to do the dirty work for the sake of its own stability.[43] Pascal Bruckner was right to detect in this aspect of the tension between the US and Europe yet another example of the Hegelian opposition between the inactive Beautiful Soul and the acting Consciousness ready to dirty its hands:

---

41   Kagan, "Power and Weakness," p. 27.
42   If, however, the European Union is more and more an impotent trans-state confederacy in need of US protection, why is the US so obviously ill at ease with it? See the convincing suggestions that the US financially supported those forces in Ireland which organized the campaign for the No to the new European treaty.
43   On the other hand, one should not forget that Europe is quite well versed in practicing double standards when this suits its interests: recall only the aforementioned role of Mitterrand's France in Rwanda. And is not Japan, arguably the first "postmodern" society, an even clearer case of relying on US military power for its security (which provoked such fury from defenders of national pride like Yukio Mishima)?

Europe has history, America is history, it is still animated by an eschatological tension directed towards the future . . . America generally begins with making mistakes, sometimes criminal ones, and then goes on to correct them. Europe makes no mistakes because it endeavors nothing. With Europe, prudence is no longer what it was for the Ancients, the art to orient oneself in an uncertain history, but the ultimate end of political action.[44]

When Bruckner writes that "America is more vulnerable than it believes, and Europe less weak than it thinks,"[45] one should be careful to note the asymmetry in this opposition: *believing* versus *thinking (i.e., knowing)*. Excessive self-confidence is a matter of belief, low self-confidence is a matter of knowledge: the US believes in itself too much, Europe does not know its true strength. This duality corresponds to the couplet action versus reflection: the US, believing in itself, acts; Europe remains inactive, endlessly questioning its weakness. To put it in Hegelese, the "truth" is here on the side of the acting Consciousness (the US).

There are, however, a series of distortions and lacunae in Kagan's and Cooper's "realistic" global picture. There is, first, the obvious fact that the "non-existing state" in "pre-modern" nations is not a *sui generis* phenomenon, the result of their (economic, social, cultural) backwardness which prevents them from finding a place in today's global world. On the contrary, this "regression" to a *de facto* pre- or sub-state is the very result of their integration into the global market and concomitant political struggles—suffice it to recall cases like Congo or Afghanistan. In other words, pre-modern sub-states are not atavistic remainders, but rather integral parts of the "postmodern" global constellation.

Then there is the no less obvious fact that the US is split between postmodernity and the "modern" nation-state in a much more complex manner than described by Kagan. One is almost tempted to say that, while Europe is "postmodern" in international relations, each European state internally remains much more "modern" than the US, while the latter, acting as a "modern" nation-state in international relations, is much more "postmodern" in its inner social, economic, and cultural organization (multiculturalism and the weakening sense of national unity, the ideology of hedonism, and so forth). With regard to its military interventions, the US oscillates between the postmodern (post-nation-state)

44   Pascal Bruckner, *La Tyrannie de la pénitence*, Paris: Grasset 2006, pp. 221–2.
45   Ibid., p. 233.

non-heroic mode (a professional army, outsourcing defense, Colin Powell's doctrine of "no casualties on our side," all battles fought outside one's own state territory—thus the shock of 9/11) and the more traditional nation-state heroic mode (soldiers called to enlist and sacrifice themselves for their country, casualties accepted as part of the cost of war). The further paradox here is that proponents of the US as a nation-state are much more isolationist (Pat Buchanan), while post-nation-state globalists are interventionists. The US as a "nation-state" is inscribed in the global order, it is not a nation-state like others, but rather a *global* nation-state, a nation-state with a global role. Which is why the US is a "rogue state" in two different modes: with relation to the other developed countries, and with regard to the pre-modern, "true" rogue states. In both cases it is an exception, but in each case in a different manner. With regard to the Kantian-inspired European Union, it takes upon itself the "rogue" character (military confrontations, double standards . . .); that is, it plays the (dubious) ethical hero who takes upon himself the necessary dirty tasks in order to protect "civilized" space; the "civilized" postmodern states can then hypocritically criticize the US while silently counting on its protection. With regard to the "ordinary" rogue states, the US is their self-sublating universalization: the "universal" rogue state which, as such, imposes and sustains global law and order. We have thus two series of states: rogue states and civilized states, with the US as the doubly-inscribed element, the rogue state among the civilized and the civilized state among the rogues.

Furthermore, the idea of a United States practicing double standards, and heroically doing the heavy lifting for a Europe luxuriating in its high principles, is misleading: what makes the US so annoying for Europeans is not its pragmatic politics and readiness to do the ugly but necessary work, but the fact that it combines its obvious practice of double standards with an excessive moralization of its politics. The US reproach to Europe is not primarily that it clings to an idealistic peace-moralism out of touch with the brutal reality of world politics, but, on the contrary, that it is all too pragmatic in accommodating itself to fundamentalist threats and human rights violations around the world. Recall how, prior to the second Iraq war, the US criticized Europe not for its idealism, but for its pragmatic opportunism and blindness to the threats lurking around the corner: the metaphor often evoked was that Europe was behaving like Chamberlain in Munich in 1938, deluding himself that a genuine peace treaty was possible with the Nazis—no wonder Rumsfeld characterized

Europe's unreadiness to participate in the attack on Iraq as being "beneath contempt."

There is also the problem of the newly emerging powers (China, India, Russia, Latin America, etc.), signaling the shift towards a polycentric world: where do they fit into the triad of pre-modern/modern/postmodern states? And, when contemporary conflicts risk escalating into a total catastrophe, up to and including the self-destruction of humanity, are we not obliged to redefine what the properly heroic thing to do might be? Can we still conceive of heroism as the simple attitude of risking-it-all for our (democratic) Cause? This brings us to the final feature: what exactly is the conflict in which the US is heroically ready to participate, in defense of the weak "postmodern" states? The struggle against a conglomerate of religious fundamentalists and corrupt dictators? Is *this* the true struggle? When Madeleine Albright defined the US as "the indispensable nation which doesn't need any counterbalance, because it balances itself,"[46] she was being truly fatuous: this self-aggrandizing Hegelian-sounding definition is simply wrong—the US is precisely *not* able to balance itself, for it has to be reminded of its limitations again and again by some external counter-force.

No wonder that Brian de Palma's *Redacted* was boycotted by the US public: it portrays rape and murder as part of the US army's obscene subculture, a form of "group solidarity" in collective transgression. The supreme irony is that the gang rape incident which the film stages happened in the summer of 2006 in Samara—and the film makes a reference to the "Appointment in Samara" story, nicely left half untold. This legend was retold by W. Somerset Maugham: a servant on an errand in the busy market of Baghdad meets Death; terrified by its gaze, he runs home to his master and asks for a horse, so that he can ride all day and reach Samara, where Death will not find him, in the evening. The good master not only provides the servant with a horse, but goes to the market himself, looking for Death to reproach it for scaring his faithful servant. Death replies: "But I didn't want to scare your servant. I was just surprised at what was he doing here when I have an appointment in Samara tonight . . ." What if the message of this story is not that a man's demise is impossible to avoid, that trying to twist free of it will only tighten its grip, but rather the exact opposite, namely that if one accepts fate as inevitable then one can break its grasp?

---

46   Quoted from ibid., p. 229.

It was foretold to Oedipus's parents that their son would kill his father and marry his mother, but the very steps they took to avoid this fate (exposing him to death in a deep forest) ensured that the prophecy would be fulfilled—without their attempt to avoid fate, fate could not have realized itself. Is this not a clear parable of the fate of the US intervention in Iraq? The US saw the signs of the fundamentalist threat, intervened to prevent it, and thereby massively strengthened it. Would it not have been much more effective to accept the threat, ignore it, and thus break its grasp? Iraq is today regressing to a pre-state condition: state power cannot enforce law and order sufficiently to contain the war amongst fundamentalist militias, which are joining forces in gradually destroying one of the positive legacies of Saddam's regime, the existence of a large, secular and well-educated middle class. The saddest news from Iraq tells the story of a massive brain-drain: as a result of religious fundamentalists' attacks on schools and hospitals, the educated middle classes are leaving the country, thus depriving it of a key element of a functioning liberal democracy.

The message of incidents like these is clear: the US is an empire in decline. Its growing negative trade balance suggests it is an unproductive predator nation: it has to suck up an influx of one billion dollars daily from other nations to pay for its consumption needs and is, as such, the universal Keynesian consumer that keeps the world economy running. This influx, which is effectively like the tithes paid to Rome in antiquity, relies on a complex economic mechanism: the US is "trusted" as the safe and stable center, so that all others, from the oil-producing Arab countries to Western Europe and Japan, and now even the Chinese, invest their surplus profits in the United States. Since this "trust" is primarily ideological and military, not economic, the problem for the US is how to justify its imperial role—it requires a permanent state of war, so it had to invent the "war on terror," offering itself as the universal protector of all other "normal" (non-"rogue") states. However, as Moishe Postone has astutely noted, the very attempt of the US to reassert itself as the global policeman is already a reaction to the emerging multi-centric global order:

> The American attempt to reassert control over the Gulf and its oil should be understood as preemptive, but in a different sense than the way the term was used by the ideologues of the Bush administration and their critics. The American action is, I would argue, a preemptive strike against the

possible emergence of Europe or China (or any other power) as a rival military as well as economic superpower, that is, as an imperial rival.[47]

With the US well advanced on the Oedipal path of self-destruction, no wonder that its hold over the global ideological imaginary is also approaching its end. Are recent trends in world cinema not an indicator of this gradual shift towards ideological multi-centricity? Is the hegemony of Hollywood not gradually breaking down with the global success of films from Western Europe, Latin America, and even China which, with films like *The Hero*, surpassed Hollywood on its home territory of grand historical spectacles and special effect action movies? Wim Wenders was right when, in a recent talk, he claimed that the time of the American Dream is approaching its end.

The standard complaint addressed by many American liberals to European Leftists was that they did not show enough sincere compassion for the victims of the 9/11 attacks. Along the same lines, the American response to European criticism is to suggest that it stems from envy and frustration at being reduced to a secondary role, from Europe's inability to accept its limitations and (relative) decline. What, however, if the truth is the exact opposite? What if these reactions are sustained by the unspoken but more fundamental reproach that Europeans do not really share the American Dream? This reproach is, in a way, fully justified. To put it bluntly, do we want to live in a world in which the only choice is between American-style civilization and the emerging Chinese authoritarian-capitalist form? If the answer is no, then the only alternative is Europe. After the American Dream, we need a European Dream.

But can Europe deliver such a thing? There are moments when one is so embarrassed by the public statements of the political leaders of one's own country that one is ashamed of being a citizen. This my reaction upon reading how the Slovene minister of foreign affairs reacted when, on Friday, June 13, 2008, the Irish voted "No" in the referendum on the Lisbon Treaty: he openly stated that European unification was too important to be left to ordinary people and their referendums. The elite sees further into the future and knows better—if they were to follow the majority, they would never achieve great transformations or realize ambitious visions. This obscene display of arrogance climaxed with the following statement: "If we were to wait for, I would say, some kind of

47   Moishe Postone, "History and Helplessness: Mass Mobilization and Contemporary Forms of Anticapitalism," *Public Culture*, 18:1, 2006.

popular initiative, the French and the Germans would today probably still be looking at each other through the cross-hairs on their guns." There is some significance in the fact that it was a diplomat from a small country who said this: the leaders of great powers cannot afford to display so directly the cynical obscenity of the reasoning which sustains their decisions — only otherwise ignored voices from small countries can do so with impunity.

The Irish "No" was a repetition of the 2005 French and Dutch "No" to the European Constitutional Treaty. Many interpretations of the Irish vote were offered, some of them contradicting each other: the "No" was an explosion of narrow European nationalism in fear of the globalization embodied by the US; alternatively, the US itself was behind the vote, since it fears the competition of a united Europe and prefers bilateral deals with weaker partners. However, such ad-hoc readings miss a deeper point: what the repetition means is that we are dealing not with an accident, a mere glitch, but with a form of long-term dissatisfaction which will persist for some time. A couple of weeks after the vote, we were able to see where the real problem lay: much more ominous than the "No" itself was the reaction of the European political elite. They had learnt nothing from the 2005 referenda — they simply did not get the message. At an EU leaders' meeting on June 19 in Brussels, after paying lip service to the duty to "respect" voters' decisions, they quickly showed their true face, treating the Irish government as a poor teacher who had failed to properly discipline or educate his retarded pupils. The Irish government was given a second chance: four extra months to correct its mistake and bring the voters back into line.

The Irish voters were not given a clear or fair choice, since the very terms of the referendum privileged the "Yes": the elite proposed a choice to the people which was effectively no choice at all — they were merely being called on to ratify the inevitable, the result of enlightened expertise. The media and the political elite presented the issue as a choice between knowledge and ignorance, between expertise and ideology, between post-political administration and old-fashioned political passions. However, the very fact that the "No" was not sustained by a coherent alternative political vision is the strongest possible condemnation of the political and mediatic elite: a monument to their inability to articulate, to translate into a political vision, the people's longings and dissatisfaction.

There was something uncanny about this referendum: its outcome was at the same time both expected and a surprise — as if we knew what would happen, but nonetheless somehow could not really believe that it would. The split reflected a much more threatening division among the voters: the majority (of the minority which bothered to vote at all) were against, although all parliamentary parties (with the exception of Sinn Féin) were emphatically for the Treaty. The same phenomenon was present in other countries, such as the neighboring UK, where, at the 2005 general election, Tony Blair was re-elected by a large majority even though opinion polls had cast him as the most hated person in the country. This gap between the explicit political choices of the voters and the same voters' dissatisfaction should trigger an alarm bell: it suggests that multi-party democracy fails to capture the gut feelings of the population, in other words that a vague resentment is accumulating which, in the absence of a proper democratic form of expression, can lead only to obscure "irrational" outbursts. When opinion polls deliver a message which directly undermines that given in an election, we have a clear case of a divided voter who, say, thinks that Tony Blair's policy is the only reasonable one, but nonetheless hates his guts.

The worst solution would be to dismiss such resistance as an expression of the ordinary voters' parochial stupidity, which merely requires better communication and explanation. Which brings us back to the unfortunate Slovene minister of foreign affairs. Not only is his quoted statement factually wrong: the great Franco-German conflicts were not caused by ordinary people's passions, they were decided by elites behind the backs of the people. It also gets wrong the role of elites: in a democracy, their role is not just to rule, but to convince the majority of the correctness of their policies, to enable people to recognize in the state's policy their own innermost strivings for justice, well-being, and so forth. In other words, if it is true that the majority "doesn't really know what it wants," that it needs an elite to guide it, then the elite has to do so in such a way that the majority recognizes itself in the message. The wager of democracy, as was once said, is that you cannot fool all the people all the time: yes, Hitler got to power democratically (although not quite . . .), but in the long term, in spite of all oscillations and confusions, the majority is still to be trusted. It is this wager that keeps democracy alive — if we drop it, we are no longer talking about democracy. The Irish vote could (and should) thus also be read as a properly political act of resistance against the growing trend towards post-politics, as a case of democratic resistance to the refusal of democracy (at least in the sense we understand it) on the part of the European elite.

The latter's utter contempt for the majority found expression in a curious but significant detail: even the Irish representative in Brussels publicly acknowledged that he had not read the full text of the Lisbon Treaty. In other words, voters were being offered a text which they were effectively not expected to know—they were supposed to trust blindly in the expertise of the Brussels elite. The tragicomedy of the European constitution thus increasingly resembles the situation in Franz Kafka's short story, "The Problem of Our Laws," about a country in which the laws are not generally known, since they are kept secret by the small group of nobles who rule the population—the people are governed by laws of which they are ignorant (and, here, more than ever, the basic metaphysical presupposition of the rule of law—ignorance is no excuse, one is guilty in the eyes of law even if one did not know the law—holds). In such a situation, the very existence of the laws is at most a matter of presumption—some decide that the laws they are trying to unravel may not even exist. The conclusion to be drawn from the story is this: since no subject knows the laws, since all are compelled to trust the interpretation of the laws proposed by the nobility, then in effect, if any law exists, it can only be whatever the nobles decide it is, for the sole visible and indubitable law imposed upon us is the will of the nobility. This is how the gap between law and power (extra-legal violence which sustains the rule of law) is (and has to be) inscribed into the legal edifice itself: as the unknowability at the heart of the law itself. Power cannot assert itself directly as naked violence: in order to function as power proper, it has to be sustained by the mystical aura of law, so that, when it violates (what appears to the subject as) its own explicit regulations, this violation is grounded in the mystical abyss of the unknowable/invisible Law.

Therein resides the lesson in the way the Brussels bureaucracy—our "nobility"—reacted to the Irish "No": Kafka's story describes not a pre-modern order of obscure authoritarianism, but the very core of the modern legal order. This is increasingly what our politics, with its "free democratic choices," is becoming: we are quite literally required to vote on (that is, confirm) complex texts which are beyond our reach. What Europe truly needs, on the contrary, is a short programmatic constitution clearly stating the principles of what "Europe" stands for as against other predominant social models (US neoliberalism, "Asian values" capitalism, and so on), perhaps—why not?—on the model of the US constitution.

And it is here that the European elites are miserably failing. If they were really ready to "respect" the voters' decisions, they would have to accept the persistent message of the people's distrust: the project of European unity, the way it is formulated now, is fundamentally flawed. What the voters are detecting is the lack of a true political vision beneath the expert clap-trap—their message is not anti-European, but amounts to a demand for *more* Europe.[48]

---

48   The confirmation that the Irish voters want another, deeper Euorpe came on October 2, 2009, when, in the repeated referendum, they voted a resounding Yes—the only problem is that this victory will enable the Brussels elite to ignore yet again the message of the first No and to go on as before.

3   Bargaining: The Return of the Critique of Political Economy

"Dare to win!"

Alain Badiou has described three distinct ways in which a revolutionary (that is, a radical emancipatory) movement might fail. First, of course, there is direct defeat: it is simply crushed by the enemy forces. Then, there is defeat in the victory itself: the movement triumphs over its enemy (temporarily, at least) only by taking over the latter's main agenda (by taking state power, either in the parliamentary-democratic form or in a direct identification of Party with State.) Finally, there is perhaps the most authentic, but also the most terrifying form of failure: guided by the correct instinct that every consolidation of the revolution into state power results in its betrayal, but unable to invent or impose a truly alternative social order, the revolutionary movement engages in a desperate strategy of protecting its purity through an "ultra-leftist" resort to destructive terror. Badiou aptly calls this last version the "sacrificial temptation of the void":

> One of the great Maoist slogans from the red years was "Dare to fight, dare to win." But we know that, if it is not easy to follow this slogan, if subjectivity is afraid not so much of fighting but of winning, it is because struggle exposes it to a simple failure (the attack didn't succeed), while victory exposes it to the most fearsome form of failure: the awareness that one has won in vain, that victory prepares repetition, restoration. That a revolution is never more than a between-two-States. It is from here that the sacrificial temptation of the void comes. The most fearsome enemy of the politics of emancipation is not repression by the established order. It is the interiority of nihilism, and the cruelty without limits which can accompany its void.[1]

---

1   Alain Badiou, *L'Hypothèse communiste*, Paris: Lignes 2009, p. 28.

What Badiou is effectively saying here is the exact opposite of Mao's "Dare to win!"—one *should* be afraid to win (to take power, to establish a new socio-political reality), because the lesson of the twentieth century is that victory ends either in restoration (return to the state-power logic) or an infernal cycle of self-destructive purification. This is why Badiou proposes replacing purification with subtraction: instead of "winning" (taking power) one maintains a distance towards state power, one creates spaces subtracted from State. This radical conclusion is based in Badiou's rejection of the standard "orthodox" twentieth-century Marxist view according to which "there is an 'objective' agent, inscribed into social reality, which carries the possibility of emancipation"; according to Badiou, therein resides the difference between the great revolutionary sequence of the twentieth century and our present time. Throughout the previous century,

> it was supposed that the politics of emancipation was not a pure idea, a will, a prescription, but was inscribed, almost programmed, in and by historical and social reality. A consequence of this conviction is that this objective agent has to be transformed into a subjective power, that this social entity has to become a subjective actor.[2]

The first thing one should note here is that the alternative Badiou presupposes—either a politics of emancipation inscribed into social reality, generated by the "objective" social process, or the purity of the communist Idea—is not exhaustive. Take Lukács's *History and Class Consciousness*—this is a work radically opposed to any kind of objectivism, or direct reference to "objective circumstances"; in other words, for Lukács, class struggle is the primordial fact, which means that every "objective" social fact is already "mediated" by struggling subjectivity (Lukács's key example: one does not wait for the "ripe" objective circumstances to make a revolution, circumstances become "ripe" for revolution through the political struggle itself). Although Lukács used the famous Hegelian couple In-itself/For-itself to describe the becoming-proletariat of the "empirical" working class as part of social reality, this does not mean that class consciousness arises out of the "objective" social process, that it is "inscribed, almost programmed, in and by historical and social reality": the very absence of class consciousness is already the outcome of the politico-ideological struggle. In other words, Lukács does not distinguish objective social

2   Ibid., p. 46.

reality from subjective political commitment — not because, for him, political subjectivization is determined by the "objective" social process, but
because there is no "objective social reality" which is not already mediated by political subjectivity.

This brings us to Badiou's dismissal of the critique of political economy:
since he conceives of the economy as a particular sphere of positive social
being, he excludes it as a possible site of a Truth-Event. However, once
we accept that the economy is always a *political* economy, a site of political
struggle — in other words that its de-politicization, its status as a neutral
sphere of "servicing the goods," is in itself always already the outcome of
a political struggle — then the prospect of a re-politicization of the economy, and thus of its re-assertion as the possible site of a Truth-Event, is
opened up. Badiou's exclusive opposition between the "corruptive" force
of economy and the purity of the communist Idea, as two incompatible
domains, introduces an almost Gnostic tone into his work: on the one
side, the noble *citoyen* struggling on behalf of the axiom of equality, on
the other, the "fallen" *bourgeois*, a miserable "human animal" striving for
profit and pleasure. The necessary outcome of such a gap is terror: it is
on account of the very purity of the communist Idea which motivates the
revolutionary process, of the lack of "mediation" between this Idea and
social reality, that the Idea can intervene into historical reality without
betraying its radical character only in the guise of self-destructive terror.
This "purity" of the communist Idea means that communism should not
serve as a predicate (designating a politics or ideology as "communist"):
the moment we use communism as a predicate, we engage in the inscription of communism into the positive order of being. And, as expected,
the ultimate culprit responsible for this short-circuit between the real of
a political Truth-Event and History in Marxism is "the Hegelian origins
of Marxism":

> For Hegel, the historical exposition of politics is effectively not an imagi-
> nary subjectivization, it is the real in person. The reason is that the crucial
> axiom of the dialectic as conceived by Hegel is that "the True is the becom-
> ing of itself," or, what amounts to the same, "Time is the being-here of
> the Notion." In this way, following Hegelian speculative reasoning, one is
> justified to think that the historical inscription, under the name of "commu-
> nism," of the revolutionary political sequences or of the disparate fragments
> of the collective emancipation, displays their truth, which resides in the
> progress according to the direction of History. The consequence of this
> latent subordination of truths to their historical sense is that one can "in

truth" speak about communist politics, communist parties or communist militants. But we can see how, today, we should avoid this adjectivization. In order to combat it, I had to assert many times that History does not exist, which is in accordance with my notion of truths, that is to say, that they do not have any direction, and, above all, the direction of a History. But, today, I have to render this verdict more precise. There is, for sure, no real of History, and it is therefore true, transcendentally true, that History cannot exist. The discontinuity of worlds is the law of appearance, and therefore of existence. However, what there is under the real condition of the organized political action, is the communist Idea, an operation linked to intellectual subjectivization, and which integrates at the individual level the real, the symbolic, and the ideological. We have to restitute this Idea by cutting its link with any predicative use. We have to save this Idea, but we also have to liberate the real from all immediate coalescence with it. Only the politics about which it would have been definitively absurd to say that they are communist can be retrieved by the communist Idea as the possible power of the becoming-Subject of individuals.[3]

To put it in the old-fashioned terms of the postmodernism debate, "History does not exist" means that there is no grand all-encompassing narrative guaranteeing the sense of history (either its meaning or direction). Badiou is here indeed close to Lyotard's postmodern thesis on the end of grand narratives: political interventions are always local, they intervene into a specific situation ("a world"). This, however, does not mean that we can simply renounce symbolic narratives and cling to the communist Idea in the real of its purity:

> If an Idea is, for an individual, the subjective operation by means of which a particular real truth is in an imaginary way projected into the symbolic movement of a History, then we can say that an Idea presents the truth as if it were a fact. Or: that the Idea presents certain facts as symbols of the real of the truth.[4]

What lurks beneath these descriptions is the good old Kantian notion of a necessary transcendental illusion: Truth is rare, elusive, fragile, it is an Event discernible only in its ambiguous traces, an Event whose actuality cannot be demonstrated by the analysis of historical reality, but is, rather, a kind of "regulative Idea." This is why "it has to be that, in the imaginary

---

3   Ibid., pp. 189–90.
4   Ibid., p. 193.

mode, the symbol comes to support the creative flight [*fuite*] of the real":[5] the pure communist Idea can become a material force, it can mobilize subjects in the service of fidelity, only if it is inscribed into a great historical narrative, projected onto historical reality, as part of the historical process. Badiou thus basically sustains the *necessity* of imaginary ideological illusion, that is, of an "illegitimate" transcendental short-circuit by means of which the fragile real is inscribed into the symbolic fiction and thus gains the consistency of a part of positive social reality. One could also say that the Idea of communism schematizes the Real of the political Event, providing it with a narrative coating and thereby making it a part of our experience of historical reality—another indication of Badiou's hidden Kantianism.

Badiou dismisses every History that goes beyond a particular World as an ideological fiction, and one should not miss the implication of his thesis that there is no general theory of History: it amounts to no less than the full abandonment of Marxist historical materialism. The irony here is that, while "creative" Marxists of the twentieth century advocated historical materialism without dialectical materialism (dismissing the latter as the regression of Marxism to a "materialist worldview," a new general ontology), Badiou aims for a dialectical materialism (or, more precisely, materialist dialectics) without historical materialism. There is no place in Badiou's theoretical edifice for historical materialism, which is neither an imaginary narrative of History nor a positive science of history as a domain of being (social reality), but the science of the real of history as well as the critique of political economy as the science of the real of capitalism.

A resuscitation of the "critique of political economy" is the *sine qua non* of contemporary communist politics. The "hard real" of the "logic of the capital" is what is missing in the historicist universe of Cultural Studies, not only at the level of content (the analysis and critique of political economy), but also at the more formal level of the difference between historicism and historicity proper. Moishe Postone is among those rare theorists who pursue the "critique of political economy," with his attempt to rethink the actuality of Marx in the conditions following the disintegration of the Communist regimes in 1990.[6]

---

5   Ibid., p. 200.
6   See Moishe Postone, "Rethinking Marx (in a Post-Marxist World)," available online at http://platypus1917.home.comcast.net.

In Defense of a Non-Marxist Marx

Although Postone is highly critical of Althusser, he, like the French philosopher, dismisses the early "humanist" Marx as deeply flawed, but posits the crucial "epistemological break" even later than Althusser does, locating it in the mid-1850s, with Marx's return to the "critique of political economy" through a renewed reading of Hegel's *Science of Logic*. It is only from this moment onwards that Marx effectively overcame his first formulation of "Marxism" (or what later became codified as the predominant form thereof) with its crude (even if superficially "dialecticized") dichotomy of "economic base" and legal and ideological "superstructure," and its naïve historicist evolutionism. The latter relied implicitly on the ahistorical absolutization of labor (the process of material production and reproduction of life) as the "key" to all other phenomena, and found its canonical expression in the "Indian Summer" text of the early Marx, the famous "Preface" to *A Contribution to the Critique of Political Economy* (1859).[7] After the "break," however, gone are all the Feuerbachian symmetrical reversals ("the dead rule over the living instead of . . ."), and gone too is the naïve opposition between the "real life process" and "mere speculation."[8] Postone's main reproach to "traditional" Marxist theory is that, at its heart, it relies on

a transhistorical—and commonsensical—understanding of labor as an activity mediating humans and nature that transforms matter in a goal-directed manner and is a condition of social life. Labor, so understood, is posited as the source of wealth in all societies and as that which underlies processes of social constitution; it constitutes what is universal and truly social. In capitalism, however, labor is hindered by particularistic and fragmenting relations from becoming fully realized. Emancipation, then, is realized in a social form where transhistorical "labor," freed from the fetters of the market and private property, has openly emerged as the regulating principle of society. (This notion, of

---

7   In this sense, one can say that after 1860 Marx was no longer a Marxist; although there is, of course, also a more refined reading of his famous statement "One thing is sure, that I am not a Marxist"—the original creator of a doctrine enters into a direct substantial relationship with it and thus cannot be its "follower": Christ was not a Christian, Hegel was not an Hegelian.

8   The Wikipedia text on Marx states as if it were self-evident that "Commodity fetishism is an example of what Engels called false consciousness, which is closely related to the understanding of ideology." But Marx *never* referred to commodity fetishism as ideology—for the simple reason that it is an "illusion" which is not part of any "ideological superstructure," but located in the very heart of the capitalist "economic" base.

course, is bound to that of socialist revolution as the "self-realization" of the proletariat.)[9]

Especially noteworthy is Postone's detailed analysis of how even the most critical "Western Marxists," who clearly saw the need to rethink Marxism in order to grasp twentieth-century capitalism, nonetheless retained its traditional core, the evolutionist-ahistorical notion of labor and productive process:

> in the face of historical developments such as the triumph of National Socialism, the victory of Stalinism, and the general increase of state control in the West, Max Horkheimer came to the conclusion in the 1930s that what earlier had characterized capitalism—the market and private property—no longer were its essential organizing principles . . . Horkheimer argued that the structural contradiction of capitalism had been overcome; society was now directly constituted by labor. Far from signifying emancipation, however, this development had led to an even greater degree of unfreedom in the form of a new technocratic form of domination. This, however, indicated, according to Horkheimer, that labor (which he continued to conceptualize in traditional, trans-historical terms) could not be considered the basis of emancipation but, rather, should be grasped as the source of technocratic domination. Capitalist society, in his analysis, no longer possessed a structural contradiction; it had become one-dimensional—a society governed by instrumental rationality without any possibility of fundamental critique and transformation.[10]

What this means is that the Heideggerian dialectic-of-Enlightenment topic of technocratic "instrumental reason," of domination grounded in the very notion of labor, of the post-political rule of labor ("administration of things"), and so on, should all be rejected as false names for the problem of how to think the failure of the Marxist revolutionary emancipatory project. Sharing with Marxism the premise that the post-capitalist society is "a social form where trans-historical 'labor,' freed from the fetters of the market and private property, has openly emerged as the regulating principle of society," the dialectic of Enlightenment merely reads it as a catastrophe rather than as emancipation: "You wanted to abolish capitalism and install the direct rule of labor? Then don't complain about totalitarianism—you got what you wanted!" This topic is therefore like

---

9   Postone, "Rethinking Marx."
10   Ibid.

a false screen, an all-too-easy direct solution, which obfuscates the true problem: the new *social* forms of domination-unfreedom in modern capitalism, but also in "totalitarianisms"—"totalitarianism" is *not* the rule of "instrumental reason." One should correct Postone himself here when he writes that

> the rise and fall of the USSR was intrinsically related to the rise and fall of state-centric capitalism. The historical transformations of recent decades suggest that the Soviet Union was very much part of a larger historical configuration of the capitalist social formation, however great the hostility between the USSR and Western capitalist countries had been.[11]

One popular intellectual parlor game among converted ex-Leftists is to identify the historical factors which paved the way for the totalitarianisms of the twentieth century: Marx? The Jacobins? Rousseau? Christianity? Plato ("from Plato to NATO . . .")? In their *Dialectic of Enlightenment*, Adorno and Horkheimer provide the most radical (self-relating) answer to this question, identifying the moment at which things took a wrong turn with the emergence of humanity, of human civilization, itself: already in "primitive" magic one can recognize the elementary contours of the "instrumental reason" which culminates in the totalitarianisms of the twentieth century. But one should be precise here and insist on the predicate "capitalist": it is not that capitalism and communism are "metaphysically the same," both expressions of instrumental reason, of the rule of labor, and so on; it is rather that, in the concrete totality of today's global society, capitalism is the determining factor, so that even its historically specific negation in "Really Existing Socialism" is part of the properly capitalist dynamic. That is to say, whence comes the Stalinist drive-to-expand, the incessant push to increase productivity, to further "develop" the scope and quality of production? Here we should correct Heidegger: it comes not from some general will-to-power or will-to-technological-domination, but from the inherent structure of capitalist reproduction which can survive only through its incessant expansion and for which this ever-expanding reproduction, not some final state, is itself the only true goal of the entire movement. When Marx describes the capitalist dynamic of expansive reproduction, he locates the roots of the very "progressivism" to which he himself often falls prey (such as when he defines communism as the

---

11   Moishe Postone, "History and Helplessness: Mass Mobilization and Contemporary Forms of Anticapitalism," *Public Culture*, 18: 1, 2006, available online at http://publicculture.org.

society in which the endless development of human potential will become an end-in-itself).

In what, then, does Marx's "epistemological break," which begins with the *Grundrisse* manuscripts and finds its ultimate expression in *Capital*, consist? Let us compare the starting point of *Capital* with the starting point of Marx's most-detailed presentation of his earlier view, in the first part of *The German Ideology*. In what is presented as a self-evident reference to "real life-process" as opposed to ideological phantasmagorias, ahistorical ideology reigns at its purest:

> The premises from which we begin are not arbitrary ones, not dogmas, but real premises from which abstraction can only be made in the imagination. They are the real individuals, their activity and the material conditions under which they live, both those which they find already existing and those produced by their activity. These premises can thus be verified in a purely empirical way . . . Men can be distinguished from animals by consciousness, by religion or anything else you like. They themselves begin to distinguish themselves from animals as soon as they begin to produce their means of subsistence, a step which is conditioned by their physical organization. By producing their means of subsistence men are indirectly producing their actual material life.[12]

This materialist approach is then aggressively opposed to idealist mystification:

> In direct contrast to German philosophy which descends from heaven to earth, here we ascend from earth to heaven. That is to say, we do not set out from what men say, imagine, conceive, nor from men as narrated, thought of, imagined, conceived, in order to arrive at men in the flesh. We set out from real, active men, and on the basis of their real life-process we demonstrate the development of the ideological reflexes and echoes of this life-process. The phantoms formed in the human brain are also, necessarily, sublimates of their material life-process, which is empirically verifiable and bound to material premises. Morality, religion, metaphysics, all the rest of ideology and their corresponding forms of consciousness, thus no longer retain the semblance of independence. They have no history, no development; but men, developing their material production and their material intercourse, alter, along with this their real existence,

---

12   Karl Marx and Friedrich Engels, *The German Ideology*, New York: International Publishers 1970, p. 42.

their thinking and the products of their thinking. Life is not determined by consciousness, but consciousness by life.[13]

This attitude culminates in a hilariously aggressive comparison: philosophy is seen as having the same relationship to the study of real life as masturbation has to the real sexual act. Here, however, problems begin: what Marx discovered with his problematic of "commodity fetishism" is a phantasmagoria or illusion which cannot simply be dismissed as a secondary reflection, because it is operative at the very heart of the "real production process." Note the very beginning of the subchapter on commodity fetishism in *Capital*: "A commodity appears, at first sight, a very trivial thing, and easily understood. Its analysis shows that it is, in reality, a very queer thing, abounding in metaphysical subtleties and theological niceties."[14] Marx does not claim, in the supposedly "Marxist" manner of *The German Ideology*, that critical analysis should demonstrate how a commodity—what appears a mysterious theological entity—emerged out of the "ordinary" real life-process; he claims, on the contrary, that the task of critical analysis is to unearth the "metaphysical subtleties and theological niceties" in what appears at first sight just an ordinary object. Commodity fetishism (our belief that commodities are magical objects, endowed with inherent metaphysical powers) is not located in our minds, in the way we (mis)perceive reality, but in our social reality itself.[15] As Kojin Karatani has perceptively noted, the circle is thereby closed: if Marx had started with the premise that the critique of religion is the beginning of all critique, and then went on to the critique of philosophy, of the state, and so forth, ending with the critique of political economy, this last brought him back to the starting point, to the "religious" metaphysical moment at work at the very heart of the most "earthly" economic activity. It is against the background of this shift that one should read the beginning of Volume I of *Capital*:

"The wealth of those societies in which the capitalist mode of production prevails, *presents itself* as 'an immense accumulation,' its unit being a

---

13   Ibid., p. 47.

14   Karl Marx, *Capital: A Critique of Political Economy, Volume One*, Chicago: Charles H. Kerr & Company, p. 81.

15   Note also the strict homology with Lacan's notion of fantasy as constitutive of every "real" sexual act: for Lacan, our "normal" sexual act precisely *is* an act of "masturbation with a real partner," that is, in it, we do not relate to the real Other, but to the Other reduced to a fantasy-object—we desire the Other insofar as s/he fits the fantasy-coordinates which structure our desire.

single commodity. Our investigation must therefore begin with the analysis of a commodity."[16]

Marx then moves on to the double nature of a commodity (use-value
and exchange-value, etc.), gradually unveiling the complex synchronous
network of capitalist society. Even here, however, there are occasional
regressions back to his earlier "Marxism," most explicitly (as noted by
some perspicuous critics) in the deceptively commonsensical definitions
of labor such as are given at the beginning of Chapter 7 of *Capital*:

> The labour-process, resolved as above into its simple elementary factors,
> is human action with a view to the production of use-values, appropriation
> of natural substances to human requirements; it is the necessary condi-
> tion for effecting exchange of matter between man and Nature; it is the
> everlasting Nature-imposed condition of human existence, and there-
> fore is independent of every social phase of that existence, or rather, is
> common to every such phase. It was, therefore, not necessary to represent
> our labourer in connection with other labourers; man and his labour on
> one side, Nature and its materials on the other, sufficed. As the taste of the
> porridge does not tell you who grew the oats, no more does this simple
> process tell you of itself what are the social conditions under which it is
> taking place, whether under the slave-owner's brutal lash, or the anxious
> eye of the capitalist, whether Cincinnatus carries it on in tilling his modest
> farm or a savage in killing wild animals with stones.[17]

Something is wrong with the process of abstraction here: "It was, therefore, not necessary to represent our labourer in connection with other
labourers; man and his labour on one side, Nature and its materials on
the other, sufficed." Really? Is not *every* production process by definition social? If we want to grasp the labor process in general, should
we not link it to "society *in general*"? Perhaps the key to what is correct
and what is mistaken in Marx's *Capital* resides in the relationship
between two "wrong" abstractions: from use-value to exchange-value,
and from social production to asocial labor. The abstraction of labor
into an asocial form is ideological in the strict sense: it misrecognizes its
own socio-historical conditions: it is only with capitalist society that the
Robinsonian category of abstract labor as asocial emerges. This abstraction is not an innocent conceptual mistake, but has a crucial social
content: it directly grounds the technocratic strain in Marx's vision of

16   Marx, *Capital, Volume One*, p. 41.
17   Ibid., pp. 204–5.

communism as a society in which the production process is dominated by the "general intellect."[18]

Perhaps the clearest example of the gap that separates *Capital* from *The German Ideology* occurs apropos money. In *Capital*, Marx analyses money in three stages: he begins with the development of the value-form, that is with the analysis of the formal determinations of value as a relationship between commodities; only then, after the concept of money is deployed "in itself," does he move on to money in the exchange process, that is to the activity of commodity owners. Finally, he presents the three functions of money: as measure of value, as means of circulation, and as actual money (which, again, functions in three ways: as treasure, payment means, and world money). The inner logic of the three functions of money is that of the Lacanian triad of the Imaginary, Symbolic, and Real: Marx begins with "ideal" money (to measure the value of a commodity, one does not need money, it is enough to imagine a certain sum of money which expresses the value of the commodity in question); he then passes to symbolic money (as a means of circulation, i.e., in order to buy and sell, we do not need money with real value [gold], since its representatives [banknotes] are good enough); but for treasure and so forth we need real money. The contrast with the methodology of *The German Ideology* could not be clearer: Marx does not begin with "real, active men" and "their real life-process," but with the

---

18   See the discussion of the *Grundrisse* and the notion of the "general intellect" in my *In Defense of Lost Causes*, pp. 354 ff. I shall merely add here that an often neglected feature is that the entire discussion of the "general intellect" from the *Grundrisse* belongs to an unpublished fragmentary manuscript—it is an experimental line of development which Marx immediately afterwards discarded, since he quickly saw that it is ultimately incompatible with his new starting point, the analysis of commodities, which focuses on commodity as a social phenomenon: "That new beginning was the category of the commodity. In his later works, Marx's analysis is not of commodities as they may exist in many societies, nor is it of a hypothetical pre-capitalist stage of 'simple commodity production.' Rather, his analysis is of the commodity as it exists in capitalist society. Marx now analyzed the commodity not merely as an object, but as the historically specific, most fundamental form of social relations that characterize that society . . . On this basis Marx proceeded to critically analyze theories that project onto history or society in general, categories that, according to him, are valid only for the capitalist epoch. This critique also holds implicitly for Marx's own earlier writings with their trans-historical projections, such as the notion that class struggle has been at the heart of all of history, for example, or the notion of an intrinsic logic to all of history or, of course, the notion that labor is the major constituting element of social life . . . Marx took the term 'commodity' and used it to designate a historically specific form of social relations, one constituted as a structured form of social practice that, at the same time, is a structuring principle of the actions, world views and dispositions of people. As a category of practice, it is a form both of social subjectivity and objectivity. In some respects, it occupies a similar place in Marx's analysis of modernity that kinship might in an anthropologist's analysis of another form of society"—Postone, "Rethinking Marx (in a Post-Marxist World)."

pure analysis of formal determinations—only at the end does he reach what "real people" do with money.[19]

However, Marx did not systematically and explicitly develop this key structuring role of the commodity form as the historical-transcendental principle of the social totality; indeed, one could argue that he was not even fully aware of this crucial breakthrough in his mature work—he was doing something new and unheard-of, and his awareness of its significance probably remained at a "Marxist" level. One should mention here, as an interesting curiosity, Engels's attempt in *Origins of the Family, Private Property and the State* to relativize or historicize the centrality of the material production process by way of supplementing labor (the production of things) with kinship (the form of the social organization of the production of humans):

> According to the materialistic conception, the determining factor in history is, in the last resort, the production and reproduction of immediate life. But this itself is of a twofold character. On the one hand, the production of the means of subsistence, of food, clothing and shelter and the tools requisite therefore; on the other, the production of human beings themselves, the propagation of the species. The social institutions under which men of a definite historical epoch and of a definite country live are conditioned by both kinds of production: by the stage of development of labor, on the one hand, and of the family, on the other. The less the development of labor, and the more limited its volume of production and, therefore, the wealth of society, the more preponderatingly does the social order appear to be dominated by ties of sex.[20]

Engels is here developing a motif found already in *The German Ideology*, where he and Marx claim that

> men, who daily remake their own life, begin to make other men, to propagate their kind: the relation between man and woman, parents and children, the family . . . The production of life, both of one's own in labour and of fresh life in procreation, now appears as a double relationship: on the one hand as a natural, on the other as a social relationship. By social

19   One could say that what Marx does for commodities, Claude Lévi-Strauss does for kinship in his *Elementary Structures of Kinship*, where he provides the elementary formal determinations of kinship relations. The interesting methodological difference is that, in the case of commodities, one begins with the role of commodities in capitalism (in which commodity production predominates), i.e., in the most developed form, while in the case of kinship, one should begin with "primitive" societies in which kinship relations functioned as the structuring principle of the entire social body.

20   Frederick Engels, *Origins of the Family, Private Property and the State*, Preface to the First Edition (1884), New York: Pathfinder Press 1972, p. 27.

we understand the co-operation of several individuals, no matter under what conditions, in what manner and to what end. It follows from this that a certain mode of production, or industrial stage, is always combined with a certain mode of co-operation, or social stage, and this mode of co-operation is itself a "productive force."[21]

(One should also note the uncannily similar passage from *Civilization and its Discontents*, where Freud claims that civilization comprises two fundamental aspects: all the knowledge and productive forces we develop to dominate external nature and gain from it adequate material products for our subsistence, *and* the network of relations which regulate how people deal with each other — or, as an American vulgarizer condensed Freud in a amusingly ideological way: "There are two businesses, the business of making money and the business of making love.")

Both Stalinist orthodoxy and critical feminism immediately recognized the explosive potential of these lines from Engels's book. Back in the 1970s and '80s, many feminists sought to identify the family as part of the mode of production, and to show how the very production of gender had to be understood as part of the "production of human beings themselves," according to norms that reproduced the heterosexually normative family. Much less well known, but no less important, is how Stalinism reacted to this passage: in the short official preface to all Stalinist editions of the book, there is a warning to readers that, in the above-quoted lines, Engels "allows an inaccuracy" and makes a claim that contradicts not only the fundamental Marxist thesis on the determining role of the mode of (material) production, but even the main body of the book itself. It would be easy to make fun of Stalinist "dogmatism" here, but there is nevertheless a genuine problem with Engels's passage — no wonder even Lukács and all "non-dogmatic" Hegelian Marxists did not know what to do with it. Engels sees a problem, but *offers only a pseudo-solution in the very terms which created the problem itself* — the "production of people" reduces its specificity to another species of production.[22]

---

21   Marx and Engels, *The German Ideology*, p. 50.

22   And, incidentally, exactly the same reproach should be raised against those partisans of "discourse analysis" who dismiss those who continue to emphasize the key structural role of the economic mode of production as representatives of "vulgar Marxism" (or, another popular catchword, "economic essentialism"): the insinuation is that such a view reduces language to a secondary instrument, locating real historical efficiency only in the "reality" of material production. There is, however, a symmetrical simplification which is no less "vulgar": that of proposing a direct parallel between language and production, that is, of conceiving — in Paul de Man style — language itself as another mode of production, the "production of sense." According to this approach, in parallel with

We should add here that not only are there "regressions" to "Marxism" in Marx's late texts, there are also, in his texts from before the late 1850s, momentary passages which point forward, towards the post-Marxist Marx. Above and beyond the obvious cases—for example, Marx's great analyses of the nineteenth-century revolutions (*The Eighteenth Brumaire*, and so on)—there are even some unexpected pearls in *Poverty of Philosophy*, where Marx presents an amusingly malicious portrait of Hegelian idealist speculation:

> Impersonal reason having outside of itself neither ground upon which to stand, nor object with which it can be composed, finds itself forced to make a somersault in posing, opposing and composing itself—position, opposition, composition. To speak Greek, we have the thesis, antithesis and the synthesis. As to those who are not acquainted with Hegelian language, we would say to them in sacramental formula, affirmation, negation, and negation of the negation. That is what it means to speak in this way. It is certainly not Hebrew, so as not to displease M. Proudhon; but it is the language of this reason so pure, separated from the individual. Instead of the ordinary individual, with his ordinary manner of speaking and thinking, we have nothing but this ordinary manner pure and simple, minus the individual.[23]

Although this passage belongs to the early "Marxist" Marx, the last proposition announces a different logic, totally at odds with the young Marx's logic (or, rather, rhetoric) of symmetrical reversals: instead of symmetrically inverting the first thesis, the second part repeats it, just cutting it short: "Instead of the ordinary individual, with his ordinary manner of speaking and thinking, we have"—*not* (as expected) an extraordinary individual (say, the transcendental Subject or the Hegelian Spirit), but—"nothing but this ordinary manner pure and simple, minus the individual."

But let us return to Postone: he is at his best when, against the formalism of "production," he demonstrates how the standpoint of the capitalist concrete-historical "totality" is missed by theories which try to

the "reification" of productive labor in its result, the commonsense notion of speech as a mere expression of some pre-existing sense also "reifies" sense, ignoring how sense is not only reflected in speech, but generated by it—it is the result of "signifying practice," as it was once fashionable to say. One should reject this approach as the worst case of non-dialectical *formalism*: it involves a hypostasis of "production" into an abstract-universal notion which encompasses economic and "symbolic" production as its two species, neglecting their radically different status.

23   Karl Marx, *The Poverty of Philosophy*, Chicago: Adamant Media Corporation 2005, p. 115.

capture the determining feature of our world with notions like "risk" or "indeterminacy":

> To the degree we choose to use "indeterminacy" as a critical social cate-gory, then, it should be as a goal of social and political action rather than as an ontological characteristic of social life. (The latter is how it tends to be presented in poststructuralist thought, which can be regarded as a reified response to a reified understanding of historical necessity.) Positions that ontologize historical indeterminacy emphasize that freedom and contingency are related. However, they overlook the constraints on contingency exerted by capital as a structuring form of social life and are, for this reason, ultimately inadequate as critical theo-ries of the present.[24]

Perhaps a more precise formulation would have been appropriate here: the experience of contingency or indeterminacy as a fundamental feature of our lives is the very form of capitalist domination, the social effect of the global rule of capital. The preponderance of indeterminacy is conditioned by the new, third, stage of "post-Fordist capitalism." Here, however, Postone may be corrected on two points. First, he sometimes seems to regress from history to historicism. For properly historical thought, as opposed to historicism, there is no contradiction between the claim that "all history hitherto is the history of class struggle" and the claim that the "bourgeoisie is the first class in history." All civilized societies were class societies, but prior to capitalism, their class structure was distorted by a network of other hierarchical orders (castes, estates, and so forth) — only with capitalism, when individuals are formally free and equal, deprived of all traditional hierarchical links, does the class structure appear "as such." It is in this (non-teleological) sense that, for Marx, the anatomy of man is key to the anatomy of the ape:

> Bourgeois society is the most developed and the most complex historic organization of production. The categories which express its relations, the comprehension of its structure, thereby also allow insights into the struc-ture and the relations of production of all the vanished social formations out of whose ruins and elements it built itself up, whose partly still uncon-quered remnants are carried along within it, whose mere nuances have developed explicit significance within it, etc. Human anatomy contains a key to the anatomy of the ape. The intimations of higher development

---

24   Postone, "History and Helplessness."

among the subordinate animal species, however, can be understood only after the higher development is already known.[25]

As for the abstraction of class, the same holds for the abstraction of labor, whose status is also historical:

Labour seems a quite simple category. The conception of labour in this general form — as labour as such — is also immeasurably old. Nevertheless, when it is economically conceived in this simplicity, "labour" is as modern a category as are the relations which create this simple abstraction . . . Indifference towards any specific kind of labour presupposes a very developed totality of real kinds of labour, of which no single one is any longer predominant. As a rule, the most general abstractions arise only in the midst of the richest possible concrete development, where one thing appears as common to many, to all. Then it ceases to be thinkable in a particular form alone. On the other side, this abstraction of labour as such is not merely the mental product of a concrete totality of labours. Indifference towards specific labours corresponds to a form of society in which individuals can with ease transfer from one labour to another, and where the specific kind is a matter of chance for them, hence of indifference. Not only the category, labour, but labour in reality has here become the means of creating wealth in general, and has ceased to be organically linked with particular individuals in any specific form. Such a state of affairs is at its most developed in the most modern form of existence of bourgeois society — in the United States. Here, then, for the first time, the point of departure of modern economics, namely the abstraction of the category "labour," "labour as such," labour pure and simple, becomes true in practice.[26]

Marx is not slipping here into the easy historicism that relativizes each universal category, rather, he is asking a much more precise Hegelian question: when do "the most general abstractions," which are as such valid for all times, "arise," when do they pass from the In-itself to the For-itself, when do they "become true in practice"? There is no teleology here, the effect of teleology is strictly retroactive: once capitalism arrives (emerging in a wholly contingent way), it provides a universal key for all other formations.

The second critical point to make with regard to Postone is that he dismisses all too quickly the class struggle as a component of the "Marxist"

---

25   Karl Marx, *Grundrisse: Foundations of the Critique of Political Economy*, New York: Penguin Classics 1993, p. 105.
26   Ibid., pp. 103–4.

determinist-evolutionary view (taken to the point of ridicule in Stalinism): the social meaning of every position in the superstructure (state, law, art, philosophy . . .) depends on which class position they "reflect." But "class struggle" in the young Lukács is precisely the transversal which undermines economic determinism: it stands for the dimension of politics at the heart of the economic. When Postone interprets the commodity form as a kind of historically specific transcendental a priori which structures the whole of social life, up to and including ideology, branding it in all its aspects with the "antinomic opposition" between "the freely self-determining individual and society as an extrinsic sphere of objective necessity," he all too quickly reduces the dimension of class struggle (social antagonism) to an ontic phenomenon which is secondary with regard to the commodity form. He thereby fails to see how class struggle is not a positive social phenomenon, an ontic component of objective social reality: it designates the very limit of social objectivity, the point at which subjective engagement co-determines what appears as social reality.

Why Masses Are Not Divided into Classes

Badiou recently summed up the core doctrine of the Marxism that deserves to be left behind in the following terms: "the masses are divided into classes, the classes are represented by parties and the parties directed by leaders."[27] Badiou here reduces classes to parts of a social body, forgetting the lesson of Louis Althusser, namely that "class struggle" paradoxically *precedes* classes as determinate social groups, that is, that every class position and determination is already an effect of the "class struggle." (This is why "class struggle" is another name for the fact that "society does not exist"—it does not exist as a positive order of being.) This is also why it is crucial to insist on the central role of the critique of *political* economy: the "economy" cannot be reduced to a sphere of the positive "order of being" precisely insofar as it is always already political, insofar as political ("class") struggle is at its very heart. In other words, one should always bear in mind that, for a true Marxist, "classes" are *not* categories of positive social reality, parts of the social body, but categories of the real of a political struggle which cuts across the entire social body, preventing its "totalization." True, there is no outside to capitalism

---

27   Filippo Del Lucchese and Jason Smith, "'We Need a Popular Discipline': Contemporary Politics and the Crisis of the Negative," interview with Alain Badiou, Los Angeles, July 2, 2007. (The unmarked quotes that follow are from the manuscript of this interview.)

today, but this should not be used to hide the fact that capitalism itself is "antagonistic," relying on contradictory measures to remain viable — and these immanent antagonisms open up the space for radical action. If, say, a co-operative movement of poor farmers in a Third World country succeeds in establishing a thriving alternative network, this should be celebrated as a genuine *political event*.

Bernard-Henri Lévy advocates an activist, universalist liberalism, opposing both the politically correct liberalism of tolerance which prohibits the critique of non-Western religious fundamentalism (accusing it of a cultural-imperialist imposition of Eurocentric notions), as well as the Leftist critique of liberalism: as Damian Da Costa has put it, Lévy wants to separate the Left, "once and for all, from what he believes to be the soft-headed liberalism of 'tolerance' on one side, and from the proto-fascist, incipiently anti-Semitic radicalism of thinkers like Slavoj Žižek on the other."[28] The flaw in this position was succinctly formulated by Scott McLemee in his review of a recent book by Lévy:

> Lévy sees the future menaced by the prospect of barbarism. He is right to worry. But amid his soliloquies, he makes gestures of warning in the wrong direction. A few years ago, Terry Eagleton wrote that it would take a transformation of the political economy of the entire planet just to make sure everyone on it had access to clean drinking water. I dare say that insight, or something like it (as opposed to, say, an irresistible hankering to go on the road to Cambodia Year Zero), is what drives most people on the left.[29]

We should thus ultimately also abandon the distinction, proposed by Rancière, between politics proper (the rise to universality of the singular "part-of-no-part") and police (the administration of social affairs), or

---

28   Damian Da Costa, "Le Rêve Gauche," *New York Observer*, October 1, 2008; available online at http://philosophysother.blogspot.com. Note the double distantiation which allows Da Costa to have his cake and eat it: he does not openly claim that I am an anti-Semitic fascist, just that I am a *proto*-fascist whose (anti-capitalist) radicalism is *incipiently* anti-Semitic. The problem with this double delimitation is that it disqualifies every radical questioning of capitalism as a "proto-fascist, incipiently anti-Semitic radicalism" — and this brings us to the underlying premise of Lévy's thesis that twenty-first-century anti-Semitism will be that of the progressives, which should be no surprise for Lévy as a self-professed partisan of the free market ("I believe in the free market," he emphatically declared in a C-SPAN interview in September 2008: *today, according to this position, every anti-capitalist position is "incipiently" anti-Semitic*. It is not difficult to perceive the extraordinary ideological-legitimizing function of this equation: it disqualifies in advance every radical critique of the hegemonic capitalist order, associating it with the worst political crime of the twentieth century.

29   Scott McLemee, "Darkness Becomes Him," *The Nation*, September 23, 2008.

Badiou's homologous distinction between politics as fidelity to an Event and policing as "servicing the goods" of a society: politics proper truly counts only insofar as it affects policing itself, radically transforming its mode. Perhaps then we should return to the very beginning, to the split in the Hegelian school between the revolutionary "young Hegelians" and the conservative "old Hegelians"? What if the "original sin" of modern emancipatory movements can be traced back to the "young Hegelian" rejection of the authority and alienation of the state? What if—a move suggested by Domenico Losurdo—the contemporary Left were to re-appropriate the "old Hegelian" *topos* of a strong State grounded in a shared ethical substance?

Badiou's dismissal of the economy as merely part of the "situation" (the given "world" or state of things) is grounded in his Rousseauean-Jacobin orientation, which leaves him stuck in the duality of *citoyen* and *bourgeois*: the latter following his interests, as a "human animal" constrained to "servicing the goods," versus the *citoyen* committed to the universality of a political Truth.[30] This duality, as we have noted, acquires in Badiou an almost Gnostic character, as the opposition between the corrupted "fallen world" of the economy and spiritual Truth. What is missing here is the properly Marxist idea of *communism* whose core principle is precisely that this corrupt state of the economy is not an eternal fate, a universal ontological condition of man, but is a state that can be radically changed such that it will no longer be reducible to the interplay of private interests. But since Badiou ignores this dimension, he has to reduce the Idea of communism to a political-egalitarian project.[31] Where does the fundamental cause of this Gnostic deviation reside—a Leftist deviation whose actual political consequences are, of course, Rightist? I would claim that it lies in the notion of the relationship between Being and Event on which it implicitly relies. Badiou—as a dialectical materialist—is aware of the idealist danger that lurks in the assertion of the irreducibility of the Event to the order of Being:

---

30   Furthermore, should politics be really given back to politics, liberated from the shadow of philosophy (or theology)? Was all radical politics not *always* "sutured" to some trans-political (philosophical, theological . . .) content?

31   Badiou's symptom here is the overblown notion of State, which effectively tends to overlap with the state (of things) in the broadest sense. Along these lines, Judith Balso claimed—at the conference on Communism in London in March 2009—that opinions themselves are part of the State. The notion of the State has to be over-expanded in this way precisely because the autonomy of "civil society" with regard to the State is ignored, so that the "State" has to cover the entire economic sphere, as well as the sphere of "private" opinions.

We must point out that in what concerns its material the event is not a miracle. What I mean is that what composes an event is always extracted from a situation, always related back to a singular multiplicity, to its state, to the language that is connected to it, etc. In fact, so as not to succumb to an obscurantist theory of creation *ex nihilo*, we must accept that an event is nothing but a part of a given situation, nothing but a *fragment of being*.[32]

The consequences of this clear statement are no less clear: there is no Beyond with regard to Being which inscribes itself into the order of Being—there is nothing but the order of Being. How can we read this absolute immanence of the Event to Being together with the assertion of their radical heterogeneity? The only way to resolve this deadlock is to accept that the line distinguishing them is not a line that separates two positive orders: within the order of Being, we will never reach a border, beyond which a different order of the Event begins. This is why there is no way—but also no need—to fully subtract ourselves from the "corrupted" order of the State: what we have to do is introduce a supplementary torsion into it, to inscribe into it our fidelity to an Event. In this way, we remain within the State, but we make the State function in a non-statal way (in a way similar to how poetry, say, takes place within language, but twists and turns it against itself, thus making it tell the truth). There is no need, then, to play the Gnostic ascetic and withdraw from fallen reality into the isolated space of Truth: while heterogeneous to reality, Truth can appear anywhere within it.

What this means is that class struggle cannot be reduced to a conflict between particular agents within social reality: it is not a difference between agents (which can be described by means of a detailed social analysis), but an antagonism ("struggle") which constitutes these agents. "Marxist" objectivism should thus be broken twice: with regard to the subjective-objective a priori of the commodity form and with regard to the trans-objective antagonism of class struggle. The true task is to think the two dimensions together: the transcendental logic of the commodity form as a mode of functioning of the social totality, and class struggle as the antagonism that cuts across social reality, as its point of subjectivization. It is indicative of this transversal role of the class struggle that the manuscript for Volume 3 of *Capital* cuts off precisely when Marx is about to provide a clear "objective" class analysis of a modern capitalist society:

---

32   Alain Badiou, *Theoretical Writings*, London: Continuum 2006, p. 43.

The first question to be answered is this: What constitutes a class? —and the reply to this follows naturally from the reply to another question, namely: What makes wage-labourers, capitalists and landlords constitute the three great social classes?

At first glance —the identity of revenues and sources of revenue. There are three great social groups whose members, the individuals forming them, live on wages, profit and ground-rent respectively, on the realization of their labour-power, their capital, and their landed property.

However, from this standpoint, physicians and officials, e.g., would also constitute two classes, for they belong to two distinct social groups, the members of each of these groups receiving their revenue from one and the same source. The same would also be true of the infinite fragmentation of interest and rank into which the division of social labour splits labourers as well as capitalists and landlords —the latter, e.g., into owners of vineyards, farm owners, owners of forests, mine owners and owners of fisheries.

[Here the manuscript breaks off.][33]

This deadlock cannot be solved with a further "objective social" analysis providing more and more refined distinctions —at some point, the process has to be cut short with a massive and brutal intervention of subjectivity: class belonging is never a purely objective social fact, but is always also the result of struggle and subjective engagement. It is interesting to note how Stalinism became involved in a similar deadlock in its search for such objective determinations of class belonging —recall the classificatory impasse the Stalinist ideologists and political activists faced in their struggle for collectivization in the years 1928–33. In an attempt to account in "scientific" Marxist terms for their effort to crush the peasants' resistance, they divided peasants into three categories (or classes): the poor peasants (no land or minimal land, working for others), natural allies of the workers; the autonomous middle peasants, oscillating between the exploited and exploiters; the rich peasants, the "kulaks" (employing other workers, lending them money or seeds, etc.), who were the exploiting "class enemy" and who, as such, had to be "liquidated." However, in practice, this classification became more and more blurred and unworkable: in a situation of generalized poverty, clear criteria no longer applied, and the other two classes of peasants often joined the kulaks in their resistance to forced collectivization. An additional category was thus introduced,

---

33   Karl Marx, *Capital: A Critique of Political Economy, Volume Three*, Chicago: Charles H. Kerr & Company 1909, p. 1031.

that of a "subkulak," a peasant who, although too poor in terms of his economic situation to be considered a *kulak* proper, nonetheless shared the "counter-revolutionary" attitude. The "subkulak" was thus

a term without any real social content even by Stalinist standards, but merely rather unconvincingly masquerading as such. As was officially stated, "by 'kulak' we mean the carrier of certain political tendencies which are most frequently discernible in the subkulak, male and female." By this means, any peasant whatever was liable to dekulakization; and the 'subkulak' notion was widely employed, enlarging the category of victims greatly beyond the official estimate of kulaks proper even at its most strained.[34]

No wonder that the official ideologists and economists finally renounced the effort to provide an "objective" definition of the kulak: "The grounds given in one Soviet comment are that 'the old attitudes of a kulak have almost disappeared, and the new ones do not lend themselves to recognition.'"[35] The art of identifying a kulak was thus no longer a matter of objective social analysis; it became a kind of complex "hermeneutics of suspicion," of identifying an individual's "true political attitudes" hidden beneath his or her deceptive public proclamations, leading *Pravda* to concede that "even the best activists often cannot spot the kulak."[36]

What all this points towards is the dialectical mediation of the "subjective" and "objective" dimensions: the "subkulak" no longer designates an "objective" social category; it designates the point at which objective social analysis breaks down and a subjective political attitude directly inscribes itself into the "objective" order—in Lacanese, the *"subkulak" is the point of subjectivization of the "objective chain": poor peasant—middle peasant—kulak*. It is not an "objective" sub-category (or sub-division) of the class of "kulaks," but simply the name for a "kulak" subjective political attitude—this accounts for the paradox that, although it appears as a subdivision of the class of "kulaks," the "subkulak" is a species that overflows

---

34   Robert Conquest, *The Harvest of Sorrow*, New York: Oxford University Press 1986, p. 119. These subdivisions were ironically referred to in Andrei Platonov's short story "Vprok (For Future Use)" from 1931, in which the "discriminations between *bedniaki, seredniaki, kulaki* and *podkulachniki* quickly become muddled, and the narrator meets a self-defined 'fighter against the secondary danger,' who cryptically explains that the 'secondary danger feeds the primary one'" (Thomas Seifrid, *Andrei Platonov*, Cambridge: Cambridge University Press 2006, p. 138). Or, as Platonov himself put it in his *Foundation Pit*, the party Activist engaged in a fierce campaign of dekulakization ends up himself in the "leftist swamp of right opposition". . .

35   Conquest, *The Harvest of Sorrow*, p. 120.

36   Ibid.

its own genus (that of kulaks), since "subkulaks" are also to be found among middle and even poor farmers. In short, the "subkulak" names political division as such, the Enemy whose presence traverses the *entire* social body of the peasantry, which is why he can be found everywhere, in all three peasant classes: the "subkulak" names the excessive element that traverses all classes, the outgrowth of which has to be eliminated.

Returning to Marx, then: there is not so much a poetic as a theoretical justice in the fact that the manuscript of the third volume of *Capital* breaks off with a class analysis: one should read this break not as a sign of the need to change the theoretical approach from objective social analysis to a more subjective one, but as an indication of the need to turn the text reflexively back onto itself, to realize that all the categories the text had analyzed up to this point, starting with the simple commodity, had involved class struggle. This is also how one should render problematic the fateful step from Lukács's *History and Class Consciousness* to Adorno and Horkheimer's *Dialectic of Enlightenment*: while both works foreground the topic of fetishism and reification — of an ideological "distortion" which functions as a kind of historical transcendental a priori of capitalist societies — in Lukács this topic is still conceived of as the obverse of a concrete dynamics of class struggle, while Adorno and Horkheimer cut this link by tracing the source of reification and alienation back to "instrumental reason," the will to technological domination/manipulation which functions as a kind of a priori of the whole of human history, but no longer rooted in any concrete historical formations. The over-arching totality is thus no longer that of capitalism, or commodity production: capitalism itself becomes one of the manifestations of instrumental reason. One can observe this "disappearance of class history" in the history of the manuscript for *Dialectic of Enlightenment* itself: when Adorno and Horkheimer revised the original 1944 manuscript for publication in 1947, the main tendency discernible in all the revisions and corrections was the erasure of references to capitalism and class struggle.[37]

The Labor Theory of Value Revisited

This, finally, brings us to the crucial question affecting any proposed revival of the Marxist critique of political economy: the question of

---

37   See Willem van Reijen and Jan Bransen, "The Disappearance of Class History in *Dialectic of Enlightenment*," in Max Horkheimer and Theodor W. Adorno, *Dialectic of Enlightenment*, Stanford: Stanford University Press 2002, pp. 248–52.

exploitation and of the so-called "labor theory of value," usually considered the weakest link in the chain of Marx's theory. Postone confronts this question head-on, starting from the premise that the "labor theory of value" is not a general (trans-historical) theory, but a theory of the specific role labor plays in capitalist society. This specificity is connected to the fact that only in capitalist societies in which commodities are produced for the market can we talk about the "double character" of labor, about the division between concrete and abstract labor. Asked about his reading of "Marx's differentiation between labor as a socially mediating activity, i.e., in its abstract dimension, on the one hand, and on the other, as a way of producing specific and concrete use-values, i.e., participating in the production of particular goods," a reading which insists that this differentiation does not exist in pre-modern forms of social organization, Postone emphasizes that

> abstract labor is not simply an abstraction from labor, i.e., it's not labor in general, it's labor acting as a socially mediating activity . . . Labor is doing something in capitalism that it doesn't do in other societies. So, it's both, in Marx's terms, concrete labor, which is to say, a specific activity that transforms material in a determinate way for a very particular object, as well as abstract labor, that is, a means of acquiring the goods of others . . . Out of this very abstract insight, Marx develops the whole dynamic of capitalism. It seems to me that the central issue for Marx is not only that labor is being exploited—labor is exploited in all societies, other than maybe those of hunter-gatherers—but, rather, that the exploitation of labor is effected by structures that labor itself constitutes. So, for example, if you get rid of aristocrats in a peasant-based society, it's conceivable that the peasants could own their own plots of land and live off of them. However, if you get rid of the capitalists, you are not getting rid of capital. Social domination will continue to exist in that society until the structures that constitute capital are gotten rid of.[38]

Postone also provided a precise answer to the reproach that Marx's labor theory involves a rather obvious logical mistake. Marx first criticizes the idea (the ideological illusion which imposes itself "at first sight") that exchange-value is a purely relational term, the result of comparing one commodity with another, not the intrinsic property of a commodity:

---

38   "Marx After Marxism: An Interview with Moishe Postone," Benjamin Blumberg and Pam Nogales, March 2008, available online at http://platypus1917.home.comcast.net.

Exchange value, at first sight, presents itself as a quantitative relation, as the proportion in which values in use of one sort are exchanged for those of another sort, a relation constantly changing with time and place. Hence exchange value appears to be something accidental and purely relative, and consequently an intrinsic value, *i.e.*, an exchange value that is inseparably connected with, inherent in commodities, seems a contradiction in terms.[39]

If this is a false appearance, what, then, is the true status of exchange-value? Here comes the surprise: although it is intrinsic rather than relational, it is *not* intrinsic in the sense of being a natural property of the commodity as object:

the exchange values of commodities must be capable of being expressed in terms of something common to them all, of which thing they represent a greater or less quantity. This common "something" cannot be a geometrical, a chemical, or any other natural property of commodities. Such properties claim our attention only in so far as they affect the utility of those commodities, make them use values. But the exchange of commodities is evidently an act characterized by a total abstraction from use value . . . As use values, commodities are, above all, of different qualities, but as exchange values they are merely different quantities, and consequently do not contain an atom of use value. If then we leave out of consideration the use value of commodities, they have only one common property left, that of being products of labor.[40]

Is not this strange universal intrinsic value—totally different in kind to all natural (physical) properties of the commodity as an object—a purely metaphysical (spiritual) property? When we look at commodities as products of abstract labor,

there is nothing left of them in each case but the same phantom-like objectivity . . . As crystals of this social substance, which is common to them all, they are values—commodity values . . . Not an atom of matter enters into the objectivity of commodity as values; in this it is the direct opposite of the coarsely sensuous objectivity of commodities as physical objects . . . Commodities possess an objective character as values only insofar as they are all expressions of an identical social substance, human labour, that their objective character as value is purely social.[41]

39   Marx, *Capital, Volume One*, p. 43.
40   Ibid., p. 44.
41   Ibid., pp. 45 and 55 (translation altered).

So what is the exact status of this "phantom-like objectivity"? Is Marx here not an ontological realist in the medieval Thomist sense, claiming that the universal has an autonomous existence within the object, but beyond its physical properties? Furthermore, does he not commit here a blatant *petitio principii*? The passage from use-value to exchange-value (based exclusively in labor time expended on the commodity) is not the passage from particular to universal: if we abstract from the concrete properties which account for the use-value of a commodity, what remains is obviously usefulness (utility) as such, as an abstract property that all commodities share; and, in an exactly symmetrical way, being-the-product-of-labor as the common property of all commodities is an abstraction from concrete particular labor which provided a particular commodity with its use-value.

The reply to this is that (exchange) value is a social category, linked to the way the social character of production is inscribed in a commodity: the relationship between use-value and (exchange) value is not one between particularity and universality, but one between the different uses of the same commodity, first as an object that satisfies some need, then as a social object, as a token of relations between subjects. Value concerns products (commodities) as social entities, it is the imprint of the social character of a commodity, and *this is why labor is its only source*—once we see that value concerns "relations between people," the claim that its source is labor becomes almost a tautology. In other words, the only source of value is human labor because value is a social category which measures the participation of each individual laborer in the totality of social labor—to claim that capital and labor are both "factors" which create value is the same as claiming that capital is, alongside the laborers, also a member of human society.

Only in capitalism is exploitation "naturalized," inscribed into the functioning of the economy, and not the result of extra-economic pressure and violence. This is why, with capitalism, we enjoy personal freedom and equality: there is no need for explicit social domination, since domination is already implicit in the structure of the production process. This is also why the category of surplus-value is crucial here: Marx always emphasized that the exchange between worker and capitalist is "just" in the sense that workers (as a rule) get paid the full value of their labor-power as a commodity—there is no direct "exploitation" here; that is, it is not that workers "are not paid the full value of the commodity they are selling to the capitalists." The exploitation occurs because labor-power as a commodity has the paradoxical character of producing more value than it is itself worth. This process is obfuscated in "bourgeois" market ideology. Let us take as a contemporary example Tim Hartford, who begins his analysis of the market economy with a "flight of fantasy," imagining "the world of truth":

> a world where markets are complete, free and competitive. In reality we're about as likely to achieve a world with complete, free and competitive markets as hotshot lawyers are to start telling the truth to everyone.
>
> You might therefore be asking yourself why you've read a chapter . . . about some bizarre economist's fantasy. The answer is that the fantasy helps us understand why economic problems arise and also helps us to move in the right direction. We know that a world of perfect markets combined with the head start approach is as good as we're going to get. When real-world economies malfunction, we know to look for the market failures — and to do our best to patch them up.[42]

The three great problems that cause market failures are scarcity power, incomplete information, and externalities. (The fourth problem — fairness — can be dealt with through the "head start" approach.) Is what Hartford presents here a rational abstraction or a fantasy *stricto sensu*, namely a construction that obfuscates its antagonisms, reducing them to secondary accidental complications? Is the pure market a *rational* symbolic fiction? Are its failures just contingent distortions or are they structurally necessary, that is, *symptoms*? The capitalist-market utopian idea is that, in principle, it is, possible to correct for market failures by taking into account externalities and the like. In a well-known passage from *Capital*, Marx ironically designated the market sphere within whose boundaries the sale and purchase of labor-power goes on as the

> very Eden of the innate rights of man. There alone rule Freedom, Equality, Property and Bentham. Freedom, because both buyer and seller of a commodity, say of labor-power, are constrained only by their own free will. They contract as free agents, and the agreement they come to, is but the form in which they give legal expression to their common will. Equality, because each enters into relation with the other, as with a simple owner of commodities, and they exchange equivalent for equivalent. Property, because each disposes only of what is his own. And Bentham, because each looks only to himself. The only force that brings them together and puts them in relation with each other, is the selfishness, the gain and the

---

42   Tim Hartford, *The Undercover Economist*, London: Abacus 2007, pp. 77–8.

private interests of each. Each looks to himself only, and no one troubles himself about the rest, and just because they do so, do they all, in accordance with the pre-established harmony of things, or under the auspices of an all-shrewd providence, work together to their mutual advantage, for the common wealth and in the interest of all.[43]

However, the moment we take a closer look on what goes on in the market exchange between the seller and the buyer of labor-power,

> we can perceive a change in the physiognomy of our dramatis personae. He, who before was the money-owner, now strides in front as capitalist; the possessor of labor-power follows as his laborer. The one with an air of importance, smirking, intent on business; the other, timid and holding back, like one who is bringing his own hide to market and has nothing to expect but — a hiding.

One specific market commodity — the worker selling his labor-power — is thus the symptom, the necessary exception which violates the ideal market rules on all accounts: in terms of scarcity power, the capitalist enjoys an a priori structural advantage; in relation to information, the capitalist's access is a priori more complete, since he organizes the whole process and deals with the market, selling the products; and as far as externalities are concerned, the capitalist can ignore them, while the worker *is* (as a person who is not *only* a worker) in himself the affected externality. According to what economists call "the law of one price," identical products on offer at the same time, in the same place, with the prices clearly visible, will go for the same price. The key consequence of this law is that it is the lowest price which gets universalized: say, if there are 19 workers applying for 18 identical jobs and one of them is ready to work for only $40 per day, they will all have to work for this sum. The same would have held in the opposite direction, but since, if we discount the exceptions, there is as a rule a surplus of workers over jobs, this "law of one price" puts workers at a big structural disadvantage. Therein resides the role of the reserve army of the unemployed: just a tiny percentage of unemployed can lower wages considerably, because their readiness to work for lower wages presents a threat to all those with jobs.[44]

---

43   Marx, *Capital, Volume One*, p. 195.
44   Hartford convincingly shows Deng's wisdom in China: instead of the shock-therapy imposed in Russia, he gradually opened up space for capitalism *at the margins*, not only in the geographic margin (exclusive "free zones") or marginal spheres of production (small artisans and services), but

What complicates the picture even further is the paradox referred to by Hartford when he talks about "the men who knew the value of nothing": we should complicate Hartford's formula here, drawing a parallel with Stephen Jay Gould's story about the relationship between the weight and price of Hershey chocolate bars: the company gradually reduced the weight of the product, then made it larger again (though not as large as it was originally) and raised the price, then again gradually diminished it, and so on—if we push this tendency to its conclusion, at some point which can be exactly calculated, the company will be selling a package with nothing in it, and this nothing will have a price which can be precisely determined. This is the profit: the price of the "nothing" we pay for when we buy something from a capitalist. The capitalist economy counts with the price of nothing, with reference to a virtual Zero which has a precise price.

This nothing is the "signifier without a signified," the brand name for which we pay when we buy, say, Coke instead of an anonymous cola drink. Imagine a totally "outsourced" company—Nike, say, which not only "outsources" its material production (to Indonesian or Central American contractors), the distribution of its products, and its marketing strategy and publicity campaigns, but also the design work itself to some selected top designer agency, and, on top of all that, borrows money from a bank. Nike will thus be "nothing in itself"—nothing *but* the pure brand mark "Nike," the "empty" Master-Signifier which connotes the cultural experience pertaining to a certain "life-style." This is where polemics against the fetishized role of the logo in our daily lives fall short: they overlook how the efficiency of different logos is parasitical upon a certain gap (between the Master-Signifier and the chain of "normal" signifiers) which pertains to language as such—we never can have a language whose terms directly designate reality, by-passing the "lifestyle" connotation.

If everything is for sale on the market, this also includes all the self-referential paradoxes: there is also a market for capitalists (who compete for loans from the banks), a market for banks, and a market for brand names themselves—for example, if an old company with a recognizable

also in the margins of production within a single company, taking into account the basic lesson of the market, which is that what really matters is the marginal cost (the cost of producing in a profitable way one more item of a product): state enterprises were not directly privatized, they were first just given the option of selling their surplus (over the state quota) on the free market. What if, far from being a limited phenomenon, this marginal role could be accepted as a model for the future—allowing capitalism a marginal space where the market economy guarantees the optimal distribution of resources?

name goes bankrupt, and all that remains is the name, this name can still be sold on. We can thus say that, when we pay more for a commodity due to its brand name, we are paying the extra price for Nothing, for the mere signifier, not for the positive qualities of the product. It is in the interest of the capitalist to maximize the part of the price of a product which covers the brand name, since this part is pure profit, payment for nothing; the ideal would be to sell a mere brand name and thus get money for nothing. Of course, this ideal is an impossible asymptotic point: a product on the actual market can never reach this pure position, since nobody is prepared to pay for nothing more than a name (except another producer who wants a previously known brand name to attach to his own products); every product thus has to appear to offer some satisfaction beyond that of its brand name: you do not buy Nike as such, but sneakers, a T-shirt or some other object to which its name is attached. The art is to find the limit point (the minimal positive content of a product and the maximum of the brand name) at which the consumer is still prepared to buy.

The process of establishing this limit point involves paradoxes of its own. A century ago, Vilfredo Pareto was the first to describe the so-called 80/20 rule of (not only) social life: 80 percent of land is owned by 20 percent of people, 80 percent of profits are produced by 20 percent of the employees, 80 percent of decisions are made during 20 percent of meeting time, 80 percent of the links on the Web point to less than 20 percent of webpages, 80 percent of peas are produced by 20 percent of the peapods and so on. As some social analysts and economists have suggested, today's explosion of economic productivity confronts us with the ultimate case of this rule: the global economy is tending towards a state in which only 20 percent of the workforce will do all the necessary work, so that 80 percent of the population will become basically irrelevant and of no use, potentially unemployed. This 80/20 rule follows from what is called "scale-free networks" in which a small number of nodes with the greatest number of links is followed by an ever larger number of nodes with an ever smaller number of links. To take an example: among any group of people, a small number of them know (have links to) a large number of other people, while the majority of people know only a small number of people — social networks spontaneously form "nodes," people with a large number of links to other people. In such a scale-free network, competition remains: while the overall distribution remains the same, the identity of the top nodes changes all the time, a latecomer replacing the earlier winners. However, some networks may pass a critical threshold beyond which competition breaks down and the winner takes all: one node grabs all the links, leaving none for the rest. This is what essentially happened with Microsoft, which emerged as the privileged node in the software industry: it grabbed all the links, that is, we have to relate to it in some way in order to communicate with other entities. The great structural question, of course, is: what defines the threshold, which networks tend to pass that threshold, beyond which point does competition break down and the winner take all?[45]

If we take this process fully into account, we will be compelled to question one of the basic presuppositions of market ideology: the idea that when, under ideal conditions, the market-mechanism is allowed a free and unencumbered run, the resulting balance—the point where supply and demand intersect, that is, when a commodity is sold for a certain price—will reflect a "natural" optimal point which is not itself contingent, or a result of the game of competition, but is that X around which supply and demand circulate, around which the price floats. What if, however, this balance-point is not "natural" but "artificial," determined by the self-referential game of the market? John Maynard Keynes captured this self-referentiality nicely when he compared the stock market to a silly competition in which the participants have to pick out the prettiest girls from a hundred photographs:

> It is not a case of choosing those which, to the best of one's judgment, are really the prettiest, nor even those which average opinion genuinely thinks the prettiest. We have reached the third degree where we devote our intelligence to anticipating what average opinion expects the average opinion to be.[46]

What if this self-referentiality inherent in the market game is so strong that *the X around which price oscillates is not given in advance but is generated by the very market process*? What this means, in somewhat simpler terms, is that *in the market, it is not the best (e.g. the prettiest girl) which wins*. The reason Microsoft triumphed over its competitors—or, in the days of video competition, VHS won over Betamax—had less to do with the inherent quality of the product in relation to the price than with the company's

---

45   See Albert-Laszlo Barabasi, *Linked*, New York: Plume 2003, Chapters 6 and 8.
46   John Maynard Keynes, *General Theory of Employment, Interest and Money*, London: Macmillan 1967, p. 156.

"luck" in exploiting market mechanisms. The self-referential mechanisms at work here are multiple; it will suffice to mention how the marketing of an object, and its supply generally, itself creates (or at least affects) the demand for it, in the same way that, as Ivan Illich convincingly demonstrated apropos the health industry, new advances in medical procedures and pharmaceuticals expand the scope of what we experience as that domain of our lives which can be treated by medical practices—in an extrapolation *ad absurdum*, our entire life, inclusive of our dying, becomes a stressful experience to be cured. Another such self-referential mechanism is availability itself: Microsoft won not because its software was "the best," but because it succeeded in imposing itself as the "standard" in its field. This explanation is not tautological, since, for a product to impose itself as the standard in its field, a lot of work has to be done which does not concern primarily its inherent qualities, but rather its marketing and distribution.

From Hegel to Marx . . . and Back

Marx's so-called "labor theory of value" is thus a kind of misnomer: it should in no way be read as claiming that one should discard exchange, or its role in the constitution of value, as a mere appearance which obscures the key fact that labor is the origin of value. One should rather conceive the emergence of value as a process of mediation by means of which value "casts off" its use—value *is* surplus-value over use-value. The general equivalent of use-values *had* to be deprived of use-value, it had to function as a pure potentiality of use-value. Essence is appearance as appearance: value is exchange-value *as* exchange-value—or, as Marx put it in a manuscript version of the changes to the first edition of *Capital*: "The reduction of different concrete private labours to this abstraction (*Abstraktum*) of the same human labour is accomplished only through exchange which effectively posits the products of different labours as equal to each other."[47] In other words, "abstract labour" is a value-relationship which constitutes itself only in exchange, it is not the substantial property of a commodity independently of its relations with other commodities. For orthodox Marxists, such a "relational" notion of value is already a compromise with "bourgeois" political economy which they dismiss as a "monetary theory of value"—however, the paradox is

---

47   *MEGA* (Marx-Engels-Gesamtausgabe), Abteilung II, Band 6, Berlin: Dietz Verlag 1976, p. 41.

that these very "orthodox Marxists" themselves effectively regress to the "bourgeois" notion of value: they conceive of value as being immanent to the commodity, as its property, and thus naturalize its "spectral objectivity" which is the fetishized appearance of its social character.

We are not dealing here with mere theoretical niceties—the precise determination of the status of money has crucial economic-political consequences. If we consider money as a secondary form of expression of value which exists "in itself" in a commodity prior to its expression—that is, if money is for us a mere secondary resource, a practical means that facilitates exchange—then the door is open to the illusion, succumbed to by Leftist followers of Ricardo, that it would be possible to replace money by simple notes designating the amount of work done by their bearer and giving him or her the right to the corresponding part of the social product—as if, by means of this direct "work money," one could avoid all "fetishism" and ensure that each worker is paid their "full value." The point of Marx's analysis is that this project ignores the formal determinations of money which make fetishism a necessary effect.

In other words, when Marx defines exchange-value as the mode of appearance of value, one should mobilize here the entire Hegelian weight of the opposition between essence and appearance: essence exists only insofar as it appears, it does not pre-exist its appearance. In the same way, the value of a commodity is not its intrinsic substantial property which exists independently of its appearance in exchange. What this means is that Marx's distinction between concrete and abstract labor is also a kind of misnomer: in a Hegelian sense, "concrete" labor (an individual working on a natural object, transforming it to make it satisfy some human need) is an abstraction from the network of concrete social relations within which it always takes place. This network of social relations inscribes itself into the category of labor precisely in the form of its opposite, of "abstract" labor, and into its product, a commodity, in the form of its value (as opposed to its use-value):

> "Concrete labor" refers to the fact that some form of what we consider laboring activity mediates the interactions of humans with nature in all societies. "Abstract labor" . . . signifies that, in capitalism, labor also has a unique social function: it mediates a new form of social interdependence . . . In a society in which the commodity is the basic structuring category of the whole, labor and its products are not socially distributed by traditional ties, norms, or overt relations of power and domination—that is, by manifest social relations—as is the case in other societies. Instead, labor

itself replaces those relations by serving as a kind of quasi-objective means by which the products of others are acquired . . . In Marx's mature works, then, the notion of the centrality of labor to social life is not a trans-historical proposition. It does not refer to the fact that material production is always a precondition of social life. Nor should it be taken as meaning that material production is the most essential dimension of social life in general, even of capitalism in particular. Rather, it refers to the historically specific constitution by labor in capitalism of the social relations that fundamentally characterize that society.[48]

It is in this precise sense that the dynamic of the commodity form is "concrete universality," the determining principle which permeates the entire social totality, generating its most abstract/formal forms of self-awareness, like the paradigmatically modern experience of the antinomy between the "freely self-determining individual and society as an extrinsic sphere of objective necessity":

> Marx's theory of value provides the basis for an analysis of capital as a socially constituted form of mediation and wealth whose primary characteristic is a tendency toward its limitless expansion . . . In Marx's terms, out of a pre-capitalist context characterized by relations of personal dependence, a new one emerged characterized by individual personal freedom within a social framework of "objective dependence." Both terms of the classical modern antinomic opposition—the freely self-determining individual and society as an extrinsic sphere of objective necessity—are, according to Marx's analysis, historically constituted with the rise and spread of the commodity-determined form of social relations.[49]

The philosopher who elaborated this antinomy between "the freely self-determining individual and society as an extrinsic sphere of objective necessity" as a key feature of modernity is, of course, Hegel. Hegel also clearly perceived the link between the antinomy in its social aspect (the coexistence of individual freedom and objective necessity in the guise of the rule of market mechanisms) and in its religious aspect (Protestantism with its antinomic motifs of individual responsibility and Predestination). This is why, philosophically, the key point here is the ambiguity of the reference to Hegel. First, there are authors, from Althusser to Karatani,

---

48   Postone, "Rethinking Marx (in a Post-Marxist World)."
49   Ibid.

who, from different theoretical positions, dismiss the reference to Hegel in Marx's critique of political economy as extraneous "coquetry" (like Lacan's later devaluation of his reference to Heidegger). Karatani, for example, insists that, although Marx's *Darstellung* of the self-deployment of capital is full of Hegelian references, the self-movement of capital is far from being equivalent to the circular self-movement of the Hegelian Notion (or Spirit): Marx's point is that this movement never catches up with itself, that it never recovers its credit, that its resolution is postponed forever, that crisis is its innermost constituent (the sign that the Whole of Capital is the non-True, as Adorno would have put it), which is why its movement is that of a "spurious infinity," forever reproducing itself:

> Notwithstanding the Hegelian descriptive style . . . *Capital* distinguishes itself from Hegel's philosophy in its motivation. The end of *Capital* is never the "absolute Spirit." *Capital* reveals the fact that capital, though organizing the world, can never go beyond its own limit. It is a Kantian critique of the ill-contained drive of capital/reason to self-realize beyond its limit.[50]

It is interesting to note that it was already Adorno who, in his *Hegel: Three Studies*, critically characterized Hegel's system in the same "financial" terms as a system living off credit that it can never pay back.[51] First, however, we must note that Hegel's Absolute is also not "absolute" in the naïve sense of achieving full self-identity: it does not end but is forever caught in an eternally repeated circle of self-reproduction—recall Hegel's image of the Idea enjoying its eternal cycle of losing itself and re-appropriating its otherness. Second, Marx's critique is precisely *not* Kantian, since he conceived the notion of limit in the properly Hegelian sense—as a *positive* motivating force which pushes capital further and further in its ever-expanding self-reproduction, not in the Kantian sense of a negative limitation. In other words, what is not visible from the Kantian standpoint is how "the ill-contained drive of capital/reason to self-realize beyond its limit" is totally co-substantial with this limit. The central "antinomy" of capital is its driving force, since the movement of capital is ultimately not motivated by the endeavor to appropriate/penetrate all empirical reality external to itself, but by the drive to resolve its inherent antagonism. In other words, capital "can never go beyond its own limit," not because some noumenal Thing resists its grasp, rather because, in a sense, it is

---

50   Kojin Karatani, *Transcritique: On Kant and Marx*, Cambridge, MA: MIT Press 2005, p. 9.
51   See Theodor W. Adorno, *Hegel: Three Studies*, Cambridge, MA: MIT Press 1994, p. 67.

blinded to the fact that *there is nothing beyond this limit,* only a specter of total appropriation generated by the limit itself.

Which brings us back to the political limitations of Karatani's vision: his project is not really communist, but an impossible Kantian dream of a "transcendental-critical" capitalism replacing the normal "dogmatic" capitalism which wants to appropriate all reality to itself. This Kantian illusion is fully realized in Karatani's reliance on LETS: the form of money that would avoid the fetishistic "transcendental illusion" and thus remain properly transcendental-critical. This is why one should refer to the (today totally neglected) work of Alfred Sohn-Rethel as the necessary companion to Karatani—what cannot but strike the eye of anyone well-versed in the history of Marxism is the conspicuous absence of any reference to this author in Karatani's book. Sohn-Rethel directly deployed the parallel between Kant's transcendental critique and Marx's critique of political economy, but in the opposite critical direction: the structure of the commodity universe *is* that of the Kantian transcendental space. That is to say, Sohn-Rethel's goal was to combine Kantian epistemology with Marx's critique of political economy. When people exchange commodities, they abstract from the specific use-value—only their value is important. Marx called this abstraction "real" because it takes place in the social reality of exchange without conscious effort, whether anybody is aware of it or not is of no importance. And, for Sohn-Rethel, this type of abstraction is the real basis of formal and abstract thinking: all of Kant's categories such as space, time, quality, substance, accident, movement, and so forth are implicit in the act of exchange. There is thus a formal identity between bourgeois epistemology and the social form of exchange, in that both involve an abstraction: it is the historical separation of exchange and use that grounds the possibility of abstract thought—both in ancient Greek and in modern societies. As the origin of the social synthesis, commodity exchange conditions the possibility of all of its thought forms—exchange is abstract and social in contrast to the private experience of use:

> What defines the character of intellectual labour in its full-fledged division from all manual labour is the use of non-empirical form-abstractions which may be represented by nothing other than non-empirical, "pure" concepts. The explanation of intellectual labour and of this division thus depends on proving the origin of the underlying, non-empirical form-abstractions . . . this origin can be none other than the real abstraction of commodity exchange, for it is of a non-empirical form-character and does not

spring from thought. This is the only way in which justice can be done to the nature of intellectual labour and of science and yet avoid idealism. It is Greek philosophy which constitutes the first historical manifestations of the separation of head and hand in this particular mode. For the non-empirical real abstraction is evident in commodity exchange only because through it a social synthesis becomes possible which is in strict spatio-temporal separation from all acts of man's material interchange with nature . . . this kind of social synthesis does not reach fruition before the eighth or seventh centuries BC in Greece, where the first introduction of coinage around 680 BC was of fundamental importance. Thus we are here confronted with the historical origin of conceptual thought in its fully developed form constituting the "pure intellect" in its separation from all man's physical capacities.[52]

Sohn-Rethel here consequently extends the scope of the social-historic mediation to nature itself: it is not only the abstraction from a particular reality which is conditioned by commodity fetishism. The very notion of nature as "objective reality" deprived of any meaning, as the domain of neutral facts opposed to our subjective values, can only emerge in a society in which the commodity form is predominant—this is why the rise of "objective" natural sciences which reduce natural phenomena to meaningless positive data is strictly correlative to the rise of commodity exchange:

It may be confusing to be told that the notion of nature as a physical object-world independent of man emerges from commodity production when it reaches its full growth of monetary economy. Nevertheless this is a true description of the way in which this conception of nature is rooted in history; it arises when social relations assume the impersonal and reified character of commodity exchange.[53]

This is Lukács's position in *History and Class Consciousness*, where he also emphatically claims that "nature is a social category": what appears as "natural" is always mediated/overdetermined by a historically specific social totality. In contrast to Karatani, the position of Lukács and Sohn-Rethel is thus that the passage from bourgeois ideology with its formalism/dualism to the revolutionary-dialectical

---

52   Alfred Sohn-Rethel, *Intellectual and Manual Labour: A Critique of Epistemology*, Atlantic Highlands, NJ: Humanities Press 1977, pp. 66–7.
53   Ibid., pp. 72–3.

thought of totality is, philosophically, the passage from Kant to Hegel. According to this second position, Hegel's dialectic is the mystified form of the revolutionary process of emancipatory liberation: the matrix should remain the same, one should merely, as Lukács put it explicitly, replace, in the role of the subject-object of history, the absolute Spirit with the proletariat. The (deservedly) famous *Grundrisse*-fragment on "Pre-capitalist modes of economic production" can also be read within this horizon, as an attempt to grasp the innermost logic of the historical process along Hegelian lines—the uniqueness of the capitalist mode of production therefore resides in the fact that, in it, "labor is torn out from its primordial immersion in its objective conditions, and, because of this, it appears on the one side itself as labor, and, on the other side, the labor's own product, as objectified labor, obtains against labor a completely autonomous existence as value."[54] The worker thus appears "as objectless, purely subjective capacity of labor, confronted with the objective conditions of production as its non-property, as a foreign property, as value which exists for itself, as capital." However, this

> *most extreme form of alienation*, wherein labour appears in the relation of capital and wage labour, and labour, productive activity appears in relation to its own conditions and its own product, is a necessary point of transition—and therefore already contains in *itself*, in a still only inverted form, turned on its head, the dissolution of *all limited presuppositions of production*, and moreover creates and produces the unconditional presuppositions of production, and therewith the full material conditions for the total, universal development of the productive forces of the individual.[55]

History is thus the gradual process of the separation of subjective activity from its objective conditions, that is from its immersion in the substantial totality; this process reaches its culmination in modern capitalism with the emergence of the proletariat, the substance-less subjectivity of workers totally separated from their objective conditions; this separation, however, is in itself already their liberation, since it creates pure subjectivity, exempted from all substantial ties, which only has to appropriate its objective conditions.

---

54   *MEGA* (Marx-Engels-Gesamtausgabe), Abteilung II, Band 1, Berlin: Dietz Verlag 1976, p. 431.
55   Marx, *Grundrisse*, p. 515.

In contrast to this Hegelian view, the third position is that Hegel's logic *is* the "logic of capital," its speculative expression; this position was systematically deployed by the so-called capital-logic school in Germany back in the 1970s, and also in Brazil and Japan.[56] The traces of this position are clearly discernible in *Capital*—for example, Marx describes the passage from money to capital in Hegelian terms as the passage from substance to subject: capital is the self-deploying and self-differentiating substance, a substance-money made subject:

> The independent form, *i.e.*, the money-form, which the value of commodities assumes in the case of simple circulation, serves only one purpose, namely, their exchange, and vanishes in the final result of the movement. On the other hand, in the circulation M-C-M, both the money and the commodity represent only different modes of existence of value itself, the money its general mode, and the commodity its particular, or, so to say, disguised mode. It is constantly changing from one form to the other without thereby becoming lost, and thus assumes an automatically active character. If now we take in turn each of the two different forms which self-expanding value successively assumes in the course of its life, we then arrive at these two propositions: Capital is money: Capital is commodities. In truth, however, value is here the active factor in a process, in which, while constantly assuming the form in turn of money and commodities, it at the same time changes in magnitude, differentiates itself by throwing off surplus-value from itself; the original value, in other words, expands spontaneously. For the movement, in the course of which it adds surplus-value, is its own movement, its expansion, therefore, is automatic expansion. Because it is value, it has acquired the occult quality of being able to add value to itself. It brings forth living offspring, or, at the least, lays golden eggs.
>
> Value, therefore, being the active factor in such a process, and assuming at one time the form of money, at another that of commodities, but through all these changes preserving itself and expanding, it requires some independent form, by means of which its identity may at any time be established. And this form it possesses only in the shape of money. It is under the form of money that value begins and ends, and begins again, every act of its own spontaneous generation . . .
>
> In simple circulation, C-M-C, the value of commodities attained at the most a form independent of their use-values, *i.e.*, the form of money;

---

56   See, among others, Helmut Reichelt, *Zur logischen Struktur des Kapitalbegriffs*, Frankfurt: Europaische Verlagsanstalt 1970, and Hiroshi Uchida, *Marx's Grundrisse and Hegel's Logic*, New York: Routledge 1988.

but that same value now in the circulation M-C-M, or the circulation of capital, suddenly presents itself as an independent substance, endowed with a motion of its own, passing through a life-process of its own, in which money and commodities are mere forms which it assumes and casts off in turn. Nay, more: instead of simply representing the relations of commodities, it enters now, so to say, into private relations with itself. It differentiates itself as original value from itself as surplus-value; as the father differentiates himself from himself qua the son, yet both are one and of one age: for only by the surplus-value of £10 does the £100 originally advanced become capital, and so soon as this takes place, so soon as the son, and by the son, the father, is begotten, so soon does their difference vanish, and they again become one, £110.[57]

Note how Hegelian references abound here: with capitalism, value is not a mere abstract "mute" universality, a substantial link between the multiplicity of commodities; from the passive medium of exchange, it turns into the "active factor" in the entire process. Instead of only passively assuming the two different forms of its actual existence (money—commodity), it appears as the subject "endowed with a motion of its own, passing through a life-process of its own": it differentiates itself from itself, positing its otherness, and then again overcomes this difference, in other words the movement is its own movement. In this precise sense, "instead of simply representing the relations of commodities, it enters . . . into private relations with itself": the "truth" of its relating to its otherness is its self-relating, i.e., in its self-movement, capital retroactively "sublates" its own material conditions, changing them into subordinate moments of its own "spontaneous expansion"—in pure Hegelese, it posits its own presuppositions. This notion of Hegelian speculation as the mystified expression of the speculative (self-) movement of capital is clearly expressed in this passage:

This *inversion* (*Verkehrung*) by which the sensibly-concrete counts only as the form of appearance of the abstractly general and not, on the contrary, the abstractly general as property of the concrete, characterizes the expression of value. At the same time, it makes understanding it difficult. If I say: Roman Law and German Law are both laws, that is obvious. But if I say: Law (*Das Recht*), this abstraction (*Abstraktum*) *realizes itself* in Roman Law and in German Law, in these concrete laws, the interconnection becoming mystical.[58]

---

57   Marx, *Capital, Volume One*, pp. 171–3.
58   Marx, *Capital, Volume One*, Appendix to the first German edition, 1867.

But, again, one should be very careful here: Marx is not simply criticizing the "inversion" that characterizes Hegelian idealism (in the style of his youthful writings, especially *The German Ideology*). His point is not that, while "effectively" Roman Law and German Law are two kinds of law, in idealist dialectics, the Law itself is the active agent—the subject of the entire process—which "realizes itself" in Roman Law and German Law. Marx's point is that this "inversion" characterizes reality itself. Let us read again the above-quoted passage:

> If now we take in turn each of the two different forms which self-expanding value successively assumes in the course of its life, we then arrive at these two propositions: Capital is money: Capital is commodities. In truth (*In der Tat*: actually), however, value is here the active factor in a process, in which, while constantly assuming the form in turn of money and commodities, it at the same time changes in magnitude, differentiates itself by throwing off surplus-value from itself; the original value, in other words, expands spontaneously.

It is "in truth" ("actually") that the relations are "inverted," that is, that the universality of value realizes itself in its two species, as money and as commodities: as in Hegelian dialectics, the universality of value is here "the active factor" (the subject). This is why we should distinguish between the way reality appears to the everyday consciousness of the individuals caught in the process, and the way reality appears "objectively," without the individuals being aware of it: this second, "objective," mystification can only be articulated through theoretical analysis. And this is why Marx wrote that "the relations connecting the labour of one individual with that of the rest appear, not as direct social relations between individuals at work, but as what they really are, material relations between persons and social relations between things"—the paradoxical claim that, in commodity fetishism, social relations appear "*as what they really are*" (as social relations between things). This overlapping of appearance and reality does not mean (as it does for commonsense) that we have no mystification, since reality and appearance coincide, but, on the contrary, that mystification is redoubled: in our subjective mystification, we follow a mystification inscribed into social reality itself. It is from this insight that one should reread the following well-known passage from *Capital*:

It is *a definite social relation of the producers* in which they *equate (gleichsetzen)* their different types of labour *as human labour*. It is not less a *definite social relation of producers*, in which they *measure* the magnitude of their labours *by the duration of expenditure of human labour-power*. But *within our practical interrelations* these *social characters* of their own labours *appear* to them *as social properties pertaining to them by nature*, as *objective* determinations (*gegenständliche* Bestimmungen) *of the products of labour themselves*, the equality of human labours as a *value-property* of the products of labour, the *measure* of the labour by the socially necessary labour-time as *the magnitude of value* of the products of labour, and finally the social relations of the producers through their labours appear as a *value-relation* or *social relation of these things*, the products of labour. Precisely because of this the products of labour *appear* to them as *commodities*, sensible-supersensible (*sinnlich übersinnliche*) or *social things*.[59]

The crucial words here are *"within our practical interrelations"* — Marx locates the fetishistic illusion not in thinking, in how we misperceive what we do and are, but in our social practice itself. He uses the same words a couple of lines below: "Therefore, *within our practical interrelations, to possess the equivalent-form* appears as *the social natural property* (*gesellschaftliche Natureigenschaft*) of a thing, as a property pertaining to it *by nature*, so that hence it appears to be *immediately exchangeable* with other things just as it exists for the senses (*so wie es sinnlich da ist*)." This is exactly how we should read Marx's general formula of the fetishistic mystification (*"sie wissen das nicht, aber sie tun es"* — they do not know it, but they are doing it): what individuals do not know is the fetishistic "inversion" they obey "within their practical interrelations," that is, in their social reality itself.

So, again, we are dealing here with *two different* levels of "mystification": first, there are the "theological niceties" of the self-movement of capital which have to be unearthed by theoretical analysis; then, there are mystifications of everyday consciousness which culminate in the so-called "Trinity formula": labor, capital, and land as the three "factors" of every production process all of which contribute to the value of the product and which are therefore remunerated accordingly — the worker gets a wage, the capitalist gets profit, and the landowner gets ground-rent. This final mystification is the result of a series of gradual displacements. First, for the capitalist, the distinction between constant and variable capital

---

59 Ibid.

(the capital invested into the means and materials of production which, through their use, just transmit their value to the product, and the capital spent on wages which, through the use of labor-power, generates surplus-value) is replaced by a more "logical" distinction between circulating and fixed capital (the capital which transmits its entire value to the product in one production cycle—materials and wages—and the capital which transmits its value to the products only gradually—buildings, machines, and other technological equipment). This displacement obfuscates the specific source of surplus-value and thus makes it much more "logical" to talk not about the rate of surplus-value (which is the ratio between variable capital and surplus-value) but about the profit rate (the ratio between all the invested capital and the surplus-value disguised as "profit").[60]

What Marx is proposing here is a *structure* in the strict "structuralist" sense of the term. What is a structure? Not just the complex articulation of elements—the minimal definition of a "structure" is that it involves (at least) two levels, so that the "deep" structure is displaced/"mystified" in the superficial "obvious" structure. A reference to Emile Benveniste's famous analysis of the active, passive, and neutral forms of the verb is helpful here: the true opposites are not active and passive (with the neutral form as the mediator between the two extremes), but active and neutral (opposed along the axis of inclusion/exclusion of the subject into the action rendered by the verb), while the passive form functions as the third term negating the common ground of the first two.[61] In the same way, the "deep" distinction between constant and variable capital is transformed into the "obvious" distinction between fixed and circulating capital, "surplus-value" is transformed into "profit," and so on.

The difference between the second and the third positions was put succinctly by Postone: "For Lukács, the proletariat is the Subject, which implies that it should realize itself (he is very much a Hegelian) whereas if Marx says capital is the Subject, the goal would be to do away with the Subject, to free humanity from an ongoing dynamic that it constitutes, rather than to realize the Subject."[62] The obvious temptation here

---

60   With speculative capital, there is yet another mystification: when a capitalist borrows money from a bank and then shares his profit with it, i.e., pays the bank part of his profit as interest, the result is a double mystification—on the one side, it appears that money as such can beget more money, which is why the bank has to be remunerated; on the other side, it appears that the capitalist is not paid for his investment—he got the money from the bank—but for what he did with the money, for his work in the organization of production. The last traces of exploitation are thus obfuscated.
61   See Emile Benveniste, *Problems in General Linguistics*, Miami: Miami University Press 1973.
62   "Marx After Marxism: An Interview with Moishe Postone."

is to project the passage from the second to the third position back onto Marx, as the passage from the *Grundrisse* to *Capital*: in the *Grundrisse*, Marx still thought that the Hegelian dialectic provided the matrix of the entire historical movement from prehistory to capitalist alienation and its "sublation" in the communist revolution; but while he was writing *Capital*, it became clear to him that the idealist mystifications of the Hegelian dialectic perfectly mirror the "metaphysical subtleties and theological niceties" which constitute the secret "inner life" of a commodity. The next temptation would be to say: but why not both? Why can we not read the second and the third positions together? If, as Marx wrote in the *Grundrisse*, capital, capitalist alienation, is in itself (that is, in an inverted form) already the hoped-for liberation from domination, can one not then say that Hegel's logic is in itself, in mystified/inverted form, already the logic of emancipation?

Which of these three positions is then the correct one? Did Marx just externally "coquette" with Hegel's dialectical terminology? Did he rely on it as a mystified formulation of the revolutionary process of emancipation? Or as an idealistic formulation of the very logic of capitalist domination? The first thing to note is that the latter reading of Hegel's dialectic does not go all the way: what, in this view, Hegel deploys is the mystified expression of the *mystification* immanent to the circulation of the capital, or, in Lacanian terms, of its "objectively-social" fantasy. To put it in somewhat naïve terms, for Marx, capital is not "really" a subject-substance which reproduces itself by way of positing its own presuppositions and so on; what this Hegelian fantasy of capital's self-generating reproduction obliterates is workers' exploitation, that is, how the circle of capital's self-reproduction draws its energy from the external (or, rather, "ex-timate") source of value, how it has to parasitize workers. So why not pass directly to the description of workers' exploitation, why bother with fantasies which sustain the functioning of the capital? It is crucial for Marx to include in the description of capital this intermediary level of "objective fantasy," which is neither the way capitalism is experienced by its subjects (they are good empirical nominalists unaware of the "theological niceties" of capital) nor the "real state of things" (of workers being exploited by capital).

So, back to our question about which of the three versions is the correct one. There is another—a fourth—position to be explored, in which one shifts the accent onto Hegel and asks a simple question: *which* Hegel is our point of reference here? Do both Lukács and the capital-logic theorists not refer to the "idealist-subjectivist" (mis)reading of Hegel, to the standard image of Hegel as the "absolute idealist" who asserted Spirit as the true agent of history, its Subject-Substance? Within this framework, Capital can effectively appear as a new embodiment of the Hegelian Spirit, an abstract monster which moves and mediates itself, parasitizing the activity of actual really-existing individuals. This is why Lukács also remains all too idealist when he proposes simply replacing Hegelian Spirit with the proletariat as the Subject-Object of History: Lukács is here not really Hegelian, but a pre-Hegelian idealist.[63] One is even tempted here to talk about Marx's "idealist inversion of Hegel": in contrast to Hegel, who was well aware that the owl of Minerva takes off only at dusk, after the fact—in other words that Thought follows Being (which is why, for Hegel, there can be no scientific insight into the future of society)—Marx reasserts the primacy of Thought: the owl of Minerva (German contemplative philosophy) should be replaced by the crowing of the Gallic rooster (French revolutionary thought) announcing the proletarian revolution—in the proletarian revolutionary act, Thought will precede Being. Marx thus sees in Hegel's motif of the owl of Minerva an indication of the secret positivism of Hegel's idealist speculation: Hegel leaves reality the way it is.

Hegel's reply might be that the delay of consciousness does not imply any naïve objectivism, so that consciousness is caught in a transcendent objective process. What is inaccessible is the impact of the subject's act itself, its own inscription into objectivity. Of course, thought is immanent to reality and changes it, but not as fully self-transparent self-consciousness, not as an Act aware of its impact. A Hegelian thus accepts Lukács's notion of consciousness as opposed to mere knowledge of an object: knowledge is external to the known object, while consciousness is in itself "practical," an act which changes its very object. (Once a worker considers himself as belonging to the ranks of the proletariat, this changes his very reality: he acts differently.) One does something, one counts oneself as (declares oneself as) the person who did it, and, on the basis of this declaration, one does something new—the proper moment of subjective transformation occurs at the moment of declaration, not at the moment of the act. This reflexive moment of declaration means that every utterance not only transmits some content, but, simultaneously, *determines how the subject relates to this content*. Even the most down-to-earth objects and

---

63   See Georg Lukács, *History and Class Consciousness*, Cambridge, MA: MIT Press 1972.

activities always contain such a declarative dimension, which constitutes the ideology of everyday life.

What one should add here is that self-consciousness is itself unconscious: we are not aware of the point of our self-consciousness. If ever there was a critic of the fetishizing effect of fascinating and dazzling "leitmotifs," it is Adorno: in his devastating analysis of Wagner, he tries to demonstrate how the Wagnerian leitmotifs serve as fetishized elements of easy recognition and thus constitute a kind of inner-structural commodification of his music.[64] It is then a supreme irony that traces of this same fetishizing procedure can be found in Adorno's own writings. Many of his provocative one-liners do effectively capture a profound insight or at least touch on a crucial point (for example: "Nothing is more true in psychoanalysis than its exaggerations"); however, more often than his partisans are ready to admit, Adorno gets caught up in his own game, infatuated with his own ability to produce dazzlingly "effective" paradoxical aphorisms at the expense of theoretical substance (recall the famous line from *Dialectic of Enlightenment* on how Hollywood's ideological manipulation of social reality realizes Kant's idea of the transcendental constitution of reality). In such cases where the dazzling "effect" of the unexpected short-circuit (here between Hollywood cinema and Kantian ontology) effectively overshadows the theoretical line of argumentation, the brilliant paradox works precisely in the same manner as the Wagnerian leitmotif: instead of serving as a nodal point in the complex network of structural mediations, it generates idiotic pleasure by focusing attention on itself. This unintended self-reflexivity is something of which Adorno undoubtedly was not aware: his critique of the Wagnerian leitmotif was an allegorical critique of his own writing. Is this not an exemplary case of the unconscious reflexivity of thinking? When criticizing his opponent Wagner, Adorno effectively deploys a critical allegory of his own writing—in Hegelese, the truth of his relation to the Other is a self-relation.

Another Hegel appears here, a more "materialist" Hegel, for whom reconciliation between subject and substance does not mean that the subject "swallows" its substance, internalizing it in its own subordinate moment. Reconciliation rather amounts to a much more modest overlapping or redoubling of the two separations: the subject has to recognize in its alienation from the Substance the separation of the Substance from

---

64   See Theodor W. Adorno, *In Search of Wagner*, London: Verso Books 2005.

itself. This overlapping is what is missed in the Feuerbachian-Marxian logic of dis-alienation in which the subject overcomes its alienation by recognizing itself as the active agent which itself posited what appears to it as its substantial presupposition. In religious terms, this overlapping would amount to the direct (re-)appropriation of God by humanity: the mystery of God is Man, "God" is nothing but the reified/substantialized version of human collective activity, and so on. What is missing here, in theological terms, is the movement of double *kenosis* which forms the very core of Christianity: God's self-alienation overlaps with the aliena-tion from God of the human individual who experiences himself as alone in a godless world, abandoned by a God dwelling in some inaccessible transcendent Beyond.

It is this double *kenosis* that the standard Marxist critique of religion as the self-alienation of humanity misses: "modern philosophy would not have its own *subject* if God's sacrifice had not occurred."[65] For subjectivity to emerge—not as a mere epiphenomenon of the global substantial onto-logical order, but as essential to Substance itself—the split, negativity, and particularization, the self-alienation, must be posited as something that takes place at the very heart of the divine Substance; in other words the move from Substance to Subject must occur within God Himself. In short, man's alienation from God (the fact that God appears to him as an inaccessible In-itself, as a pure transcendent Beyond) must coincide with the alienation of God from Himself (the most poignant expression of this is, of course, Christ's "Father, father, why have you forsaken me?" on the cross): finite human "consciousness only represents God because God re-presents itself; consciousness is only at a distance from God because God distances himself from himself."[66]

This is why standard Marxist philosophy oscillates between the ontol-ogy of "dialectical materialism" which reduces human subjectivity to a particular ontological sphere (no wonder that Georgi Plekhanov, the creator of the term "dialectical materialism," also described Marxism as "dynamized Spinozism"), and the philosophy of *praxis* which, from the young Lukács onwards, takes collective subjectivity which posits/medi-ates every objectivity as its starting point and horizon, and is thus unable to think its genesis from the substantial order, the ontological explosion, the "Big Bang," which gives rise to it.

---

65   Catherine Malabou, *The Future of Hegel: Plasticity, Temporality and Dialectic*, New York: Routledge 2005, p. 111.
66   Ibid., p. 112.

In the Hegelian "reconciliation" between subject and substance, there is no absolute Subject which, in total self-transparency, appropriates and internalizes all objective substantial content. But "reconciliation" also does not mean (as it does in German Idealism from Hölderlin to Schelling) that the subject should renounce its *hubristic* perception of itself as the axis of the world and accept its constitutive "de-centering," its dependence on some primordial abyssal Absolute which is beyond/beneath the subject-object divide, and, as such, also beyond the subjective conceptual grasp. The subject is not its own origin: Hegel firmly rejects Fichte's notion of the absolute I which posits itself and is nothing but the pure activity of this self-positing. But the subject is also not just a secondary accidental appendix or outgrowth of some pre-subjective substantial reality: there is no substantial Being to which the subject can return, no encompassing organic Order of Being in which the subject has to find its proper place. "Reconciliation" between subject and substance means acceptance of this radical lack of any firm foundational point: the subject is not its own origin, it is secondary, dependent upon its substantial presuppositions; but these presuppositions do not have a substantial consistency of their own and are always retroactively posited. The only "absolute" is thus the process itself:

> That "the truth is the whole" means that we should not look at the process that is self-manifestation as a deprivation of the original Being. Nor should we look at it only as an ascent to the highest. The process is already the highest . . . The *subject* for Hegel is . . . nothing but the active relationship to itself. In the subject there is nothing underlying its self-reference, there is *only* the self-reference. For this reason, there is only the process and nothing underlying it. Philosophical and metaphorical models such as "emanation" (neo-Platonism) or "expression" (Spinozism) present the relationship between the infinite and the finite in a way that fails to characterize what the process (self-manifestation) is.[67]

And this is also how one should approach Hegel's outrageously "speculative" formulations about Spirit being its own result, a product of itself: while "Spirit has its beginnings in nature in general,"

> the extreme to which spirit tends is its freedom, its infinity, its being in and for itself. These are the two aspects but if we ask what Spirit is, the immediate answer is that it is this motion, this process of proceeding

---

67   Dieter Henrich, *Between Kant and Hegel*, Cambridge, MA: Harvard University Press 2008, pp. 289–90.

from, of freeing itself from, nature; this is the being, the substance of spirit itself.[68]

Spirit is thus radically de-substantialized: Spirit is not a positive counter-force to nature, a different substance which gradually breaks and shines through the inert nature, it is *nothing but* this process of freeing-itself. Hegel directly disowns the notion of Spirit as some kind of positive Agent which underlies the process:

> Spirit is usually spoken of as subject, as doing something, and apart from what it does, as this motion, this process, as still something particular, its activity being more or less contingent . . . it is of the very nature of spirit to be this absolute liveliness, this process, to proceed forth from naturality, immediacy, to sublate, to quit its naturality, and to come to itself, and *to free itself*, it being itself only as it comes to itself as such a product of itself; *its actuality being merely that it has made itself into what it is*.[69]

If, then, "it is *only* as a result of itself that it is spirit,"[70] this means that the standard discourse on the Hegelian Spirit which alienates itself, and then recognizes itself in its otherness and thus reappropriates its content, is deeply misleading: the self to which Spirit returns is produced in the very movement of this return, or, in other words, that to which the process of return is returning is produced by the very process of returning. Recall here the unsurpassed concise formulations from Hegel's *Logic* on how essence

> presupposes itself and the sublating of this presupposition is essence itself; conversely, this sublating of its presupposition is the presupposition itself. Reflection therefore *finds before it* an immediate which it transcends and from which it is the return. But this return is only the presupposing of what reflection finds before it. What it thus found only *comes to be* through being *left behind* . . . For the presupposition of the return-into-self—that from which essence *comes*, and is only as this return—is only in the return itself.[71]

---

68   G. W. F. Hegel, *Hegel's Philosophie des subjektiven Geistes / Hegel's Philosophy of Subjective Spirit*, Dordrecht: Riedel 1978, pp. 6–7.
69   Ibid.
70   Ibid.
71   *Hegel's Science of Logic*, Atlantic Highlands: Humanities Press International 1989, p. 402. Various nationalist movements with their striving to "return to the origins" are exemplary here: it is the very return to the "lost origins" which literally constitutes what was lost, and, in this sense, the Nation/notion—as a spiritual substance—is the "product of itself."

When Hegel says that a notion is the result of itself, that it provides its own actualization, this claim—which, initially at least, cannot but appear extravagant (the notion is not simply a thought activated by the thinking subject, but possesses a magic property of self-movement)—is to be approached, as it were, from the opposite side: Spirit as the spiritual substance is a substance, an In-itself, which sustains itself *only* through the incessant activity of the subjects engaged in it. For example, a nation exists *only* insofar as its members take themselves as members of this nation and act accordingly, it has absolutely no content, no substantial consistency, outside this activity; and the same goes for, say, the notion of communism—this notion "generates its own actualization" by way of motivating people to struggle for it.

This Hegelian logic is at work in Wagner's universe up to and including *Parsifal*, whose final message is profoundly Hegelian: "The wound can be healed only by the spear that smote it [*Die Wunde schliesst der Speer nur der Sie schlug*]." Hegel says the same thing, although with the accent shifted in the opposite direction: Spirit is itself the wound it tries to heal; that is, the wound is self-inflicted.[72] What is "Spirit" at its most elementary? It is the "wound" of nature: the subject is the immense—absolute—power of negativity, of introducing a gap or cut into the given and immediate substantial unity, the power of *differentiating*, of "abstracting," of tearing apart and treating as self-standing what in reality is part of an organic unity. This is why the notion of the "self-alienation" of Spirit (of Spirit losing itself in its otherness, in its objectivization, in its result) is more paradoxical than it may appear: it should be read together with Hegel's assertion of the thoroughly non-substantial character of Spirit: there is no *res cogitans*, no thing which also has the property of thinking, Spirit is nothing but the process of overcoming natural immediacy, of the cultivation of this immediacy, of withdrawing-into-itself or "taking off" from it, of—why not?—alienating itself from it. The paradox is thus that there is no self that precedes Spirit's "self-alienation": the very process of alienation creates/generates the "self" from which Spirit is alienated and to which it then returns. Spirit's self-alienation is the same as, fully coincides with, its alienation from its Other (nature), because it constitutes itself through its "return-to-itself" from its immersion in natural Otherness. In other words, Spirit's return-to-itself creates the very dimension to which it returns.

---

72   G. W. F. Hegel, *Aesthetics*, Volume 1, Oxford: Oxford University Press 1998, p. 98.

What this also means is that communism should no longer be conceived as the subjective (re-)appropriation of the alienated substantial content—all versions of reconciliation which take the form "the subject swallows the substance" should be rejected. So, again, "reconciliation" is the full acceptance of the abyss of the de-substantialized process as the only actuality that exists: the subject has no substantial actuality, it comes second, it emerges only through the process of separation, of overcoming its presuppositions, and these presuppositions are also only a retroactive effect of the same process of their overcoming. The result is thus that there is, at both extremes of the process, a failure or a negativity inscribed into the very heart of the entity we are dealing with. If the status of the subject is thoroughly "processual," it means that it emerges through the very failure to fully actualize itself. This brings us again to one possible formal definition of the subject: a subject tries to articulate ("express") itself in a signifying chain, this articulation fails, and by means of and through this failure, the subject emerges: the subject is the failure of its signifying representation—this is why Lacan writes the subject of the signifier as $\$$, as "barred." In a love letter, the very failure of the writer to formulate his declaration in a clear and effective manner—his vacillations, the letter's fragmentary nature, and so on—can in themselves be proof (perhaps are the necessary and only reliable proof) that the professed love is authentic: here, the very failure to deliver the message properly is the sign of its authenticity. Were the message to be delivered smoothly, it would only invite the suspicion that it is part of a calculated approach, or that the writer in fact loves himself, or the charm of his writing, more than he loves his beloved, that his love-object is effectively just a pretext for engaging in the narcissistically satisfying activity of writing.

And the same goes for substance: substance is not only always already lost, it only comes to be through its loss, as a secondary return-to-itself—which means that substance is always already subjectivized. In the "reconciliation" between subject and substance, both poles thus lose their firm identity. Take the case of ecology: radical emancipatory politics should aim neither at complete mastery over nature nor at a humble acceptance of the predominance of Mother-Earth. Rather, nature should be exposed in all its catastrophic contingency and indeterminacy, and human agency assumed in the total unpredictability of its consequences. Viewed from this perspective of the "other Hegel," the revolutionary act no longer involves as its agent the Lukácsian substance-subject, that agent who knows what it is doing while doing it.

Proletarians or Rentiers?

One needs this "other Hegel" especially in order to grasp the central problem we are facing today: how does the late-capitalist predominance (or even hegemonic role) of "intellectual/immaterial labor" affect Marx's basic scheme of the separation of labor from its objective conditions, and of the revolution as the subjective re-appropriation of those conditions? The paradox is that while this "immaterial labor" no longer involves the separation of labor from its immediate "objective" conditions (workers own their computers, etc., which is why they can make contracts as autonomous producers), nevertheless the "substance" of "immaterial labor" (what Lacan called the "big Other," the network of symbolic relations) cannot be "appropriated" by collective subject(s) the way the substance of material labor can be. The reason is very precise: the "big Other" (the symbolic substance) is the very network of intersubjective ("collective") relations, as such its "appropriation" can only be achieved if intersubjectivity is reduced to a single subject (even if it is a "collective" one). At the level of the "big Other," "reconciliation" between subject and substance can no longer be conceived as the subject's (re-)appropriation of the substance, but only as the reconciliation of subjects mediated by substance.

It is against this background that we should measure the ambiguity of what is arguably the Left's only original economic idea of the last few decades: the basic (citizen's) income, that is, a form of rent ensuring the dignified survival of all citizens, in particular those who have no other resources. The term "rent" as used in Brazil (*renta basica*) should be taken seriously here: the introduction of a basic rent brings to a conclusion the becoming-rent of profit which characterizes contemporary capitalism. After the rent paid to those who have privatized parts of the "general intellect" (like Bill Gates, who collects rent for enabling people to participate in global networking), and the rent collected by those who dispose of scarce natural resources (oil, etc.), finally, the work force, the third element in the production process, would also be paid a rent. On what is this rent based? As its other name ("citizen's income") indicates, it is a rent paid to all the citizens of a state, privileging them over non-citizens. (This, perhaps, also explains why the idea of demanding some minimal social work as a condition for receiving this rent is seldom discussed: the point is precisely that we are dealing with a rent, something citizens receive on account of the mere fact of being citizens of a state, independently of what they do.) Brazil was the first country to pass a law guaranteeing a minimum income: in 2004, President Lula signed the law guaranteeing "an unconditional basic income, or citizenship income" for every Brazilian citizen or foreigner resident for five years or more. The payment will be of equal value, payable in monthly amounts and sufficient to cover "minimal expenses in food, housing, education and health care," taking into account "the country's level of development and budgetary possibilities." While this "basic citizenship income" will be realized in steps, at the discretion of the executive, and giving priority to the neediest layers of the population, it is nonetheless viewed as an important breakthrough, grounded in a long tradition of social struggle:

> In the last quarter of the 19th century, a real social, economic and political organization was born in Canudos, a municipality in the state of Bahia, in the Northeast of Brazil, created on the grounds of a complex religious system, and headed by Antônio Conselheiro. This community developed a "mutual, cooperative and solidary concept of work." In Canudos, which once held a population of 24 thousand people and 5,200 homes, there was a kind of socio-mystical, religious, assisting, community power inspired by the "equalitarian fraternity of primitive Christian communism," in which there was no hunger. "They all worked together. *Nobody had anything. Everybody worked the soil, everybody labored. Harvested . . . Here's yours . . . Here's yours. Nobody got more nor less.*" Conselheiro had read Thomas More, and his experiences were similar to those of utopian socialists Fourier and Owen. Canudos was razed by the Brazilian army, and Antônio Conselheiro was beheaded in 1897.[73]

The movement in support of a basic citizen's income is also growing in other countries: in South Africa, it has received support from several institutions; in Europe, some followers of Toni Negri are working on a similar legislation for the European Union, and so on. But the truly surprising case is that of Alaska: the Alaska Permanent Fund is a constitutionally established fund managed by a semi-independent corporation; it was established in 1976, when the oil from Alaska's North Slope began flowing into the market, enabling the state to spend at least 25 percent

---

73   Quoted from http://www.exclusion.net.

of proceeds on helping the poor and raising levels of social welfare. In theoretical terms, the first to elaborate the idea was the Brazilian economist Antonio Maria da Silveira who, already in 1975, published a book called *Redistribution of Income*. Today, the main proponent of the idea of a basic income is Philippe Van Parijs, who hailed the new Brazilian law as "a deep reform which belongs in the same category as the abolition of slavery or the adoption of universal suffrage." Parijs's idea is that a capitalist society offering a substantial and unconditional basic income to all its members would be capable of reconciling equality and freedom, resolving the old deadlock whereby more of the one entails less of the other.[74] Relying on Rawls and Dworkin, Parijs claims that such a society beyond traditional capitalism and socialism would be both just and feasible, and would promote a genuine freedom to make choices. In today's society, one cannot really choose to stay at home in order to raise children or to start a business—such freedom would be feasible only if, as a form of income redistribution, a society were to tax the "scarce" commodity of well-paid jobs. But Parijs's idea is that the dynamic of capitalism can be combined with Rawls's notion of a just society as one that maximizes the least advantaged individual's "real freedom," the freedom to choose what one prefers. In short, the only possible moral justification for capitalism would lie in its productivity being harnessed to provide the highest sustainable basic income.

Parijs thus offers a real "Third Way" beyond capitalism and socialism: the very profit-seeking process which sustains capitalist productivity is to be "taxed" to provide for the poor. In contrast to Canudos and other socialist utopias where all members have to work, working or not working is here a truly free choice: the freedom to choose not to work is added to the capitalist society of free choice as a genuine option. If there is exploitation in such a society, it lies not so much in the exploitation of the workers by the capitalists as in the exploitation of the productive strata of both capitalists and workers by the non-workers: those who receive the rent are not the parasites at the top of the social scale (noblemen, priests), but those at the bottom. Furthermore, the minimum income would increase workers' negotiating power, since they would be able to refuse any job offer they considered outrageous or unacceptable; moreover, it would support consumption (giving a boost to demand) and thus help the economy to thrive.

---

74 Developed in his *Real Freedom for All: What (If Anything) Can Justify Capitalism?*, Oxford: Clarendon 1995.

It is easy to note here the link of the theory of the basic income with the "cultural capitalist" notion of a commodity itself containing or providing the remedy against the consumerist excess: in the same way as you do your ecological or social duty by buying a product (the price of a Starbucks cappuccino includes money for organic agriculture, for helping the poor, etc.), the practice of basic income is making capitalism work for the common good: the more capitalists profit, the more they will provide for the welfare of those at the bottom . . . The "Consumtariat" (the idea that, in developed societies, the lower class is no longer a proletariat but a class of consumers kept satisfied with cheap, mass-produced commodities, from genetically modified food to digitalized mass culture)[75] becomes a reality with basic income: those excluded from the production process are paid the basic income not only for reasons of solidarity, but also so that their demand will fuel production and thus prevent crises.

We should be attentive to the presuppositions behind the basic income solution: first, we remain within capitalism—social production remains predominantly capitalist, and redistribution is imposed from the outside by the state apparatus. After 1989, most of the few remaining Communist countries which survived made every possible concession to capitalism, allowing unconstrained market exploitation, giving away everything except the essential: the power of the Communist Party. The basic income society is a kind of symmetrical reversal of this capitalist socialism: it too would give away everything, everything except the essential: the smooth running of the capitalist machine. The basic income idea is the most radical version of Welfare State distributive justice, of the attempt to make capitalism work for social welfare. As such, it presupposes a very strong state, a state able to enforce and control such a radical redistribution. (Along these lines, one can even imagine a worldwide basic income system, in which rich states support poor ones in a regulated way.) The basic income would make it possible to accept and render functional the trend towards the marginalization of 80 percent of the population within the economy.

It should come as no surprise, then, that Peter Sloterdijk, the liberal-conservative *enfant terrible* of contemporary German thought, has arrived at a similar conclusion. Sloterdijk's diagnosis of the contemporary predicament is that in our developed Western societies the balance between the two basic life forces, *eros* and *thymos*, desire grounded in

---

75   See Alexander Bard and Jan Soderqvist, *Netocracy: The New Power Elite and Life After Capitalism*, London: Reuters 2002.

lack and need and pride grounded in self-assertive generosity, has been fatally disturbed: lack and need have priority over excess and generous giving, guilt and dependence over pride and self-assertion, precarious-ness over excess.[76] We are paralyzed by cowardice when confronted with prideful self-assertion and giving: "We have practically no under-standing for the complementary dimension of the life of the human soul, the pride, the honor, the generosity, the having and the bequeath-ing, the whole scale of giving virtues which belong to the complete thymotic life."[77] Consequently, "only a kind of political-psychological reformation"[78] can help us to break out of this "lethargocratic basic atmosphere." And Sloterdijk adds here a nice multiculturalist twist: our focus on lack is Eurocentric and, as such, prevents us from dealing adequately with other cultures: "our thinking, caught in the categories of lacking and needing, prohibits us from grasping even approximately the numerous pride-cultures which continue to exist on the earth together with their life-projects in which the man possesses a plus and demands honor."[79] Sloterdijk would not be Sloterdijk if he had not drawn from this simple diagnosis a far-reaching and provocative conclusion: previ-ously, we thought that only the (united) poor could save the world, but the twentieth century has shown the catastrophic consequences of this attitude, the destructive violence which is engendered by universalized resentment. Now, in the twenty-first century, we should finally have the courage to accept that only the rich can save the world—exceptionally creative and generously giving individuals like Bill Gates and George Soros have done more for the struggles for political freedom and against disease than has any state intervention.

Sloterdijk's diagnosis should not be confused with the usual conserva-tive-liberal rant against the so-called "resentment Left"; the central idea is that we have had enough of the "welfare tyranny" that abounds in our "democratic despotism"; as in the Middle Ages, personal pride is today the greatest sin, and our fundamental right is more and more simply the "right to dependence": "Welfare is today a drug on which more and more people depend. A good human idea turned into a kind of opium for the people."[80] What makes Sloterdijk interesting is that he understands his

---

76   See Peter Sloterdijk, "Aufbruch der Leistungstraeger," *Cicero*, November 2009, pp. 95–107.
77   Ibid., p. 96.
78   Ibid., p. 97.
79   Ibid.
80   Norbert Bolz, "Wer hat Angst vor der Freiheit?," *Cicero*, November 2009, p. 70.

proposal as a strategy to secure the survival of modern Europe's greatest economico-political achievement, the social democratic Welfare State. According to Sloterdijk, our reality—in Europe, at least—is "objective" social democracy as opposed to "subjective" social democracy. We should distinguish between the social democracy associated with the panoply of political parties that claim this label, and social democracy as the "formula of a system" which

> precisely describes the political-economic order of things, which is defined by the modern state as the state of taxes, as the infrastructure-state, as the state of the rule of law and, not least, as the social state and the therapy state. Consequently, in the systemic actuality of the Western nation-states, we are always dealing with two social democracies which we should carefully keep apart if we want to avoid confusion. We encounter everywhere a phenomenal and a structural social democracy, a manifest and a latent one, one which appears as a party and another which is more or less irreversibly built into in the very definitions, functions, and procedures of modern statehood as such.[81]

This "really-existing semi-socialism" is today approaching its limits. Although our societies prosper through the (re)distribution of wealth generated by the creative minority, both political poles deny this fact: the Left denies it because, if it were to admit it, it would have to accept that the Left itself lives off the exploitation of the rich and successful; the Right denies it because, if it didn't, it would have to accept that it is really part of the social-democratic Left. Such denials worked for as long as the political scene was focused on a nation-state playground in which a large "popular" people's party was able to make a pact between the wider population and the productive minority; today, however, with global migration and exchange, this "social-national synthesis" is becoming less and less workable. Therein resides, for Sloterdijk, the lesson of the 2009 German elections: the great losers were both the "people's parties" (the Social Democrats as well as the CSU/CDU), while the winners were the Liberal Democrats who, not wanting to represent the whole of society, deliberately restrict themselves to standing for the productive minority. In order to maintain "objective social democracy," it is therefore crucial to grant this creative and "tax-active" strata the social recognition they deserve: they are not the "exploiters," not the takers, but the givers in

---

81   Sloterdijk, "Aufbruch der Leistungstraeger," p. 99.

our societies, those on whose creativity our entire welfare hinges. This is why, according to Sloterdijk, we should finally correct the old mistake, for which Ricardo and Marx are mainly responsible, of recognizing only "labor" as the value-generating agency:

> Arguably there is in the entire history of ideas no other case of a theoretical mistake which entailed such large practical consequences. On this mistake is based a system, virulent up until today, of calumniating the bearers of creativity, whose reign extends over two hundred years, from the early socialists to the post-Communists.[82]

We should create a "new semantic," a new space of hegemonic ideas in which the culture of pride, and the recognition of the achievers (not only fiscal, but also moral), will have its proper place.

However, one might respond, is not the lesson of the ongoing financial crisis exactly the opposite? Most of the gigantic sums involved in the bail-out are going precisely to those Ayn Randian deregulated "titans" who failed in their "creative" schemes and thereby caused the meltdown. It isn't the great creative geniuses who are now helping lazy ordinary people, it's the ordinary taxpayers who are helping these failed "creative geniuses." Furthermore, is it not the case that, instead of blaming the egalitarian "resentment Left" for the preponderance of *eros* over *thymos*, Sloterdijk would do better to recall his own earlier point that it is capitalism itself which, in its very core, is driven by a perverted *eros*, by a lack which becomes ever deeper the more it is satisfied? Therein resides the superego core of capitalism: the more profit you amass, the more you need. Aware of all this, and referring to Georges Bataille's notion of the "general economy" of sovereign expenditure, which he opposes to the "restrained economy" of capitalism's endless profiteering, Sloterdijk sketches the outlines of capitalism's split from itself, its immanent self-overcoming: capitalism culminates when it "creates out of itself its own most radical—and the only fruitful—opposite, totally different from what the classic Left, caught in its miserabilism, was able to dream about."[83] His positive mention of Andrew Carnegie shows the way: the sovereign self-negating gesture of the endless accumulation of wealth is to spend that wealth on things beyond price and outside market circulation: the arts and sciences, public health, and so on. This

---

82   Ibid., p. 106.
83   Peter Sloterdijk, *Zorn und Zeit*, Frankfurt: Suhrkamp 2006, p. 55.

concluding "sovereign" gesture enables the capitalist to break out of the vicious cycle of endlessly expanded reproduction, of making money in order to earn more money. When he donates his accumulated wealth for the public good, the capitalist self-negates himself as the mere personi-fication of capital and its reproductive circulation: his life acquires meaning. Expanded reproduction is no longer taken as an end in itself. Furthermore, the capitalist thereby accomplishes the shift from *eros* to *thymos*, from the perverted "erotic" logic of accumulation to public recognition and reputation. What this amounts to is nothing less than an elevating of figures such as Soros or Gates into personifications of the inherent self-negation of the capitalist process itself: their charity work—in the form of immense donations to public welfare—is not just a personal idiosyncrasy. Whether sincere or hypocritical, it is the logical end-point of capitalist circulation, necessary from the strictly economic standpoint, since it allows the capitalist system to postpone its crisis. It re-establishes balance—a kind of redistribution of wealth to the truly needy—without falling into a fateful trap, namely the destructive logic of resentment and enforced statist redistribution of wealth which can only end in generalized misery. It also avoids, one might add, the other standard way of re-establishing a kind of balance and asserting *thymos* through sovereign expenditure, namely war. This paradox signals a sad predicament of ours: contemporary capitalism cannot reproduce itself on its own. It needs extra-economic injections of charity to sustain the cycle of social reproduction. The proximity of Sloterdijk and Van Parijs cannot but strike the eye: from opposite ends, they both reach the same practical conclusion—both aim to justify capitalism by way of making it serve the social-democratic Welfare State.

One problem with Sloterdijk's position is precisely that of *thymos*, of people's pride and dignity: how does the fact that my welfare depends on charity affect my pride? The basic income idea seems to avoid this by respecting the dignity of the receivers, since the income is not the result of private charity, but a state-regulated right of every citizen; nevertheless, its division of society into "basic" and "productive" citi-zens poses uncharted problems of resentment. Furthermore, precisely because the minimum required for a dignified life is not only a matter of material needs to be satisfied but (also) a matter of social relations, of envy and resentment, one could argue that there is no "just measure" of the basic income, ensuring it is set neither too low, thereby condemning the non-workers to humiliating poverty, nor too high and so devaluing productive effort. All these problems point towards the utopian nature of the basic income project: yet another dream of having one's cake and eating it, of (cons)training the capitalist beast to serve the cause of egalitarian justice.

But today's historical conjuncture does not compel us to drop the notion of the proletariat, or of the proletarian position — on the contrary, it compels us to radicalize it to an existential level beyond even Marx's imagination. We need a more radical notion of the proletarian subject, a subject reduced to the evanescent point of the Cartesian *cogito*, deprived of its substantial content. It would be easy, all too easy, to raise a critical "Marxist" argument against this universalization of the notion of the proletariat: one should distinguish the general process of "proletarianization" (reduction to the minimum of substanceless subjectivity) from the specific Marxian point regarding the "proletariat" as the exploited productive class deprived of the fruits of its labor. Indeed, it is obvious that what distinguishes the Marxian "proletariat" from the "proletarianization" of the people living in an ecological wasteland, deprived of their collective "symbolic substance," reduced to a "post-traumatic" shell, and so on, is that only the Marxian "proletariat" is the exploited creator of all wealth — which is why it is only the Marxian "proletariat" that can re-appropriate it, recognizing within it its own "alienated" product. The problem is that the rise of "intellectual" labor (scientific knowledge as well as practical *savoir-faire*) to a hegemonic position (the "general intellect") undermines the standard notion of exploitation, since it is no longer labor-time which serves as the source and ultimate measure of value. But what this means is that the concept of exploitation needs to be radically re-thought.

Measured by the strict Marxist standards, Venezuela (like Saudi Arabia, etc.) is now unambiguously *exploiting* other countries: the main source of its wealth, oil, is a natural resource, its price is a rent which does not express value (whose sole source is labor): Venezuelans are enjoying a form of collective rent from the developed countries, rent gained by the fact of possessing scarce resources. The only way one can talk about the exploitation of Venezuela here is to abandon Marx's labor theory of value for the neo-classical theory of three factors of production (resources, labor, capital), each of which contributes to the value of the product. Only if, applying this theory, we claim that a developed country is not paying the full price for oil ("full" price being defined as the price that would have been reached in conditions of frictionless market competition), can we say that, prior to Chávez's rule, Venezuela was "exploited." We cannot have it both ways: something has to go, either Marx's labor theory of value or the notion of exploitation of the developing countries through robbing them of their natural resources.

The diminishing role of direct physical labor is gradually changing the role and motivation of strikes. In the classic era of capitalism, workers went on strike to get better wages, working conditions, and so on, counting on their indispensability—without their labor, machines stood still, losing the owners large amounts of money. Today, since workers can increasingly be replaced by machines or by outsourcing the entire productive process, striking—where it occurs at all—is more a protest act addressed primarily to the general public rather than owners or managers, its goal being simply to maintain jobs by making the public aware of the terrifying predicament that awaits the workers if they lose their jobs (and a typical strike now occurs in a factory which plans to radically curtail or close down production). This is the possibility not taken into account by Marx: the very process of the rise of the "general intellect," and of the marginalization of physical labor measured by time, instead of undermining capitalism by way of rendering capitalist exploitation meaningless, can be used to render workers more impotent and defenseless, using their potential uselessness itself as a threat against them.

Against this background, one can also elaborate in a new way the relationship between the exploited and their exploiters. It was clear already to Marx that the exploiters (the owners of the means of production, that is, of the objective conditions of the production process) are a stand-in for the alienated-objective Other (the capitalist is the agent of "dead" past work). Human subordination of nature is thus reflected in the split within humankind itself, where the relation is inverted: the general productive relationship between humankind and nature is that between subject and object (humanity as a collective subject asserts its domination over nature through its transformation and exploitation in the productive process); within humankind itself, however, productive workers as the living force of domination over nature are themselves subordinated to those who are the agents of, or stand-ins for, subordinated objectivity. This paradox was clearly perceived already by Adorno and Horkheimer in their *Dialectic of Enlightenment*, where they show how domination over nature necessarily entails the class domination of people over other people. The question to be raised here concerns the classical Marxian notion of proletarian revolution: is it not all too subjectivist, conceiving communism as the final victory of subject over substance? This does not mean that we have to accept the necessity of social domination; we should, rather, accept the "primacy of the objective" (Adorno): the way to rid ourselves of our masters is not for humankind itself to become a collective master over nature, but to recognize the imposture in the very notion of the Master.

Interlude 3.   The Architectural Parallax

My knowledge of architecture is limited to some idiosyncratic data: my love for Ayn Rand and her architecture-novel *The Fountainhead*;[1] my admiration for baroque Stalinist "wedding-cake" *kitsch*; my dream of a house composed only of secondary spaces and places of passage — stairs, corridors, toilets, store-rooms, kitchen — with no living room or bedroom. The danger I am courting is thus that what I have to say will oscillate between the two extremes of unfounded speculation and architectural commonplace.

But maybe, just maybe, my use of the notion of parallax will justify the risk involved in my venturing some remarks on architecture based on this concept (which I have borrowed from Kojin Karatani).[2] "Parallax," according to its common definition, is the apparent displacement of an object (the shift of its position against a background), caused by a change in observational position that provides a new line of sight. The philosophical twist to be added, of course, is that the observed difference is not simply "subjective," thanks to the fact that it is the same object existing "out there" which is seen from two different points of view. It is rather that, as Hegel would have put it, subject and object are inherently "mediated," so that an "epistemological" shift in the subject's point of view always reflects an "ontological" shift in the object itself.

The parallax gap is thus not just a matter of shifting perspective (from one standpoint, a building looks a certain way — if I move a little bit, it looks different); things get interesting when we notice that the gap is inscribed into the "real" building itself — as if the building, in its very material existence, bears the imprint of different and mutually exclusive

---

1   We should mention here Brigitte Reimann's *Franziska Linkerhand* (first published after the author's death in 1974, but in a censored form), a classic of GDR literature: a true anti-*Fountainhead*, it concerns the struggle of a young woman architect to construct buildings which would be livable in for ordinary people.
2   See Kojin Karatani's *Transcritique: On Kant and Marx*, Cambridge, MA: MIT Press 2003.

perspectives. When we succeed in identifying a parallax gap in a building, the gap between the two perspectives thus opens up a place for a third, virtual building. In this way, we can also define the creative moment of architecture: it concerns not merely or primarily the actual building, but the virtual space of new possibilities opened up by the actual building. Furthermore, the parallax gap in architecture means that the spatial disposition of a building cannot be understood without reference to the temporal dimension: the parallax gap *is* the inscription of our changing temporal experience when we approach and enter a building. It is a little bit like a cubist painting, presenting the same object from different perspectives, condensing into the same spatial surface a temporal extension. Through the parallax gap in the object itself, "time becomes space" (which is Claude Lévi-Strauss's definition of myth).

It is in this sense that, when confronted with an antinomic stance in the precise Kantian sense of the term, we should renounce all attempts to reduce one aspect to the other (or, a fortiori, to enact a kind of "dialectical synthesis" of opposites). The task is, on the contrary, to conceive of all possible positions as responses to a certain underlying deadlock or antagonism, as so many attempts to resolve this deadlock. This brings us immediately to so-called postmodern architecture which, sometimes, seems to enact the notion of parallax in a directly palpable way. Think about Liebeskind or Gehry: their work often appears as a desperate (or joyous) attempt to combine two incompatible structuring principles within the same building (in the case of Liebeskind, horizontal/vertical and oblique cubes; in the case of Gehry, traditional house with modern—concrete, corrugated iron, glass—supplements), as if two principles were locked in a struggle for hegemony.

Postmodernism and Class Struggle

In his seminal essay on Gehry, Fredric Jameson reads his plans for individual houses as an attempt to mediate tradition (old ornamented wooden structures) and alienated modernity (the iron, concrete and glass). The result is an amphibious building, a freakish combination, an old house to which, like a cancerous outgrowth, a modern concrete-iron part is annexed. In his first landmark project, the renovation of his own home in Santa Monica (1977–78), Gehry "took a modest bungalow on a corner lot, wrapped it in layers of corrugated metal and chain-link, and poked glass structures through its exterior. The result was a simple house extruded into surprising shapes and surfaces, spaces and views."[3] Jameson discerns a quasi-utopian impulse in this "dialectic between the remains of the traditional (rooms from the old house, preserved like archaic dream traces in a museum of the modern), and the 'new' wrappings, themselves constituted in the base materials of the American wasteland."[4] This interaction between the space of the preserved old house and the interstitial space created by the wrapping generates a new space, a space which "poses a question fundamental to thinking about contemporary American capitalism: that between advanced technological and scientific achievement and poverty and waste."[5] A clear indication, to my Marxist mind, that architectural projects are answers to a problem which is ultimately socio-political.

But are we justified in using the (now already half-obsolete) term "postmodernism"? Insofar as post-'68 capitalism forms a specific economic, social, and cultural unity, this very unity justifies the name "postmodernism." Although many warranted criticisms were made of postmodernism as a new form of ideology, one should nonetheless admit that, when Jean-François Lyotard, in his *The Postmodern Condition*, elevated the term from merely describing certain new artistic tendencies (especially in writing and architecture) to designating a new historical epoch, there was an element of authentic *nomination* in his act: "postmodernism" effectively functioned as a new Master-Signifier which introduced a new order of intelligibility into the confused multiplicity of historical experience. We can thus easily apply to architecture the Lacanian triad of the Real, the Symbolic, and the Imaginary, vaguely corresponding to the triad of realism, modernism, and postmodernism. First, there is the reality of the physical laws one has to obey if a building is to stand up, of the concrete functions it has to fulfill, of the needs it has to satisfy (people should be able to live or work in it; it should not cost too much)—all the panoply of pragmatic-utilitarian considerations. Then, there is the symbolic level: the (ideological) meanings a building is supposed to embody and convey. Finally, there is the imaginary space: the experience of those who will live or work in the building—how does it feel to them? We might argue that one of the defining feature of postmodernism is the autonomization of each of these three levels: function is dissociated from form and so forth.

---

3   Hal Foster, "Why All the Hoopla?," *London Review of Books*, August 23, 2001.
4   Fredric Jameson, *Post-Modernism, or, the Cultural Logic of Late Capitalism*, London: Verso 1991, p. 276.
5   Ibid.

If ever there was an example of architecture in which the symbolic function predominated, it was in Communist Albania, where its leader Enver Hoxha, obsessed with protecting the country from foreign invasion, ordered the construction of over 10,000 small concrete cupola-like bunkers (mostly about six yards in parameter) which are strewn all over Albania (the poorest country in Europe with 1.5 million inhabitants). Obviously, the role of these bunkers was neither real (as a means of military defense they were worthless) nor imaginary (they were certainly not built with the pleasurable experience of those trained to use them in mind), but for purely symbolic reasons: to serve as a sign of Albania's determination to defend itself at all costs.[6]

To these three levels of architecture—the real, the symbolic, and the imaginary— one should add a fourth: *virtual architecture*. Second Life is a thriving 3-D space of virtual communities in which one buys part of a virtual space shared by others, composes the identity of one's own avatar, and then goes on to build a home, do business, interact with others, and so on—even China is moving in with its own version. The key difference with regard to multi-player internet games like Warcraft is that in Second Life there are no pre-established rules and tasks, and one must form one's own identity from scratch. (And of course, this leads to ethical and legal problems: there have already been cases of virtual pedophilia.) The phenomenon is becoming more and more important—according to some estimates, within a couple of years, more than three quarters of internet users (over a billion people) will also inhabit a virtual universe of the kind on offer in

---

6   In his short novel *The Pyramid* (London: Harvill Press 1996), Ismail Kadare underpins this symbolic function with a real one. The novel begins with the Pharaoh Cheops announcing to his advisors that he does not want to build a pyramid like his predecessors. Alarmed by this suggestion, advisors point out that pyramid building is crucial to preserving his authority: some generations earlier, prosperity made the people of Egypt more independent, and they began to doubt and resist the Pharaoh's authority. When Cheops decides that Egypt's prosperity must be diminished, his advisors examine the different options for bringing this about (engaging in war with neighboring countries; artificially provoking a natural catastrophe—like disturbing the flow of Nile and thus ruining agriculture) but they are all rejected as being too dangerous (should Egypt lose the war, the Pharaoh himself and his elite may lose power; a natural catastrophe might expose the inability of those in power to control the situation and thus generate chaos). So they return to the idea of building a pyramid so large that its construction will mobilize the full resources of the country and so drain its prosperity—sapping the energies of its populace will keep everyone in line. The project turns the country into an emergency state for two decades, with the Pharaoh's secret police busy uncovering sabotage plots and organizing Stalinist-style arrests, public confessions, and executions. The novel concludes with a report on how the Pharaoh's wise and ingenious insight was practiced again and again throughout later history, most recently and originally in Albania where, instead of one big pyramid, thousands of little bunkers did the same job.

Second Life.[7] The irony is that this community has its own money, "Linden Dollars," which have a fixed rate of exchange with "real" dollars. That is to say, within this universe, one's avatar has to shop—has to buy clothes, food, cars, houses, and so on, since most players cannot program them. And who sells these items? Other players who can do the programming. There is a Second Lifer fashion designer who sells shirts and jackets for other players' avatars: in real life, he was not earning enough, so he moved to Second Life, making sketches of the clothes and then hiring an inexpensive programmer to digitalize the designed items. His earnings in real money terms are three times more than they were in his real-life job, plus he has no problems with physical workers or raw materials—once the design is digitalized, selling thousands of each item involves just making so many copies, which costs nothing. No wonder Second Life has been praised for offering a space of "pure" frictionless capitalism.

In his modernist manifesto *Ornament and Crime*, from 1908, Adolf Loos drew from the axiom that "form follows function" the demand for the "elimination of ornament": "The evolution of culture marches with the elimination of ornament from useful objects." For Loos, ornaments were "immoral" and "degenerate," so their suppression was necessary for regulating modern society. Interestingly, he took as one of his examples the tattooing of the Papuans—Loos considered the Papuans not to have evolved to the moral and civilized levels of modern man, who, should he tattoo himself, would be considered either a criminal or a degenerate. We should add here that, in our everyday lives, ideology is at work especially in the apparently innocent reference to pure utility—one should never forget that, in the symbolic universe, "utility" functions as a reflexive notion, that is, it always involves the assertion of utility as meaning (for example, someone who lives in a large city and drives a Land Rover is unlikely to be leading the kind of no-nonsense, "down to earth" life suggested by his choice of car; rather, he owns such a vehicle in order to signal that he leads his life under the sign of a no-nonsense, "down to earth" attitude).

The "architecturally correct" opposition between authentic function and vulgar display can be illustrated by the contrast between a simple water pump and a gold tap: the one a simple object satisfying a vital need, the other suggesting an excessive display of wealth. However, one should always be careful in such cases to avoid the trap signaled by John Berger

---

7   See the report "Alternate Universe," in *Newsweek*, July 30, 2007, pp. 36–45.

in his *Success and Failure of Picasso* where he notes acidly that Picasso's blue period, "because it deals pathetically with the poor, has always been the favorite among the rich."[8] Upon a closer look, one soon discovers that this opposition is overdetermined by a much more complex and ambiguous background. Anyone who visits real slums (like the Brazilian *favelas*) cannot help noticing how the improvised patchwork buildings, even if made from remainders of corrugated iron and wood, are full of often ridiculously excessive kitsch decorations, including (fake, of course) gold taps. It is (mostly) poor people who dream about gold taps, while rich people like to imagine the simple functionality of household equipment — providing a simple water pump is how Bill Gates seeks to help poor Africans, while the poor Africans themselves would probably embellish it as soon as possible with "kitsch" ornamentation. It is like the ironic remark made by an observer of the Yeltsin years in Russia that ordinary women who wanted to appear attractive dressed like (the common idea of) prostitutes (heavy red lipstick, cheap jewels, and so on), while real prostitutes preferred to mark their distinction by wearing simple but expensive "business" suits. Indeed, as a saying popular among the poor who participate in carnivals in Brazil goes: "Only the rich like modesty; the poor prefer luxury."

In contrast to Loos, Robert Venturi emphasized the importance of a building communicating meaning to the public, which necessitates incorporating non-functional elements into the building — he wittily changed Mies van der Rohe's maxim "less is more" into "less is a bore." What, again, we should add here is that modernist functionalist austerity is always reflexive; it also communicates meaning: the "functionality" of a high modernist building is the message the building emanates. It is not simply that it *is* functional, it *declares itself as* being such, but with the irony that this declaration can often be at the expense of the building's real functionality: modernist buildings designed without superfluous ornament and simply to fulfill their function end up by precisely not fulfilling their declared functions — the people who live in them often feel constrained and uneasy. It is the excessive, non-functional elements of a building which make it actually "functional," that is, livable. In classic modernism, a building was supposed to obey one all-encompassing code, while with postmodernism we have a multiplicity of codes. This can be either a multiplicity (ambiguity) of meanings — what Charles Jencks

---

8   John Berger, *The Success and Failure of Picasso*, New York: Pantheon 1989, p. 3.

called "alluded metaphor" (is the Sydney Opera House the growth of a blossom or a series of turtles copulating?) — or a multiplicity of functions, from performance to shopping and eating (Snøhetta's National Opera House in Oslo, designed to appeal to a younger generation, tries to appear "cool" by imitating sleek stealth-bomber lines; furthermore, the roof inclines into the fjord and doubles as a swimming platform).

As has been often remarked, postmodernism can be said to stand for the *deregulation* of architecture — for a radical historicism where, in a globalized pastiche, everything is possible, anything goes. Pastiche works like "empty parody": a radical historicism within which the whole of the past is equalized in a synchronicity of the eternal present. The exact functioning of pastiche should be specified with concrete examples and analysis. Let me take an extreme case: in Moscow, there are a couple of exclusive new apartment blocks, designed for the *nouveaux riches*, which perfectly imitate the style of the Stalinist neo-Gothic Baroque (Lomonosov University, the Palace of Culture in Warsaw, etc.). To grasp their ideological meaning, let me focus on another, even more extreme, phenomenon, linked to a recent art scandal in Russia. At the beginning of December 2008, the prestigious Kandinsky Prize, the highest art prize in Russia (financially supported by the Guggenheim Foundation and Deutsche Bank), was given to Alexey Belyaev-Guintovt. As expected, this caused a great commotion in art circles, not only in Russia but also in the West, on account of Belyaev's outspoken politico-ideological orientation: his paintings directly and crudely display his "National-Bolshevism," an eclectic mixture of Russian Orthodox-patriotic motifs and the "Stalino-Fascist" anti-liberal "totalitarian" motifs of discipline, sacrifice, and so on, all rendered in a kitschy Stalinist Romantic-realist baroque style. Belyaev is a member of philosopher Alexander Dugin's pro-Kremlin Eurasian movement, which calls for "union with our great Eastern neighbours" and anticipates the "blinding dawn of the new Russian Revolution — fascism as limitless as our lands, and red as our blood." Its catechism features phrases such as "Strength Begets Strength" and "Our Goal is Absolute Power!" How are we to read Belyaev's success? One should begin by openly identifying his "class basis." Predictably, Belyaev's glorification of violence, imperial domination, blood, soil, and war, expressed in a self-consciously triumphal neo-Stalinist aesthetic, mixing crimson with gold leaf to confirm its redundant imperialist messages, is not only criticized but also ferociously rejected by the three main ideologico-artistic orientations in Russia — namely, "authentic" Orthodox conservatives, pro-Western liberals, and (whatever remains of) the Left—who all dismiss Belyaev as a clown and performer not to be taken seriously as an artist. This constellation was reflected in the very competition for the prize, where Belyaev unexpectedly beat the anti-Communist veteran Boris Orlov's *Parade of Astral Bodies* and the Communist Dmitry Gutov's *Used*. Orlov's work (which had been expected to win) is a collection of sculptural hybrids (including heads of German eagles and tails of Soviet airplanes covered with black cloth) which pour out of a replica of Malevich's *Black Square* hung on the wall. The point, of course, is that *Black Square*, this emblem of modernism and the Russian avant-garde, stands also for the crimes that modernity perpetrated under the Nazi and Soviet empires—by clearing away the past, erasing the texture of tradition to leave only the minimal difference of black and white, Malevich unwittingly creates the space in which "totalitarian" violence can thrive. (Platonov's *Foundation Pit* can also be read at this level: the digging of the foundation for the gigantic "Proletarian Home" creates a massive empty square; the construction of the building itself was never even begun.) Belyaev's work has the same content as Orlov's, but deprived of the dialectical tension with the *Black Square* background which provides the critical edge: in Belyaev, we have only the "totalitarian" content, directly staged in an affirmative mode. How could this have happened and what does it mean? As the socialist league VPERED [Forward!] explained:

It is not that the curators and critics in the jury of the Kandinsky Prize are fascist sympathizers . . . The problem is that they are ultra-liberals. Their market utopianism makes no distinction between right and left, brown and red, fascism and communism; it sees irony lurking around every corner to make everything nice and normal again. "We didn't talk about the artist's political convictions," says jury member Alexander Borovsky, head of the Russian Museum's contemporary art department. Borovsky also claims that Belyaev's work is a distanced, playful take on the etatist zeitgeist. But there is nothing playful in Belyaev's calls for Russian tanks to roll on Tbilisi, to execute the Georgian president, to create a "Greater Serbia" or to "liberate" the former Soviet republics under the banner of a Eurasian (read: Russian) Empire . . . It is this indifference that unites the obscure "left-nationalist," essentially postmodern ideology of Eurasianism and the pan-aestheticism of the Russian business and media elites who control the board of the Kandinsky Prize. "Let a thousand flowers bloom!" "All ideologies are equal!" "Art beyond politics!" cry all these respectable people as one, thus legitimizing increasingly overt expressions of genuinely felt

fascism in the public sphere. Their indifference is a form of complicity
. . . The presence of figures like Belyaev testifies to the ruling elite's rapid
drift toward fascism in a moment of crisis. This elite is already deeply
reactionary and anti-democratic, having accumulated its capital violently
through shock privatization and expropriation. Five years ago, it began
using contemporary art as a means of civic legitimation, establishing its
hegemony over the more liberal, glamorous side of cultural life during the
Putin "normalization."[9]

The key to Belyaev's success definitely resides in the way he "integrates
Russia's Soviet hangover with its hyper-capitalist present"—it is, however,
crucial to analyze the precise modality of this integration (or, to put it in
more contemporary theoretical terms, articulation). The self-perception
of the engaged public is that of playful indifference: is what Belyaev is
doing with "totalitarian" symbols not the ultimate triumph over "totalitarianism"—he can play with it, act as if he believes in it, and nonetheless
its ideological efficacy is totally suspended? "Russia's Soviet hangover"
is thus acted out, reduced to an impotent pastiche. Ironic, postmodern
"Stalino-Fascism" should thus be considered as the final stage of Socialist
Realism, in which the formula is reflectively redoubled, becoming its own
pastiche. So why should we not read Belyaev's use of "totalitarian" motifs
as a case of postmodern irony, as a comic repetition of the "totalitarian"
tragedy? Marx famously wrote that history occurs first as tragedy, then
as farce—the ancient Greeks said farewell to their gods in the form of
Lukianus's satires, making fun of them. However, as many perspicuous
commentators have noticed, sometimes this order can be reversed: what
begins as a farce ends up as a tragedy. Throughout the late 1920s, for
instance, Hitler and his fringe party were universally mocked as clownish
buffoons.

The "class basis" of Belyaev and his pals is thus the new Russian capitalist elite which sees itself as ideologically indifferent, "apolitical," caring
only about money and success, despising all great Causes. The "spontaneous ideology" of this new bourgeoisie appears, paradoxically, as the
opposite of their vulgar "passion of the real" (pleasure, money, power):
a (no less vulgar) pan-aestheticism—all ideologies are equal, equally
ridiculous, they are useful only to provide spicy aesthetic excitement, so
the more problematic they are, the more excitement they generate. And

---

9   VPERED Socialist Movement, Chto Delat Platform, "An Open Letter on the 2008 Kandinsky
Prize" (December 8, 2008).

exactly the same goes for the new apartment blocks built in the style of a neo-Stalinist architecture which *pretends to pretend*—it (and its public) think that they are just playing a game, but what they are unaware of is that, independently of their playful attitude, the game has the potential to get serious. Their "playful indifference" conceals the reality of the ruthless exercise of power: what they stage as aesthetic spectacle is reality for the masses of ordinary people. Their indifference towards ideology is the very form of their complicity with the ruling ideology.

This indifference bears witness to how, in postmodernism, the parallax is openly admitted, displayed—and, in this way, neutralized: the antagonistic tension between different standpoints is flattened out into an indifferent plurality of standpoints. "Contradiction" thus loses its subversive edge: in a space of globalized permissiveness, inconsistent standpoints cynically co-exist—cynicism is the reaction of "So what?" to inconsistency. One ruthlessly exploits natural resources but also contributes to Green causes—so what? Sometimes, the thing itself can serve as its own mask—the most effective way to obfuscate social antagonisms being to openly display them.

The Incommensurability

But perhaps we have gone too fast. Let me step back and address the basic issue: how does an ideological edifice (real architectural edifices included) deal with social antagonisms? In his classic *The Political Unconscious*, Fredric Jameson proposed a perspicuous ideologico-critical reading of Claude Lévi-Strauss's interpretation of the unique facial decorations of the Caduveo Indians from Brazil:[10] they use "a design which is symmetrical but yet lies across an oblique axis . . . a complicated situation based upon two contradictory forms of duality, and resulting in a compromise brought about by a secondary opposition between the ideal axis of the object itself [the human face] and the ideal axis of the figure which it represents." Jameson comments: "Already on the purely formal level, then, this visual text has been grasped as a contradiction by way of the curiously provisional and asymmetrical resolution it proposes for that contradiction."[11] (Incidentally, does this not sound like a map of Manhattan, where the symmetrical design of streets and avenues is cut across by the oblique axis of Broadway? Or, at the architectural level,

---

10   See Claude Lévi-Strauss, *Tristes Tropiques*, New York: Atheneum 1971, pp. 176 ff.
11   Fredric Jameson, *The Political Unconscious* (1981), new edition, London: Routledge 2002, p. 63.

like a typical Liebeskind building with its tension between vertical and crooked lines?) In the next, crucial, move, Lévi-Strauss interprets this imagined formal resolution of an antagonism as (not a "reflection," but) a symbolic act, a transposition-displacement of the basic social imbalance-asymmetry-antagonism of Caduveo society. The Caduveo are a hierarchical society, and their

> nascent hierarchy is already the place of the emergence, if not of political power in the strict sense, then at least of relations of domination: the inferior status of women, the subordination of youth to elders, and the development of a hereditary aristocracy. Yet whereas this latent power structure is, among the neighboring Guana and Bororo, masked by a division into moieties which cuts across the three castes, and whose exogamous exchange appears to function in a nonhierarchical, essentially egalitarian way, it is openly present in Caduveo life, as surface inequality and conflict. The social institutions of the Guana and Bororo, on the other hand, provide a realm of appearance, in which real hierarchy and inequality are dissimulated by the reciprocity of the moieties, and in which, therefore, "asymmetry of class is balanced . . . by symmetry of 'moieties."[12]

Is this not also our predicament? In bourgeois societies, we are split between formal-legal equality sustained by the institutions of a democratic state, and class distinctions enforced by the economic system. We live the tension between, on the one hand, politically correct respect for human rights, and so forth, and growing inequalities, gated communities, and exclusions on the other. And exactly the same goes for architecture: when a building embodies democratic openness, this appearance is never a mere appearance—it has a reality of its own, it structures the way individuals interact in their real lives. The problem with the Caduveo was that (like today's non-democratic states) they lacked this appearance— they were not "lucky enough to resolve their contradictions, or to disguise them with the help of institutions artfully devised for that purpose. . . . since they were unable to conceptualize or to love this solution directly, they began to dream it, to project it into the imaginary." The facial decorations are "a fantasy production of a society seeking passionately to give symbolic expression to the institutions it might have had in reality, had not interest and superstition stood in the way."[13] (Note the refined texture

---

12   Ibid., pp. 63–4.
13   Lévi-Strauss, *Tristes Tropiques*, pp. 179–80.

of Levi-Strauss's analysis—Jameson himself seems to miss a dimension when he summarizes its result: Caduveo facial art "constitutes a symbolic act, whereby real social contradictions, insurmountable in their own terms, find a purely formal resolution in the aesthetic realm,"[14] and, in this sense, "the aesthetic act is itself ideological, and the production of aesthetic or narrative form is to be seen as an ideological act in its own right, with the function of inventing imaginary or formal 'solutions' to irresolvable social contradictions."[15])

However, Lévi-Strauss deserves here a precise and close reading: it is not that, simply and directly, Caduveo facial decorations formulate an imaginary resolution of real contradictions; it is rather that they supplement the lack of a properly functioning "appearance" which could be inscribed into their very social and institutional organization. In other words, we are not dealing with a longing for real equality, but with the longing for a *proper appearance*.[16] This is why Jameson is fully justified in talking about the "political unconscious": there is a coded message in formal architectural play, and the message delivered by a building often functions as the "return of the repressed" of the official ideology. Recall Wittgenstein's insight: what we cannot directly talk about can be shown by the form of our activity. What the official ideology cannot openly talk about may be revealed in the mute signs of a building.

This brings us to an unexpected result: it is not only that the fantasy embodied in the mute language of buildings can articulate the utopia of justice, freedom, and equality betrayed by actual social relations; this fantasy can also articulate a *longing for inequality*, for a clear-cut hierarchy and for class distinctions. Jameson takes Stanley Kubrick's *The Shining*, another film focused on architecture, as exemplary of this ambiguity of utopian impulses. As we all know, the film (based on Stephen King's novel) takes place in a large modern mountain hotel, closed for winter, and occupied by a single family looking after it.[17] The hotel is, of course, a cursed building haunted by spirits of the past—but which spirits? It is here that Jameson finds the film disturbing:

14   Jameson, *The Political Unconscious*, p. 64.
15   Ibid.
16   Does the same not hold for Niemeyer's plan of Brasilia, this imaginary dream of the resolution of social antagonisms which supplements not the reality of social antagonisms, but the lack of an ideologico-egalitarian mechanism which might cover them up with a properly functioning appearance?
17   Already this basic situation cannot but evoke rich associations: while in Japan one may be squeezed in a subway crowd and still feel at a distance from others, in *The Shining*, even a large abandoned hotel is not large enough for a single family whose members feel crowded out and explode in aggression and violence.

the drive towards community, the longing for collectivity, the envy of other, achieved collectivities, emerges with all the force of a return of the repressed: and this is finally, I think, what *The Shining* is all about. Where to search for this "knowable community," to which, even excluded, the fantasy of collective relations might attach itself? It is surely not to be found in the managerial bureaucracy of the hotel itself, as multinational and standardized as a bedroom community or a motel chain . . . Where the novel stages the "past" as a babel of voices and an indistinct blast of dead lives from all the generations of historical inhabitants in the hotel's history, Kubrick's film foregrounds and isolates a single period, multiplying increasingly unified signals: tuxedoes, roadsters, hipflasks, slicked-down hair parted in the middle . . . That generation, finally, is the twenties, and it is by the twenties that the hero is haunted and possessed. The twenties were the last moment in which a genuine American leisure class led an aggressive and ostentatious public existence, in which an American ruling class projected a class-conscious and unapologetic image of itself and enjoyed its privileges without guilt, openly and armed with its emblems of top-hat and champagne glass, on the social stage in full view of the other classes. The nostalgia of *The Shining*, the longing for collectivity, takes the peculiar form of an obsession with the last period in which class consciousness is out in the open: even the motif of the manservant or valet expresses the desire for a vanished social hierarchy, which can no longer be gratified in the spurious multinational atmosphere in which Jack Nicholson is hired for a mere odd job by faceless organization men. This is clearly a "return of the repressed" with a vengeance: a Utopian impulse which scarcely lends itself to the usual complacent and edifying celebration, which finds its expression in the very snobbery and class consciousness we naively supposed it to threaten.[18]

And, *mutatis mutandis*, does the same not hold for Stalinist neo-Gothic architecture? Does it not enact the "return of the repressed" of the official egalitarian-emancipatory socialist ideology, the weird desire for hierarchy and social distinctions? The utopia enacted in architecture can also be a conservative utopia of regained hierarchical order. (The same perhaps also holds for the monumental public buildings from the Roosevelt era, like the central post office in New York. No wonder the NYU central building in downtown Manhattan looks like Lomonosov University in Moscow . . .)

The architectural background of *The Shining* is thus crucial — the murderous madness which explodes can only be explained in the

---

18   Fredric Jameson, "Historicism in *The Shining*," in *Signatures of the Visible*, London: Routledge 1992, pp. 82–98; available online at http://www.visual-memory.co.uk/amk/doc/0098.html.

terms of the tension (or incommensurability) between the lone family and the gigantic empty building they occupy. In this sense, one can even read *Psycho*, Alfred Hitchcock's masterpiece, as the staging of an architectural antagonism: is Norman not split between the two *houses*, the modern horizontal motel and the mother's vertical Gothic house, forever running between the two, never finding a proper place of his own? In this sense, the *unheimlich* character of the film's end means that, in his full identification with the mother, he finally found his *heim*, his home. In modernist works like *Psycho*, this split is still visible, while the main goal of contemporary postmodern architecture is to obfuscate it. Suffice it to recall the "New Urbanism," with its return to small family houses in small towns, with front porches, recreating the cozy atmosphere of the local community—clearly, this is a case of architecture as ideology at its purest, providing an imaginary (although "real" in the sense of materialized in the actual disposition of houses) solution to a real social deadlock which has nothing to do with architecture and everything to do with late capitalist dynamics. Gehry's work offers a more ambiguous case of the same antagonism: he takes one of the two poles of the antagonism—an old-fashioned family house or a modernist concrete-and-glass building—and then either submits it to a kind of cubist anamorphic distortion (curving walls and windows, etc.) or combines the old family home with a modernist supplement. So here is my hypothesis: if the Bates Motel had been built by Gehry, directly combining the old house and the modern motel into a new hybrid entity, there would have been no need for Norman to kill his victims, since he would have been relieved of the unbearable tension that compels him to run between both places—he would now have a third place of mediation between the two extremes.

The hypothesis, furthermore, is that today's gigantic performance and arts complexes, arguably the paragon of contemporary architecture, effectively try to impose themselves as architectural zero-institutions: their conflictual meanings (entertainment and high art, the profane and the sacred, the exclusive and the popular) cancel each other out, resulting in the presence of meaning as such, as opposed to non-meaning—their meaning is to have meaning, to be islands of meaning in the flow of our meaningless daily existence. By way of offering a brief insight into the parallax nature of their structure, let me turn to Jameson's description of Rem Koolhaas's project for the Bibliothèque Nationale de France: the enormous box that houses the library

rebukes traditional conceptions of the shell or the shape by its very enor-
mity, attempting . . . by the prosaic nature of the form to escape formal
perception altogether. What this nonform specifically negates . . . is the
grandest of modernist, Corbusean conceptions of the essentially expressive relationship between the interior and its outer plastic lines and walls,
which were to shed their rigidity and simply follow their functions in
such a way as to correspond aesthetically to the rather different realities
within.[19]

This *expressive correspondence* between the inside (the division of a building
into rooms and spaces for different activities) and the outside of a building
thus shifts towards radical *incommensurability*: "the functions, the rooms,
the interior, the inner spaces, hang within their enormous container like
so many floating organs."[20] These formal shifts in the relation between
outside and inside "reincorporate the paradoxes of private property after
the end of civil society (in the case of a library, by way of the dialectic of
the property of information, or by way of the more classic antinomy of a
public space that is privately owned)."[21]

However, one should not misunderstand this emphasis on the incommensurability between outside and inside as a critique (relying on the
demand for the continuity between the two). The incommensurability between outside and inside is a transcendental a priori—in our most
elementary phenomenological experience the reality we see through a
window is always minimally spectral, not as fully real as the closed space
we are in. This is why, when driving a car or looking through a window
of a house, one perceives the reality outside in a weirdly de-realized state,
as if one were watching a performance on screen; on opening the window,
the direct impact of the external reality always causes a minimal shock;
we are, as it were, overwhelmed by its proximity. This is also why, when
we enter the closed space of a house, we are often surprised: the inside
volume seems larger than the outside frame, as if the house were larger
from the inside than from the outside.

On the southern side of the demilitarized zone that divides North
from South Korea, the South Koreans built a unique visitors site: a
theater building with a large screen-like window in front, opening onto
the North. The spectacle people observe when they take their seats to

---

19   Fredric Jameson, *The Seeds of Time*, New York: Columbia University Press 1994, p. 135.
20   Ibid., p. 136.
21   Ibid., p. 135.

look through the window is reality itself (or rather, a kind of "desert of the real"): the barren demilitarized zone with its walls and so forth, and beyond, a glimpse of North Korea. As if to comply with the fiction, North Korea then built a fake model village with beautiful houses in full view of the window; in the evening, the lights in all the houses are turned on at the same time, and their inhabitants are supplied with good clothes and obliged to take a stroll every evening—a barren zone is thus given a fantasmatic status, elevated into a spectacle, solely by being enframed. Something similar happens in Peppermint Bay, a community center in Tasmania (designed by Terroir Pty Ltd), where the function area is located opposite an oak tree at the end of a labyrinthine route. From a large hall inside the centre, the big ancient tree on the grass outside can be seen through a windowpane which covers an entire wall and whose zig-zag form vaguely fits the shape of the tree. What we see through the window (the tree, but also the grass and water in the background) is an attractive natural landscape—though seen as such from inside the building, with the window functioning as a frame. We thus have to distinguish between two outsides: the outside itself (where the tree is seen directly from the grass) and the inside-outside (the outside seen from inside). The two are not the same: in the second case, the outside is no longer simply the encompassing unity containing the inside, but is itself simultaneously enclosed by the inside (or, one might say, nature is enclosed by culture). Likewise, North Korea may appear sublime—when viewed from the safe spot in South Korea; conversely, democracy may appear sublime, when viewed from an authoritarian or "totalitarian" regime. Bernard Tschumi's New Acropolis Museum, built in front of the hill on which the Parthenon stands, also relies on a similar effect: on reaching the third floor, one sees through a wide window frame the "thing itself," the Parthenon—the fact of its being viewed through the frame, and not directly, only enhances its sublime appearance.[22]

What this mutual encroachment indicates is that inside and outside never cover the entire space: there is always the excess of a third space which gets lost in the division into outside and inside. In human dwellings, there is an intermediate space which is disavowed: we all know

---

22   There can also be a false inside. In the ZKM house in Karlsruhe, there is a TV screen in front of the entrance to the main toilet area, showing continuously on its black and white screen the inside of a small toilet cube with an empty toilet bowl. After the first moment of relief (thank God the toilet is free, I'm desperate!), I become aware that it will no longer be empty when I enter, so that I will be seen defecating. It is only then that the obvious truth strikes me: it is, of course, a pre-recorded tape that we see, not the actual inside of the restroom . . .

it exists, but we do not really accept its existence—it remains ignored and (mostly) unsayable. The main content of this invisible space is of course excrement (in the plumbing and sewers), but it also includes the complex network of electricity supplies, digital links, etc.—all contained in the narrow spaces between walls or under floors. Of course we know well enough how our excrement leaves the house, but our immediate phenomenological relation to it is more radical: it is as if the waste disappears into some netherworld, beyond our sight and out of our world.[23] Similarly, in relation to another person's body, we know very well that he or she sweats, defecates, and urinates, but we abstract from this in our daily relations—these features are not part of the image of our fellow-man. We rely on this space, but ignore it—no wonder then that, in science-fiction, horror films, and techno-thrillers, this dark space between the walls is where horrible threats lurk (from spying machines to monsters or animals like cockroaches and rats). Recall also, in science-fiction architecture, the topos of a building with an extra floor or room not included in the building's plan (and where, of course, terrifying things dwell).

What can architecture do here? One possibility is to re-include this excluded space in a domesticated form. At 509 meters above ground, the Taipei 101 Tower in Taiwan was until recently the tallest building on Earth. Since Taiwan is often hit by typhoons, the problem was how to control the swinging that would occur when the building was exposed to strong winds. The solution was original: to reduce lateral vibrations, a gigantic steel ball weighing 606 tons is suspended from the 92nd floor, reaching down to the 87th; the ball is connected to pistons which drive oil through small holes, thus damping down the vibrations. What makes this solution especially interesting is that it is not treated as the building's hidden secret, but is publicly displayed as its main attraction. That is to say, sitting in the magnificent restaurant, on the one side the panorama of the city is visible through the windows, while on the other, one can watch the gigantic ball gently swinging. But this transparency is, of course, a pseudo-transparency, like that of the stalls in big food supermarkets where food is prepared in front of our eyes (fruit juice is squeezed, meat and vegetables are fried . . .).

---

23   This is why it is most unpleasant to observe one's excrement coming back up from the pipes into the toilet bowl—something like the return of the living dead . . .

The Envelope . . .

So, back to postmodern architecture: the ambiguously "meaningful" form in which the building is wrapped — often a primitive mimetic symbolism, such as the entire building resembling an animal (turtle, bird, bug . . .) — is not an expression of its inside but is just imposed upon it. The link between form and function is cut, there is no causal relationship between the two — form no longer follows function, function no longer determines form, and the result is a generalized aestheticization. This aestheticization reaches its climax in contemporary performance-arts venues whose basic feature is the gap between skin and structure. What are the basic architectural versions of this gap? The non-expressive, zero-level is represented by some of Koolhaas's buildings, like the above-mentioned project for the Bibliothèque Nationale de France: here the envelope is simply a neutral enormous box that, in its interior, houses the multiple functional spaces which "hang within their enormous container like so many floating organs." (It is the same with many shopping malls contained within grey rectangular boxes.)

Some of Liebeskind's projects (exemplarily the Wohl Center at Bar-Ilan University, Ramat-Gan, Israel) reflect the gap between the protective skin and the inner structure in the "skin" itself: the same external form (enormous box) is multiplied, relying on the contrast between the straight vertical/horizontal lines and the diagonal lines of the external walls. The result is a hybrid effect, as if the same building were a condensation of two (or more) asymmetrical cubes — as if the same formal principle (a cubic box) was applied on different axes. A weird tension and imbalance, a conflict of principles, are thus directly inscribed into the form, as if the actual building lacked a single anchoring point and perspective.

The next step is the minimal aestheticization of the external container: it is no longer just a neutral box, but a round shell protecting the jewel inside. Formally, the contrast between outside and inside is usually that between the roundness of the skin and the straight lines of the inner structures — a round envelope (an egg-like cupola) envelops the box-like vertical-horizontal buildings inside, like the "giant teacups" of the Oriental Art Centre in Shanghai, or, by the same architect (Paul Andreu), the National Grand Theater of China in Beijing, with its giant metal-glass cover, an eggshell protecting the performance buildings. The Kinder Surprise, one of the most popular confectionery products on sale in Central Europe, is a chocolate egg wrapped in colorful paper; inside one will find a small plastic toy (or the parts from which a toy can be constructed) — one can indeed claim, then, that the National Grand Theater of China is a kind of gigantic Kinder Surprise. This motif of protecting the jewel reaches its climax in the project for the new Marinski Theater in St. Petersburg: the functional box-like theater building in black marble (an eighteenth-century palace) is cocooned by a freestanding irregular glacé structure, a "lamella."

The aestheticization of the "skin" culminates in the so-called "sculptural Gehry buildings" where the outer structure enveloping the functional interior is no longer just a shell, but a meaningful sculpture in its own right. For example: the Performing Arts Center in Bard College whose skin is a curved aluminum bug-cockroach form; or the Walt Disney Concert Hall in Los Angeles with its curved metallic forms without windows; or the Jay Pritzker Pavilion in Chicago Millennium Park which tries to achieve the "Bilbao effect," that is to create a vibrant public space in the midst of the city's concrete jungle. One should also mention here the Tenerife Auditorium in Santa Cruz, whose skin looks like a giant sea-bird trapped by the encroaching half-moon (or sickle-like) wing.

There is yet another variation on this gap between skin and content — the so-called "terrain buildings" where the surface-skin is constructed as a direct continuation of the surrounding terrain, with the undulations of a hill covered by grass and so on (recall the hobbits' dwellings in *The Lord of the Rings*). The Yokohama International Port Terminal (designed by Foreign Office Architects) is exemplary here: a public space whose roof functions as an open plaza, continuous with the surface of the nearby park: "Rather than developing the building as an object or figure on the pier, the project is produced as an extension of the urban ground," as the designers themselves described their work. The Yokohama Terminal can thus be seen as the extreme case where, in a way, the whole Inside of the building is reduced to the interstitial space between the skin/envelope (the green or wooden surface) and the body of the earth, squeezed in the flattened domain between the two. Not surprisingly, the actual effect of such buildings is the very opposite of the intended "naturalization" (seamless immersion into natural environs): nature itself is thereby de-realized, that is, it appears as if a "natural" surface of grass is an artificial skin concealing complex machinery.

And, to conclude, the relationship between outside and inside can also be turned around, as in the case of Tate Modern in London where a once decaying abandoned megalith (the power station) is retained as the exterior envelope, with all the internal walls and floors totally restructured and modernized. (The same goes for the Eastgate Theatre and Arts Center in Peebles (UK): of the old disused church, only the Victorian Gothic façade was kept, while the main body behind was rebuilt in modern glazed style.)

The very relationship between urbanism and architecture is thus to be historicized: it changes with postmodernism, where the difference is progressively blurred: postmodern buildings tend to function as their own urban spaces (like parks inside malls, self-contained capsule-worlds).[24] In this way, the public space is privatized to such an extent that it potentially suspends the very dialectical tension between private and public. A shopping mall building is like a box with a world inside, separated from the outside by a plain grey wall or by dark glass panels which just reflect the outside, providing no insight or hint of what goes on within.

The central semiotic mystery of performance-arts venues is the mystery of this redoubling: why a house within a house, why does a container itself have to be contained? Does this (sometimes freakish) display of inconsistency and excess not cry out for a diagnosis, functioning as it does as a symptom, a message encoded in the mess? What if this redoubling renders the "contradiction" of a public space which is privately controlled, of a sacred space of art which should be open to profane amusement? A close analysis of the "envelope" that encompasses many such buildings brings us to the same conclusion. Alejandro Zaera Polo's ongoing work on the concept of the architectural envelope is focused on the border between outside and inside, instead of on the internal organization of the inside: he defines "envelope" as the membrane which separates the Inside of a building from its Outside.[25] As such, the envelope (the outward appearance of a building's volume) is the oldest and most primitive architectural element which materializes the division between exterior and interior and is therefore automatically politically charged. In his detailed elaboration, Zaera Polo distinguishes four typological forms: flat horizontal, flat vertical, vertical, and spherical/cubic; each type possesses a number of features which make it suited for representations and functions which can be linked to certain social and political effects. However, more interesting than these detailed differentiations is the way Zaera Polo grounds the

---

24   One is tempted here to conceive the triad of urbanism-architecture-design as a Hegelian triad of the Universal, Particular, and Singular, where architecture is the mediator, drawing the line of separation between the outer space (the domain of urbanism) and inner space (whose arrangement is the domain of design or inner decoration).

25   Alejandro Zaera Polo, "The Politics of the Envelope: A Political Critique of Materialism," *Volume* 17, pp. 76–105; available online at: http://c-lab.columbia.edu.

notion of the envelope in a very precise idea of late-capitalist dynamics based on the work of Gilles Deleuze and Peter Sloterdijk.

Zaera Polo's starting point is what one is tempted to call "neo-capitalist Deleuzianism" (no jibe intended). Deleuze and Guattari proposed a certain conceptual network—the opposition between the molecular and the molar, production and representation, difference and identity, the nomadic multitude and the hierarchical order, etc.—within which one pole is the generative force and the other its shadowy represen-tation: the multitude is productive, and is as such reflected in a distorted way in the theater of representation. To put it in a brutally simplified way, the problem is: how does this network relate to capitalism? There are two opposing answers. Deleuze and Guattari's own is a Marxist one: even if capitalism is a force of "de-territorialization," unleashing the productivity of the multitude, this productivity remains constrained within the confines of a new "re-territorialization," that of the capitalist framework of profit which encloses the entire process; only in commu-nism can the nomadic productivity of the multitude be fully unleashed. The opposite answer is that given by advocates of the post-'68 "new spirit of capitalism": for them, it is Marxism itself which remains caught in the totalizing-representational logic of the Party-State as the unitary agent regulating social life, and it is capitalism which is today the only effective force of nomadic molecular productivity. Paradoxically, one should admit that there is more truth in the second answer: although Deleuze and Guattari are right in conceiving the capitalist framework as an obstacle to fully released productivity, they here make the same mistake as did Marx himself, ignoring how the obstacle is (like the Lacanian *objet a*) a positive condition of what it enframes, so that, by abolishing it, we paradoxically lose the very productivity it was obstructing.

Zaera Polo is thus justified in inscribing his Deleuzianism on the capi-talist side:

> There are two basic forms of political structures that have historically organized exchange and flow of resources, skills and command structures in time and space: markets and bureaucracies. They are the two domains where architects may try to construct their agency. Within the global economy the market has become predominant as a mechanism of organi-zation capable of integrating a larger number of agents in its processes within a shorter time. Bureaucracies are organizations of power which are based on a hierarchical totality operating in stable conditions for extended periods of time and can hardly survive the pace of change and level of

complexity required by a global economy. While within bureaucracies the agents and their relationships are fixed over time, markets are organizations that organize power through a complex and constantly changing set of agents and factors. As the form of political organization better suited to integrate ever expanding domains, the market is a powerful force behind the failure of ideology and utopia as effective political devices, as they would require a centralized power if they were to be implemented. The market is probably a better milieu to articulate the current proliferation of political interests and the rise of micro-politics . . . Those advocates of ideology who hope for a return to a state-driven, ideologically-enlightened society as a remedy to the miseries of the market economy and as an alibi for the reconstruction of a representative, significant, even utopian architecture would do well to remember the miseries of bureaucracies and consider how possible institutional interventions can be channelled through the huge machine of markets to prevent them from becoming sclerotic.[26]

Consequently, one should drop all anti-market ideological utopianism and fully endorse the fact that the global market "is the primary milieu of contemporary architectural politics"—that is, one should operate within the system of global capitalism. The great feature of globalization is the hitherto unprecedented unleashing of the powers of de-territorialization—the process described long ago by Marx in the famous passage from *The Communist Manifesto*: "All fixed, fast-frozen relations, with their train of ancient and venerable prejudices and opinions are swept away, all new-formed ones become antiquated before they can ossify. All that is solid melts into air, all that is holy is profaned . . ."[27] This does not mean, however, that everything is gradually turning into formless social slime: de-territorialization itself creates the need for new modes of delimitation, now no longer the old hierarchic fixed walls, but a multiplicity of "envelopes," "bubbles," as "containers of liquid reality":

Globalization has propelled a set of spatial typologies primarily determined by the capacity to conduct flow. Architects have tried to engage with this borderless space, the "space of flows," by dissolving the envelope as an obstacle to flow and spatial continuity and presenting an image of the world as a chaotically flowing magma. However a new picture is

---

26   Ibid., p. 103.
27   Karl Marx and Frederick Engels, *The Communist Manifesto*, Harmondsworth: Penguin Books 1985, pp. 83–4.

emerging in the form of bubbles and Information Technology, Economic foams, containers of a liquid reality.[28]

Here enters Peter Sloterdijk and his monumental *Spheres* trilogy: far from advocating a return to pre-modern containment, Sloterdijk was the first to propose what one can call a "provincialism for the global era":

the world as a foamy space filled with bubbles and balloons of different scales and qualities. This capsular society and its phenomena such as global provincialism, the politics of climatization and social uteri describe a new paradigm that requires not just a reconsideration of the technologies and economics of the building envelope, but of its political, social and psychological implications.[29]

So what are the political implications of the "current appetite for the envelope as a device of insulation and immunization"? Zaera Polo is well aware that the interior of a building is thoroughly determined by demands for efficiency and so forth; his wager is that the envelope—in its independence from the functional contents—can become a potential space of freedom, of aesthetic autonomy, purveying its own message:

While most other aspects of the architectural project are now in the control of other agents (e.g., project managers, specialist contractors) that ensure the efficiency of the project delivery, the increasing faceless-ness of the client gives architects license to invent the building's interface. The envelope has become the last realm of architectural power, despite the discipline's inability to articulate a theoretical framework capable of structuring its renewed importance. Mobilizing a political critique of the envelope capable of addressing its multiple attachments and complexi-ties may enable us to frame architecture not merely as a representation of the interests of a client, of a certain political ideology or an image of utopia, but as an all-too-real, concrete, and effective political agency able to assemble and mediate the interests of the multiplicities that converge on the architectural project.[30]

In contrast to the old-fashioned forms of radical politics that tend to act as a single agency with the goal of undermining the system, the new efforts

---

28   Zaera Polo, "The Politics of the Envelope," p. 78.
29   Ibid.
30   Ibid., p. 79.

to enact a redistribution of power work at the sub-political level of local interventions:

> Instead of resorting to predefined and all-encompassing political ideologies or utopian references to frame the practices of architecture, we aim to map possible correlations between architectural strategies and political effects in order to mobilize the discipline on a sub-political level. The question now is not whether certain architecture is aligned to the right, to the left or to a certain political party—as in earlier embodiments of architectural politics—but rather what architectural strategies may trigger effects on the distribution of power . . . There is a growing number of new forms of political action which herald both the emergence of different political qualities (such as affects) and domains (such as everyday life). Contemporary politics are giving way to a new wave of powerful material habitats, artificial environments, artificial organizations, belongings and attachments, which are literally redefining political surroundings in which we are and co-exist. Both governmental agencies and corporate organizations are moving toward multiple layers of governance with intensified connections between them . . . As a result, the challenge to power can only be selective and a division of political labour has to be addressed by multiple disciplines operating independently and simultaneously . . . A singular politics of resistance is no longer capable of challenging contemporary forms of instituted power.[31]

However, as Zaera Polo has to admit, apart from the (relative) aesthetic and political autonomy it provides (and the obvious environmental function), the envelope also serves as a security device: "The design of spherical envelopes has consequently focused recently on the construction of the surface itself, both as an environmental and security device and as the locus of symbolic representation." The security task is here not the same as that of traditional walls protecting the inside from external dangers: the fateful difference is that the envelope secures a privatized public space: "A more permeable definition of the property boundary is more likely to effectively accommodate a fluid relationship between private and public *in an age when the public realm is increasingly built and managed by private agents*" (emphasis added). So, from the Deleuzian poetry of fluid de-territorialization, we are back to the task of how to enact and protect the (private) enclosure of public spaces. If traditional architecture was an attempt to enclose the inside from the outside, today it often tries to

---

31   Ibid., p. 102.

enclose the outside itself, that is, to create a protected/screened outside, separated from the "wild" outdoors. The envelope which isolates a (set of) building(s) is thus the urban-architectural version of the enclosure of the commons: not only the interior of a house, but its exterior itself is cordoned-off and "climatized"—not only with regard to heat and air quality, but also with regard to the undesired presence of potentially "toxic" subjects:

> Sloterdijk's "politics of climatization" points to a process in which growing sectors of urban space are given to private agents to develop and maintain: gardeners, event managers and private security agents are part of the design of these *atmospheres*. Koolhaas' *junkspace* is another description of the same phenomenon of sanitization of ever-larger areas of the city, providing a safe environment, assuming we are prepared to surrender police duties to private security services.[32]

This tendency reached its peak (for the time being at least) in the "Crystal Island" project in Moscow, recently announced by Norman Foster—"2.5 million square meters under a single envelope, the world's biggest building, approximately five times the size of the Pentagon building. The project is described as an example of sustainability, able to improve the environmental performance of the building by swallowing ever larger areas of the city under a single envelope designed to enhance natural ventilation and daylight."[33] Officially "progressive" ideology and politics (such as New Labour in the UK) likes to celebrate such projects as models of the "revitalization" of decaying city centers; however, Zaera Polo is right to ask the question "whether this is actually a regeneration of the urban centres, as New Labour claims, or whether it is the takeover of the inner cities by a sort of alien organization with air-conditioning and private security."[34] This brings us to the social antagonism these buildings try to resolve. On the one hand, to build a performing-arts venue rates "as a holy grail for architects": "Unlike the more conventional types of buildings, such as offices, housing and even civic architecture, which have to conform to the streetscape, a performing-arts venue can afford to be bold and unusual, to stand out."[35] However, this space for creative freedom is counteracted

---

32   Ibid., p. 84.
33   Ibid.
34   Ibid., p. 85.
35   Michael Hammond, *Performing Architecture: Opera Houses, Theatres and Concert Halls for the Twenty-First Century*, London and New York: Merrell 2006, pp. 24–5.

by the demand for the building's multi-functionality—venue managers cannot

> simply rely on performances themselves to provide a sufficient attraction; the building must create an "experience" and a "sense of place" for its increasingly demanding audience. It is with such intangibles that events can really win against home entertainment. Thought must be given to all aspects of a visit, from the foyers and bars to the facilities and ease of access.[36]

This demand, however, is not merely financial but profoundly ideological—it reflects a "cultural tension":

> The perception that public funds are being spent on "elitist" buildings has always been an Achilles heel for these projects, leaving them open to attacks from all quarters, and in today's more transparent and politically correct society it is the issue of inclusion more than any other that has influenced the design of contemporary performing spaces. As a result, the performing-arts venue has had to be redefined for the twenty-first century. The new generation of buildings must be part of the public realm, with access to only the core areas being restricted by the requirement for a ticket. These venues include public activities within and around the complex, attracting a wider range of visitors.[37]

. . . of the Class Struggle

This constant effort to counteract the threat of "elitism" signals a series of oppositions which performance-arts buildings have to deal with: public/private, open/restrained, elite/popular—all variations on the basic motif of the class struggle (which, we are told, no longer exists in our societies). The space of these oppositions delineates the problem to which performance-arts buildings are proposed solutions.

Claude Lévi-Strauss mentions one of the native American tribes whose members claim that all dreams have a hidden sexual meaning—all *except the overtly sexual ones*: here, precisely, one has to look for another secret meaning. The same goes for class antagonism: every non-class issue (ecological, feminist, racist) can be interpreted through the prism of class antagonism, except for the direct reference precisely to class

---

36   Ibid., p. 25.
37   Ibid., p. 26.

antagonism, which (because it is a necessarily distorted displacement of the "true" antagonism) needs to be referred to another antagonism. When Pat Buchanan "codes" in class terms his opposition to multiculturalism and feminism, his racism, and so forth, or when Nixon was perceived as "lower-class" in contrast to Kennedy, here the very direct class reference functions as a screen dissimulating the true link between class antagonism and the issue at stake (feminism, racism, and so on).

Class antagonism itself can function as a means to mystify class antagonism—it cannot "signify itself," but it can obfuscate itself. Republican strategy masterfully exploits the flaws of liberal-democratic politics: its patronizing care for the poor, combined with an underground thinly disguised indifference, contempt even, for blue-collar workers; its politically correct feminism, combined with a secret distrust of powerful women. Sarah Palin was a hit on both scores: parading both her working-class husband and her femininity.

Earlier generations of women politicians (Golda Meir, Indira Gandhi, Margaret Thatcher, up to a point even Hillary Clinton) were what is usually referred to as "phallic" women: they acted as "iron ladies" who imitated and tried to outdo male authority, to be "more men than men themselves." In a recent comment in *Le Point*, Jacques-Alain Miller pointed out how Sarah Palin, on the contrary, proudly displays her femininity and motherhood. She has a "castrating" effect on her male opponents not by way of being more manly than them, but by using the ultimate feminine weapon, the sarcastic put-down of puffed-up male authority—she knows that male "phallic" authority is a posture, a semblance to be exploited and mocked. Recall how she mocked Obama as a "community organizer," exploiting the fact that there was something sterile in Obama's physical appearance, with his diluted black skin, slender features, and big ears. Here we have "post-feminist" femininity without a complex, uniting the features of mother, prim teacher (glasses, hair in a bun), public person, and, implicitly, sex object, proudly displaying the "first dude" as a phallic toy. The message is that she "has it all"—and that, to add insult to injury, it was a Republican woman who had realized this Left-liberal dream. It is as if she simply *is* what Left-liberal feminists *would like* to be. No wonder that the Palin effect is one of false liberation: drill, baby, drill! We can combine the impossible: feminism and family values, big corporations and blue-collar workers. What this means is that—in Hegelese—the class struggle encounters itself in its oppositional determination (*gegensätzliche Bestimmung*), in its distorted/displaced form, as one among many social

struggles. And, in exactly the same way, "anti-elitist" populism in architecture is the mode of appearance of its opposite, of class differences.

So how does the anti-elitist architecture of performance-arts venues fit
these coordinates? Its attempt to overcome elitist exclusivity fails, since it
reproduces the paradoxes of upper-class liberal openness — its falsity, and
failure to achieve its goal, is the falsity and limitation of our tolerant liberal
capitalism. The effective message of the "political unconscious" of these
buildings is *democratic exclusivity*: they create a multi-functional egalitarian open space, but the very access to this space is invisibly filtered and
privately controlled. In more political terms, performance-arts venues try
to enact *civic normality in a state of emergency (exception)*: they construct an
"open" space which is cocooned, protected, and filtered. (This logic is
taken to an extreme in shopping malls in some Latin-American countries,
well protected by security personnel armed with machine guns.)

As such, performance-arts venues are utopian spaces which exclude
junkspace:[38] all the foul-smelling "leftovers" of the city space. To use a term
coined by Deleuze, a contemporary big city is a space of "disjunctive inclusion": it *has to include* places whose existence is not part of its "ideal-ego,"
which are *disjoined* from its idealized image of itself. The paradigmatic
(but by far not the only) such places are slums ("favelas" in Brazil), places
of spatial deregulation and chaotic mixture, of architectural "tinkering/
bricolage" with ready-made materials. (It would be interesting to study
in detail the great suburban slums as an architectural phenomenon
with a wild aesthetic of its own.) In between these two extremes — the
"self-conscious" architecture meant to be noted and observed as such,
as exemplified by performance-arts venues, and the spontaneous self-
organization of junkspace — there is the large, mostly invisible domain
of "ordinary" architecture, the thousands of "anonymous" buildings,
from apartment blocks to garages and shopping malls, which are meant
just to function, not to be noted in the press or architectural journals.
Should we be surprised to discover how these three modes of architecture
correspond to three great strata of our societies: the managers, lawyers,
show-business personalities, and other top "immaterial workers"; (whatever remains of the) ordinary working class; and finally the excluded (i.e.
those living in the slums)?

Performance-arts venues function as exceptions: artificial islands of
meaning in our meaningless existence, utopian enclosures sticking out

38   A term coined by Rem Koolhaas; see his "Junkspace," in Rem Koolhaas/OMA, *Content*,
Cologne: Taschen 2004, pp. 166–7.

from the ordinary reality of our cities. As such, they unite the opposites: they are sacred and profane, like secular churches—and the way a visitor relates to them is with a mixture of sacred awe and profane consumption. They inspire awe with their majestically sublime features, but the object of this awe is again ambiguous: is it the High Art whose temples they are, or the capitalist corporations which stand behind them? Hal Foster was right in his remark that

> the individuality of Gehry's architecture does seem more exclusive than democratic. Rather than "forums of civic engagement," his cultural centers appear as sites of spectacular spectatorship, of touristic awe . . . Such is the logic of many cultural centers today, designed, alongside theme parks and sports complexes, to assist in the corporate "revival" of the city—its being made safe for shopping, spectating and spacing out.[39]

This brings us to what is false about the anti-elitism of performance-arts venues: it is not that they are secretly elitist, it is their very anti-elitism, its implicit ideological equation of great art with elitism. Difficult as it may sometimes be for the broad public to "get into" Schoenberg or Webern, there is nothing "elitist" about great art—great art is by definition universal and emancipatory, potentially addressing us all. When, in "elite" places like the old Met in New York, the upper classes gathered for an opera performance, their social posturing was in blatant contradiction with the works performed on stage—to see Mozart and the rich crowd as belonging to the same space is an obscenity. There is a well-known story from the early years of the Met when a high-society lady, one of the opera's great patrons, arrived late, half an hour into the first act; she demanded that the performance be interrupted for a couple of minutes and the lights be turned on so that she could inspect the dresses of other ladies with her opera glasses (and, of course, her demand was granted). If anything, Mozart belonged to the poor in the upper stalls who spend their last hard-earned dollars to see the opera. Far from making the exclusive temple of high art more accessible, it is the very surroundings of expensive cafeterias and so forth which are really exclusive and "elitist." Recall what Walter Benjamin wrote about the Garnier opera palace in Paris: the true focus of the opera is not the performance hall but the wide oval staircase on which high-society ladies display their fashionable clothes and gentlemen meet for a casual smoke—this social life was the true focus of opera life,

---

39   Foster, "Why All the Hoopla?"

"what it was really about." In terms of Lacan's theory, if enjoyment of the performance on stage was what drew the public in, the social game played out on the staircases before the performance and during the intermissions was the foreplay which provided the *plus-de-jouir*, the surplus-enjoyment that made it really worth coming.[40] And the same also holds for today's performance-arts venues — the truth of their democratic anti-elitism is the cocooning protective wall of the "skin." It is this very additional protective "skin" which is responsible for the effect of the Sublime generated by these buildings. As Hal Foster notes, Jameson

> used the vast atrium of the Bonaventure Hotel in Los Angeles designed by John Portman as a symptom of a new kind of architectural Sublime: a sort of hyper-space that deranges the human sensorium. Jameson took this spatial delirium as a particular instance of a general incapacity to comprehend the late capitalist universe, to map it cognitively. Strangely, what Jameson offered as a *critique* of postmodern culture many architects (Frank Gehry foremost among them) have taken as a *paragon*: the creation of extravagant spaces that work to overwhelm the subject, a neo-Baroque Sublime dedicated to the glory of the Corporation (which is the Church of our age). It is as if these architects designed not in contestation of the "cultural logic of late capitalism" but according to its specifications.[41]

In short, even such an acute critic as Jameson was too naïve here: what the cultural critic discerns through painful analysis is openly admitted by the object of his critique. There is, however, another question to be raised: why should our human sensorium not be deranged? Is such deranging not also a way to awaken us from our daily ideological slumber? Here there is a very simple but trenchant dilemma that confronts us: if we live in an alienated and commodified society, what should architecture do? Make us aware of the alienation by making us feel uncomfortable, shocked and awed, or provide a false semblance of a nice life which obliterates the truth? For Nikos Salingaros, the pursuit of formal or critico-ideological concerns in place of adapting to nature and the needs of ordinary human beings defines "bad architecture" which makes people uncomfortable or

---

40   Taking this logic to an absurd extreme, one could imagine a building which would consist *only* of a gigantic circular staircase, with elevators taking us to the top, so that what is usually just a means, a route to the true goal, would become the main purpose — one would go to such a building simply to take a slow walk down the stairs. Does the Guggenheim Museum in New York not come pretty close to this, with the art exhibits de facto reduced to decorations designed to make the long walk more pleasant?

41   Hal Foster, "The ABCs of Contemporary Design," *October*, 100 (Spring 2002), p. 191.

physically ill. Salingaros's targets were the star postmodern architects who emphasized meaning at the expense of the concrete experience of the people who used their buildings. Take Bernard Tschumi—from the premise that there is no fixed relationship between architectural form and the events that take place within it, he drew a socio-critical conclusion: this gap opens up the space for critical undermining. Architecture's role is not to express an extant social structure, but to function as a tool for questioning that structure and revising it. Salingaros's counter-argument would be: should we then make ordinary people uncomfortable and ill at ease in their buildings, just to impose on them the critico-ideological message that they live in an alienated, commodified, and antagonistic society? Koolhaas was right to reject what he dismissively calls architecture's "fundamental moralism," and to doubt the possibility of any directly "critical" architectural practice—however, our point is not that architecture *should* somehow be "critical," but that it *cannot not* reflect and interact with social and ideological antagonisms: the more it tries to be pure and purely aesthetic and/or functional, the more it reproduces these antagonisms.

Spandrels

Is there a way out of this deadlock? There is no easy way out, for sure. The first step is, of course, the shift of focus from the "great" symbolic projects such as performance-arts venues (which are meant to be "noted") to the "anonymous" buildings springing up everywhere and in which the vast majority of people will spend almost all of their time: a true revolution would involve changing something here, in the way these "anonymous" projects are conceived and enacted. (In the same way, cinema theorists noted that a true revolution in cinema is to be located not in eccentric shots or camera movements—those which are meant to be noted, like Hitchcock's famous crane shots—but rather in the transformation involved in the filming of, say, an everyday conversation between two characters.) There are some interesting attempts in this direction, like the works of the Lacaton & Vassal tandem in France, whose goal is to halve the price of a building per square unit and to return to the density of housing in ancient crowded European towns which involves much less energy-use in terms of temperature regulation and transport (see their architectural school building in Nantes, a low-cost multifunctional building—school, local music center, space for community meetings—but multifunctional in a totally different way to the celebrated "multifunctionality" of the representative performance-arts venues).

But even the performance-arts venues open up new and unexpected possibilities. There is an interesting new phenomenon which emerges with the assertion of the gap between skin and structure — an unexpected interstitial space. Something similar happened long ago in modern painting — one of the minimal definitions of modernist painting concerns the function of its frame. The frame of the painting in front of us is not its true frame; there is another, invisible, frame, implied by the structure of the painting, the frame that enframes our perception of the painting, and these two frames by definition never overlap — there is an invisible gap separating them. The pivotal content of the painting is not rendered in its visible part, but is located in this dis-location of the two frames, in the gap that separates them. This dimension in-between-the-two-frames is obvious in Malevich, in Edward Hopper,[42] or in Munch's "Madonna" — the droplets of sperm and the small fetus-like figure from "The Scream" squeezed in between the two frames.

Do we not find something similar in some of the performance-arts venues, like the Kimmel Center for the Performing Arts in Philadelphia, where the same third space is generated? Its two halls are like "two jewels in a glass case," covered by a gigantic roof: "the vast vaulted roof of folded steel and glass creating a spectacular indoor-outdoor experience."[43] Beneath the vault, on the top of boxes, there are terraces with greenery, located in the space between inside and outside. There are open entries on both sides, "creating a sheltered extension of the sidewalk outside, and blurring the distinction between the city and the outside."[44] This "open space inside," this outside which is inside, open to access, is full of cafés, free puppet shows, and so on. The same holds for the Esplanade National Performing Arts Centre in Singapore: above the buildings there is a giant metal and glass fish-like "skin," a "buffer zone, or bio-climactic environment, that would moderate the climate between the fully conditioned and sealed environments of the two major black-box performance spaces

42   Recall his lone figures in office buildings or diners at night, where it seems as if the picture's frame has to be redoubled with another window frame — or, in the portraits of his wife close to an open window, exposed to the sun's rays, the opposite excess of the painted content itself with regard to what we effectively see, as if we see only the fragment of the whole picture, the shot with a missing counter-shot.

43   Hammond, *Performing Architecture*, p. 42.

44   Ibid.

and the ever-changing external environment."[45] This "interstitial space" opened up by the "disconnection between skin and structure" plays a crucial role:

> For many, the real magic of this building is the dramatic sense of place in the "leftover" spaces between the theatres and the enclosure. The curvaceous shapes of these public areas are the by-products of two separate design processes—those of the acoustic- and logistic-driven performing zones, and the climactic- and structure-driven envelope.[46]

Is this space—which offers not only exciting views of both inside and outside, but also hidden corners in which to take a stroll or to rest—not a potential utopian space?

One name for this interstitial space between the skin and the content of a building is *poche* (French for "pocket"). Poche refers primarily to a plan or drawing of a building in which solid objects are completely blacked in, in order to get a better idea of the geometry of the physical space by outlining it; more generally, it refers to all the "uncanny" spaces ignored in the overall scheme of a building.[47] It also has, however, a much more specific meaning specified by the Badiouian term "subtraction": the thickening of walls to create a "subtractive space"; this space is created by carving through a large wall, cutting halls and chambers into it. Poche allows for the creation of unique movements through a building; it is useful not only for shaping the floor plan of a structure, and for the design of both the roof and floor, it also allows us to cut through a structure horizontally to create a visually pleasing flow of movement (for example, one way to get light into a structure is to cut through the roof leaving slits that allow more light in). To put it in clumsy Hegelese, poche reflects the dialectic of the envelope and the body into the thickened envelope itself: the envelope itself is blown into the body out of which additional interiors are carved. This is why poche can also be inverted in "virtual poche," in which what appears as the thickness of poched walls is actually void: if "poche" designates the carving of halls and chambers into an actual thick wall, "virtual poche" stands for a spatial disposition of (normal thin) walls which creates the illusion that the space delineated by these walls is enveloped by (or carved into) a thick wall.

---

45   Ibid., pp. 65–7.
46   Ibid., p. 67.
47   See Anthony Vidler, *The Architectural Uncanny*, Cambridge, MA: MIT Press 1994.

The notion of "exaptation," originally introduced by Stephen Jay Gould and Richard Lewontin, may be of some relevance here.[48] There are two types of exaptations: (1) adaptations that initially arose through natural selection and were subsequently co-opted for another function ("co-opted adaptations"); (2) features that did not arise as adaptations through natural selection but rather as side effects of adaptive processes and that have been co-opted for a biological function ("co-opted spandrels").[49]

Gould's favorite example was the human chin, whose presence is an incidental consequence of the differential growth rate of two bones in the lower jaw. The dentary bone which carries the teeth elongates more slowly than the jawbone itself, so the chin juts out. In our ape-like ancestors the jawbone grows more slowly so no chin develops.[50]

What should draw our attention here is that Gould and Lewontin borrowed the architectural term "spandrel" (using the pendentives of San Marco in Venice as an example) to designate that class of forms and spaces that arise as necessary by-products of another, independent, design decision, and not as adaptations employed directly for their utility in themselves.

In architecture, the prototypical spandrel is the triangular space "left over" on top, when a rectangular wall is pierced by a passageway capped with a rounded arch. By extension a spandrel is any geometric configuration of space inevitably left over as a consequence of other architectural decisions. Thus, the space between the floor and the first step of a staircase or the horizontal course between the lintels of a horizontal line of windows and the bottom of the row of windows on the floor just above are also called spandrels. By generalization . . . a spandrel is any space necessarily and predictably shaped in a certain way, and not explicitly designed as such, but rather arising as an inevitable side consequence of another architectural decision (to pierce a wall with a rounded arch, to build a stair at a certain height from the floor, to construct a multistoried building with windows in rows).[51]

48   See Stephen Jay Gould and Richard Lewontin, "The Spandrels of San Marco and the Panglossian Paradigm: A Critique of the Adaptationist Programme" (1979), reprinted in *The Richness of Life: The Essential Stephen Jay Gould*, New York: W. W. Norton 2007.
49   See David M. Buss et al., "Adaptations, Exaptations, and Spandrels," American Psychologist 53: 5, 1998, pp. 533–48; available online at http://sscnet.ucla.edu.
50   Richard C. Lewontin, "The Triumph of Stephen Jay Gould," *New York Review of Books*, 55: 2, February 14, 2008.
51   Stephen Jay Gould, "The Exaptive Excellence of Spandrels as a Term and Prototype," *Proceedings of the National Academy of Sciences* 94: 20, September 30, 1997, pp. 10750–5.

The spaces between the pillars of a bridge can thus be used by homeless persons for sleeping, even though such spaces were not designed for providing such shelter. And just as church spandrels may incidentally become the locus for decorations such as portraits of the four evangelists, so anatomical spandrels may be co-opted for uses for which they were not selected in the first place.

Do spandrels not then open up the space for architectural exaptations? And does this procedure not expand to buildings themselves, such that a church or train station might be exapted into an art gallery, etc.? Are the "interstitial spaces" created by the "disconnection between skin and structure" in performance-arts venues not such spandrels, functionally empty spaces open for exaptation? The struggle is up for grabs here—the struggle over who will appropriate them. These "interstitial spaces" are thus the proper place for utopian dreaming—they remind us of architecture's great politico-ethical responsibility: much more is at stake in architectural design than may at first appear. Recall William Butler Yeats's well-known lines: "I have spread my dreams under your feet / Tread softly because you tread on my dreams." Since they refer also to architecture, the warning to architects is: when making your plans, tread softly because you tread on the dreams of the people who will live within and gaze upon your buildings.

4 Depression: The Neuronal Trauma, or, the Rise of the Proletarian Cogito

Cogito Against Historicism

What underlies this topic of the *cogito* is the status of the so-called "Western exception" which culminates in European modernity: the shift from the organic Whole to Universality (which introduces a cut/rupture into the Whole, opposing Universality to particular content), from particular spiritualized lifeworlds to a global secular order, and so on. Hegel conceives this shift as the passage from the Ancient Greek aesthetic Whole of the *polis* to Christian abstract universality; on a closer look, we can see how the shift repeats itself three times in Western history: first, as the move from *mythos* to *logos*, that is, the break of Greek philosophy from the traditional mythic universe; then, as the Christian break with the pagan cosmos which culminates in the "irrational" rejection of the world, the withdrawal into the non-thought of the "night of the world"; finally, as the modern "disenchantment" of reality, the rise of the Cartesian subject opposed to the mute and meaningless infinite universe. For today's anti-modernist partisans of a new post-secular "holistic paradigm," things went fatally wrong when Plato privileged abstract notional thinking over thought embedded in a concrete lifeworld; or when Christianity posited the believer as an abstract individual, not as a member of a concrete community; or when Cartesian modernity broke with the pre-modern universe of mythic meaning. For such partisans, the whole idea of secular modernism and universalism is a freakish idiosyncrasy in the history of the human species, the root of our ecological and other forms of crisis — ultimately, secular modernism is an impossible position, an illusion; "we were never modern" (as Bruno Latour puts it).

When, in the 1830s, Adolphe de Custine visited Russia, his experience there illustrated an interesting and properly Hegelian point: the very object of his inquiry alienated itself from him as he approached it. That is to say, Custine went to Russia searching for an immediate organic order; he wanted to find a society which, in contrast to Western Europe—with its ongoing disintegration of organic links caused by the modern economy and the French Revolution—remained hierarchically ordered and grounded in tradition. What he found, however, was the exact opposite: what Russia lacked was precisely the organic unity of society; instead, he found a fragile mixture of brutal order and complete chaos. Not only, beneath the appearance of total power and order, was there immense chaos; state power itself functioned chaotically, exposed as it was to the whims of the Tsar. (This feature—chaos behind the appearance of order and totalitarian control—persists even today, and was strikingly present in the Soviet era.[1]) "Organic unity" thus reveals itself to be the mode of appearance of its opposite, of inherent instability—the "secret" of despotic societies is that they never did find their "*inneres Gestalt*," their inner form; this holds also for Fascism, torn as it always was between modernism and the return to tradition. This is why, resisting any such "organic" temptation, it is absolutely crucial for emancipatory politics to remain faithful to the universalist/secular project of modernity. Consequently, one should reject the claim that the ongoing transition to a multi-centric world (in which Western culture is no longer privileged) compels us to renounce every projection of a universal history, no matter how critical, including the Marxist vision of historical progress. Let us take one of the most articulate "postcolonial" critiques of the Marxist "historicism," Dipesh Chakrabarty's *Provincializing Europe*.[2]

The irony of Chakrabarty's book is that, in criticizing historicism, it reduces it to a rather narrow "stageist" theory which posits a linear historical development (from traditional societies to modern secularized universal ones), thereby practically ignoring the predominant use of the term in contemporary cultural studies, a use fully endorsed and practiced by Chakrabarty himself: the radical historical relativization of every culture and lifeworld. That is to say, Chakrabarty criticizes Marx for unproblematically endorsing the universality of the "logic of capital" and its constitutive moments (like abstract labor), ignoring how, in each of its actually existing forms, this universality is always colored by a historically specific lifeworld and thus cannot be directly applied to other cultures—every such extension should rather involve a long and patient work of translation.

1   See Irena Gross, *The Scar of Revolution*, Berkeley: University of California Press 1991.
2   Dipesh Chakrabarty, *Provincializing Europe: Postcolonial Thought and Historical Difference*, Princeton: Princeton University Press 2000.

According to Chakrabarty, if we accept the "stageist" notion of historical evolution, then our very critique of colonialism and support for
anti-colonial struggles will surreptitiously rely on colonialist notions. For
a Eurocentric progressivist Marxist, when Third World peasants rebel
against colonial rule, they do so by means of pre-political traditional-
religious forms of protest, that is, they are "not yet" at the level of a
modern political (secular) movement; ultimately, they remain in the "waiting room" of history and need time to shed their archaic practices and
become properly educated in the ways of modernity. Furthermore, every
refinement or complication of the Marxist theory (appeals to "uneven
development," the "synchronicity of the synchronous," etc.) still relies on
the stageist model, which, according to Chakrabarty, should be definitively abandoned: since there is no universal standard of historical stages,
there is nothing "incomplete" in the co-existence of "modern" forms of
political life with "traditional" practices.

> If Indian modernity places the bourgeois in juxtaposition with that which
> seems prebourgeois, if the nonsecular supernatural exists in proximity
> to the secular, and if both are to be found in the sphere of the political,
> it is not because capitalism or political modernity in India has remained
> "incomplete".[3]

Consequently, when India was integrated into the global capitalist
network, the pre-modern life practices which persisted should in no
way be dismissed as "the mere survival of an antecedent pre-capitalist
culture": "This was capitalism indeed, but without bourgeois relations
that attain a position of unchallenged hegemony; it was a capitalist dominance without a hegemonic bourgeois culture."[4] Chakrabarty refers here
to India's much-celebrated effortless combination of traditional spirituality (with its diversity of everyday life practices and rituals) and digital
modernity; it is this combination that effectively makes India a model,
demonstrating that a "worldless" global capitalism can co-exist with a
plurality of particular lifeworlds.[5] (One can even discern here echoes
of the notion of alternate modernities, where India could be replaced

3   Ibid., pp. 14–15.
4   Ibid., p. 15.
5   As for the cultural level of this collaboration, the Oscar-winning film *Slumdog Millionaire* brings
together the worst of both Western market-consumerism and Eastern spiritualism, with Eastern
karma giving a helping hand to its financial success—the film is effectively a case of the worst of
Eastern and Western ideologies supplementing and reinforcing each other.

with other cultures: the Latin-American combination of modernity with pre-modern indigenous "magical" practices; the Japanese and Chinese combination of modernity with "Asian values"; including also the touchy topic of Islam and modernity.)

Chakrabarty is not, however, engaged in a simplistic dismissal of Marxist universalism: in a refined dialectical way, he admits it is "both indispensable and inadequate in helping us to think through the various life practices" of social and political developments in Third World countries.[6] Furthermore, this combination of "modern" and "pre-modern" elements is a necessary constituent of every "really existing" capitalism, Western versions included; in other words, one should read "the expression 'not yet' deconstructively as referring to a process of deferral internal to the very being (that is, logic) of capital": "It is as though the 'not yet' is what keeps capital going."[7] Here Chakrabarty introduces a distinction between "History 1 (H1)"—the immanent history of capital which posits its own presuppositions—and "History 2 (H2)"—all those lifeworld elements and processes which cannot be reduced to moments of capital's self-reproduction. H1 is abstract-universal, it articulates the decontextualized logic of the Enlightenment, while H2 refers to concrete lifeworlds. The point, of course, is that since H1 is always contaminated by H2,

> no historical form of capital, however global its reach, can ever be a universal. No global (or even local, for that matter) capital can ever represent the universal logic of capital, for any historically available form of capital is a provisional compromise made up of History 1 modified by somebody's History 2. The universal, in that case, can only exist as a place holder, its own place always usurped by a historical particular seeking to present itself as the universal.[8]

It is here, however, that the problems arise: the very fact that one has to distinguish H1 and H2 indicates the special status of H1. How then do we account for this distinction? Can we ultimately reduce H1 to being an effect of H2? In other words, can the process of European secularization be conceived as itself fully grounded in the European lifeworld? Chakrabarty indicates a positive answer:

---

6   Chakrabarty, *Provincializing Europe*, p. 6.
7   Ibid., p. 65.
8   Ibid., p. 70.

The phenomenon of "political modernity"—namely, the rule by modern institutions of the state, bureaucracy, and capitalist enterprise—is impossible to *think* of anywhere in the world without invoking certain categories and concepts, the genealogies of which go deep into the intellectual and even theological traditions of Europe.[9]

The next logical step is to reject the assumption that "the gods and spirits are in the end 'social facts,' that the social somehow exists prior to them":

One empirically knows of no society in which humans have existed without gods and spirits accompanying them. Although the God of monotheism may have taken a few knocks—if not actually "died"—in the nineteenth-century European story of "the disenchantment of the world," the gods and other agents inhabiting practices of so-called "superstition" have never died anywhere. I take gods and spirits to be coeval with the human, and think from the assumption that the question of being human involves the question of being with gods and spirits.[10]

Chakrabarty mentions here the well-known figure of the Indian software programmer who, each morning before going to work, offers gifts to his local divinity: for the Western "stageist," this programmer lives simultaneously in universes which are "centuries apart." But is the non-problematic simultaneity of such attitudes—in other words the "normalized" co-existence of the universality of modernization and of particular lifeworlds—not one of the defining features of postmodernity? As many observers have noted, postmodernity is not the overcoming of modernity but its fulfillment: in the postmodern universe, pre-modern "leftovers" are no longer experienced as obstacles to be overcome by progress towards a fully secularized modernization, but as something to be unproblematically incorporated into the multicultural global universe—all traditions survive, but in a mediated "de-naturalized" form, that is, no longer as authentic ways of life, but as freely chosen "life-styles." Therein resides the cunning of postmodernity: the Indian programmer is allowed his traditional rituals—and his belief that, through these practices, he remains in touch with his authentic lifeworld—but the rituals themselves have already been "mediatized" and incorporated into global capitalism, rendering possible its smooth functioning. (Heidegger, Chakrabarty's main reference, was well aware of this "trans-functionalization" of traditions into components

9   Ibid., p. 4.
10   Ibid., p. 16.

of global technological machinery.) Such coexistence holds not only for India, but is present everywhere, including in the most developed Western societies. It is here that one should apply the properly dialectical notion of totality: capitalism functions as a "totality," in other words, elements of pre-existing lifeworlds and economies (including money) are gradually re-articulated as its own moments, "exapted" with a different function. What this means is that the line separating H1 and H2 is by definition blurred: parts of H2 "found" by capitalism to be external to it, become permanently re-articulated as its integral elements.

To put it in more abstract methodological terms, one should here draw a clear distinction between the imaginary ideal and conceptual ideality. In German, this is the distinction between *ideal* and *ideel*—like the distinction between "ideal science"—a fully formalized scientific structure we are endlessly approaching—and the "ideal structure" of a science, which renders the notional structure of the existing sciences. What Marx describes as the "logic of capital" is not an ideal which cannot ever be fully realized because it always remains contaminated by particular lifeworlds, but the notional structure of existing capitalism. There is no need for "translation" here, since the same formal matrix regulates all capitalist processes, no matter how different are the lifeworlds within which they occur. Chakrabarty confronts this problem when he proposes a critical reading of Marx's analysis of abstract labor: he rejects the predominant "substantialist" reading according to which "abstract labor" designates a real or ideal property of labor. Abstract labor should rather be understood

as a performative, practical category. To organize life under the sign of capital is to act *as if* labor could indeed be abstracted from all social tissues in which it is always embedded and which make any particular labor— even the labor of abstracting—concrete . . . Notice Marx's expression: "The abstraction . . . becomes true in practice." Marx could not have written a clearer statement indicating that abstract labor was not a substantive entity, not physiological labor, not a calculable sum of muscular and nervous energy. It referred to a practice, an activity, a concrete performance of the work of abstraction, similar to what one does in the analytical strategies of economics when one speaks of an abstract category of "labor".[11]

This opposition, however, is all too crude and exclusive, in that it does not leave any space for the actual status of abstract labor in Marx.

11   Ibid., p. 54.

Abstract labor is neither "substantial" nor a performance—it is, of course, a social category and, in this sense, "performative," but as such it has an *actuality* of its own, as the structure of the actual network of social relations. Again, there is no need for translation here, since, *in the social field, "as if" is the thing itself*—abstraction is actualized in the act of exchange: "The reduction of different concrete private labours to this abstractum of equal human labour proceeds only through exchange, which actually equates products of different labour with each other."[12] The performative status of abstract labor is thus in no way "less real" than its substantial status: when an Indian capitalist trades with European companies, or when an Indian worker sells his labor-power, these acts are, of course, differently perceived in different lifeworlds, but the "truth" is in their abstraction, not in their concrete (cultural or other) content. In other words, the concrete (cultural) content is ultimately an ideological fake: *a mask obfuscating the reign of abstraction.* To return to Chakrabarty's example: the Indian programmer thinks that in the core of his being he remains faithful to his traditional lifeworld, but his "truth" is his inclusion in the global capitalist machine. With modernity, the lifeworld loses its immediacy—Heidegger was well aware of this, which is why he perceived European modernity as harboring the "danger" of a "worldless" universe, as a threat to authentic lifeworlds.

When critics of universality emphasize its violent character as a highly risky imposition,[13] one is tempted to reply by paraphrasing the famous answer given by the interrogator to Winston Smith, when, in Orwell's *1984*, he doubts the existence of the Big Brother: "It is you who doesn't exist!" Does the universal dimension to which we refer really exist? But what if it is our particular identity which does not exist, that is, which is always already traversed by universalities, caught up in them? What if, in today's global civilization, we are more universal than we think, and it is our particular identity which is a fragile ideological fantasy? Furthermore, and even more importantly, by taking particular lifeworld identities as his starting point, Chakrabarty ignores how universality manifests itself through the gaps, failures, and antagonisms at the heart of those very

12   Karl Marx, "Ergänzungen und Veränderungen zum ersten Band des Kapitals," MEGA, Part 2, Vol. 6, 1987, p. 41.
13   To proclaim something universal is always a risky hypothesis, we cannot ever be sure that the universality we propose is not colored by our particular position, so the construction of universals is a long process, a form of patient and infinite work which can only asymptotically approximate its goal.

identities. As Susan Buck-Morss puts it, "universal humanity is visible at the edges":

> rather than giving multiple, distinct cultures equal due, whereby people are recognized as part of humanity indirectly through the mediation of collective cultural identities, human universality emerges in the historical event at the point of rupture. It is in the discontinuities of history that people whose culture has been strained to the breaking point give expression to a humanity that goes beyond cultural limits. And it is in our empathic identification with this raw, free, and vulnerable state, that we have a chance of understanding what they say. Common humanity exists in spite of culture and its differences. A person's non-identity with the collective allows for subterranean solidarities that have a chance of appealing to universal, moral sentiment, the source today of enthusiasm and hope.[14]

The standard complaint about how global capitalism corrodes and destroys particular lifeworlds should be countered by the claim that such lifeworlds are invariably based on some form of domination and oppression, that to a greater or lesser extent they conceal hidden antagonisms, and that any emerging emancipatory universality therein is the universality of those who have no "proper place" within their particular world, a universality that forms the lateral link between the excluded in each lifeworld.[15]

The political consequences of the loss of an authentic lifeworld in a global economy in which abstractions reign can easily be discerned in contemporary China. The Western liberal media had their laugh when, in August 2007, the Chinese State Administration of Religious Affairs passed "Order Number Five," a law due to come into effect in the following month, which covered "the management measures for the reincarnation

---

14   Susan Buck-Morss, *Hegel, Haiti, and Universal History*, Pittsburgh: University of Pittsburgh Press 2009, p. 133.
15   The fate of the Portuguese language in Angola is exemplary of the paradoxes of decolonization. Prior to decolonization, a large majority of people in Angola spoke their own tribal languages, with only the narrow elite educated by the colonizers speaking Portuguese. After independence was declared in 1975, the ensuing civil war caused large resettlements of the population: fleeing the fighting, millions took refuge in the capital Luanda where, in order to understand each other, they had recourse to the only universal language at their disposal, Portuguese. It was thus only after decolonization that the language of the colonizer fully penetrated the entire social body and emerged as the predominant language of the newly independent nation-state. Does this paradox not lie at the core of all independent postcolonial states: their independence signifies not a return to a pre-colonial condition, but the adoption of that very form of the nation-state brought by the colonizers?

of living Buddhas in Tibetan Buddhism." This "important move to institu-
tionalize the management of reincarnation" stipulates the procedures by
which one is to reincarnate—in short, it prohibits Buddhist monks from
reincarnating without government permission: no one outside China can
influence the reincarnation process, and only monasteries in China can
apply for permission.

Before we explode in rage at the totalitarian Chinese Communists who
now want to control the lives of their subjects even after their deaths
(imagine a bureaucrat answering a candidate with: "Sorry, but all high
posts for reincarnation have already been occupied in your region; we can
only allow you to reincarnate as a dog or a pig. . ."), we should remember that such measures were familiar enough in early modern European
history. The Peace of Augsburg in 1555, the first step towards the Peace
of Westphalia in 1648, which ended the Thirty Years War, declared the
local Prince's religion to be the official religion of a region or country
(*cuius regio, eius religio*). This resulted in the acceptance or toleration of
Lutheranism in Germany by Catholics; however, when a new ruler of a
different religion took power, large groups of people had to convert. The
first big institutional move towards religious tolerance in modern Europe
thus involved the paradox of the same type as the Chinese Order Number
Five: religious belief, supposedly a matter of the individual's innermost
spiritual experience, is to be regulated at the whim of a secular prince.

The Chinese government is regulating something it not only tolerates,
but even supports. Its concern is not with religion per se, but with social
"harmony"—the political dimension of religion. In order to counter the
social disintegration caused by capitalist development, Chinese officials
now celebrate religions and traditional ideologies which sustain social
stability, from Buddhism to Confucianism—the very ideologies that had
been targets of the Cultural Revolution. In April 2006, Ye Xiaowen,
China's top religious official, told the Xinhua News Agency that "religion is one of the important forces from which China draws strength,"
and singled out Buddhism for its "unique role in promoting a harmonious society," the official formula for combining economic expansion with
social development and care; the same week, China hosted the World
Buddhist Forum.

The stakes involved in the legislation concerning reincarnation became
clear when, in the ongoing struggle between the Chinese authorities
and the Dalai Lama, the Chinese acted as protectors of ancient Tibetan
traditions against modernization. In November 2007, in reaction to the

announced Chinese legislation, the Dalai Lama proclaimed that his successor would probably not be chosen by reincarnation but by more modern democratic means: he suggested that some kind of representative religious body like the conclave in the Vatican should select his successor. This time, it was the Chinese government which counter-attacked by defending reincarnation as the method of choice, accusing the Dalai Lama of abandoning ancient Tibetan traditions because of vested political interests.

The role of religion in China as a force of stability against the capitalist dynamic is thus officially sanctioned—what bothers the Chinese authorities in the case of sects like the Falun Gong is merely their independence from state control. In the same vein, the problem with Tibetan Buddhism resides in an obvious fact which one tends to forget: namely that the traditional power structure in Tibet, headed by the Dalai Lama, is theocratic. The Dalai Lama unites religious and secular power—so when we are talking about his reincarnation, we are talking about a method of choosing a head of state. It is then a bit strange to hear those who complain about the non-democratic Chinese pressure on Tibet worry about the rights of the Dalai Lama—a non-democratically elected leader if ever there was one.[16]

Over the last few years, the Chinese have changed their strategy in Tibet, increasingly relying more on ethnic and economic colonization than on military coercion, rapidly transforming Lhasa into a Chinese version of the capitalist Wild West with karaoke bars and Disney-like "Buddhist theme parks" for Western tourists. In short, what the media image of brutal Chinese soldiers terrorizing Buddhist monks conceals is the much more effective American-style socio-economic transformation: within a decade or two, Tibetans will be reduced to the same status as that of Native Americans in the United States. It seems that the Chinese Communists have finally learnt the lesson: what is the oppressive power of secret police, prison camps, and Red Guards destroying ancient monuments, compared to the power of unbridled capitalism to undermine all traditional social relations?

Perhaps we find China's reincarnation laws so outrageous not because they are alien to our sensibility, but because they spell out so openly the secret of what we are all up to. Are not the Chinese doing only what all "civilized" governments do: respectfully tolerating what they do not take

16   Although an argument can be made that reincarnation is one way of practicing election by lot, which was indeed a democratic means widely used in Ancient Greece.

quite seriously, while trying to contain its possible political consequences through legislation?

It is all too easy to laugh at the idea of an atheist power regulating (and thereby admitting the existence of) something that, in its eyes, does not exist. However, do *we* believe in it? In Peter Shaffer's *Equus* (1973), the police ask Martin Dysart, a psychiatrist, to treat the seventeen-year-old Alan Strand who, inexplicably, has blinded six horses at the stable where he worked. Dysart discovers that, when Alan was a child, his mother, a devout Catholic, read to him daily from the Bible, while his atheist father, concerned that Alan was taking an unhealthy interest in the more violent aspects of the Bible, destroyed a picture of the crucifixion that Alan had at the foot of his bed, replacing it with one of a horse. The father tells Dysart that one night he saw Alan kneeling in front of the picture of the horse, chanting a made-up genealogy of horses parodying that of Christ in the Bible, which ends with "Equus" — Alan deified horses to make up for his failure to integrate paternal authority. Quite naturally, Alan gets a job at a stable, where he becomes erotically fixated on a stallion called Nugget, secretly taking him for midnight rides, riding him bareback and naked, enjoying the feeling of the power of the animal and the smell of the sweat. One evening, Jill, a fellow worker, suggests that they go to the stable to have sex; but as Alan hears the horses moving around, his nervousness makes him unable to get an erection. He threatens Jill with a hoof pick; after she escapes, he blames the spirit of Equus for his embarrassment, and punishes the six horses by blinding them for seeing his shame. At the end of the play, Dysart doubts whether he can really help Alan: his treatment would stamp out Alan's intense sexual-religious life. But Dysart also notices how, although he is deeply interested in old pagan spirituality, his own life is sterile, since it took him such a long time to recognize in front of him, in Alan, the living presence of what he was searching for in old artefacts.[17]

When the Taliban forces in Afghanistan destroyed the Bamiyan statues, were we, the benevolent Western observers outraged at this horror, not all Dysarts?[18]

---

17   Although the best-known Dysart was Richard Burton, who played the role on Broadway and in the cinema version, two other actors who have played the part evoke much more interesting associations: Anthony Hopkins and Anthony Perkins — Dysart: between Hannibal Lecter and Norman Bates!

18   *Equus* is usually read in a New Age way, as a play celebrating the living force of re-awakened pagan spirituality; however, the play's narrative sustains the opposite message: pagan spirituality explodes when our Western (Christian) religion fails, when the symbolic Law it guarantees collapses. What appears more "primordial" is thus a secondary reaction, a myth concocted to fill in the hole of the suspended paternal Law. In a way, Alan is a "horseman" like the little Hans, Freud's child

What this also means is that, before we succumb to bemoaning the "alienating" effect of the fact that "relations between persons" are being replaced by "relations between things," we should keep in mind the opposite, *liberating*, effect: displacement of the fetishism onto "relations between things" de-fetishizes "relations between persons," allowing them to acquire "formal" freedom and autonomy. While, in a market economy, I remain de facto dependent, this dependence is nonetheless "civilized," enacted in the form of a "free" market exchange between myself and other persons instead of in the form of direct servitude or even physical coercion. It is easy to ridicule Ayn Rand, but there is a grain of truth in the famous "hymn to money" from her *Atlas Shrugged*:

> Until and unless you discover that money is the root of all good, you ask for your own destruction. When money ceases to become the means by which men deal with one another, then men become the tools of other men. Blood, whips and guns or dollars. Take your choice — there is no other.[19]

But did not Marx say something similar in the formula just quoted, regarding how, in a commodity economy, "relations between people assume the guise of relations among things"? In the market economy, relations between people can appear as relations of mutually recognized freedom and equality: domination is no longer directly enacted and visible as such. What is problematic is the underlying premise of Rand's statement: that the only choice is between direct and indirect relations of domination and exploitation.

So what about the standard critique of "formal freedom" — that it is, in a way, even worse than direct servitude, since, in the case of the latter, at least I am not deluded into thinking that I am free. One reply on this point is Herbert Marcuse's aforementioned motto "freedom is the condition of liberation": in order to demand "actual freedom," I already have to experience myself as basically and essentially free — only as such can I experience my actual servitude as unworthy of my human condition. In order to experience this antagonism between my freedom and the actuality of my servitude, however, I have be recognized as formally free: the demand for my actual freedom can arise only out of my "formal" freedom. In other words, in exactly the same way as, in the development

---

patient — with the key difference that here the horse is not an object of phobia but an object of excessive *jouissance*, of the non-castrated paternal libido.

19   Ayn Rand, *Atlas Shrugged*, London: Penguin Books 2007, p. 871.

of capitalism, the formal subsumption of the production process under capital precedes its real subsumption, formal freedom precedes actual freedom, creating the latter's conditions. That very force of abstraction which dissolves organic lifeworlds is simultaneously the resource of emancipatory politics.

The philosophical consequences of this real status of abstraction are crucial: they compel us to reject the historicist relativization and contextualization of different modes of subjectivity, and to assert the "abstract" Cartesian subject (the *cogito*) as something which today corrodes from within all different forms of cultural self-experience—no matter how much we see ourselves as embedded in a particular culture, the moment we participate in global capitalism, this culture is always already de-naturalized, effectively functioning as one specific and contingent "way of life" of abstract Cartesian subjectivity. If, however, modern philosophy is inaugurated with the rise of the Cartesian *cogito*, where do we stand today with regard to the latter? Are we really entering a post-Cartesian era, or is it only now that our unique historical constellation enables us to discern the full significance of the *cogito*?

The Freudian Unconscious Versus the Cerebral Unconscious

What makes our historical moment unique? Let us begin with an unexpected case: George Soros is undoubtedly an honest humanitarian whose Open Society foundation more or less single-handedly saved critical social thinking in the post-Communist countries. Yet a decade or so ago, the same George Soros engaged in speculation on the currency market, exploiting differences in exchange rates to make hundreds of millions of dollars. This massively successful operation also caused untold suffering, especially in South-East Asia, where hundreds of thousands lost their jobs, with all the attendant consequences. Such is today's "abstract" violence at its purest: at the one extreme, financial speculation pursued in its own sphere, with no obvious links to the reality of human lives; at the other extreme, a pseudo-natural catastrophe which hits thousands like a tsunami, for no apparent reason. Today's violence is like a Hegelian speculative "infinite judgment," positing the identity of these two extremes.

The psychological consequences of this rise in new forms of "abstract" violence are the topic of Catherine Malabou's *Les nouveaux blessés* (*The*

New Wounded).[20] If the Freudian name for the "unknown knowns" is the Unconscious,[21] the Freudian name for the "unknown unknowns" is *trauma*, the violent intrusion of something radically unexpected, something the subject was absolutely not ready for, and which it cannot integrate in any way. Malabou has proposed a critical reformulation of psychoanalysis along these lines, taking as her starting point the delicate echoes between the internal and external Real in psychoanalysis. For Freud and Lacan, external shocks, unexpected brutal encounters or intrusions, owe their properly traumatic impact to the way they touch on a pre-existing traumatic "psychic reality." Malabou rereads along these lines Lacan's account of the Freudian dream "Father, can't you see I'm burning?" The contingent external encounter of the real (the candle falls, setting alight the cloth covering the dead child; the smell of the smoke disturbs the father on his night-watch) triggers the true Real, the unbearable fantasy-apparition of the dead child reproaching his father. In this way, for Freud (and Lacan), every external trauma is "sublated," internalized, owing its impact to the way a pre-existing Real of "psychic reality" is aroused through it. Even the most violent intrusions of the external real—say, the shocking effect of wartime bombings on the victims—owe their traumatic effect to the resonance they find in perverse masochism, in the death drive, in unconscious guilt-feelings, and so on. Today, however, our socio-political reality itself imposes multiple versions of external intrusions, traumas, which are just that, brutal but meaningless interruptions that destroy the symbolic texture of the subject's identity. First, there is external physical violence: terror attacks like 9/11, the "shock and awe" bombing of Iraq, street violence, rape, and so on, but also natural catastrophes, earthquakes, hurricanes. Then there is the "irrational" (meaningless) destruction of the material base of our inner reality (brain-tumors, Alzheimer's disease, organic cerebral lesions, etc.), which can utterly change, destroy even, the victim's personality. Finally, there are the destructive effects of socio-symbolic violence (such as social exclusion). (Note how this triad echoes the triad of commons: the commons of external nature, of inner nature, of symbolic substance.) Most of these forms of violence have, of course, been known for centuries, some even from the prehistory of humanity. What is new today is that, since we live in a "disenchanted" post-religious era, they are much more likely to be directly experienced as meaningless

---

20   Catherine Malabou, *Les Nouveaux blessés*, Paris: Bayard 2007.
21   "Analysis came to announce to us that there is knowledge that is not known, knowledge that is based on the signifier as such." Jacques Lacan, *Encore*, New York: Norton 1998, p. 96.

intrusions of the Real, and for this very reason, although utterly different in nature, they appear to belong to the same series and produce the same effect. (Recall the historical fact that rape was categorized as trauma only in the twentieth century.)[22]

There is yet another distinction one should bear in mind here. While for us, in the developed West, trauma is as a rule experienced as a momentary violent intrusion which disturbs our normal daily lives (a terrorist attack, an earthquake or tornado, being mugged or raped . . .), for those in a war-torn country like Sudan or Congo trauma is the permanent state of things, a way of life. They have nowhere to retreat to, and cannot even claim to be haunted by the specter of a earlier trauma: what remains is not the trauma's specter, but the trauma itself. It is almost an oxymoron to refer to them as "post-traumatic" subjects, since what makes their situation so traumatic is the very *persistence* of trauma.

Malabou's basic reproach to Freud is that, when confronted with such cases, he succumbs to the temptation to look for meaning: he is not ready to accept the direct destructive power of external shocks—they can destroy the psyche of the victim (or, at least, wound it in an irremediable way) without resonating with any inner traumatic truth. It would obviously be obscene to link, say, the psychic devastation of a "Muselmann" in a Nazi camp to his masochistic tendencies, death drive, or guilt feelings. He (like the victim of multiple rape, torture, and so on) is not devastated by unconscious anxieties, but by a "meaningless" external shock which can in no way be hermeneutically appropriated or integrated: for the wounded brain,

> there is no possibility of being present at its own fragmentation or at its own wound. In contrast to castration, there is no representation, no phenomenon, no example of separation, which would allow the subject to anticipate, to wait for, to fantasize what could be a break in cerebral connections. One cannot even dream about it. There is no scene for this Thing which is not one. The brain in no way anticipates the possibility of its own damage. When this damage occurs, it is another self which is affected, a "new" self founded in misrecognition.[23]

---

22   We can witness a unique combination of the social and personal dimensions of trauma in contemporary China, where interest in psychoanalysis is growing against the background of the trauma of the Cultural Revolution, with old memories of lives wounded and destroyed in those turbulent years continuing to haunt the present. Information supplied by Molly Rothenberg (New Orleans).

23   Malabou, *Les Nouveaux blessés*, p. 235.

For Freud, when external violence grows too strong, we simply exit the psychic domain proper: "either the shock is re-integrated into a pre-existing libidinal frame, or it destroys the psyche and nothing is left." What he cannot envisage is that the victim, as it were, survives its own death: all different forms of traumatic encounter, independently of their specific nature (social, natural, biological, symbolic), lead to the same result—a new subject emerges which survives its own death, the death (or erasure) of its symbolic identity. There is no continuity between this new "post-traumatic" subject (the victim of Alzheimer's or other cerebral lesions, and so on) and its old identity: after the shock, it is literally a new subject which emerges. Its features are well known: a lack of emotional engagement, profound indifference and detachment—it is a subject who is no longer "in-the-world" in the Heideggerian sense of engaged embodied existence. This subject lives death as a form of life—his or her life is the death drive embodied, a life deprived of erotic engagement; and this holds for the henchman no less than for his victims. If the twentieth century was the Freudian century, so that even its worst nightmares were read as (sado-masochistic) vicissitudes of the libido, will the twenty-first be the century of the post-traumatic disengaged subject, whose first emblematic figure, that of the Muselmann, is multiplying in the guise of refugees, terror victims, survivors of natural disasters or of family violence? Common to all these figures is the sense that the cause of the catastrophe remains libidinally meaningless, resisting any interpretation:

> the victims of socio-political traumas present today the same profile as the victims of natural catastrophes (tsunamis, earthquakes, floods) or grave accidents (serious domestic accidents, explosions, fires). We have entered a new era of political violence where politics draws its resources from the renunciation of the political sense of violence. . . . All traumatizing events tend to neutralize their intention and to assume the lack of motivation proper to chance incidents, the feature of which is that they cannot be interpreted. *Today, the enemy is hermeneutics.* . . . This erasure of sense is not only discernible in countries at war, it is present *everywhere*, as the new face of the social which bears witness to an unprecedented psychic pathology, identical in all cases and in all contexts, *globalized*.[24]

Insofar as the violence of traumatizing events consists in the way they cut the subject off from its reserves of memory, "the speech of these patients

---

24   Ibid., pp. 258–9.

does not have any revelatory meaning, their illness does not constitute a kind of truth with regard to the subject's past history."[25] In this lack of sense, "social conflicts are deprived of the dialectics of political struggle proper and become as anonymous as natural catastrophes."[26] We are thus dealing with a heterogeneous mixture of nature and politics, in which "politics cancels itself as such and takes on the appearance of nature, and nature disappears in order to assume the mask of politics. This *global heterogeneous mixture of nature and politics is characterized by the global uniformization of neuropsychological reactions*."[27] Global capitalism thus generates a new form of illness which is itself global, indifferent to the most elementary distinctions such as that between nature and culture.

In the case of such an intrusion of the raw real, "*all hermeneutics is impossible*":[28] the trauma remains external to the field of sense, it cannot be integrated into it as a mere deterrent which triggers the resuscitation of a latent psychic trauma. This is what Freud cannot (or, rather, refuses to) think: for him, external traumas like brain lesions are "psychically mute,"[29] they can only have a psychic impact when a sexual trauma resonates within them. In other words, the enemy the psyche is fighting when it encounters a trauma is ultimately always an "internal enemy." Freud refuses to consider the psychic impact of a violent intrusion which remains external to sense, which precludes "the possibility of being fantasized";[30] he refuses to envisage the psychic consequences of traumatic intrusions which cannot be integrated into a psychic staging—such as indifference, the loss of affect. It is crucial that, in such cases, the limits that separate history from nature, "sociopathy" from "neurobiology," are blurred: the terror of the concentration camp and an organic brain lesion can produce the same form of autism.

Such detached psyches are "beyond love and hate: one should call them neither sadistic nor masochistic."[31] Against Malabou, however, the difference between pleasure and *jouissance* should be fully acknowledged: while it is clear that the dialectical reversals of pleasure fail to capture the traumatic cases evoked by Malabou, the intrusion of a numbing *jouissance* is definitely relevant here. In many of the cases reported by Oliver

25   Ibid., p. 345.
26   Ibid., p. 267.
27   Ibid., p. 260.
28   Ibid., p. 29.
29   Ibid., p. 33.
30   Ibid., p. 35.
31   Ibid., p. 323.

Sacks in his *Musicophilia*, the patient haunted by compulsive music feels a great release when he learns that his hallucinations are caused by an organic brain lesion or some other kind of physical malfunctioning, not by psychological madness—in this way, the patient no longer has to feel subjectively responsible for his own hallucinations, they become just a meaningless objective fact. Is there not, however, also a possible escape from some traumatic truth at work in this release? Sacks reports on the case of David Mamlok, an old Jewish immigrant from Germany who was haunted by musical hallucinations:

> When I asked Mr. Mamlok what his internal music was like, he exclaimed, angrily, that it was "tonal" and "corny." I found this choice of adjectives intriguing and asked him why he used them. His wife, he explained, was a composer of atonal music, and his own tastes were for Schoenberg and other atonal masters, though he was fond of classical and, especially, chamber music, too. But the music he hallucinated was nothing like this. It started, he said, with a German Christmas song (he immediately hummed this) and then other Christmas songs and lullabies; these were followed by marches, especially the Nazi marching songs he had heard growing up in Hamburg in the 1930s. These songs were particularly distressing to him, for he was Jewish and had lived in terror of the *Hitlerjugend*, the belligerent gangs who had roamed the streets looking for Jews.[32]

Did the organic stimulus here not re-awaken old traumas of obscene religio-political kitsch? Although Sacks is aware of how organically caused disturbances like musical hallucinations get invested with meaning (why *these* songs and not others?), nonetheless all too often the immediate reference to organic causes tends to obliterate the repressed traumatic dimension.

In the new form of subjectivity (autistic, indifferent, deprived of affective engagement), the old personality is not "sublated" or replaced by a compensatory formation, but thoroughly destroyed—destruction itself acquires a form, becomes a (relatively stable) "form of life"—what we have is not simply the absence of form, but the form of (the) absence (of the erasure of the previous personality). More precisely, the new form is less a form of life than a form of death—not an expression of the Freudian death drive, but, more directly, the *death of the drive*.

---

32   Oliver Sacks, *Musicophilia*, New York: Alfred A. Knopf 2007, pp. 56–7.

As Deleuze pointed out in *Difference and Repetition*, death is always double: the Freudian death drive means that the subject wants to die, but to die in its own way, according to its own inner path, not as the result of an external accident. There is always a gap between the two, between the death drive as "transcendental" tendency and the contingent accident which kills me. Suicide is a desperate (and ultimately failed) attempt to bring the two dimensions together. There is a nice scene in a Hollywood horror movie in which a desperate young woman, alone in her bedroom, is about to kill herself when suddenly the horrible creature attacking the city breaks into the room and attacks her—the woman then fights back desperately, since although she wanted to die, this was not the death she wanted.

Insofar as the "new wounded" are radically cut off from their past, inso-far as their wound suspends all hermeneutics, insofar as there is ultimately nothing to interpret here, such a "deserted, emotionally disaffected, indif-ferent psyche is also not (any longer) able to transfer. We live in the epoch of the end of transference. The love for the psychoanalyst or the therapist means nothing to a psyche which can neither love nor hate."[33] In other words, these patients seek neither to know nor not to know—when in treatment, they do not position their psychiatrist or analyst in the role of the subject supposed to know. What, then, should the therapist do in such conditions? Malabou endorses Daniel Wildloecher's position: she or he should "become the subject of the other's suffering and of its expression, especially when this other is unable to feel anything whatsoever"—or, as Malabou herself puts it, the therapist should "assemble [*recueillir*] for the other his/her pain."[34] These formulae are full of ambiguities: if there is no transference whatsoever, then the question is not only how this collecting/assembling affects the patient (does it do them any good whatsoever?), but, even more radically, how we can be at all sure that it is really the patient's suffering we are assembling. What if the therapist, in imagining how the patient must suffer, can only imagine how the patient's depriva-tions must appear to someone who still has, say, an intact memory, and is thus able to imagine what it would be like to be deprived of it? What if the therapist thus misreads blessed ignorance as unbearable suffering? No wonder Malabou's formula of "assembling the other's pain" recalls the problem of witnessing the Holocaust: the problem the survivors of the camps encountered is not only that witnessing is impossible—that it

33   Malabou, *Les Nouveaux blessés*, p. 346.
34   Ibid.

always has an element of prosopopoeia, that another has to collect/assemble their pain, since the true witness is always already dead and we can only speak on his behalf—but also a symmetrical problem at the opposite end: there is no proper public, no listener to adequately receive the testimony. The most traumatic dream Primo Levi had in Auschwitz was about his survival: the war is over, he is reunited with his family, telling them about his life in the camp, but they gradually become bored, start to yawn, and, one after another, leave the table, so that finally Levi is left alone. A fact from the Bosnian war in the early 1990s illustrates the same point: many of the girls who survived brutal rape experiences killed themselves later on, after they had rejoined their communities and found that there was no one who was really ready to listen to them, to accept their testimony. In Lacan's terms, what is missing here is not only another human being, the attentive listener, but the "big Other" itself, the space of the symbolic inscription or registration of my words. Levi made the same point in his direct and simple way when he said that what the Nazis did to the Jews was so irrepresentable in its horror that even if someone were to survive the camps, he would not be believed by those who were not there—they would simply declare him a liar or a madman!

While Malabou focuses on cases where a neuronal change has traumatic subjective effects, would it not have been even more unsettling to consider cases where such a change might have passed unnoticed? In May 2002, it was reported that scientists at New York University had attached a computer chip, able to receive signals, directly to a rat's brain, enabling them to control the rat's movements by means of a steering mechanism (as in a remote-controlled toy car). For the first time, the "will" of a living animal agent, its "spontaneous" decisions about the movements it will make, were taken over by an external machine. Of course, the great philosophical question here is how the unfortunate rat "experienced" these movements which were effectively decided from outside. Did it continue to "experience" them as spontaneous (in other words, was it totally unaware that its movements were being steered?), or was it aware that "something was wrong"? More crucially, what if an identical experiment were to be performed with humans—which, ethical issues notwithstanding, ought not to be much more complicated, technically speaking, than in the case of the rat? In the latter case, it might be argued that one should not apply to the rat the human category of "experience," but in the case of a human being one could indeed ask whether the subject of the experiment would remain totally unaware that their movements were being steered, or whether they would realize that "something was wrong". And how, precisely, would this "external power" appear—as something "inside one," an unstoppable inner drive, or as simple external coercion? If the subject remained totally unaware that their "spontaneous" behavior was being steered from the outside, could one really pretend that this would have no consequences for our notion of free will?

We can add another gruesome traumatic experience to those enumerated by Malabou. In "Le prix du progrès," one of the fragments that conclude *Dialectic of Enlightenment*, Adorno and Horkheimer quote the argument of the nineteenth-century French physiologist Pierre Flourens against medical anesthesia using chloroform: Flourens claims that it can be proven that the anesthetic works only on our memory's neuronal network. So, while being butchered alive on the operating table, we feel the terrible pain throughout, but later, on coming round, we do not remember it. Should we not read this scene as a perfect staging of the inaccessible Other Site of the fundamental fantasy that can never be fully subjectivized, assumed by the subject? Such premonitions are regularly confirmed: "anesthesia awareness"—where the patient is mentally alert (and terrified) while supposedly under full general anesthesia—continues to be reported between 100 and 200 times daily in the United States alone. The patient is paralyzed, unable to speak, and totally unable to communicate his or her awareness; the actual pain of the operation may or may not be felt, but the patient is fully aware of what is happening, feeling as if they cannot breathe, and unable to communicate any distress because of the muscle relaxant. The most traumatic cases occur when patients who have experienced full awareness explicitly recall it afterwards: the result is an enormous trauma generating post-traumatic stress disorder, leading to long-lasting after-effects such as nightmares, night terrors, flashbacks, insomnia, and in some cases even suicide.

Is the trauma of which Malabou speaks not a trauma experienced as such because it is so unsettling from within the horizon of meaning—in other words, is the absence of a meaningful Self traumatic only if we expect its presence? If so, then why should we not surmise that these cold, indifferent, disengaged subjects are *not* suffering at all? That, once their old persona has been erased, they enter a blessed state of indifference, and only appear to us to be undergoing unbearable suffering? What if *les nouveaux blessés* are literally the new blessed ones? What if the logic of the old medical joke about Alzheimer's ("The bad news is we've discovered you have severe Alzheimer's disease. The good news is you will have already forgotten the bad news by the time you get home") applies here, so that, when the patient's old personality is destroyed, the very measure of their suffering also disappears? Is Malabou not then guilty of the same mistake for which she reproaches psychoanalysis: the mistake of not being able to think the absence of meaningful engagement, of reading disengaged indifference from within the horizon of such engagement? To put it another way, does she not forget to include herself, her own desire, in the observed phenomenon? In an ironic reversal of her claim that the autistic subject is unable to enact transference, perhaps it is her own transference that she fails to take into account when she portrays the autistic subject's immense suffering. This subject is primordially an enigmatic impenetrable Thing, totally ambiguous, such that one cannot but oscillate between attributing to it immense suffering and blessed ignorance. What characterizes it is the lack of recognition in a double sense: we do not recognize ourselves in it, there is no empathy possible, *and* the autistic subject, on account of its withdrawal, does not recognize *us*, its partner in communication.

Malabou rejects the autonomy of psychic life, in the Freudian sense of an autonomous "psychic reality," of the libido as psychic energy different from neuronal (brain) energy. For her, the Freudian libido is based on the suspension (or exclusion) of neuronal energy; more precisely, on Freud's refusal to admit the brain's ability to enact self-affection, to engage in self-regulatory self-modeling. As she puts it: "The psychic energy is in a way a rhetorical detour of the neuronal energy"[35]—when the endogenous brain excitation cannot be released within the nerve system itself, it changes into psychic energy which may find release in rhetorical displacements; in short, "rhetoric supplants the silence of the neuronal system"; "The unconscious is structured like a language only insofar as the brain does not talk."[36] Today's brain sciences have invalidated the Freudian hypothesis with their discovery of the "emotional brain," which can generate self-representations and regulate its life through affects: "Emotion is a reflexive structure by means of which the vital regulation affects itself."

One should thus counterpose to the Freudian sexual unconscious the "cerebral unconscious," the self-representative activity of the brain which incessantly constructs the cartography of its own states and thereby affects itself. Malabou strictly opposes this cerebral self-affection (self-relating) to that self-affection which is the self-awareness of the

---

35   Ibid., p. 73.
36   Ibid., p. 74.

(conscious) subject, and which was "deconstructed" by Derrida in his detailed analysis of the paradoxes and deadlocks involved in "hearing-oneself-talking." Nobody can be aware of the workings of his or her own brain; there is no subjectivization possible of the neuronal process of self-affection: "Cerebral self-affection is the unconscious of subjectivity."[37] There is only one way in which the subjective experience of the auto-affection of one's own brain can occur: in the guise of the suffering caused by brain damage.

When the libidinal unconscious undergoes a traumatic encounter, it reacts by "regression," withdrawing from higher-level engagement and interaction to a more primitive mode of functioning. When the cerebral process of self-affection is disturbed, there is no space or more fundamental level to which the subject can return: its substance is erased, the Self which survives this destruction is literally a new Self, its identity an "identity by default," that of an impassive disengaged subject deprived even of the capacity to dream.

Malabou's thesis here is both radical and very precise. Her point is not simply to add to the Freudian libidinal unconscious another, cerebral, unconscious. The problem is rather that the Freudian unconscious only makes sense when (or if) we refuse to admit—we erase the possibility of—the cerebral unconscious. What this means is that the "cerebral unconscious" is not just a mechanism for explaining those processes which cannot be accounted for in terms of the libidinal unconscious: once we admit the cerebral unconscious, the libidinal unconscious loses its grounding. It is only this cerebral unconscious, irreducible to the Lacanian triad Imaginary-Symbolic-Real, which is the truly *material* unconscious.[38] The cerebral unconscious is not the imaginary—its self-modeling is not narcissistic self-mirroring; it is not symbolic—its traces do not re-present the subject within a structure of meaning; and it is not real in the Lacanian sense of the Thing as the ultimate incestuous libidinal object of "psychic reality," since it is radically external to the libido, to sexuality.

Nothing distinguishes the Freudian unconscious and the cerebral unconscious more clearly than the way they relate to death: as Freud emphasized repeatedly, the libidinal unconscious is "undead," it does not know (cannot represent) its own death, it acts as if it were immortal, indestructible; but our brain never acts as if it is immortal: the

---

37   Ibid., p. 85.
38   Ibid., p. 235.

cerebral unconscious is destructible and "knows" itself (models itself) as such.

The second distinction concerns sexuality, or Eros as the counter-pole to Thanatos. If the cerebral unconscious is mortal, the Freudian unconscious is sexual, where, as Malabou puts it in very precise terms, Freudian "sexuality" designates not merely a constrained content (sexual practices), but the very formal structure of the relationship between Outside and Inside, between the external incident/accident and its *Aufhebung*/integration into the internal libidinal process it triggers. "Sexuality" is thus the name for this passage from contingency to necessity, from *Ereignis* to *Erlebnis*: it is through its integration into a pre-existing frame of "psychic reality" that the external accident is "sexualized." The mediator between the two is *fantasy*: in order to "arouse" me, the external accident, this pure shock, has to touch on my fantasy, my pre-existing fantasmatic frame has to resonate within it. Fantasy enacts the "stitch [*soudure/Verloetung*]" between the outside and the inside. The activity of unconscious fantasizing is "primordially repressed," into the radical (non-subjectivizable) unconscious, yet as such it remains strictly psychic, irreducible, and autonomous with regard to the brain's activity: it is the outside of the psychic inside itself, its level of ex-timacy.

One should nonetheless render problematic the very term "cerebral unconscious": it designates not only "blind" neuronal process but also the reflexivity of that process, the fact that the brain incessantly "reflects" itself, registering and regulating its process on the model of what Damasio calls the "proto-Self." However, in what precise sense does this proto-Self deserve to be called "unconscious"? Does such reflexivity not remain a "blind" natural self-regulatory process? Does Malabou's very formal definition of the cerebral unconscious not point in this direction? She locates the basic formal condition of the cerebral unconscious in the fact that, when we are thinking, it is never the brain itself which perceives itself, that is, we cannot ever reflexively become aware of how our brain is working when we are thinking—the "cerebral unconscious" is then this self-regulating and self-representing of the brain which forever remains closed to us.

However, insofar as Malabou continues to talk about the "cerebral unconscious" as something *more* than such a blind self-regulatory process, she runs the risk of regressing to a pre-modern organicist-idealist figure of a spiritual Form inherent to matter as such (along the Aristotelian lines of the soul as the inherent form of a body). Is what she presents as her more radical materialism—there is no need for a specific psychic domain or level; the brain itself can reflect itself—not a covert re-spiritualization of matter?

How, then, do the two different figures of radical Otherness relate to each other: the "cerebral" otherness of a meaningless neuronal Real, and the abyss of the Neighbor-Thing? Linked to this is another obvious gap in Malabou's line of argumentation: while she tries to demonstrate how cerebral lesions generate trauma totally independently of the sexualized libidinal economy, she never raises the opposite question: namely, how *does* the sexualized universe of meaning arise? Is Freudo-Lacanian theory not still required in order to explain the rise of sexualized-symbolic subjectivity?

Malabou formulates the problem in the terms of the difficulty of truly reaching beyond the pleasure principle: what Freud calls "beyond the pleasure principle," the death drive, is really itself another roundabout assertion of the pleasure principle, not its true beyond. Einstein's theory of relativity offers here unexpected parallels with Lacanian theory. The starting point of the theory of relativity is the strange fact that, for every observer, no matter in what direction and how fast he moves, light moves at the same speed; in an analogous way, for Lacan, no matter whether the desiring subject approaches or runs from his or her object of desire, this object seems to remain at the same distance from the subject. Who has not experienced the nightmarish situation in a dream: the more I run away, the more I remain in the same place? This paradox can be neatly solved by introducing the difference between the object and the cause of desire: no matter how close I get to the object of desire, its cause remains at a distance, totally elusive. Furthermore, the general theory of relativity solves the antinomy between the relativity of every movement with regard to the observer and the absolute velocity of light, which moves at a constant speed independently of the point of observation, with the notion of curved space. In a homologous way, the Freudian solution to the antinomy between the subject's approaching or running away from his object of desire, and the "constant speed" (and distance from him) of the object-cause of desire, resides in the *curved space of desire*: sometimes the shortest way to realize a desire is to by-pass its object-goal, to post- pone the encounter with it. What Lacan calls the *objet petit a* is the agent of this curvature: the unfathomable X on account of which, when we confront the object of our desire, more satisfaction is provided by danc- ing around it than by directly going for it. And is what happens in the case of a post-traumatic subject not the *destruction* of the *objet a*? This is why such a subject is deprived of an engaged existence and reduced to indifferent vegetation. No wonder, then, that in her confrontation with Lacan—when she argues that, contrary to all appearances, both Freud and Lacan cannot really think the dimension "beyond the pleasure principle," since every destructive trauma is re-eroticized—Malabou totally ignores Lacan's key distinction between pleasure (*Lust*, *plaisir*) and enjoyment (*Geniessen*, *jouissance*): what is "beyond the pleasure principle" is enjoyment itself, it is the drive as such. The basic paradox of *jouissance* is that it is both impossible *and* unavoidable: it is never fully achieved, always missed, but, simultaneously, we can never get rid of it—every renunciation of enjoyment generates an enjoyment in renunciation, every obstacle to desire generates a desire for an obstacle and so forth. This reversal provides the minimal definition of surplus-enjoyment: it involves the paradoxical "pleasure in pain." That is to say, when Lacan uses the term *plus-de-jouir*, one has to ask a naïve, but crucial question: in what does this surplus consist? Is it merely a qualitative increase of ordinary pleasure? The ambiguity of the French expression is decisive here: it can mean "surplus of enjoyment" as well as "no enjoyment"—the surplus of enjoyment over mere pleasure is generated by the presence of the very opposite of pleasure, namely pain. Surplus-enjoyment is thus precisely that part of *jouissance* which resists being contained by the homeostasis, by the pleasure principle. (And since Malabou refers—among others—to the "Muselmann" of the Nazi camps as a pure figure of the death drive beyond the pleasure principle, one is almost tempted to claim that it is precisely the "Muselmann" who, due to his libidinal disengagement, can effectively act upon the pleasure principle: his minimal gestures are fully instrumentalized, he strives to eat when hungry, and so on.)

Here Malabou seems to pay the price for her all too naïve reading of Freud, taking him too "hermeneutically," failing to distinguish between the true core of Freud's discovery and the different ways he himself misunderstood the scope of that discovery. Malabou accepts Freud's dualism of drives as it is formulated, ignoring those precise readings (from Lacan to Laplanche) which convincingly demonstrated that this dualism was a false way out, a theoretical regression. So, ironically, when Malabou contrasts Freud and Jung, emphasizing Freud's dualism of drives against Jung's monism of the (desexualized) libido, she misses the crucial paradox: it is at this very point, when he resorts to the dualism of drives, that Freud is *at his most Jungian*, regressing to a pre-modern mythic agonism of opposed primordial forces. How then are we to grasp properly what eluded Freud and pushed him into this dualism? When Malabou takes it that, for Freud, Eros always relates to and encompasses its opposite Other, the destructive death drive, she—following Freud's own misleading formulations—conceives of this opposition as a conflict of two opposed forces, and not, more precisely, as the inherent self-blockage of the drive. The "death drive" is not an opposing force with regard to the libido, but a constitutive gap which distinguishes the drive from instinct (significantly, Malabou prefers translating *Trieb* by "instinct")—always derailed, caught in a loop of repetition, marked by an impossible excess. Deleuze, on whom Malabou otherwise constantly relies, made this point clear in his *Difference and Repetition*: Eros and Thanatos are not two opposing drives that compete and combine their forces (as in eroticized masochism); there is only one drive, the libido, striving for enjoyment, and the "death drive" is the curved space of its formal structure:

> [it] plays the role of a transcendental principle, whereas the pleasure principle is only psychological. For this reason, it is above all silent (not given in experience), whereas the pleasure principle is noisy. The first question, then, is: How is it that the theme of death, which appears to draw together the most negative elements of psychological life, can be in itself the most positive element, transcendentally positive, to the point of affirming repetition? . . . Eros and Thanatos are distinguished in that Eros must be repeated, can be lived only through repetition, whereas Thanatos (as transcendental principle) is that which gives repetition to Eros, that which submits Eros to repetition.[39]

How, then, do we pass from animal sexuality (instinctual coupling) to properly human sexuality? By submitting animal sexuality (its "life instinct") to the death drive. The death drive is the transcendental form which makes sexuality proper out of animal instincts. In this sense, the disengaged indifferent de-libidinalized subject is indeed the pure subject of the death drive: in this subject, only the empty frame of the death drive as the formal-transcendental condition of libidinal investments survives, deprived of all content. It is weird that Malabou, who quotes from Deleuze's *Difference and Repetition* in her book, ignores these passages which directly bear on her topic, providing an elegant solution to her

---

39   Gilles Deleuze, *Difference and Repetition*, New York: Columbia University Press 1994, pp. 16, 18.

question of why Freud was unable to find positive representations of the death drive.

The Libidinal Proletariat

Perhaps pushing the envelope a bit, one is tempted to say that the subject deprived of its libidinal substance is the "libidinal proletariat." When Malabou develops her key notion of "destructive plasticity," of the subject who continues to live on after its psychic death (the erasure of the narrative texture of its symbolic identity that sustained its libidinal investments and engagements), she touches on a key point: the reflexive reversal of the destruction of form into the form acquired by destruction itself. In other words, when we are dealing, say, with a victim of Alzheimer's, it is not merely that his or her awareness is severely constrained, that the scope of the Self is diminished—we are literally no longer dealing with the same Self. After the trauma, *another* subject emerges, we are talking to a stranger.

This may appear to be the very opposite of what goes on in a Hegelian dialectical process, in which we are dealing with a continuous metamorphosis of the *same* substance-subject which develops in complexity, mediates and "sublates" its content into a higher level: is not the whole point of the dialectical process that, precisely, we never go through a zero-point, that the past content is never radically erased, that there is no radically new beginning?

The question concerns the subject's radical finitude. Heidegger is consistent in developing all the consequences of the radical assertion of finitude—it involves a series of self-referential paradoxes. That is to say, when Heidegger claims that the ultimate failure, the breakdown of the entire structure of meaning—the withdrawal from engagement and care, the possibility that the totality of *Dasein*'s engagements "collapses into itself; the world has the character of completely lacking significance"[40]— is the innermost possibility of *Dasein*, when he claims that *Dasein* can succeed in its engagement only against the background of a possible failure—"the interrelational structure of the world of Care can fail in such a catastrophic way that *Dasein* will appear not as the world-embedded, open-to-meaning, engaged agent in a shared world that is, but, all at once as it were, as the null basis of a nullity"[41]—he is not just making the

---

40   Martin Heidegger, *Being and Time*, New York: HarperCollins 2008, p. 231.
41   Robert Pippin, *The Persistence of Subjectivity*, Cambridge: Cambridge University Press 2005, p. 64.

decisionist-existentialist point about how "being a subject means being able to fail to be one,"[42] about how the choice is ours and utterly contingent, with no guarantee of success. His point is rather that the historical totality-of-meaning into which we are thrown is always already, "constitutively," thwarted *from within* by the possibility of its utmost impossibility. Death, the collapse of the structure of meaning and care, is not an external limit which, as such, would enable *Dasein* to "totalize" its meaningful engagement; it is not the final quilting point that "dots the i's" of one's life-span, enabling one to totalize a life-story into a consistent meaningful narrative. Death is precisely that which *cannot* be included into any meaningful totality, its meaningless facticity is a permanent threat to meaning, its prospect a reminder that there is no final way out.[43] The consequence of this is that the choice is not a direct choice between success and failure, between an authentic and an inauthentic mode of existence: since the very notion that one can successfully totalize one's life in an all-encompassing structure-of-meaning is the ultimate inauthentic betrayal, the only true "success" *Dasein* can have is to heroically confront and accept its ultimate failure.

However, it is here that one should be very precise: this outline of a continuous "dialectical" metamorphosis is not Hegelian, but an example of "dynamized Spinozism" or organicism—the same Substance (Life) maintains itself through its metamorphoses. The logic of dialectical transitions is entirely different, since it involves a radical trans-substantiation: true, after negation/alienation/loss, the subject "returns to itself," but this subject is not the same as the substance that underwent the alienation—it is constituted in the very movement of returning-to-itself. In a properly Hegelian-Freudian-Lacanian way, one should thus draw a radical conclusion: *the subject is* as such *the survivor of its own death*, a shell which remains after it is deprived of its substance; this is why Lacan's matheme for the subject is *$*—the barred subject. It is not that Lacan *can* think the rise of a new subject surviving its death/disintegration—for Lacan, the subject as such is a "second subject," a formal survivor (the surviving form) of the loss of its substance, of the noumenal X called by Kant the "I or he or it (the thing) that thinks."

---

42   Ibid., p. 67.
43   Here we approach the topic of Heidegger and psychiatric clinics: what about that withdrawal from engagement which is *not* death but the psychotic breakdown of a living human being? What about the possibility of "living in death," of vegetating without a care, like the Muselmann in the Nazi camps?

When Malabou insists that the subject who emerges after a traumatic wound is not a transformation of the old subject, but literally a new one, she is well aware that the identity of this new subject does not arise from a *tabula rasa*: many traces of the old subject's life-narrative survive, but they are totally restructured, torn out of their previous horizon of meaning and inscribed into a new context. The new subject

> profoundly modifies the vision and the content of the past itself. On account of its pathological force of deformation and of its destructive plasticity, such a [traumatic] event effectively introduces into psychic life *inauthenticity, facticity*. It creates *another history*, a *past which doesn't exist*.[44]

But does this not hold already for radical historical breaks? Are we not dealing all the time with what Eric Hobsbawm called "invented traditions"? Does not every new epoch rewrite its past, rearticulating it into a new context? Malabou is at her theoretical best when she makes a fine critical point about those brain scientists, from Luria to Sacks, who insist on supplementing the naturalist description of brain lesions, and so on, with a subjective description of how the biological wound not only affects the subject's particular abilities (loss of memory, inability to recognize faces, etc.), but changes their entire psychic structure, the fundamental way they perceive themselves and their world. (The first great classic is here Alexander Luria's unsurpassable *The Mind of a Mnemonist*, a description of the inner universe of a man who was condemned to absolute memory, unable to forget anything.) These scientists remain all too "humanist": they focus on the victim's attempts to cope with his or her wound, to build a supplementary life-form that will somehow enable them to reintegrate into social interaction (in Sacks's *The Man Who Mistook His Wife For a Hat*, the cure is found in the man's undisturbed musical sense: although he cannot recognize the face of his wife or his other companions and friends, he can identify them through their sounds.) Luria, Sacks, et al., thereby avoid fully confronting the true traumatic heart of the matter: not the subject's desperate effort to recompense for the loss, but the subject of this loss itself, the subject which is the positive *form* this loss assumes (the disengaged impassive subject). They make their job too easy by passing directly from the neuronal devastation to the subject's efforts to cope with the loss, avoiding the true difficulty: the subjective form of this devastation itself.

---

44   Malabou, *Les Nouveaux blessés*, p. 252.

For Malabou, even Lacan succumbs to this temptation of "stitching" with his notion of the Thing (*das Ding*) as the ultimate libidinal object, the all-erasing abyss of incestuous *jouissance* which equals death. At this ultimate, asymptotic point of the coincidence of opposites, *Ereignis* and *Erlebnis*, the outside and the inside, fully overlap. As Malabou puts it in very precise terms, the Thing is Lacan's name for the horizon of ultimate destruction which is impossible-real, an always deferred anticipation, a threat of an unimaginable X always to come and never here. The destruction of every horizon remains a horizon of this destruction, the lack of encounter remains the encounter of lack. The Thing is real, but a real transposed into "psychic reality," it is the way the subject experiences/represents the very impossibility of experiencing/representing.

Lacan's name for the transcendental Inside which finds resonance in external traumatic intrusion is "separation": prior to any empirical traumatic loss is the "transcendental" separation constitutive of the very dimension of subjectivity, in its multiple guises, from birth-trauma to symbolic castration. Its general form is that of the separation from the partial object which survives as the specter of the undead *lamella*.

Here, perhaps, Lacan introduces a logic which is not taken into account by Malabou: castration is not only a threat-horizon, a not-yet/always-to-come, but, simultaneously, something which always already happens: the subject is not only under the threat of separation, it *is* the effect of separation (from substance). Furthermore, insofar as a traumatic encounter generates anxiety, we should bear in mind that, for Lacan, what the subject is exposed to in anxiety is precisely the loss of the loss itself — Lacan here turns Freud around: anxiety is not the anxiety of separation from the object, but the anxiety of the object(-cause of desire) coming too close to the subject. This is why trauma belongs to the domain of the uncanny in the fundamental ambiguity of that term: what makes the uncanny uncanny is its proximity, the fact that it is the coming-into-visibility of something too close to us.

So, when Malabou — with a critical edge vis-à-vis Lacan — defines the intrusion of the traumatic real as separation from separation itself, she thereby repeats Lacan's notion of psychotic breakdown as the loss of the loss: what is lacking in psychosis is ultimately lack itself, the gap of "symbolic castration" that separates me from my symbolic identity, from the virtual dimension of the big Other. Consequently, when Malabou insists that in the true trauma of the real it is not just that the subject lacks its objective supplement, but that the subject itself is lacking (goes missing, disintegrates), does she not echo Lacan's notion of the subject's disintegration caused by the psychotic over-proximity of the object?

What Freud cannot think is "destructive plasticity," that is, the subjective form assumed by the very destruction of the self, the direct form of the death drive: "It is as if there is no intermediary between the plasticity of the good form and elasticity as the mortifying erasure of all form. *In Freud, there is no form of the negation of form.*"[45] In other words, Freud fails to consider

> the existence of a specific form of psyche produced by the presence of death, of pain, of the repetition of a painful experience. He should have done justice to the existential power of improvisation proper to an accident, to the psyches deserted by pleasure, in which indifference and detachment have taken over, and which nonetheless remain psyches. What Freud is looking for when he talks about the death drive is precisely the form of this drive, the form he doesn't find insofar as he denies to destruction its own specific plasticity. . . . The beyond of the pleasure principle is thus the work of the death drive as the giving-form to death in life, as the production of those individual figures which exist only in the detachment of existence. These forms of death in life, fixations of the image of the drive, would be the "satisfying" representatives of the death drive Freud was for such a long time looking for far away from neurology.[46]

These figures are "not so much figures of those who want to die as figures of those who *are already dead*, or, rather, to employ a strange and terrible grammatical twist, who *have already been dead*, who have 'experienced' death."[47]

Although it is impossible to miss the Hegelian resonances of this notion of "negative plasticity," of the form through which destructivity/negativity itself acquires positive existence, the strange fact is that Malabou—herself the author of a path-breaking book on Hegel—not only totally ignores Hegel in *Les Nouveaux blessés*, but even here and there drops hints that this negative plasticity is "non-dialectizable" and, as such, beyond the scope of the Hegelian dialectic. She sees here not only a task for psychoanalysis, but also a properly *philosophical* task of reconceptualizing the notion of the subject so as to include in it this zero-level of the subject of the death drive: "the only philosophical issue today is the elaboration of a new

---

45   Ibid., p. 273.
46   Ibid., pp. 322, 324.
47   Ibid., p. 326.

materialism which precisely refuses to envisage any, even the smallest, separation not only between brain and thought, but also between brain and the unconscious."[48] Malabou is right to emphasize the philosophical dimension of the new autistic subject: in it, we are dealing with the zero-level of subjectivity, with the formal conversion of the pure externality of the meaningless real (its brutal destructive intrusion) into the pure internality of the "autistic" subject detached from external reality, disengaged, reduced to a persisting core deprived of all substance. The logic is here again that of the Hegelian infinite judgment: the speculative identity of meaningless external intrusion and of the pure detached internality — it is as if only a brutal external shock can give rise to the pure interiority of the subject, of the void that cannot be identified with any determinate positive content.

The properly philosophical dimension of the study of the post-traumatic subject resides in this recognition that what appears as the brutal destruction of the subject's (narrative) substantial identity is also the moment of its birth. The post-traumatic autistic subject is the "living proof" that the subject cannot be identified (does not fully overlap) with the "stories it tells itself about itself," with the narrative symbolic texture of its life: when all this is taken away, something (or, rather, *nothing*, but a *form* of nothing) remains, and this something is the pure subject of the death drive.

The Lacanian subject as $ is thus a response *to and of* the real: a response *to* the real of the brutal meaningless intrusion; and a response *of* the real, that is, a response which emerges when the symbolic integration of the traumatic intrusion fails, reaches its point of impossibility. As such, the subject at its most elementary is indeed "beyond the unconscious": an empty form deprived even of unconscious formations encapsulating a variety of libidinal investments.

We should nonetheless apply even to the post-traumatic subject the Freudian notion that a violent intrusion of the real counts as trauma only insofar as a previous trauma resonates in it — *in this case, the previous trauma is that of the birth of subjectivity itself*: a subject is "barred," as Lacan says, it emerges only when a living individual is deprived of its substantial content, and this constitutive trauma is what is repeated in the later traumatic experience. This is what Lacan aims at with his claim that the Freudian subject is none other than the Cartesian *cogito*: the *cogito* is not an

---

48   Ibid., p. 342.

"abstraction" from the reality of living actual individuals with their wealth of properties, emotions, abilities, and relations, etc.; on the contrary, it is this "wealth of personality" which functions as the imaginary "stuff of the I," as Lacan put it; the *cogito* is, on the contrary, a very real "abstraction," an "abstraction" which functions as a concrete subjective attitude. The post-traumatic subject, the subject reduced to an empty substance-less form of subjectivity, is the historical "realization" of the *cogito* — recall that, for Descartes, the *cogito* is the zero-point of the overlapping of thinking and being, that point at which the subject, in a way, neither "is" (it is deprived of all positive substantial content) nor "thinks" (its thinking is reduced to the empty tautology of thinking that it thinks).

Is, then, the post-traumatic subject also another name for the Neighbor as Thing, for the abyss/void of the Other beyond every empathy and identification? Is what makes the confrontation with a post-traumatic subject so unbearable — so *traumatic*, precisely — the very fact that, in this encounter, we are confronted with a Neighbor deprived of the clothing of "fellow-man"? Yes and no: although there is an obvious proximity between the two, the Neighbor as Thing is *not* simply the Cartesian *cogito* (or its appearance in reality in the guise of the post-traumatic subject). The Neighbor stands for the abyss of the Other's desire, for the enigma of *Che vuoi?*, while the post-traumatic subject is precisely deprived of this enigmatic depth — it is flat, lacking any depth, any impenetrable density.

So, when Malabou claims that the post-traumatic subject cannot be accounted for in the Freudian terms of the repetition of a past trauma (since the traumatic shock erases all traces of the past), she remains all too fixed on the traumatic content and forgets to include in the series of past traumatic memories the very erasure of substantial content, the very subtraction of the empty form from its content. In other words, precisely insofar as it erases all substantial content, the traumatic shock *repeats* the past, namely the past traumatic loss of substance which is constitutive of the very dimension of subjectivity. *What is repeated here is not some ancient content, but the very gesture of erasing all substantial content.* This is why, when a human subject falls victim to a traumatic intrusion, the outcome is the empty form of the "living-dead" subject, but when the same thing happens to an animal, the result is simply total devastation. In the case of the human subject, what remains after the violent intrusion which erases all substantial content is the pure form of subjectivity, a form which must have already been there.

To put it another way, the subject is the ultimate case of what Freud described as the experience of "feminine castration" which grounds fetishism: the experience of encountering nothing where we expected to see something (a penis). If the fundamental philosophical question is "Why is there something rather than nothing?", the question raised by the subject is "Why is there nothing where there should be something?" The latest form of this surprise occurs in the brain sciences: one looks for the "material substance" of consciousness only to find that there is "nobody home"—just the inert presence of a piece of meat called the "brain." So where is the subject here? Nowhere: it is neither the self-acquaintance of awareness, nor, of course, the raw presence of brain matter. When one looks an autistic subject (or a "Muselmann") in the eye, one may also have this sense of an "empty house," where, unlike in the case of a dead object like the brain, one expected to find someone/something inhabiting the empty space. This then is the subject at its zero-level: like an empty house where "no one is home":

> to kill in cold blood, to "explode oneself" . . . to organize terror, to give to terror the face of a chance event emptied of sense: is it really still possible to explain these phenomena by way of evoking the couple sadism and masochism? Do we not see that their source is elsewhere, not in the trans-formations of love into hate, or of hate into indifference to hate, but in a beyond of the pleasure principle endowed with its own plasticity which it is time to conceptualize?[49]

The rise of such a detached subject, a survivor of its own death, relates directly to a feature of today's global capitalism nicely rendered by the title of Naomi Klein's book *The Shock Doctrine*. There is, however, an even more radical question to be asked here: how does the rise of such a detached subject relate to the ongoing process of "enclosing" the commons, the process of the proletarianization of those who are thereby excluded from their own substance? Do the three versions of proletarianization not fit perfectly the three contemporary figures of the Cartesian subject?

The first figure, corresponding to the enclosure of external nature, is, unexpectedly perhaps, Marx's notion of the *proletarian*, the exploited worker whose product is taken away from him, reducing him to a subjec-tivity without substance, to the void of pure subjective potentiality whose actualization in the labor process equals its de-realization.

---

49   Ibid., p. 315.

The second figure, linked to the enclosure of symbolic "second nature," is that of a *totally "mediatized" subject*, fully immersed in virtual reality: while "spontaneously" he thinks that he is in direct contact with reality, his relationship to reality is in fact sustained by complex digital machinery. Recall Neo, the hero of *The Matrix*, who all of a sudden discovers that what he perceives as everyday reality is constructed and manipulated by a mega-computer—is his position not precisely that of the victim of the Cartesian *malin génie*?

The third figure, corresponding to the enclosure of our "inner" nature, is, of course, the post-traumatic subject: to get an idea of the *cogito* at its purest, its "degree zero," one need only come face to face with an autistic "monster"—a painful and disturbing spectacle. This is why we resist so adamantly the specter of the *cogito*.

Interlude 4.   Apocalypse at the Gates

My Own Private Austria

Hegel was fully aware of how the weight added to an event by its symbolic inscription "sublates" its immediate reality—in his *Philosophy of History*, he provided a wonderful characterization of Thucydides' history of the Peloponnesian war: "In the Peloponnesian War, the struggle was essentially between Athens and Sparta. Thucydides has left us the history of the greater part of it, and his immortal work is the absolute gain which humanity has derived from that contest."[1] One should read this judgment in all its naivety: in a way, from the standpoint of world history, the Peloponnesian war took place so that Thucydides could write a book about it. The term "absolute" should also be given its due: from the relative perspective of our finite human interests, the numerous tragedies of the Peloponnesian war (the suffering and devastation it caused) are, of course, infinitely more important than a mere book; from the standpoint of the Absolute, however, it is the book that matters.

This is the question to be raised when one talks about Radovan Karadžić as a poet: in the name of which poem did he commit slaughter? According to the Serbian media, Karadžić (disguised as Dabić) often went to a bar where old Serbian poetry was regularly performed, accompanied by a "gusle" (a traditional single-string instrument), beneath pictures of both Karadžić and Ratko Mladić proudly displayed on the wall. He once recited a newly composed poem about himself—already seeing himself as the hero of an epic that would be sung by a distant future generation. So, one is tempted to say, again thousands had to die and suffer in order that a future epic poem about the war might be written.

Outrageous as it may sound, one wants to say that something similar holds for that subterranean Austrian reality into which we got a glimpse

---

1   Hegel, *Philosophy of History*, Part II, Section II, Chapter 3, "The Peloponnesian War"; available online at http://www.marxists.org.

with the case of Josef Fritzl: here, the work of Austrian playwright and novelist Elfriede Jelinek is "the absolute gain which humanity has derived" from such terrifying crimes. For decades, Jelinek has uncompromisingly described the violence of men against women in all its forms, including women's own libidinal complicity in their victimization. Mercilessly, she has brought to light the obscene fantasies that underlie Middle European respectability, fantasies which crawled into public space with the Fritzl affair, which indeed has the "unreality of a 'bad' fairy tale."[2] No wonder Jelinek has for decades been a thorn in the side of Austrian conservatives, who dismiss her as a degenerate publicizing her depraved private fantasies. During an election campaign, Jörg Haider's Freedom Party even used posters with the simple question: *"Jelinek oder Kultur?"* — do you want true culture or Jelinek? The answer is clear: the true formula is *"Jelinek oder das Unbehagen in der Kultur"* — Jelinek stages the obscene discontent that lies at the very core of our culture, her work in this respect being similar to that of the rock band Rammstein.

There is, of course, at least one obvious difference between Thucydides and Jelinek: Thucydides arrived after the event, to write a history of the war, while Jelinek is perhaps even more than a contemporary, a precursor writing a history of the future, detecting in the present the potential for forthcoming horrors. This temporal reversal — wherein the symbolic depiction precedes the fact it depicts, history as story precedes history as real event — is an indicator of the condition of late modernity in which the real of history assumes the character of a trauma.

When we think we really know a close friend or relative, it sometimes happens that, all of a sudden, this close person does something — utters an unexpectedly vulgar or cruel remark, makes an obscene gesture, casts a cold indifferent glance where compassion was expected — which makes us aware that we do not really know him or her: we become suddenly aware that there is a total stranger in front of us. At this point, the fellow-man changes into a Neighbor. This is what happened in a devastating way with Josef Fritzl: from being a kind and polite fellow, he suddenly changed into a monstrous Neighbor — to the great surprise of the people who met him daily and simply could not believe that this was the same person. Josef Fritzl, *mon prochain* . . .

Freud's idea of the "primordial father (*Urvater*)," which he developed in his *Totem and Taboo*, is usually met with ridicule — and justly so, if we

---

2   Nicholas Spice, "Up from the Cellar," *London Review of Books*, June 5, 2008, p. 3.

take it as a seriously meant anthropological hypothesis arguing that, at the very dawn of humanity, the "ape-men" lived in groups dominated by an all-powerful father who kept all women for his own exclusive sexual (ab)use, and that, after the sons rebelled and killed the father, he returned to haunt them as a totemic figure of symbolic authority, giving rise to feelings of guilt and imposing the prohibition of incest. What if, however, we read the duality of the "normal" father and the primordial father with unlimited access to incestuous enjoyment not as a fact about the earliest history of humanity, but as a libidinal fact, a fact about "psychic reality," which accompanies "normal" paternal authority like its obscene shadow, prospering in the murky depths of unconscious fantasies? This obscene underground is discernible through its effects—in myths, dreams, slips of tongue, symptoms—and, sometimes, it enforces its direct perverse realization (as Freud noted, perverts realize what hysterics only fantasize about).

Did not the very architectural arrangement of the Fritzl house—the "normal" ground and upper floors supported (literally and libidinally) by the underground windowless space of total domination and unlimited *jouissance*—materialize the "normal" family space redoubled by the secret domain of the obscene "primordial father"? Fritzl created in his cellar his own utopia, a private paradise in which, as he told his lawyer, he spent hours on end watching TV and playing with the youngsters while Elisabeth prepared dinner. In this self-enclosed space, even the language the inhabitants shared was not the common vernacular, but a kind of private language: it is reported that the two sons Stefan and Felix communicate in a bizarre dialect, with some of their sounds being "animal-like."

The case of Fritzl validates Lacan's pun on perversion as *père-version*, a version of the father—it is crucial to note how the secret underground apartment complex materializes a very precise ideologico-libidinal fantasy, an extreme version of the father-domination-pleasure nexus. One of the mottos of May '68 was "all power to the imagination"—and, in this sense, Fritzl is also a child of '68, ruthlessly realizing his fantasy. This is why it is misleading, even outright wrong, to describe Fritzl as "inhuman"—if anything, he was, to use Nietzsche's title, "human, all too human." No wonder Fritzl complained that his own life had been "ruined" by the discovery of his secret family. What makes his reign so chilling is precisely the way his exercise of power and his *usufruct* of the daughter were not just cold acts of exploitation, but were accompanied by an ideologico-familial justification (he did what a father should do, protecting his children from drugs and other dangers of the outside world), as well as by occasional displays of compassion and human consideration (he did take the sick daughter to the hospital, for example). These acts were not chinks of warm humanity in his armor of coldness and cruelty, but expressions of the same protective attitude which led him to imprison and violate his children.

Fritzl claimed he had noted that Elisabeth wanted to escape from home—she was coming back late, looking for a job, had a boyfriend, was possibly taking drugs, and he wanted to protect her from all that. The contours of the obsessive strategy are clearly recognizable here: I will protect her from the dangers of the outside world even if it means destroying her. According to the media, Fritzl defended himself thus: "If it weren't for me, Kerstin wouldn't be alive today. I'm no monster. I could have killed them all. Then there would have been no trace. No-one would have found me out." What is crucial here is the underlying premise: as a father, he had the right to exercise total power over his children, including sexual *usufruct* and killing; it was thanks to his goodness that he showed some consideration and did not fully exercise that power. As every psychoanalyst can confirm, we often find traces of such an attitude even in the most "normal" and caring of fathers: all of a sudden, the kind father explodes into a father-Thing, convinced that his children owe him everything, their very existence, that they are absolutely indebted to him, that his power over them is limitless, that he has the right to do whatever he wants in order to take care of them.

Fritzl's own "psychological" explanation (that Elisabeth reminded him of his mother, a tyrannical matriarch) is, of course, a ridiculous example of a commonsensical imitation of Freudian jargon. But one should avoid the trap here of putting the blame on patriarchal authority as such, seeing in Fritzl's monstrosity the ultimate consequence of the paternal Law, as well as the opposite trap of blaming the disintegration of that Law. Such an attitude is neither a component of "normal" paternal authority (the measure of its success is precisely the ability to set the child free, to let him or her move out into the outside world) nor a sign of its failure (in the sense that the void of "normal" paternal authority is supplemented, filled in, by the ferocious figure of the all-powerful "primordial father"), but rather both simultaneously: a dimension which, under "normal" circumstances, remains virtual, was actualized in the Fritzl case.

The attempts to blame Austrian particularity make the same ideological error as those who dream of an "alternate modernity" to the predominant liberal-capitalist one: by shifting the blame onto contingent Austrian circumstances, they want to keep paternity as such blameless and innocent, that is, they refuse to see the potential for such acts in the very notion of paternal authority. And, incidentally, it is rather comic to see critical analysts blaming the Fritzl affair on the Austrian sense of orderliness and need to maintain appearances, of turning a blind eye and refusing to take a closer look even when something is obviously wrong, whilst simultaneously hinting at the Austrians' dark Nazi past—does one not usually associate Nazism rather with the opposite "totalitarian" stance, that of spying on one's neighbors in order to detect any subversive activity and denounce it to the police?[3]

This, of course, does not mean that all debate about the "Austrian" character of the Fritzl crime should be rejected: one should just be aware that the excessive violence of the "primordial father" assumes in every particular culture certain specific fantasmatic features. Instead of the silly attempts to blame Josef's terrible crime on Austria's past or its excessive sense of orderliness and outward show, we should rather link the figure of Fritzl to a much more respectable Austrian myth, that of the von Trapp family immortalized in *The Sound of Music*—another family living in a secluded castle, under a father's benevolent military authority protecting them from the evil outside world, and with the generations strangely mixed up (Sister Maria, like Elisabeth, of a generation between the father and the children). The kitsch aspect is relevant here: *The Sound of Music* is the ultimate kitsch phenomenon, and what Fritzl created in his basement also displays features of a realized kitsch family life: the happy family getting ready for dinner, the father watching TV with the children while mother prepares the food. However, one should not forget that the kitsch imagery we are dealing with here is not Austrian but belongs to Hollywood and, more generally, to Western popular culture: Austria in *The Sound of Music* is not the Austrians' Austria, but the mythic Hollywood image of Austria. And yet, over the last few decades, the Austrians themselves have started to "play Austrians," as if identifying with the Hollywood image of their own country.

---

3   Turning a blind eye to what one does not want to see was, of course, also part of the Nazi universe, but at a different level: it involved pretending not to know about the horrible crimes committed by the state, like the killing of the Jews. What is needed here is a more precise analysis of different types of turning a blind eye: obviously one should not place in the same category the attitude of pretending not to notice the Holocaust, and the basic politeness of pretending not to notice when our neighbor looks awful or makes some embarrassing blunder.

The parallel can be extended to include the Fritzl-version of some of the most famous scenes from *The Sound of Music*. One can imagine the frightened children gathered around mother Elisabeth, in fear of the storm of the father's imminent arrival, and mother calming them down with a song about "some of their favorite things" to focus their minds on, from the toys bought by father to their most popular TV show. Or else a reception upstairs in the Fritzl villa to which the underground children are exceptionally invited, and then, when the time for bed comes, the children performing for the assembled guests the song "Aufwiedersehen, Goodbye" and departing one after the other. Truly, in the Fritzl house, the basement, if not the hills, was alive with the sound of music.

Ludicrous as *The Sound of Music* is, as one of the worst cases of Hollywood kitsch, one should take very seriously the sacred intensity of the universe of the film, without which its extraordinary success cannot be accounted for: the power of the film resides in its obscenely direct staging of embarrassingly intimate fantasies. The film's narrative turns on resolving the problem stated by the nuns' chorus in the introductory scene: "How do you solve a problem like Maria?" The proposed solution is the one mentioned by Freud in an anecdote: "Penis normalis, zwei mal taeglich . . ." Recall what is arguably the most powerful scene in the film: after Maria escapes from the von Trapp family and returns to the nunnery, unable to deal with her sexual attraction towards Baron von Trapp, she cannot find peace there, since she is still longing for the Baron; in a memorable scene, the Mother Superior advises her to return to the von Trapp family and try to sort out her relationship with the Baron. She delivers this message in a weird song, "Climb Every Mountain," whose surprising motif is: Do it! Take the risk and try everything your heart wants! Do not allow petty considerations to stand in your way! The uncanny power of this scene resides in its unexpected display of the spectacle of desire, an *eros energumenes* which renders the scene literally *embarrassing*: the very character who one would expect to preach abstinence and renunciation turns out to be a champion of maintaining fidelity to one's desire. In other words, while Mother Superior undoubtedly is a superego figure, she is so in Lacan's sense, for whom the true superego injunction is "Enjoy!" One can well imagine, along these lines, Josef Fritzl visiting his priest, confessing his passionate desire to imprison and rape his daughter, and the priest answering: "Climb every mountain . . ." (Or, as a matter of fact—literally, much closer to the facts—a young priest confessing to his superior his pedophile lust, and receiving the same reply.)

The key fantasmatic scene of the film is the one after the children and Maria return from their trip to Salzburg, dirty and wet. At first, the angry Baron plays the strict disciplinarian father, coldly dismissing them and reprimanding Maria. Later, however, when he returns to the house and hears them singing "The Hills are Alive" in chorus, he immediately breaks down and shows his true gentle nature—he starts to hum the tune and then joins them in song, after which they all embrace as father and children are reunited. The father's laughably theatrical disciplinarian rituals and orders are thus shown up for what they are: a mask of the very opposite, a soft and gentle heart. But what has this to do with Fritzl? Was he not a fanatical disciplinarian with no soft spot? Not exactly. While Fritzl's power was used to enforce his dream, he was not a cold disciplinarian, but rather precisely someone who was too much "alive with the sound of music" and wanted to realize his dream in a private space of his own.

In the last years of the Communist regime in Romania, Nicolae Ceauşescu was asked by a foreign journalist how he justified the constraints on foreign travel imposed on Romanian citizens—was this not a violation of their human rights? Ceauşescu answered that these constraints were there to protect an even higher and more important human right, the right to a safe homeland, which would have been threatened by too much free travel. Was he not reasoning here like Fritzl, who also protected his children's "more fundamental" rights to a safe home, where they would be protected from the dangers of the outside world? In other words, to use Peter Sloterdijk's terms, Fritzl protected his children's right to live in a safe self-enclosed sphere, while, of course, reserving for himself the right to transgress the barriers all the time, including visiting Thai sex tourist resorts, the very embodiment of the kind of danger he wished to protect his children from. Remember that Ceauşescu also saw himself as a caring paternal authority, a father protecting his nation from foreign decadence; and, as in all authoritarian regimes, the basic relationship between the ruler and his subjects was also one of unconditional love. Furthermore, in caring for his own home, the city of Bucharest, Ceauşescu made a proposal which strangely recalls the architecture of the Fritzl house: in order to solve the problem of the polluted river which runs through the city, he planned to dig beneath the existing river bed *another* wide channel into which all the dirt would be directed, so that there would have been two rivers, the deep one containing all the pollution, and the surface one for the happy citizens to enjoy . . .

The Ubuism of Power

Does the fact that events like the Fritzl affair—in their different variations (including pedophilia in the Church)—are becoming increasingly
common not point towards the imminence of what one can only designate
with the old-fashioned-sounding term "a moral apocalypse"? What did
Badiou mean when, in answer to a journalist's question, he said that one
of our problems today is that there is too much freedom? Perhaps an
extreme example of what he was getting at can be seen in the moral vacuity portrayed in the documentary *Freemen: When Killers Make Movies*, shot
in Medan, Indonesia, in 2007.[4] It reports on a case of obscenity which
reaches extreme proportions: a film, made by Anwar Congo and his
friends, who are now respected politicians, but were once gangsters and
death-squad leaders who played a key role in the 1966 killing of about 2.5
million alleged Communist sympathizers, mostly ethnic Chinese. *Freemen*
is about "killers who have won, and the sort of society they have built."
After their victory, their crimes were not relegated to the status of the
"dirty secret," the founding crime whose traces are to be obliterated—on
the contrary, the killers boast openly about the details of their massacres
(the way to strangle a victim with a wire, the way to cut a throat, how to
rape a woman in the most pleasurable way). In October 2007, Indonesian
state TV produced a talk show celebrating Anwar and his friends; in the
middle of the show, after Anwar says that their killings were inspired by
gangster movies, the beaming moderator turns to the cameras and says:
"Amazing! Let's give Anwar Congo a round of applause!" When she asks
Anwar if he fears the revenge of the victim's relatives, he replies: "They
can't. When they raise their heads, we wipe them out!" When his henchman adds, "We'll exterminate them all!" the studio audience explodes into
exuberant cheers. One has to see this to believe it possible. But what
also makes *Freemen* extraordinary is the level of reflexivity between documentary and fiction—the film is, in a way, a documentary about the real
effects of living a fiction:

> To explore the killers' astounding boastfulness, and to test the limits of their
> pride, we began with documentary portraiture and simple re-enactments
> of the massacres. But when we realized what kind of movie Anwar and
> his friends really wanted to make about the genocide, the re-enactments

---

4   Final Cut Film Productions 2009, Copenhagen, directed by Joshua Oppenheimer and Christine
Cynn.

became more elaborate. And so we offered Anwar and his friends the opportunity to dramatize the killings using film genres of their choice (western, gangster, musical). That is, we gave them the chance to script, direct and star in the scenes *they had in mind when they were killing people*.[5]

Did they reach the limits of the killers' "pride"? They almost did when they proposed to Anwar that he play the victim of his tortures in a re-enactment; when a wire is placed around his neck, he interrupts the performance and says "Forgive me for everything I've done." But this proves to be a temporary lapse which does not lead to any deeper crisis of conscience—his heroic pride immediately takes over again. Probably the protective screen which prevented any deeper moral crisis was the very fact of being filmed: as in their past real acts of murder and torture, they experienced their activity as an enactment of cinematic models, which enabled them to experience reality itself as a fiction. As great admirers of Hollywood (they started out as organizers and controllers of the black market in cinema tickets), they acted out parts in their massacres, imitating a movie gangster, cowboy or even a musical dancer.

Here the "big Other" enters, not only with the fact that the killers modeled their crimes on the cinematic imaginary, but also and above all with the much more important fact of society's moral vacuum: what kind of symbolic texture (the set of rules which draw the line between what is publicly acceptable and what is not) must a society be composed of if even a minimal level of public shame—which would compel the perpetrators to treat their acts as a "dirty secret"—is suspended, and such a monstrous orgy of torture and killing can be publicly celebrated decades after it took place, and not even as an extraordinary crime necessary for the public good, but as an ordinary acceptable pleasurable activity? The response to be avoided here is, of course, the easy one of placing the blame either directly on Hollywood or on the "ethical primitiveness" of Indonesia. The starting point should rather be the dislocating effects of capitalist globalization which, by undermining the "symbolic efficacy" of traditional ethical structures, creates such a moral vacuum.

A look at Berlusconi's Italy may be instructive here. We are, of course, still far from Indonesia's freemen, but the first steps in their direction are being taken even in Italy: the public display of private obscenities, the indecent confessions on TV shows, the shameless mixture of politics

---

5   Quoted from the publicity material of Final Cut Film Productions.

and private business interests, all this gradually creates a dangerous moral vacuum. On September 4, 2009, Niccolo Ghedini, Berlusconi's lawyer, said that Berlusconi "is ready to go to court to explain that not only is he not a big lecher but is also not impotent,"[6] thereby taking one step further in public obscenity. One shudders to imagine how exactly Berlusconi would "explain" his potency?[7] Gone are the days when the Right was characterized by its stiff manners and the Left engaged in "vulgar" outbursts—today, as the Right becomes more and more openly vulgar (and is France not following closely behind? Is there not a clown-ish Berlusconian side also to Sarkozy?), it is perhaps the task (or one of the tasks) of the Left to restore some simple good manners.

The ongoing "Ubuism" of power—the term was coined by Foucault, with reference to Alfred Jarry's *Ubu Roi*, in order to characterize the obscene/crazy sovereignty of a decadent power—stands in stark contrast to the two twentieth-century "totalitarianisms" of Fascism and Stalinism, both of which insisted on the untouchable dignity of those at the summit of power. In a Stalinist regime, obsessed with saving appearances, it is unimaginable for someone to mock the Leader or for the Leader to make fun of himself, of his great mission—if something like this happens, it is experienced as a catastrophe, panic sets in. In today's "Ubuized" poli-tics, the impossible becomes possible, and this kind of self-mockery takes place all the time, while power continues to function smoothly.

The task is to restore civility, not a new ethical substance. Civility is not the same as custom (in the strong sense of *Sittlichkeit*, "mores," that is, the substantial ethical base of our social activity)—civility, on the contrary, and to put it in somewhat simplified terms, *supplements the lack or collapse of the substance of mores*. Civility stands for custom (or, rather, what remains of custom) after the fall of the big Other: it assumes the key role when subjects encounter a lack of substantial ethics, in other words when they find themselves in predicaments which cannot be resolved by way of relying on the existing ethical substance. In such situations, one has to improvise and invent new rules ad hoc; but, to be able to do so—to have at one's disposal the intersubjective space in which, through complex interaction, a solution can be agreed upon—this interaction has

---

6   Quoted from lifeinitaly.com.

7   One may even suspect that, with the public display of his potency, Berlusconi is mobilizing the ancient pagan mythic link between the potency of the king and the health and prosperity of his country: the virility of the king is the key to the prosperity of his nation. As long as the Fisher King is incapacitated by his wound, the country will be stricken by plague and other disasters . . .

to be regulated by a minimum of civility. The more the "deep" substantial ethical background is missing, the more a "superficial" civility is needed.

Along the same lines, one should *respect* rather than dismiss the lower-class rejection of elitist-vanguard artistic provocations (which are, in any case, now fully integrated into the dynamics of the art market). The retrospective "Andres Serrano: Works 1983–93" at the New Museum of Contemporary Art in New York City notoriously caused a scandal: Serrano's photograph "Piss Christ," which depicts a crucifix immersed in urine, became an exhibit in the congressional debate about whether the state should support artists (such as Serrano, a grant recipient) whose work scorns the standards of common decency thought to be shared by the taxpayers who support the state. Predictably, Left liberals exploded at this attack — Michael Benson's note in *New York Times* was typical of the kind of defense mounted:

> Like Robert Mapplethorpe, Mr. Serrano struggles against inhibitions about the human body. His use of bodily fluids is not intended to arouse disgust but to challenge the notion of disgust where the human body is concerned. It is possible to see Mr. Serrano's use of bodily fluids as pure provocation. But you can also believe that Mr. Serrano views them as a form of purification. The fluids make us look at the images harder and consider basic religious doctrine about matter and spirit.[8]

The problem with this defense is that it works all too well: its logic covers almost everything. Let us say I were to publish a video clip depicting in detail how I defecate, how the anal hole gradually gets wider until the excremental sausage falls out, while also showing the stupidly satisfied/relaxed expression on my face when the business is over — could one claim then that "Mr. Žižek struggles against inhibitions about the human body. His use of bodily excrement is not intended to arouse disgust but to challenge the notion of disgust where the human body is concerned. It is possible to see Mr. Žižek's use of bodily excrement as pure provocation. But you can also believe that Mr. Žižek views it as a form of purification — the body gets purified by ejecting excrement. The excrement makes us look at the images harder and consider basic religious doctrine about matter and spirit"? Maybe then, just maybe, Chávez was right in banning some US TV series on Venezuelan TV as being morally problematic.

---

8   Michael Benson, "Andres Serrano: Provocation and Spirituality," *New York Times*, December 8, 1989.

Back in the 1960s, when the Pepsi Cola company introduced Diet Pepsi, the song accompanying the Super Bowl XL commercial concluded with the refrain "brown and bubbly"; not surprisingly, the commercial was immediately withdrawn, since it generated immediate associations with diarrhea. Why did the publicity company not notice this obvious association? Were they simply blind, or—a more paranoid option—did they think that the anal association would satisfy the secret coprophagic longings of the public? Perhaps we can imagine, in a not too distant future, a time when such tasteless direct references to excrement will be perfectly normal—with the same Pepsi advertisement this time *not* being withdrawn.

What is missing in liberalism is what, following Marx, one can call the "base" of freedom. However, this awareness of the need for such a "base" should not lure us into trusting the traditional ethical substance of "common decency" among ordinary people: faced with the present ecological, biogenetic, and other challenges, this domain of traditional "organic" mores has literally *lost its substance*—one can no longer rely on it to provide a kind of "ethical mapping," enabling us to find our way out of the present conundrums. How, then, does the public political space function in such a de-substantialized universe?

Recall the psychoanalytic distinction between *acting out* and the *passage à l'acte*: acting out is a spectacle addressing a figure of the big Other, which leaves the big Other undisturbed in its place, while the *passage à l'acte* is a violent explosion which destroys the symbolic link itself. Is this not our predicament today? The massive demonstrations against the US attack on Iraq back in 2003 were exemplary of a strange symbiotic relationship, parasitism even, between power and the anti-war protesters. Their paradoxical outcome was that both sides were satisfied. The protesters saved their beautiful souls—they had made it clear that they did not agree with the government's policy on Iraq—while those in power could calmly accept it, even profit from it: not only did the protests do nothing to prevent the (already decided upon) attack on Iraq, paradoxically, they even provided an additional legitimization for it, best rendered by none other than George Bush, whose reaction to the mass demonstrations protesting his visit to London was: "You see, this is what we are fighting for: so that what people are doing here—protesting against their government policy—will be possible also in Iraq!"

The celebration by people like Habermas of the pan-European movement against the Iraq war was thus perhaps a little bit misplaced and facile: the whole affair was rather a supreme case of a fully co-opted acting out. Our predicament is that the only alternatives appear to be violent outbursts like those that erupted in the French suburbs a few years ago — *l'action directe*, as one of the post-'68 Leftist terrorist organizations called itself. What is needed instead is the act proper: a symbolic intervention capable of undermining the big Other (the hegemonic social link), of re-arranging its coordinates.

Welcome to the Anthropocene

This moral vacuum is but one dimension of the apocalyptic times in which we live. It is easy to see how each of the three processes of proletarianization (mentioned in the previous chapter) refer to an apocalyptic point: ecological breakdown, the biogenetic reduction of humans to manipulable machines, total digital control over our lives. At all these levels, things are approaching a zero-point, "the end time is near" — here is Ed Ayres's description: "We are being confronted by something so completely outside our collective experience that we don't really see it, even when the evidence is overwhelming. For us, that 'something' is a blitz of enormous biological and physical alterations in the world that has been sustaining us."[9] At the geological and biological level, Ayres enumerates four "spikes" (or accelerated developments) asymptotically approaching a zero-point at which the quantitative expansion will reach its point of exhaustion and will bring about a qualitative change. These four spikes are: population growth, consumption of resources, carbon gas emissions, and the mass extinction of species. In order to cope with this threat, our collective ideology is mobilizing mechanisms of dissimulation and self-deception which include the direct will to ignorance: "a general pattern of behavior among threatened human societies is to become more blinkered, rather than more focused on the crisis, as they fail."[10]

The recent shift in how those in power are reacting to global warming is a blatant display of such dissimulation. On June 27, 2008, it was reported in the media that, according to scientists from the National Snow and Ice Data Center in Boulder, Colorado, the Arctic sea-ice is melting away much faster than had been predicted: the North Pole may be briefly ice-free by September 2010. Until recently, the predominant reaction to similar ominous news items was a call for emergency measures: we are

---

9   Quoted in Holmes Rolston, "Four Spikes, Last Chance," *Conservation Biology* 14:2, 2001, pp. 584–5.
10   Ibid.

approaching an unthinkable catastrophe, and the time to act is quickly running out. Lately, however, we hear more and more voices enjoining us to be positive about global warming. The pessimistic predictions, so we are told, should be seen a more balanced context. True, climate change will bring increased resource competition, coastal flooding, infrastructure damage from melting permafrost, stresses on animal species and indigenous cultures, all this accompanied by ethnic violence, civil disorder, and local gang rule. But we should also bear in mind that the hitherto hidden treasures of a new continent will be disclosed, its resources will become more accessible, its land more suitable for human habitation. Already in a year or so, cargo ships will be able to take a direct northern route through the Arctic, cutting the consumption of fuel and thereby reducing carbon emissions. Big businesses and state powers are already looking for new economic opportunities, which concern not only (or even primarily) "green industry," but much more simply the potential for further exploitation of nature opened up by climatic changes.

The contours of a new Cold War are thus appearing on the horizon — and, this time, it will be a conflict literally fought in very cold conditions. On August 2, 2007, a Russian team planted a titanium capsule with a Russian flag under the ice caps of the North Pole. This assertion of the Russian claim to the Arctic region was done neither for scientific reasons nor as an act of political and propagandistic bravado. Its true goal was to secure for Russia the vast energy riches of the Arctic: according to current estimates, up to one quarter of the world's untapped oil and gas sources may lie under the Arctic Ocean. Russia's claims are, predictably, opposed by four other countries whose territory borders on the Arctic region: the United States, Canada, Norway, and Denmark (through its sovereignty over Greenland).

While it is difficult to estimate the soundness of these predictions, one thing is sure: an extraordinary social and psychological change is taking place right in front of our eyes — the impossible is becoming possible. An event first experienced as real but impossible (the prospect of a forthcoming catastrophe which, however probable it may be, is effectively dismissed as impossible) becomes real and no longer impossible (once the catastrophe occurs, it is "renormalized," perceived as part of the normal run of things, as always already having been possible). The gap which makes these paradoxes possible is that between knowledge and belief: we *know* the (ecological) catastrophe is possible, probable even, yet we do not *believe* it will really happen.

A decade ago, the legitimation of torture or the participation of neo-Fascist parties in a West European government would have been dismissed as ethical disasters which could "never really happen"; once they happened, we immediately got accustomed to the new situation, accepting it as obvious. Recall too the infamous siege of Sarajevo from 1992 to 1995: the fact that a "normal" European city of half a million inhabitants was encircled, starved, bombed, its citizens terrorized by sniper fire, etc., and that this went on for three years, would have been considered unimaginable before 1992 — surely the Western powers would simply break the siege and open a safe corridor to the city? Indeed, when the siege began, even the citizens of Sarajevo thought it a short-term event, sending their children to safety "for a week or two, till this mess is over." And then, very quickly, the siege was "normalized."

This same immediate passage from impossibility to normalization is clearly discernible in the way state powers and big capital relate to ecological threats like the melting ice caps. Those very same politicians and managers who, until recently, dismissed fears of global warming as the apocalyptic scaremongering of ex-communists, or at least as based on insufficient evidence — and who thus assured us that there was no reason for panic, that, basically, things would carry on as usual — are now all of a sudden treating global warming as a simple fact, as just another part of "carrying on as usual." In July 2008, CNN repeatedly broadcast a report called "The Greening of Greenland," celebrating the new opportunities that the meltdown offers to Greenlanders — they can already grow vegetables on open land, and so on. The obscenity of this report lies not only in its focusing on a minor benefit of a major catastrophe, but also in the fact that, adding insult to injury, it plays on the double meaning of "green" in our public speech ("green" for vegetation; "green" for ecological concern), associating the fact that more vegetables can be grown in Greenland because of global warming with a rise in ecological awareness. Are not such phenomena yet another example of how right Naomi Klein was when, in her book *The Shock Doctrine*, she described the way global capitalism exploits catastrophes (wars, political crises, natural disasters) to get rid of "old" social constraints and impose its agenda on the "clean slate" created by the disaster? Perhaps the forthcoming ecological crises, far from undermining capitalism, will serve as its greatest boost.

What gets lost in this shift is any proper sense of what is going on, of all the unexpected traps the catastrophe hides. For example, one of the unpleasant features of our predicament is that the very attempt to counteract certain ecological threats may contribute to the worsening of others. (For example, the hole in the ozone layer helps shield the interior of the Antarctic from global warming, so as the hole is repaired, the Antarctic could quickly catch up with the rest of the Earth in terms of warming.) One thing at least is sure: over the last few decades, it has been fashionable to talk about the predominant role of "intellectual labor" in our post-industrial societies—however, materiality is now reasserting itself with a vengeance in all its aspects, from the forthcoming struggles over scarce resources (food, water, energy, minerals) to environmental pollution. So, while we should definitely exploit the opportunities opened up by global warming, we should never forget that we are dealing with a tremendous social and natural catastrophe, which we should do everything possible to alleviate. In adopting a "balanced view" we act like those who plead for a more "balanced view" of Hitler: true, he killed millions in the camps, but he also abolished unemployment and inflation, built new highways, made the trains run on time . . .

This new constellation provides the starting point for Dipesh Chakrabarty's elaboration of the historico-philosophical consequences of global warming, the main one being the collapse of the distinction between human and natural histories: "For it is no longer a question simply of man having an interactive relation with nature. This humans have always had . . . Now it is being claimed that humans are a force of nature in the geological sense."[11] That is to say, the fact that "humans— thanks to our numbers, the burning of fossil fuel, and other related activities—have become a geological agent on the planet,"[12] means that they are able to affect the very balance of life on Earth, so that—"in itself" with the Industrial Revolution, "for itself" with global warming—a new geological era began, baptized by some scientists as the "Anthropocene." The way humankind is forced to perceive itself in these new conditions is as a *species*, as one of the species of life on earth. When the young Marx described humanity as a "species being [*Gattungswesen*]," he meant something quite different: that, in contrast to animal species, only humans are a "species being," that is a being which actively relates to itself as a species and is thus "universal" not only in itself, but also for itself. This universality first appears in its alienated-perverted form with capitalism, which connects and unites all of humanity within the same world market;

---

11   Dipesh Chakrabarty, "The Climate of History: Four Theses," *Critical Inquiry* 35: 2, Winter 2009, p. 209.
12   Ibid.

with modern social and scientific development, we are no longer just one mere species among others or yet another aspect of the natural condition. For the first time in history, we, humans, collectively constitute ourselves and are aware of it, so that we are also responsible for ourselves: the mode of our survival depends on the maturity of our collective reason. The scientists who talk about the Anthropocene, however, "are saying something quite the contrary. They argue that because humans consti-tute a particular kind of species they can, in the process of dominating other species, acquire the status of a geologic force. Humans, in other words, have become a natural condition, at least today."[13] The standard Marxist counter-argument here is that this shift from the Pleistocene to the Anthropocene is entirely due to the explosive development of capi-talism and its global impact—which confronts us with the key question: how are we to think the link between the social history of Capital and the much larger geological changes of the conditions for life on Earth?

> If the industrial way of life was what got us into this crisis, then the ques-tion is, Why think in terms of species, surely a category that belongs to a much longer history? Why could not the narrative of capitalism—and hence its critique—be sufficient as a framework for interrogating the history of climate change and understanding its consequences? It seems true that the crisis of climate change has been necessitated by the high-energy-consuming model of society that capitalist industrialization has created and promoted, but the current crisis has brought into view certain other conditions for the existence of life in the human form that have no intrinsic connection to the logics of capitalist, nationalist, or socialist iden-tities. They are connected rather to the history of life on this planet, the way different life-forms connect to one another, and the way the mass extinction of one species could spell danger for another. . . . In other words, whatever our socio-economic and technological choices, whatever the rights we wish to celebrate as our freedom, we cannot afford to desta-bilize conditions (such as the temperature zone in which the planet exists) that work like boundary parameters of human existence. These param-eters are independent of capitalism or socialism. They have been stable

---

13   Ibid., p. 214. With the recent devastating earthquakes in the interior of China, the notion of the Anthropocene has acquired a new actuality: there are good reasons to suppose that the main cause of the earthquakes, or at least of their unexpected strength, was the construction of the gigantic Three Gorges dams nearby, which resulted in the creation of large artificial lakes; the additional pressure on the surface seems to influence the balance of the underground cracks and thus contribute to the earthquake. Something as elementary as an earthquake should thus also be included in the scope of phenomena influenced by human activity.

for much longer than the histories of these institutions and have allowed human beings to become the dominant species on earth. Unfortunately, we have now ourselves become a geological agent disturbing these parametric conditions needed for our own existence.[14]

In contrast to nuclear war, which would be the result of a conscious decision of a particular agent, climate change "is an unintended consequence of human action and shows, only through scientific analysis, the effects of our actions as a species."[15] This threat to the very existence of humanity creates a new sense of "we" which truly encompasses all of humanity:

> Climate change, refracted through global capital, will no doubt accentuate the logic of inequality that runs through the rule of capital; some people will no doubt gain temporarily at the expense of others. But the whole crisis cannot be reduced to a story of capitalism. Unlike in the crises of capitalism, there are no lifeboats here for the rich and the privileged (witness the drought in Australia or recent fires in the wealthy neighborhoods of California).[16]

The most appropriate name for this emerging universal subject may be "species": "Species may indeed be the name of a placeholder for an emergent, new universal history of humans that flashes up in the moment of the danger that is climate change."[17] The problem is that this universal is not a Hegelian one, which arises dialectically out of the movement of history and subsumes-mediates all particularities: it "escapes our capacity to experience the world,"[18] so it can only give rise to a "negative universal history,"[19] not Hegelian world history as the gradual, immanent self-deployment of freedom.

With the idea of humans as a species, the universality of humankind falls back into the particularity of an animal species: phenomena like global warming make us aware that, with all the universality of our theoretical and practical activity, we are at a certain basic level just another living species on planet Earth. Our survival depends on certain natural parameters which we automatically take for granted. The lesson of global warming is that the freedom of humankind was possible only against the

---

14   Chakrabarty, "The Climate of History," pp. 217–18.
15   Ibid., p. 221.
16   Ibid.
17   Ibid.
18   Ibid., p. 222.
19   Ibid.

background of stable natural parameters of life on earth (temperature, the composition of the air, sufficient water and energy supplies, and so on): humans can "do what they like" only insofar as they remain marginal enough so as not to seriously perturb natural preconditions. The limitation of our freedom that becomes palpable with global warming is the paradoxical outcome of the very exponential growth of our freedom and power, that is, of our growing ability to transform nature around us, up to and including destabilizing the very framework for life. "Nature" thereby literally becomes a socio-historical category, but not in the exalted Lukácsian sense (the content of what counts for us as "nature" is always overdetermined by a historically specified social totality structuring the transcendental horizon of our understanding of nature); rather, in the much more radical and literal (ontic) sense of something that is not just a stable background of human activity, but is affected by it in its most basic components. What is thereby undermined is the basic distinction between nature and human history, according to which nature blindly follows its course, and just has to be explained, while human history has to be understood—and even if its global course is out of control, functioning as a fate going against the wishes of most people, this "fate" is a result of the complex interaction of many individual and collective projects and acts, based upon certain understandings of what our world is. In short, in history, we confront the result of our own endeavors.[20]

Chakrabarty seems to miss here the full scope of the properly dialectical relationship between the basic geological parameters of life on earth and the socio-economic dynamic of human development. Of course, the natural parameters of our environment are "independent of capitalism or socialism"—they harbor a potential threat to all of us, independently of economic development, political system, etc. However, the fact that their stability has been threatened by the dynamic of global capitalism nonetheless has a stronger implication than the one allowed by Chakrabarty: in a way, we have to admit that *the Whole is contained by its Part*, that the fate of the Whole (life on earth) hinges on what goes on in what was formerly one of its parts (the socio-economic mode of production of one of the species on earth). This is why we have to accept the paradox that, in the

---

20   Radical libertarians emphasize the unconstrained human freedom which can be limited only by the freedom of others, while conservatives point out that freedom is a gift which comes with responsibility, guilt even. To this couple, one should add the radical reductionist-naturalist position of "neither freedom nor guilt/responsibility"; there is, however, a fourth, and perhaps the most interesting, position: the inverse of freedom without responsibility/guilt—*guilt/responsibility without freedom*. We are not free, but nonetheless responsible and thus guilty.

relation between the universal antagonism (the threatened parameters of the conditions for life) and the particular antagonism (the deadlock of capitalism), the key struggle is the particular one: one can solve the universal problem (of the survival of the human species) only by first resolving the particular deadlock of the capitalist mode of production. In other words, the commonsense reasoning which tells us that, independently of our class position or our political orientation, we will all have to tackle the ecological crisis if we are to survive, is deeply misleading: the key to the ecological crisis does not reside in ecology as such.

The December 2009 Copenhagen talks between the top representatives of 20 great powers about how to fight global warming failed miserably—the result was a vague compromise without any fixed deadlines or obligations, more a statement of intentions than a treaty. The lesson is bitter and clear: the state political elites serve capital, they are unable and/or unwilling to control and regulate capital even when the very survival of the human race is ultimately at stake. Fredric Jameson's old quip holds today more than ever: it is easier to imagine a total catastrophe which ends all life on earth than it is to imagine a real change in capitalist relations—as if, even after a global cataclysm, capitalism will somehow continue . . . One argument more for the fact that, when our natural commons are threatened, neither market nor state will save us, but only a properly communist mobilization. All one has to do here is to compare the reaction to the financial meltdown of September 2008 with the Copenhagen conference of 2009: save the planet from global warming (alternatively: save the AIDS patients, save those dying for lack of funds for expensive treatments and operations, save the starving children, and so on)—all this can wait a little bit, but the call "Save the banks!" is an unconditional imperative which demands and receives immediate action. The panic was here absolute, a trans-national, non-partisan unity was immediately established, all grudges between world leaders momentarily forgotten in order to avert *the* catastrophe. We may worry as much as we want about global realities, but it is Capital which is the Real of our lives.

Consequently, as suggested earlier, we should not say that capitalism is sustained by the egotistic greed of individual capitalists, since their greed is itself subordinated to the impersonal striving of the capital itself to reproduce; what we really need is more, not less, enlightened egotism. The conflict between capitalism and ecology may appear to be a typical conflict between pathological egotistic-utilitarian interests and a properly ethical care for the common good of humanity. Upon a closer look, however, it immediately becomes clear that the situation is exactly the opposite: it is our ecological concerns which are grounded in a utilitarian sense of survival, and as such lack the properly ethical dimension, simply standing for enlightened self-interest, or, at its highest, for the interest of future generations (assuming, of course, that we ignore the New Age spiritualist notion of the sacredness of life as such, of the right of the environment to preservation, etc.). The ethical dimension in this situation is rather to be found in capitalism's drive towards its own ever-expanding reproduction: a capitalist who dedicates himself unconditionally to the capitalist drive is effectively ready to put everything, including the survival of humanity, at stake, not for any "pathological" gain or goal, but simply for the sake of the reproduction of the system as an end-in-itself—*fiat profitus pereat mundus* might be his motto. As an ethical motto, this is of course weird, if not downright evil—however, from a strict Kantian perspective, we should recognize that what makes it seem repulsive to us is our purely "pathological" survivalist reaction: a capitalist, insofar as he acts "in accordance with his notion," is someone who faithfully pursues a universal goal, without regard for any "pathological" obstacles . . .

Perhaps the key to the limitations of Chakrabarty's position lies in his simplified notion of the Hegelian dialectic. Is the idea of a "negative universal history" really anti-Hegelian? On the contrary, is the idea of a multiplicity (of humans) totalized (brought together) through a negative external limit (a threat) not Hegelian *par excellence*? Furthermore, is it not the case that for Hegel *every* universality is ultimately "negative," in the precise sense that it has to appear as such, in opposition ("negative relationship") to its own particular-determinate content (recall Hegel's theory of war)? Hegel may appear to celebrate the *prosaic* character of life in a well-organized modern state where disturbances are overcome in the tranquility of private rights and the security of the satisfaction of needs: private property is guaranteed, sexuality is restricted to marriage, the future is safe. In this organic order, universality and particular interests appear reconciled: the "infinite right" of subjective singularity is given its due, individuals no longer experience the objective state order as a foreign power intruding on their rights, they recognize in it the substance and frame of their very freedom. However, Gérard Lebrun asks here the fateful question: "Can the sentiment of the Universal be dissociated from this appeasement?"[21] The answer is clear: yes, and this is why war

---

21   Gérard Lebrun, *L'Envers de la dialectique. Hegel à la lumière de Nietzsche*, Paris: Editions du Seuil 2004, p. 214.

is necessary—in war, universality reasserts its right over and against the concrete-organic appeasement inherent in prosaic social life. Is the necessity of war thus not the ultimate proof that in fact, for Hegel, every social reconciliation is doomed to fail, that *no organic social order can effectively contain the force of abstract-universal negativity*? This is why social life is condemned to the "spurious infinity" of the eternal oscillation between stable civic life and wartime perturbation.

In other words, Chakrabarty's dismissal of Hegelian universality only holds if we reduce what Hegel calls "concrete universality" to the organic-corporate model of a universal order within which every particular moment plays its determinate role, contributing to the wealth of the All. If, however, we recognize that Hegelian "concrete universality" designates a universal which enters into dialectical tension with its own particular content—in other words, that every universality can only posit itself "as such" in a negative way—then the idea of nature as not only forming the stable background to human activity, but also as harboring an apocalyptic threat to the human species, appears profoundly Hegelian.[22]

Versions of the Apocalypse

There are at least three different versions of apocalypticism today: Christian fundamentalist, New Age, and techno-digital-post-human. Although they all share the basic notion that humanity is approaching a zero-point of radical transmutation, their respective ontologies differ radically: techno-digital apocalypticism (whose main representative is Ray Kurzweil) remains within the confines of scientific naturalism, and identifies at the level of the evolution of the human species the contours of its transmutation into the "post-human"; New Age apocalypticism gives the transmutation a spiritualist twist, interpreting it as the shift from one mode of "cosmic awareness" to another (usually from the modern dualist-mechanistic stance to one of holistic immersion); finally, Christian fundamentalists read the apocalypse in strictly biblical terms, searching

---

22   The crucial speculative problem here is the relation between the two negativities: the negativity of nature as the radical Other which always poses a minimal threat to humanity, ultimately the threat of humanity's annihilation due to some totally meaningless external shock (like a gigantic asteroid hitting the earth), and the negativity of human subjectivity itself, its destructive impact on nature. To what extent can we say that, in confronting the Otherness of Nature, humanity is confronting its own essence, the negative core of its own being? Speculatively, this is obviously true, since nature appears as a threatening Otherness only from the standpoint of a subject who perceives itself as opposed to nature: in the threatening negativity of nature, the subject receives back the mirror-image of its own negative relationship towards nature.

for (and finding) signs that the final battle between Christ and the Anti-Christ is nigh, that things are approaching a critical turn. Although this last version is considered the most ridiculous, though still dangerous in terms of its content, it is the one closest to a radical "millenarian" emancipatory logic.

Let us first look at techno-digital apocalypticism. A preview of what awaits us here is a wearable "gestural interface" called "SixthSense," developed by Pranav Mistry, a member of the Fluid Interfaces Group at the MIT Media Lab.[23] The hardware — a small webcam which dangles from one's neck, a pocket projector, and a mirror, all connected wirelessly to a smartphone in one's pocket — forms a wearable mobile device. The user begins by handling objects and making gestures; the camera recognizes and tracks the user's hand gestures and the physical objects using computer-vision-based techniques. The software processes the video stream data, reading it as a series of instructions, and retrieves the appropriate information (texts, images, etc.) from the internet; the device then projects this information onto any physical surface available — all surfaces, walls, and physical objects around the wearer can serve as interfaces. Here are some examples of how it works: in a bookstore, I pick up a book and hold it in front of me; immediately, I see projected onto the book's cover its reviews and ratings. If I want to check the time, I merely draw a circle on my left wrist, and the projector displays a clock on my right arm. When I hold my fingers out at arm's length and form a square, the system recognizes this gesture as "framing a scene," snaps a photo and saves it. (Afterwards, I can manipulate the photos by projecting them onto any wall and giving instructions with my hands — dragging the images with my fingertips, etc.) On the way to the airport, I hold up my airline ticket, and, for example, the words "flight delayed for 40 minutes" will be projected onto it. While reading a newspaper, I point at an image and alternative images or video clips providing more information will be projected onto the surface. I can navigate a map displayed on a nearby surface, zoom in, zoom out or pan across, using intuitive hand movements. I draw a sign of @ with my finger and a virtual PC screen with my email account is projected onto any surface in front of me; I can then write messages by typing on a virtual keyboard. And one could go much further here — just think how such a device could transform sexual interaction. (Suffice it to

---

23   Apart from numerous reports in the media, see the concise description under "SixthSense" on Wikipedia.

concoct, along these lines, a sexist male dream: just look at a woman, make the appropriate gesture, and the device will project a description of her relevant characteristics—divorced, easy to seduce, likes jazz and Dostoevsky, good at fellatio, etc.) The surprise is the low cost of this device: a current prototype system costs only about $350 to build, so one can imagine its potentially widespread appeal.

In this way, the entire world becomes a "multi-touch surface," while the whole internet is constantly mobilized to supply additional data allowing me to orient myself. Mistry emphasized the physical aspect of this interaction: until now, the internet and computers isolated the user from the surrounding environment; the archetypal internet user is a geek sitting alone in front of a screen, oblivious to the reality around him. With SixthSense, I remain engaged in physical interaction with objects: the alternative "either physical reality or the virtual screen world" is replaced by a direct interpenetration of the two. The projection of information directly onto the real objects with which I interact creates an almost magical and mystifying effect: things appear to continuously reveal—or, rather, emanate—their own interpretation.

The first thing to note here is that SixthSense does not really represent a radical break with our everyday experience; rather, it openly stages what was always the case. That is to say, in our everyday experience of reality, the "big Other"—the thick symbolic texture of knowledge, expectations, prejudices, and so on—continuously fills in the gaps in our perception. For example, when a Western racist sees a poor Arab in the street, does he not "project" a complex of prejudices and expectations onto the Arab and thus "perceive" him in a certain way? This is why SixthSense presents us with another case of ideology at work in technology: the device imitates and materializes the ideological mechanism of (mis)recognition which overdetermines our everyday perceptions and interactions. The question is to what extent the open staging of this mechanism might undermine its efficiency.

If there is one scientist-capitalist who, even more than Bill Gates, perfectly exemplifies the third "spirit of capitalism" with its non-hierarchic and anti-institutional creativity, its humanitarian and ethical concerns, and so on, it is Craig Venter, with his idea of DNA-controlled production. Venter's field is synthetic biology, in which a life is forged not by Darwinian evolution but created by human intelligence. Venter's first breakthrough was to develop "shotgun sequencing," a method for analyzing the human genome faster and more cheaply than ever before;

he published his own personal genome, the first time any individual's DNA had been sequenced (incidentally, it revealed that Venter is at risk of Alzheimer's, diabetes, and hereditary eye disease). He then announced his next great project: to build an entirely synthetic organism, which could be used to save the world from global warming. In January 2008, he constructed the world's first completely synthetic genome of a living organism: using laboratory chemicals, he recreated an almost exact copy of the genetic material found inside a tiny bacterium. This largest man-made DNA structure is 582,970 base pairs in length; it was pieced together from four smaller (but still massive!) strands of DNA by utilizing the transcription power of yeast, and is modeled on the genome of a bacterium known as *Mycoplasma genitalium* (common in the human reproductive tract, it was chosen purely because it has a relatively tiny genome). "The lab-made genome has not so far resulted in a living microbe that functions or replicates. But Dr. Venter said it is just a matter of time before they figure out how 'to boot it up' by inserting the synthetic DNA into the shell of another bacterium."[24] This success opens the way for creating new types of micro-organisms that could have numerous applications: as green fuels to replace oil and coal; to digest toxic waste or absorb greenhouse gases, etc. Venter's dream is effectively to create the first "trillion-dollar organisms"—patented bugs that could excrete bio-fuels, generate clean energy in the form of hydrogen, or even produce tailor-made foods:

> Imagine the end of fossil fuels: a cessation of ecologically devastating drilling operations, deflation of the political and economic power of neoconservative oil barons, and affordable, low-emission transportation, heating, and electricity. The impact of this technology is profound, and it doesn't stop there. By discovering the details of biochemical and metabolic pathways, we can more closely mimic their elegance and efficiency to solve problems that plague industrial civilization. Maybe we'll engineer a primitive, self-sustaining bio-robot that feeds on CO_2 and excretes O_2. Perhaps we could remove mercury from our water supplies. The limitations are not known, but the possibilities are awe-inspiring.[25]

There are, as Venter admits, also more sinister possibilities; for example, it will be possible to synthesize viruses like Ebola, or to build new

---

24   Carolyn Abraham, "Lab-made Genome Gives New Life to Ethics Debate," available at theglobeandmail.com.
25   Ian Sample, "Frankenstein's Mycoplasma," *Guardian*, June 8, 2007.

pathogens. But the problem runs deeper: such extreme genetic engineering will create substantially different organisms—we will find ourselves in a new terrain full of unknowns. The problem lies in our limited understanding of how DNA works: even if we can put together a sequence of synthetic DNA, we cannot predict how it will actually perform, how its components will interact. DNA communicates with a cell by prompting it to make proteins, and we are far from fully understanding the relationship between a given DNA sequence, the proteins it generates, and the final properties of an organism. These dangers are heightened by the absence of any public control over what goes on in bioengineering—independent of any democratic oversight, profiteering industrialists are tinkering with the building-blocks of life. Venter tried to allay the fears of an emerging *Blade-Runner*-like society:

> The movie [*Blade Runner*] has an underlying assumption that I just don't relate to: that people want a slave class. As I imagine the potential of engineering the human genome, I think, wouldn't it be nice if we could have 10 times the cognitive capabilities we do have? But people ask me whether I could engineer a stupid person to work as a servant. I've gotten letters from guys in prison asking me to engineer women they could keep in their cell. I don't see us, as a society, doing that.[26]

Venter may not see it, but the requests he is bombarded with certainly prove that there is a social demand for the creation of a serving sub-class. Ray Kurzweil offered a different rebuttal of these fears:

> The scenario of humans hunting cyborgs doesn't wash because those entities won't be separate. Today, we treat Parkinson's with a pea-sized brain implant. Increase that device's capability by a billion and decrease its size by a hundred thousand, and you get some idea of what will be feasible in 25 years. It won't be, "OK, cyborgs on the left, humans on the right." The two will be all mixed up.[27]

While this is in principle true (and one can here vary endlessly the Derridean motif of how our humanity is always already supplemented by artificial prostheses), the problem is that, with the decrease in size by a factor of a hundred thousand, the prosthesis is no longer experienced as such, but becomes invisible, part of our immediate-organic

26   Quoted in ibid.
27   Quoted in ibid.

self-experience, so that those who technologically control the prosthesis control us in the very heart of our self-experience.[28]

There are even more radical questions to be raised here, questions which concern the very limits of our desire (and readiness) to know: what will prospective parents do when informed that their child will have the genes for Alzheimer's? The recent new buzzword "previvor" (a person who does not have cancer but possesses a genetic predisposition to develop the disease, a "pre-survivor") renders perfectly the anxiety of such advance knowledge.

Scientists at the Beijing Genomics Institute (BGI) have completed the fourth human genome to be sequenced worldwide; they plan to use their genome database to "solve problems related to Chinese-specific genetic diseases" as well as to improve diagnosis, prediction, and therapy. Such phenomena are just the tip of the iceberg of a process going on in China about which not much is heard, in a media preoccupied by the troubles in Tibet and so on: namely, the expansion of the biogenetic revolution. While we in the West are mired in endless debates on the ethical and legal limits of biogenetic experiments and procedures (stem cells, yes or no? how far should we be allowed to intervene into the genome — only to prevent diseases, or also to enhance physical and even psychic properties in order to create a newborn that fits our desires?), the Chinese are simply pressing ahead without restraint, in a model example of smooth co-operation between state agencies (such as their Academy of Sciences) and private capital. In short, both branches of what Kant would have called the "private" use of reason (the state and capital) have joined hands at the expense of the absent "public" use of reason (a free intellectual debate in an independent civil society on what is happening: how such might developments infringe on the individual's status as an ethically autonomous agent, and so on, not to mention the possible political misuses). Things are proceeding fast on both fronts, not only towards the dystopian vision of the state controlling and steering the biogenetic mass of its citizens, but also in a race for profits: billions of US dollars are being invested in Chinese labs and clinics (the biggest one in Shanghai) in order to develop commercial clinics targeting rich Western foreigners who, thanks to legal prohibitions, will not

28   In the case of Habermas, the paradox is that, insofar as the creation of artificial life is the accomplishment of (one of the strands of) modernity, it is Habermas himself who abstains from accomplishing the project of modernity, that is, he prefers modernity to remain an "unfinished project," setting a limit to the unfolding of its potential.

be able to get such treatments in their own countries. The problem is, of course, that in the global context any legal prohibitions are fast becoming meaningless: their main effect will be to strengthen the commercial and scientific advantage of Chinese and other facilities—Shanghai thus has every chance of becoming a dystopian megalopolis like the anonymous city in *Blade Runner*.

The time is approaching when we will have to invert the standard complaint that our relations with other people are increasingly mediated by digital machinery, to the extent that, between every face-to-face contact, there always is an interface: the prospect for the near future is the explosive development of direct links between computers (and other media) themselves, which will then communicate, make decisions, etc., on our behalf, and simply present us with the final results of their interaction. (For example, when we withdraw money from a cash machine, the machine informs our bank, whose computer sends the information to our PC via email.) Already today, there are more connections between computers themselves than between computers and their human users— one could apply Marx's formula here also, insofar as relations between computer-things are replacing relations between persons. What if, out of this interaction, a form of self-organization emerges capable of imposing its own agenda, so that human users no longer control and dominate the digital network but are themselves used by it?

The big-budget techno-thriller *Eagle Eye* (2008, D. J. Caruso) deals with this prospect in all its ambiguity—no wonder the film flopped at the box office, for interesting ideological reasons. Here is a brief outline of its plot[29]—it starts with a standard accident in the "war on terror": the US Army has a lead on a suspected terrorist in the Middle East, but as the man is a recluse, getting a positive ID proves difficult, and the computer system which processes all military data recommends that the mission be aborted. The Secretary of Defense agrees, but the President orders the mission be carried out anyway. This turns into a political disaster when all those killed turn out to be civilians, and retaliatory bombings are carried out in response. Now the heroes of the film are introduced, two ordinary US citizens, Jerry Shaw (a Stanford dropout) and Rachel Holloman (a young single mother whose son Sam is a trumpet player). One day, when Jerry returns home, he finds his apartment filled with weapons, explosives, and forged documents. He receives a phone call

---

29   Courtesy of Wikipedia.

from an unknown woman, who explains that the FBI is about to appre-
hend him in 30 seconds and that he must escape. Not believing her, he
is arrested by the FBI, but the unknown woman again arranges Jerry's
escape over a phone and has him join up with Rachel, who has been
coerced by the same unknown woman into assisting Jerry, with a threat
to kill her son. The woman (still just a voice on the phone) helps the pair
to avoid the police and FBI units, demonstrating an ability to remotely
control virtually any networked device, such as traffic lights, cell phones,
and even automated cranes. Jerry and Rachel are led to an electronics
store where the woman-voice introduces herself to them: she turns out
to be a top-secret supercomputer called "Autonomous Reconnaissance
Intelligence Integration Analyst" (Ariia), which gathers intelligence from
all over the world and can control virtually anything electronic. In light
of the mistake made by the president at the beginning of the film, Ariia
has decided that the executive power is a threat to the public good and
must be eliminated. Ariia plans to destroy the president's cabinet, leaving
the secretary of defense, who agreed with the recommendation to abort
the mission, as his successor. She explains to Jerry and Rachel that she
is trying to help the people of the United States. Rachel is given an necklace, which, unbeknownst to her, contains explosives, and sent to watch
the president's State of the Union address. The speech is introduced with
a performance given by Sam's class, and the trigger that will set off the
explosive necklace is set to activate when Sam plays a high F on his trumpet, corresponding to the word "free" in the last stanza of the US national
anthem. In the end, everything turns out OK thanks to the heroic work of
the honest FBI agents; the explosion is averted, Sam is saved, and Rachel
and Jerry are united as a couple.

Is Ariia not simply a rational agent, effectively acting in the interests
of the people of the United States? Would it not be the best for the US
if her plan were to succeed? Ariia is ready to sacrifice dozens of innocent bystanders—but so was the president when he agreed to the original
attack that ended up killing dozens of Arab civilians. The ambiguity of
the film is that it remains unclear whether this irony is intended or not.[30]

---

30   At a more visceral level, one cannot resist the fairy-tale logic that underlies the scenes in which
Jerry and Rachel repeatedly succeed in escaping from the FBI. It is as if they move in an enchanted
universe in which they are not simply confronting enemies against a neutral background of reality—the very texture of reality is guided by a magic hand which twists it to their profit: when the cars
pursuing them get too close, cranes block their way; when, running from police, they enter a subway
station, the timetable display tells them which direction to take. Is this not the ultimate paranoid
dream, the dream that reality is not made of neutral inert stuff indifferent to our struggles, but is an

How does the digitalization of our lives affect the hermeneutic horizon of our everyday experience? According to a CNN report from May 29, 2008, monkeys with sensors implanted in their brains have learned to control a robot arm with their thoughts, using it to feed themselves fruit and marshmallows. In the experiment at the University of Pittsburgh School of Medicine, a pair of macaque monkeys were fitted with electrodes the width of a human hair that transmitted signals from areas of the brain linked to movements. The scientists behind the experiment say it will lead to the creation of brain-controlled prosthetic limbs for amputees or patients with degenerative disorders. The first prototype is already operative: a wheelchair-mounted robotic arm controlled by thought alone has been created at the University of South Florida.[31] The device gives people with amyotrophic lateral sclerosis (ALS) or full body paralysis—who have fully functional brains, but no way to express their thoughts—the ability to perform simple day to day functions that would otherwise be impossible. EEG scans offer one way for patients with ALS to communicate with the outside world; by fitting patients with a head cap equipped with electrodes and filled with an electrically conductive gel, scientists can monitor particular kinds of electrical impulses coursing through the brain. In this case, the scientists monitor a particular brain wave called P300; reading P300 waves is basically like reading a person's thoughts, but only in the most coarse kind of way. For the wheelchair-mounted robotic arm, the person in the wheelchair looks at directional arrows flashing across a small screen; when the arrow points in the direction that they want to go, their brain lights up on the EEG, and the wheelchair or robotic arm moves accordingly. Even Stephen Hawking's proverbial little finger—the minimal link between his mind and the outside world, the only part of his paralyzed body that he can move—will thus no longer be necessary: the mind will be able *directly* to

---

artificial mechanism guided by a benevolent intelligence? The logic which (in its weaker version) is usually turned against the hero (recall *Enemy of the State*, in which, thanks to the complex system of surveillance, the enemy always seems to know where Will Smith is) works here *for* the heroes—with the inevitable implication that, since the controlling agency is by definition evil, the heroes must be unwittingly coerced instruments of an evil big Other which controls our reality.

Arguably the most poetic scene in the film occurs when the heroes enter Ariia—the inside of a big round cupola with blinking "neurons"—as if they had entered the head, the very brain, of the female voice that was addressing them. The charm (and, simultaneously, the key ideological manipulation) of the scene is that although we see the impersonal-mechanical "brain" working, the computer remains subjectivized, the spectral female voice continues to address the humans as partners in a dialogue.

31   See Eric Bland, "Wheelchair Arm Controlled by Thought Alone," *Discovery News*, available online at dsc.discovery.com.

cause objects to move, it is the brain itself which will serve as the remote control machine.

Recent research points towards the uncanny fact that the secret US defense agencies are involved in wide-ranging and long-term projects to develop the means to control human emotions and attitudes remotely, by attacking brains with precise electromagnetic waves. Since it is already possible to identify the brainwaves that materially support particular emotional attitudes (fear, hatred, courage), the idea is to bombard the brain with similar artificially generated waves in order to produce or thwart the targeted emotion. A similar procedure has already been tested in the context of treating veterans for post-traumatic effects: by identifying the material support of traumatic memory traces in the brain and then exposing the brain to specific waves, these traces can be erased, with limited short-term memory loss as an undesired side-effect. While the scope of these practices is unknown, it seems clear there are sufficient grounds for assuming that the agencies involved are engaged in a major effort to exploit the possibility of collapsing the difference between "inside" and "outside," directly linking the "wiring" of the brain to external technologically manipulable processes.

The ideal that regulates this research is the possibility of eventual full control of past and future at the psychic level. The strategy is always the same: an invention is first presented as a brilliant new remedy for some debilitating illness (so that no one can oppose it), and is then extended to other fields. There is already extensive research into genetic and biochemical interventions which might selectively erase a subject's traumatic past and thereby enable, say, a victim of torture or rape to regain normalcy — the problem arises, of course, when such a procedure is expanded to include a more total control of traces of the past. Rich prospective parents can already afford to have their unborn child's brain scanned for traces of possible future mental weaknesses (low IQ, criminal tendencies . . .) — and, again, what would be the consequences of the possible universalization of this procedure? One has to avoid here a double trap: the utopian dream of a benevolent "cleansing" of the brain, of protecting it from illnesses and removing the traces of past traumas, but also the false doomsday perspective which treats all such interventions into the brain as signaling the "end of humanity."

The "World Transhumanist Association" — founded in 1998 by Nick Bostrom and David Pearce — has set itself the task of addressing these problems. It describes itself as "an international nonprofit membership organization which advocates the ethical use of technology to expand human capacities."[32] Its premise is that human development, in evolutionary terms, has not reached anything like an endpoint: all kinds of emerging technologies—neuropharmacology, artificial intelligence and cybernetics, nanotechnologies—have the potential, it says, to enhance human abilities. As Bostrom puts it: "a few years ago, the discussions would typically revolve around the question, 'Is this science fiction? Or are we dealing in realistic future possibilities?' Now the discussions tend to start from the position that, yes, it will be increasingly possible to modify human capacities. The issue now is whether we should do it. And, if so, what are the ethical constraints?" In contrast to Nietzsche's notion of the "overman" aiming at a "moral and cultural transcendence" (a select few endowed with strong willpower and great refinement would throw off the shackles of traditional morality and convention, and so rise above the rest of humanity), the transhumanist idea of the "post-human" aims at a society in which everybody will have access to enhancement technologies:

> transhumanists advocate increased funding for research to radically extend healthy lifespan and favor the development of medical and technological means to improve memory, concentration, and other human capacities. Transhumanists propose that everybody should have the option to use such means to enhance various dimensions of their cognitive, emotional, and physical well-being. Not only is this a natural extension of the traditional aims of medicine and technology, but it is also a great humanitarian opportunity to genuinely improve the human condition.

Consequently, the main ethical concerns are those of accessibility and the question of who is transforming whom:

> It's one thing if we are talking about adult, competent citizens deciding what to do with their own bodies. If, on the other hand, we are thinking of modifying children, or selecting embryos, then there is another set of ethical questions that arise. There is a further set of ethical questions relating to access. If some of the technologies, as they well might, turn out to be very expensive, then what mechanisms should be in place to ensure fairness?[33]

---

32   John Sutherland, "The Ideas Interview: Nick Bostrom," *Guardian*, May 9, 2006.
33   Nick Bostrom, "Transhumanism: The World's Most Dangerous Idea?", available at nick-bostrom.com.

To prevent state or private institutions deciding our fate, the choice of whether to avail oneself of such enhancement options should generally reside with the individual—but is this sufficient protection?

With all their warnings about how we are on the brink of a post-human era, transhumanists effectively remain too humanist. That is to say, when they describe the possibility of intervening in our biogenetic base and changing our very "nature," they somehow presuppose that the autonomous subject freely deciding on his or her acts will still be present, deciding on how to change its "nature." They thus take the split between the "subject of the enunciated" and the "subject of enunciation" to its extreme: on the one hand, as the object of my interventions, I am a biological mechanism whose properties, including mental ones, can be manipulated; on the other hand, I (act as if I) am somehow exempt from this manipulation, an autonomous individual who, acting at a distance, can make the right choices. But what about the prospect of the loop being closed, so that my very power of decision-making is already "meddled with" by biogenetic manipulation, and the autonomous individual is no longer there? This is why there always seems to be something shallow, boring even, about all transhumanist meditations: they basically ignore the problem and, like their critics, avoid the core of the question with which they appear to be dealing: how will biogenetic and other inter-ventions affect the very definition of humanity? Both transhumanists and their critics unproblematically cling to the standard notion of a free autonomous individual—the difference is that transhumanists simply assume that it will survive the passage into the post-human era, while their critics see post-humanity as a threat to be resisted.

Taken to an extreme, techno-digital apocalypticism assumes the form of so-called "tech-gnosis" and passes over into New Age apocalypticism. What looms on the horizon of the "digital revolution" is thus the prospect of human beings acquiring the capacity for what Kant and other German Idealists called "intellectual intuition [*intellektuelle Anschauung*]"—that form of intuition which immediately generates the object it perceives, closing the gap that separates (passive) intuition and (active) produc-tion—a capacity hitherto reserved for the infinite divine mind. With the appropriate neurological implants, it will be possible to switch from our "common" reality to an alternative computer-generated reality without all the clumsy machinery of today's Virtual Reality (the awkward glasses and gloves, etc.), since the signals will directly reach our brain, by-passing our sensory organs. Dan Brown's *The Lost Symbol* is an exemplary case of the spiritualist mystification of these ongoing scientific breakthroughs: the fact that the brain sciences are slowly unraveling the neuronal processes which support thinking is mystified into the New Age notion of thought itself directly "influencing" material processes. Furthermore, this spiritualist mystification is supplemented by a piece of vulgar materialism: the novel claims that thought itself has a separate material existence of its own. The New Age announced by the novel, the shattering transformation which will affect humanity, involves overcoming the gap separating thinking from reality: humans will reawaken their spiritual potential and become like gods in the precise sense of being able to directly influence the world by thought alone. Magic and science, faith and knowledge, will thus be reconciled, with ancient faith acquiring scientific experimental confirmation. Against *The Lost Symbol*, one should insist that the symbol as such (the symbolic order in which humans dwell) is the symbol of a loss—that is to say, what the novel presents as a loss (the gap between thinking and reality) is the very feature which sustains our freedom of thinking. It is the gap itself which preserves us from immediate immersion in reality, allowing thought to distance itself from reality—in short, the true miracle of thinking is precisely that which *The Lost Symbol* perceives as the obstacle to be overcome.[34]

One favorite Janus-faced notion mobilized by the New Age spiritualists is the notion of synchronicity derived from quantum physics: the precise quantum notion of synchronicity (two separate particles are interconnected in such a way that the spin of one of them affects the spin of the other faster than the time it takes for light to travel between them) is read as a material manifestation of a "spiritual" dimension linking events beyond the network of material causality: "Synchronicities are the jokers in nature's pack of cards for they refuse to play by the rules and offer a hint that, in our quest for certainty about the universe, we have ignored some vital clues."[35]

In standard New Age cognitive mapping, the "Left" stands for the unconscious and unknown, and the "Right" for consciousness and

---

34   Although *The Lost Symbol* is a truly bad novel, there are two further features worth noting. The first is that it continues the desexualization of the couple already present in *The Da Vinci Code*: nothing happens, there is no erotic tension between Robert Langdon and the heroine (Deborah Solomon), and it is as if all the extraordinary things going on out there fill in this gap at the novel's center. The second is that, even more than in Brown's previous novel, *The Lost Symbol* fixes the coordinates of the new genre of the religious thriller with alternation between tense action and amateurish historical explanations.

35   F. David Peat, *Synchronicity: The Bridge Between Nature and Mind*, New York: Bantam 1987, p. 3.

wakefulness. Accordingly, the tragedy of the political Left over the last two centuries is supposedly that it has limited itself to matters of social justice and economic equality, forgetting about the need for a "deeper" shift from mental-rational consciousness to the recognition of a hidden dimension accessible only to intuition: "The Left fought for the 'rights' of man, while ignoring the 'lefts' of man and woman."[36] In the radical version of New Age spiritualism, the looming material crisis (the ecological catastrophe) is reduced to a mere "material expression of a psycho-spiritual process, forcing our transition to a new and more intensified state of awareness."[37]

This brings us back to the three "spirits of capitalism," which effectively form a kind of Hegelian triad of the "negation of negation": the individualist Protestant-ethic subjectivity of the entrepreneur, supplanted by the corporate "organization man," returns in the new guise of the infinitely plastic "creative" capitalist. It is crucial to note that the two shifts are not at the same level: the first concerns the normative content within the same symbolic form (of the Ego-Ideal and the ideal-ego), while the second shift abandons the very form of the symbolic Law, replacing it with a vague superego injunction. Is there a "fourth spirit" of capitalism, one which would repeat the move from the individual to the collective, from the Protestant ethic to the organization man, but at the level of the "third spirit," that is, which would do to the "third spirit" what the "second spirit" did to the first? One could argue that this "fourth spirit" is precisely no longer a spirit of capitalism, but already a name (one of the names) of communism. Here is a New Age spiritualist version of the new social order expected to emerge as a secondary effect of the deeper spiritual shift:

> If we are graduating from nation-states to a noospheric state, we may find ourselves exploring the kind of nonhierarchical social organization— a "synchronic order" based on trust and telepathy—that the Hopi and other aboriginal groups have used for millennia. If a global civilization can self-organize from our current chaos, it will be founded on cooperation rather than a winner-takes-all competition, sufficiency rather than surfeit, communal solidarity rather than individual elitism, reasserting the sacred nature of all earthly life.[38]

---

36   Daniel Pinchbeck, *2012*, New York: Jeremy P. Tarcher / Penguin 2007, p. 213.

37   Ibid., p. 392.

38   Ibid., p. 394.

Does this description—if we scratch away its spiritualist coating—not render a kind of communism? How, then, are we to get rid of the coating? The best antidote to the spiritualist temptation is to bear in mind the basic lesson of Darwinism: the utter contingency of nature. Why are bees dying in massive numbers, especially in the US where, according to some sources, the death toll has reached up to 80 percent of the population? This catastrophe could have a devastating effect on our food supply: about one-third of the human diet comes from insect-pollinated plants, and the honeybee is responsible for 80 percent of that pollination. This is how one should imagine a possible global disaster: no big bang, just a small-scale interruption with devastating global consequences. One cannot even say that all we need do is restore the situation to its natural balance. To what balance? What if bees in the US and Europe have already adapted to a certain degree and mode of industrial pollution?

There is an air of mystery to the collapse of the bee population: although the same thing is happening simultaneously all around the (developed) world, local investigations point to different causes—the poisonous effects of pesticides on the bees, their loss of spatial orientation caused by the electronic waves of our communication machines, and so on. This multiplicity of causes makes the link between cause and effect uncertain—and, as we know from history, whenever there is a gap between cause and effects, the temptation to look for a deeper Meaning arises: what if, beneath the natural causes, there is a deeper spiritual cause? How else are we to account for the mysterious synchronicity of a phenomenon which is, from the standpoint of natural science, caused by different factors in different places? Here enters so-called "spiritual ecology": are beehives not a kind of slave colony, concentration camps where bees are ruthlessly exploited? So is Mother Earth striking back at us for our exploitation? The best antidote to this spiritualist temptation is to bear in mind that, in this case too, there are things we know that we know (e.g., the bees' vulnerability to pesticides), things we know that we do not know (say, how bees react to human-caused radiation), but also, and above all, there are unknown unknowns and unknown knowns. There will be aspects of how bees interact with their environment which are not only unknown to us, but of which we are not even aware. And there are many "unknown knowns" affecting our perception of bees: all the anthropocentric prejudices that spontaneously color and bias our study of them.

The most unsettling aspect of such phenomena is the disturbance caused in what Lacan called "knowledge in the real": the "instinctual" knowledge which regulates animal and plant activity. This obscure knowledge can run amok. When the winter is too warm, plants and animals misread the temperature as a signal that spring has already begun and so start to behave accordingly, thus not only rendering themselves vulnerable to later onslaughts of cold, but also perturbing the entire rhythm of natural reproduction. In all probability, something of this kind is happening to bees.

While we cannot gain full mastery over our biosphere, it is unfortunately in our power to derail it, to disturb its balance so much that it runs wild, wiping us away in the process. Take the recently discovered vast frozen peat bog in western Siberia (the size of France and Germany combined): it has started to thaw, potentially releasing billions of tons of methane, a greenhouse gas 20 times more potent than carbon dioxide, into the atmosphere. This should be read together with the report from May 2007 that researchers at the Albert Einstein College of Medicine "have found evidence that certain fungi possess another talent beyond their ability to decompose matter: the capacity to use radioactivity as an energy source for making food and spurring their growth."[39] Ideas are already circulating on how the "radiation-munching fungi could be on the menu for future space missions. 'Since ionizing radiation is prevalent in outer space, astronauts might be able to rely on fungi as an inexhaustible food source on long missions or for colonizing other planets,'" noted one of the scientists.

Instead of succumbing to terror at this prospect, it is in such cases that one should keep an open mind towards new possibilities, bearing in mind that "nature" is a contingent multi-faceted mechanism in which catastrophes can lead to unexpectedly positive results—as in Robert Altman's film *Short Cuts*, in which a catastrophic car accident brings about an unexpected friendship.[40]

Just as it would be wrong to dismiss environmentalism as "a fundamentalist religion adopted by urban atheists looking to fill a yawning spiritual gap plaguing the West,"[41] there is no reason to treat the eco-skep-

---

39   Kate Melville, "Chernobyl Fungus Feeds On Radiation," available at www.scienceagogo.com.

40   With regard to this inherent instability of nature, the most consistent proposal was made by a German ecological scientist back in the 1970s: since nature is changing constantly and the conditions on Earth will render the survival of humanity impossible within a couple of centuries, the collective goal of humanity should not be to adapt itself to nature, but to intervene in it even more forcefully with the aim of freezing its change, so that the Earth's ecology will remain basically the same, thus enabling humanity's survival. This extreme proposal renders visible the truth of ecology.

41   Adam Morton, "The Sceptic's Shadow of Doubt," *The Age* (Sydney), May 2, 2009, p. 4.

tics as being similar to Holocaust deniers—there is a double lesson to be learned from them about global warming: (1) how much ideology is indeed invested in ecological concerns; and (2) how little we really know about the actual consequences of our activity in the natural environment.

An openness to radical contingency is difficult to maintain—even a rationalist like Habermas cannot do so. His late interest in religion breaks with the traditional liberal concern for the humanist, spiritual, and other content hidden in the religious form; what interests him now is the form itself: people who *really* fundamentally believe and are ready to put their lives at stake for that belief, displaying a raw energy and unconditional engagement missing from the anemic-skeptical liberal stance—as if the embrace of such a commitment could revitalize our post-political desiccation of democracy. Habermas is reacting here to the same problem as Chantal Mouffe with her "agonistic pluralism": how to reintroduce passion into politics? Is he, however, thereby not engaged in a kind of ideological vampirism, sucking the energy from naïve believers without being ready to abandon his own basically secular-liberal stance, so that full religious belief remains a kind of fascinating and mysterious Other? But as Hegel already showed apropos the dialectic of Enlightenment and faith in his *Phenomenology of Spirit*, such counter-posing of formal Enlightenment values to fundamental-substantial beliefs is false, amounting to an untenable ideologico-existential position. What we should do, by contrast, is fully assume the identity of the two opposed moments— which is precisely what an apocalyptic "Christian materialism" does do, in bringing together both the rejection of a divine Otherness and the element of unconditional commitment.

5   Acceptance: The Cause Regained

In 1968, Structures Walked the Streets: Will They Do So Again?

These words, of course, refer to Jacques Lacan's reaction to the well-known anti-structuralist graffito on the Paris walls in May '68: "structures do not walk the streets"—in other words, one cannot explain the large student and workers' demonstrations of '68 in terms of structuralism (which is why some historians even posit 1968 as the year that separates structuralism from post-structuralism, with the latter, so the story goes, being much more dynamic and open to active political interventions). Lacan's answer was that this, precisely, is what happened in May '68: structures *did* descend onto the streets, i.e., the explosive events were ultimately the result of a structural shift in the basic social and symbolic texture of modern Europe—the result, in Lacan's terms, of the passage from the Master's discourse to the University discourse.[1]

How right Lacan was when he described modernity as marked by the rise of the "University discourse" becomes clear when we focus on the phrase "to serve the people": not only is the leader legitimized by serving the people, the king himself has to reinvent his function as the "highest servant of the people" (as Frederick the Great put it). Crucially, there is no one who does not serve but is simply being served: ordinary people serve the state or the People, while the state itself serves the people. This logic reaches its climax in Stalinism where the entire population serves: ordinary workers are supposed to sacrifice their well-being for the community, the leaders work night and day, serving the people (although

---

1   See Jacques Lacan, *The Other Side of Psychoanalysis (Seminar, Book XVII)*, New York: Norton 2007. One of the great slogans of postmodern political theory is "governance versus sovereignty": instead of centralized sovereign power, we get a dispersed network of agents taking measures, imposing regulations, etc. In Lacanian terms, what we have here is a vision of S_2, the chain of expert-knowledge, functioning without S_1, the Master-Signifier. In other words, governance is power turned into administration, relieved of its radical responsibility—this is why one should insist on sovereignty as an irreducible aspect of power.

their "truth" is S_1, the Master-Signifier). The agency being served, the People, has no substantial positive existence: it is the name for the abyssal Moloch that every existing individual serves. The price of this paradox is, of course, a further set of self-referential paradoxes: the people as individuals serve themselves as the People, their Leaders directly embody their universal interest as the People, and so on.

In his fragment "Couriers," Kafka provides a glimpse into the world without a Master-Signifier:

> They were given the choice between becoming kings or the couriers of kings. In the manner of children, they all wanted to be couriers; as a result, there are only couriers. They gallop through the world shouting to each other messages that, since there are no kings, have become meaningless. Gladly would they put an end to their miserable existence, but they dare not, because of their oaths of service.

Would it not be refreshing to find individuals naïvely ready to adopt the position of the Master, simply claiming "I *am* the one you are serving!" without this position of the Master being alienated in the knowledge of their Servants-Leaders?

Lacan's succinct critical formula concerning the glorious events of May '68 was "truth goes on strike [*la vérité fait la grève*]": "With the weight of truth on us at each instant of our existence, what good fortune to have only a collective relationship with it."[2] It was as if, in a strange version of the reversal that characterizes the *point de capiton*, the series of truths each one has to struggle with, the individualized symptoms, were exchanged for one big collective Truth: I follow the Truth, and I do not have to deal with other truths. This collective Truth, of course, is no truth at all: in it, truth is on strike, the proper dimension of truth is suspended. This situation could not last, and we should consider ourselves fortunate that the new power which emerged after the collapse of this Truth (the triumphant return of de Gaulle once the euphoria was over—the old-new Master which, as Lacan put it, the hysterical revolutionaries wanted and got) was not more tyrannical than the preceding one (as happened with the French Revolution and with the October Revolution, once the enthusiasm waned): "This is Lacan's liberal thesis, and it was a *tour de force* to manage to present it to students who were very far from that

---

2   Jacques Lacan, *Le Séminaire XVI: D'un autre à l'Autre*, Paris: Editions du Seuil 2006, p. 289.

perspective."[3] Miller is right: Lacan's thesis is effectively liberal, in the precise sense that it obliterates the Real which one encounters at the collective level. The political as such is here devalued as a domain of imaginary and symbolic identifications; by definition, it involves a misrecognition. The basic premise of liberalism is the nominalism of truth: truth is individual, the social can only provide a neutral frame for the interaction and self-realization of individuals. What if, however, the collective is not merely the level of imaginary and symbolic identifications? What if, in it, we encounter the Real of antagonisms?

Furthermore, was the explosion of '68 really the passage from the Master's discourse to the University discourse? Was it not, rather, the crisis of a certain form of the University discourse, that French "republican" form which had been dominant since the French Revolution? The figure of Hegel is crucial here. Hegel is, on the one side, the first figure of the University discourse: late in his life, he was a professor in Berlin at the university reorganized by Humboldt as the first modern university—all previous great universities (the Sorbonne, Oxford) were still rooted in theological discourse. On the other side, Hegel is not yet fully a figure of the University discourse: what resists that discourse in Hegel is his central notion of Absolute Knowledge, which is absolutely incompatible with the open exploratory spirit of the University discourse—no wonder that the whole of post-Idealist modernity defines itself through its opposition to Hegel, as a specific way of negating the "absurd" position of Absolute Knowledge.[4]

Was Lacan then right to conceptualize this shift as a transition from the Master's discourse to the University discourse? Did he not know that the University discourse characterizes the basic underlying discursive structure of modernity as such, of post-traditional societies which, no longer reliant on a Master's undisputed authority, demand that every authority be justified before the tribunal of Reason? Did Lacan not designate the Soviet Union—a country of hierarchic-administrative-central authority if there ever was one—as the purest embodiment of the University discourse? What effectively happened in the aftermath of '68 was the rise of a new "spirit of capitalism": the hierarchical Fordist structure of the production process was gradually abandoned and replaced with a

---

3   Jacques-Alain Miller, "A Reading of the Seminar *From an other to the Other* II," *lacanian ink* 30, p. 16.
4   The key question is: is Hegel's Absolute Knowledge really a theologico-metaphysical remainder, or does it signal the fact that, on account of his place in the interstice between the two epochs, Hegel was able to see and articulate something which, immediately afterwards, with the rise of the great anti-Idealists (Schopenhauer, Feuerbach, Marx, Kierkegaard), once again became invisible?

network-based form of organization founded on employee initiative and autonomy in the workplace. In place of a hierarchical-centralized chain of command there were now networks with a multitude of participants, organizing work in the form of teams or projects, intent on customer satisfaction, and a general mobilization of workers thanks to their leaders' vision. This new "spirit of capitalism" triumphantly recuperated the egalitarian and anti-hierarchical rhetoric of 1968, presenting itself as a successful libertarian revolt against the oppressive social organizations of corporate capitalism *and* of "really existing" socialism.[5]

On closer analysis, we should probably distinguish between the two phases of this "cultural capitalism," as exemplified by a shift in the logic of advertising. In the 1980s and 1990s, it was the direct reference to personal authenticity or quality of experience that predominated, without any direct ideological coloring, while, over the last decade, one can note the increasing mobilization of socio-ideological motifs (ecology, social solidarity): the experience referred to here is that of being part of a larger collective movement, of caring for nature and for the ill, the poor and the deprived, of doing something to help. TOMS Shoes, a company founded in 2006, provides an example of this "ethical capitalism" taken to an extreme. The company's policy rests

> on a simple premise: with every pair you purchase, TOMS will give a pair of new shoes to a child in need. One for One. Using the purchasing power of individuals to benefit the greater good is what we're all about. . . . Of the planet's six billion people, four billion live in conditions inconceivable to many. Let's take a step towards a better tomorrow.[6]

The motto "One for One" provides the key to unraveling the ideological mechanism that sustains TOMS Shoes: the very relationship between egotistic consumerism and altruistic charity becomes one of exchange; that is, the sin of consumerism (buying a new pair of shoes) is paid for and thereby erased by the awareness that someone who really needs shoes received a pair for free. The process thus reaches its climax: the very act of participating in consumerist activity is simultaneously presented as a participation in the struggle against the evils ultimately caused by capitalist consumerism.

If one reads *logos* in the Heideggerian manner, as the primordial

---

5   For a more detailed analysis of this "cultural capitalism," see Slavoj Žižek, *First as Tragedy, Then as Farce*, London: Verso 2009, where I rely on Luc Boltanski and Eve Chiapello, *The New Spirit of Capitalism*, London: Verso 2005.

6   See tomsshoes.com. I owe this reference to Ryan Hatch.

"gathering" of sense which opens up a world, then one can effectively interpret the big company *logo* as the latest stage of *logos*: a logo is not just a sign designating certain properties or qualities, it "gathers" a multiplicity of meanings into a single Name and thus "opens up" a whole world. *Levi's* does not just point towards the alleged properties of a pair of jeans, it sustains a whole world of meaning(s) which provides the background against which we experience what it is to wear jeans, the "world" which comes with wearing jeans.

The semantic density, the surplus-charge of meaning with which our daily lives are burdened, is thus becoming more and more palpable: you cannot even drink a cup of coffee or buy a pair of shoes without being reminded that your act is overdetermined by ecology, poverty, and so on. Pepsi Cola has pushed the manipulation of this humanitarian surplus to an unexpected level of reflexivity: consumers are not only promised that part of the company's profit will go to humanitarian and other causes, they are even solicited for ideas about how to spend the money and then offered a chance to vote on which idea will be implemented:

> Pepsi has always been about refreshment. But what if, instead of just refreshing people, Pepsi helped to refresh the world? . . . If you've got an idea about how to make the world a better place—whether it's saving something, creating something, or fixing something—we want you to tell us about it. Then you vote to decide which ideas are the best. We'll award millions of dollars in Pepsi Refresh Grants to put the winning ideas into action.[7]

The surplus is thus opened up to us, the consumers: as we consume, we are also given the "freedom of choice" to express our preferred ideological commitment.

What should be avoided at all costs here are facile generalizations which accept the ideological core of such consumer self-perception as an accurate reflection of contemporary society, and which thus contribute to the blurring of key distinctions, such as the following: "We no longer live in a world of masters and slaves, capitalists and proletarians, or citizens, but in a world of consumers, either real or virtual."[8] Instead, we should analyze how those aspects of '68 which were successfully integrated into the hegemonic capitalist ideology can be (and are) today mobilized not

---

7   Ad on p. 6D of *USA Today*, November 10, 2009.
8   Gérard Wajcman, "Intimate Extorted, Intimate Exposed," *Umbr(a)* 2007, p. 49.

only by liberals, but also by the contemporary Right, in their struggle against any form of "Socialism." Emblematic here is the topic of "freedom of choice" and its central role in the resistance to President Obama's healthcare reforms in the US.

9/11 did mark the end of a certain postmodernity: the one associated with the happy Clintonite 1990s, the age of irony and political correctness. After 9/11, there were signs everywhere of the return of "grand" ideologies: from Latin American Leftist populism to Arab anti-Western mobilizations, new causes emerged—and the same process is discernible in the West itself. Hegel remarked that evil can also reside in the very gaze which perceives the world around it as permeated by evil. Think about a religious fundamentalist who sees signs of sin and corruption everywhere in modern society—is the true evil not his suspicious gaze itself? Does the true evil not lie in that attitude of total blindness to the achievements of modern secular permissive societies, from women's rights to religious tolerance and the fight against racism? Hegel's observation certainly applies to Sarah Palin who, in an online comment on August 7, 2009, called Obama's health plan "downright evil": "The America I know and love is not one in which my parents or my baby with Down Syndrome will have to stand in front of Obama's 'death panel' so his bureaucrats can decide, based on a subjective judgment of their 'level of productivity in society,' whether they are worthy of health care." The standard Republican claim that the reform plans will lead to rationing, with the government determining which medical procedures a patient can have, is here supplemented with the additional spice of ideological fantasy: the image of Obama's "death panels" deciding in true Stalinist mode who lives and who dies, imposing the criterion of the "level of productivity." However, beyond the ridiculous idiosyncrasies of the conservative "culture war," a more general point deserves to be made about freedom of choice.

Some of us remember the infamous old Communist tirades against merely "formal" bourgeois freedom—absurd as they were, there is a pinch of truth in the distinction between "formal" and "actual" freedom: "formal" freedom is that freedom to choose *within* the coordinates of the existing power relations, while "actual" freedom grows when we can change the very coordinates of our choices. A manager of a company in crisis has the "freedom" to fire workers A or B, etc., but not the freedom to change the situation which has imposed this choice on him. The moment we approach the healthcare debate in this way, the "freedom to choose" appears in a different light. True, a large part of the population will be effectively delivered of the dubious "freedom" to worry about who will cover their medical costs, the "freedom" to find their way through the intricate network of financial and other decisions. Being able to take basic healthcare for granted — to count on it like one counts on the water or electricity supply without worrying about choosing a water or electricity company — they will simply gain more time and energy to dedicate their lives to other things. An imposed additional choice can affect the background set which forms the condition-base of freedom and can thus diminish our actual freedom of choice. Freedom and regulation are not opposites: we are effectively able to make free choices only because a thick background of regulations sustains this freedom, because we can rely on the fact that there is some kind of rule of law to appeal to if we are attacked or robbed, because we can expect with reasonable certainty a minimum of civility when we interact with others, etc. *And* also because we can rely on guaranteed healthcare and thus do not have to worry all the time about illness . . . The lesson to be learned is thus that freedom of choice operates only when a complex network of legal, educational, ethical, economic, and other conditions form an invisible thick background to the exercise of our freedom. This is why, as a counter-position to the ideology of choice, countries like Norway should be held up as models: although all the main agents respect a basic social agreement and ambitious social projects are enacted in a spirit of solidarity, productivity and dynamism remain at extraordinarily high levels, flatly denying the common wisdom that such a society ought to be stagnating.

The extreme ideological manipulation of the idea of "freedom of choice" can be linked to the way popular anti-consumerist ideology has recently been dealing with the topic of poverty, effectively presenting it as a matter of personal choice. There are plenty of books and articles in lifestyle journals advising us on how to "step out of consumerism" and adopt a way of life free of the compulsion to possess the latest products. The ideological bias here is obvious: by presenting poverty as a (free) choice, it psychologizes an objective social predicament. Former Slovene President Janez Drnovšek, a cold technocrat turned foolish self-taught New Ager, used to answer ordinary people's letters in a popular weekly magazine. In one letter, an old lady complained that due to her tiny pension she was not able to eat meat or to travel; the president's answer was that she should be glad about her situation — simple food without meat is healthier, and, instead of indulging in tourist travel, she could

embark on a spiritually much more satisfying inner journey, the exploration of her own true Self.[9]

It is thus not enough to vary the standard motif of the Marxist critique:
"although allegedly we live in a society of choices, the choices left to us
are effectively trivial, and their proliferation masks the absence of true
choices, choices that would change the basic features of our lives . . ."
While this is true, the problem is rather that we are forced to choose
without having at our disposal the kind of knowledge that would enable
us to make a proper choice—more precisely, what renders us unable to
act is not the fact that we "don't yet know enough" (about whether, say,
human industry is really responsible for global warming, and so on) but,
on the contrary, the fact that we know too much *while not knowing what to
do* with this mass of inconsistent knowledge, not knowing how to subordinate it to a Master-Signifier. (The ecological crisis is paradigmatic here.)
This brings us to the tension between S_1 and S_2: the chain of knowledge
is no longer totalized/quilted by Master-Signifiers. The exponential,
uncontrollable growth of scientific knowledge functions in the mode of
an acephalous drive, and this push-to-knowledge unleashes a power that
is not that of mastery: a power proper to the exercise of knowledge as
such. The Church senses this lack, eagerly offering itself as the Master
who will guarantee that the explosion of scientific knowledge remains
within "human limits" and will not overwhelm us—a vain hope, of course.

Some time ago, Ulrich Beck deployed the notion of the "risk society,"
focusing on how our fundamental subjective stance has passed from "I am
hungry" to "I am afraid."[10] What generates fear today is the causal non-
transparency of the threats involved: not so much the transcendence of the
causes as their immanence (we don't know to what extent we are ourselves
bringing about the danger). We are not impotent in the face of some natural
or divine Other; we are becoming all too potent, without understanding our
own power. Risks are cropping up everywhere, and we rely on the scientists
to cope with them. But here lies the problem: the scientists/experts are the
subjects supposed to know, but they do not know. The becoming-scientific
of our societies has a doubly unexpected feature: while we increasingly rely
on experts even in the most intimate domains of our experience (sexuality

---

9   What such an ideological approach misses is how "consumerism" is ultimately conditioned by the
ever-expansive circulation of capital itself. To give a boost to the car industry and thus counteract the
economic slowdown, the German government passed a measure paying those who own a car over
ten years old and want to buy a new car a couple of thousand euros to scrap the old car—an act of
encouraging consumerism which is clearly opposed to environmental prudence.
10   See Ulrich Beck, *Risk Society*, London: Sage Publications 1992.

and religion), this universalization only transforms the field of scientific knowledge into an inconsistent and antagonistic non-All. The old Platonic division between the pluralism of opinions (*doxa*) and a single universal scientific truth is replaced by a world of conflicting "expert opinions" themselves. And, as is always the case, such universalization involves self-reflexivity: as Beck perspicuously notes, today's threats are not primarily external (natural), but are self-generated by human activities linked to scientific advances (the ecological consequences of industry, the psychic consequences of uncontrolled biogenetics, and so on), such that the sciences are simultaneously (one of) the source(s) of risk, the sole medium we have to grasp and define the risk, as well as (one of) the source(s) of coping with the threat, of finding a way out[11] — Wagner's "*Die Wunde schliest der Speer nur, der Sie schlug*" ("The wound can only be healed by the spear that made it") thus acquires a new relevance.

The paradigmatic category which reveals this helplessness of science while simultaneously covering it up with a deceptive screen of expert assurance is "limit value": how much can we still "safely" pollute our environment? how much fossil fuel can we burn? how much of a poisonous substance does it take to threaten our health? (or, in a racist version, how many foreigners can our community integrate without losing our identity?) and so on. The obvious problem here is that, thanks to the non-transparency of the situation, every "limit value" has the aspect of a fiction, of an arbitrary symbolic intervention into the real — can we be really sure that the level of sugar in the blood prescribed by the doctors is the correct one, so that above it we are in danger and beneath it we are safe? Are "limit values" not rather cases of what Thomas Schelling called "focal points"? According to Schelling, real human interactions are not governed only by pure strategic calculus (which can be formalized), but by focal points that are "invisible under a mathematical formulation of the problem. Schelling did not believe that game theory was useless, merely that most human interactions were so shot through with ambiguity that these focal points could be the ultimate guide to what might or should happen."[12] Here is Schelling's most famous example: I arrange with a friend to meet him next day in New York, but, due to a breakdown of communication, neither of us knows where and when to meet. When Schelling asked his students what to do, the majority

11   Even if we blame scientific-technological civilization for global warming, we still need the same science not only to define the scope of the threat, but often even to perceive it — the "ozone hole" can be "seen" in the sky only by scientists.

12   Tim Harford, *The Logic of Life*, London: Abacus 2009, p. 53.

suggested going to the clock at Grand Central Station at noon—that being the meeting point which has imposed itself as the most "obvious" (to a person from our culture, of course), independently of all strategic calculations. The reasoning here is more complex than it may appear: when I look for the focal point, I do not merely try to guess what will be the most obvious point for both of us—the question I try to answer is "what do I expect the other to expect that I expect of him?" When I go to the Grand Central clock at noon, I do so because I expect my friend to expect me to expect him to go there. In negotiations, the "focal point" can be an "irrational" commitment (in the sense of not grounded in any rational strategic calculation) which fixes a non-negotiable feature: for the State of Israel, control over the whole of Jerusalem is "non-negotiable"; ahead of salary negotiations, a trade union leader announces that he will never settle for less than a 5 percent raise, and so on. While there are, of course, always ways to compromise while sticking to the letter of one's engagement (say, the trade union leader can accept that the 5 percent raise will be gradual, spread over five years), such an engagement raises the stakes: one cannot abandon its letter without "losing face." In contrast to purely strategic reasoning, such commitment is not psychological but properly *symbolic*: it is "performative," grounded in itself ("I say so because I say so!")—and we can clearly see how "limit value" is ultimately just another case of Schelling's "focal point," which is itself another name for what Lacan called the "quilting point," and, later, the Master-Signifier.

But was the passage from Master to University discourse—or from one "spirit of capitalism" to another—all that really happened in the events of '68, such that all the drunken enthusiasm about freedom was just a means for replacing one form of domination with another? (Recall Lacan's challenge to the students: "You are hysterics who demand a new master. You will get one.") More likely, '68 was not a single event but an ambiguous one in which different political tendencies struggled for hegemony. This would account for the fact that, while the May events were appropriated by the hegemonic ideology as an explosion of sexual freedom and anti-hierarchic creativity, Nicolas Sarkozy could say in his electoral campaign of 2007 that his great task was to help France finally get over '68. (One should not, of course, miss the irony of this remark: the fact that Sarkozy, with his clownish outbursts and marriage to Carla Bruni, could have become French president, is in itself one effect of the changes in mores brought about by May '68.) There is, then, "their" and "our" May '68, with the latter—the link between the students' protests and the workers' strikes—today largely forgotten.

If, then, as Badiou claims, May '68 was the end of an epoch, signaling (together with the Chinese Cultural Revolution) the final exhaustion of the great revolutionary-political series which started with the October Revolution, where do we stand today? If we consider our predicament from the perspective of '68, the analysis should be guided by the prospect of a radical alternative to parliamentary-democratic capitalism: are we constrained to withdraw and act from different "sites of resistance," or can we still imagine a more radical political intervention? This is the true legacy of '68, at the core of which was a rejection of the liberal-capitalist system, a *no* to the totality of it, best encapsulated in the formula *Soyons réalistes, demandons l'impossible!* The true utopia is the belief that the existing global system can reproduce itself indefinitely; the only way to be truly "realistic" is to think what, within the coordinates of this system, cannot but appear as impossible. How are we to prepare for this radical change, to lay the foundations for it? The least we can do is to look for traces of the new communist collective in already existing social or even artistic movements. What is therefore needed today is a refined search for "signs coming from the future," for indications of this new radical questioning of the system. Here, we can count on some unexpected allies.

On March 8, 2008, at 2:55 p.m. precisely, 3,000 people on the Place du Trocadéro in Paris suddenly stood still like statues, repeating an event a couple of months earlier in New York when an even larger number of people took part in a "freeze" at Grand Central Station.[13] The point was to "put magic back into the city": "to show that one can occupy an urban space in an alternative manner, very different from the purpose for which it was designed . . . It's a very instinctive way of being together without necessarily knowing each other or sharing anything else but that one exceptional moment."[14] The instigators of such events are well aware that such acts, hovering as they do between protest and tomfoolery, belong to a post-Left space: "We want to show that it is possible to occupy a public space in a radical and entertaining manner, without actually breaking the law."[15] This strategy of interrupting the smooth flow of our participation in the routines of daily life can also assume more radical forms: in Los Angeles, groups of digital artists and militant engineers arrange for all incoming audio and video transmissions in a limited residential area to be cut, and then film the perplexed inhabitants as they venture outside, not knowing what to do, disconnected from their daily infusion of the

---

13   Antoine Couder, "We Own the Streets," *Aéroports de Paris Magazine*, 04/08, pp. 16–20.
14   Francois Bellanger from Transit Consulting, quoted in ibid.
15   Arthur Lecaro, a spokesman for Aristopunks, quoted in ibid.

media-drug. (Of course, it is easy to imagine the possible recuperation of these phenomena by the establishment: a postmodern manager, say, encouraging his employees to practice a "protest minute," "disconnecting" from their daily work in order to just "freeze," or to do something more extravagant like jumping up and down, to refresh their energies.)

There is no message in such acts, they are cases of what, in the golden era of structuralism, Roman Jakobson called the "phatic" function of language, the use of language to maintain a social relation through ritualized formulas such as greetings, chit-chat about the weather, and related formal niceties of social communication. This is a feature flash mobs share with what appears to be their radical opposite: explosions of "irrational" mob violence. But although the two may appear to be opposed—the raw violence of burning cars and killing against the harmless aesthetic spectacle—there is a deeper "identity of the opposites" at work here. One can say that 1968, 1989 and 2005 form a kind of Hegelian triad: the revolt of May '68 failed politically (capitalism returned triumphant) but, in a way, won socially (by thoroughly overhauling the substance of social mores through sexual liberation, new individual freedoms, stronger positions for women, post-patriarchal forms of authority, and so on); the anti-Communist revolt in 1989 won politically (Communism did indeed disintegrate), but lost socially (the new post-Communist society with its combination of wild capitalism and nationalism is not what the dissidents were fighting for). Those who want a kind of truce between these two politically opposed movements ('68 was anti-capitalist and critical of parliamentary democracy, while '89 wanted parliamentary democracy) usually point out that they share an underlying libertarian commitment to individual freedom and creativity against all forms of social constraint and oppression. However, from a more radically critical standpoint, one should render problematic this very libertarian kernel, locating in it a shared ideological commitment. The third moment, then, is the events of 2005, the burning of cars in the Paris suburbs, a kind of moment of truth of the entire movement: the revolt of '68 was quickly appropriated by the ruling ideology, so that its ultimate after-effect was the overturning, not of capitalism, but of the enemy of the capitalist Free World: Really-Existing Socialism. In 2005, we got what remains of '68 once we subtract '89 from it, the realization of its actual political potential—pure irrational revolt without any program.

Badiou has reflected on the fact that we live in a social space which is progressively experienced as "worldless."[16] Within such a space,

---

16   Alain Badiou, "The Caesura of Nihilism," lecture delivered at the University of Essex, September 10, 2003.

"meaningless" violence is the only form protest can take. Even Nazi anti-Semitism, however ghastly it was, opened up a world: it described its critical situation by positing an enemy in the form of "the Jewish conspiracy"; it named a goal and the means of achieving it. Nazism disclosed reality in a way which allowed its subjects to acquire a global cognitive map, and which included a space for their meaningful engagement. Capitalism, however, is the first socio-economic order which *de-totalizes meaning*: there is no global "capitalist worldview," no "capitalist civilization" proper: the fundamental lesson of globalization is precisely that capitalism can accommodate itself to all civilizations, from Christian to Hindu or Buddhist, from West to East. Capitalism's global dimension can only be formulated at the level of truth-without-meaning, as the "real" of the global market mechanism. This is why the famous Porto Alegre motto "Another world is possible!" is too simplistic; it fails to register that right now we already live less and less within what can be called a world, so that the task is no longer just to replace the old one with a new one, but . . . what? The first indications are given in art.

Signs From the Future: Kafka, Platonov, Sturgeon, Vertov, Satie

There are two contrasting figures of idiocy in our lives. The first is the (occasionally) hyper-intelligent subject who "doesn't get it," who understands a situation "logically," missing its hidden contextual rules. For example, when I visited New York for the first time, a café waiter asked me: "How was your day?" Misunderstanding the remark as a real question, I answered him truthfully ("I'm dead tired, I've got jetlag . . ."), and of course he looked at me as if I were a complete idiot. One exemplary case of such idiocy was Alan Turing, a man of extraordinary intelligence, but also a proto-psychotic unable to follow implicit contextual rules. In literature, it is hard to ignore Jaroslav Hašek's good soldier Schwejk, who, when he saw his comrades shooting from their trenches at the enemy soldiers, ran into no man's land shouting: "Stop shooting, there are people on the other side!" The archetype of such idiocy is, however, the naïve child from Andersen's tale who points out that the emperor is naked—thereby missing the fact that, as Alphonse Allais put it, we are all naked underneath our clothes.

The second and inverse form of idiocy is that of those who fully identify with commonsense, who are wholly in favor of the "big Other" of appearance. In a long series of figures—beginning with the Greek Chorus in the role of canned laughter or canned crying, always ready to comment on the action with some commonplace wisdom—one at least should mention the classic "stupid" partners of the great detectives: Holmes's Watson, Poirot's Hastings. These figures do not only serve as a foil for the detective's greatness; indeed, in one of the novels, Poirot tells Hastings that he is indispensable to the detective work: immersed in common sense, Hastings reacts to the scene of a crime the way the murderer who wanted to erase the traces of his act expected the public to react; it is then only by including in his analysis this expected reaction of the "big Other" that the great detective can solve the crime. The greatness of Kafka resides (among other things) in his unique ability to present the first figure of idiocy in the guise of the second figure, as something entirely normal and conventional (recall the extravagantly "idiotic" reasoning in the long debate between the priest and Josef K. which follows the parable on the Door of the Law). "Josephine the Singer, or the Mouse Folk"[17] is Kafka's very last story, written immediately prior to his death, and so could be considered as Kafka's testament, his last word (while writing it, he knew he was dying). Is "Josephine" then the allegory of the fate of Kafka-the-artist himself? Yes and no. When Kafka was writing the story, he had already lost his voice due to his inflamed throat (moreover, he was, like Freud, tone-deaf as regards music). Even more important is the fact that while at the story's end Josephine disappears, Kafka himself *wanted* to disappear, to erase all traces after his death (recall his order to Max Brod to burn all his manuscripts). But the true surprise is that what we get in the story is not the expected existential anguish mixed with slimy eroticism—it is, rather, a simple story of Josephine, the singing mouse, and her relation to the mice people (the translation of *Volk* as "folk" introduces a totally unwarranted populist dimension). Although Josephine is widely admired, the narrator (an anonymous "I") casts doubt on the quality of her singing:

> So is it singing at all? Is it not perhaps just a piping? And piping is something we all know about, it is the real artistic accomplishment of our people, or rather no mere accomplishment but a characteristic expression of our life. We all pipe, but of course no one dreams of making out that our piping is an art, we pipe without thinking of it, indeed without noticing it, and there are even many among us who are quite unaware that piping is one of our characteristics. So if it were true that Josephine does not sing

17   Franz Kafka, "Josephine the Singer, or the Mouse Folk," in *The Basic Kafka*, New York: Pocket Books 1984, p. 128; available online at fortunecity.com.

but only pipes and perhaps, as it seems to me at least, hardly rises above the level of our usual piping—yet, perhaps her strength is not even quite equal to our usual piping, whereas an ordinary farmhand can keep it up effortlessly all day long, besides doing his work—if that were all true, then indeed Josephine's alleged vocal skill might be disproved, but that would merely clear the ground for the real riddle which needs solving, the enormous influence she has.

As the narrator puts it, "this piping of hers is no piping"—a line which cannot but recall the title of Magritte's famous painting, so that one can imagine a painting of Josephine piping with the title: "This Is Not Piping." The first topic of the story is the enigma of Josephine's voice: if there is nothing special about it, why does it generate such admiration? What is "in her voice more than voice itself"? As Mladen Dolar has observed, her meaningless piping (a song deprived of meaning, that is, reduced to the object-voice) functions like Marcel Duchamp's *urinoir*—it is an art object not because of any inherent material properties, but only because Josephine occupies the place of an artist—in herself, she is exactly the same as all "ordinary" members of the people. Here, singing is thus the "art of minimal difference"—what differentiates her voice from others' voices is of a purely formal nature.[18] In other words, Josephine is a purely differential marker: she does not bring to her public—the people—any deep spiritual content; what she produces is the difference between the people's "utter silence" and their silence "as such," marked as silence by way of its opposition to her singing. Why, then, if Josephine's voice is the same as all the others', is she needed, why do people gather to listen to her? Her piping-singing is a pure pretext—ultimately, the people gather for the sake of gathering:

> Since piping is one of our thoughtless habits, one might think that people would pipe up in Josephine's audience too; her art makes us feel happy and when we are happy we pipe; but her audience never pipes, it sits in mouselike stillness; as if we had become partakers in the peace we long for, from which our own piping at the very least holds us back, we make no sound. Is it her singing that enchants us or is it not rather the solemn stillness enclosing her frail little voice?

The last line reiterates the key point: what matters is not her voice as such, but the "solemn stillness," the moment of peace, of withdrawal from

---

18   See Chapter 7 in Mladen Dolar, *A Voice and Nothing More*, Cambridge, MA: MIT Press 2006.

hard work, that (listening to) her voice brings about. Here the socio-political content becomes relevant: the mice people lead harsh and tense lives, difficult to bear, their existence is always precarious and threatened, and the very precarious character of Josephine's piping functions as a stand-in for the precarious existence of the entire mice people:

> Our life is very uneasy, every day brings surprises, apprehensions, hopes, and terrors, so that it would be impossible for a single individual to bear it all did he not always have by day and night the support of his fellows; but even so it often becomes very difficult; frequently as many as a thousand shoulders are trembling under a burden that was really meant only for one pair. . . . This piping, which rises up where everyone else is pledged to silence, comes almost like a message from the whole people to each individual; Josephine's thin piping amidst grave decisions is almost like our people's precarious existence amidst the tumult of a hostile world. Josephine exerts herself, a mere nothing in voice, a mere nothing in execution, she asserts herself and gets across to us; it does us good to think of that.

Josephine "is thus the vehicle for the collectivity's affirmation of itself: she reflects their collective identity back to them"; she is needed because "only the intervention of art and the theme of the great artist could make it possible to grasp the essential anonymity of the people, who have no feeling for art, no reverence for the artist."[19] In other words, Josephine "causes [the people] to assemble in silence — would this be possible without her? She constitutes the necessary element of exteriority that alone permits immanence to come into being."[20] This brings us to the logic of the exception constitutive of the order of universality: Josephine is the heterogeneous One through which the homogeneous All of the people is posited (perceives itself) as such.

Here, however, we see why the mouse community is not a hierarchic community with a Master, but rather a radically egalitarian "communist" community: Josephine is not venerated as a charismatic Mistress or Genius, her public is fully aware that she is just one of them. So the logic is not even that of the Leader who, with her exceptional position, establishes and guarantees the equality of her subjects (who are equal in their shared identification with their Leader) — Josephine herself has

---

19   Fredric Jameson, *The Seeds of Time*, New York: Columbia University Press 1994, p. 125.
20   Ibid.

to dissolve her special position into this equality. This brings us to the central part of Kafka's story, the detailed, often comical description of the way Josephine and her public, the people, relate to each other. Precisely because the people are aware that Josephine's function is just to assemble them, they treat her with egalitarian indifference; when she "demands special privileges (exemption from physical labor) as a compensation for her labor or indeed as a recognition of her unique distinction and her irreplaceable service to the community,"[21] her request is denied:

> For a long time back, perhaps since the very beginning of her artistic career, Josephine has been fighting for exemption from all daily work on account of her singing; she should be relieved of all responsibility for earning her daily bread and being involved in the general struggle for existence, which—apparently—should be transferred on her behalf to the people as a whole. A facile enthusiast—and there have been such—might argue from the mere unusualness of this demand, from the spiritual attitude needed to frame such a demand, that it has an inner justification. But our people draw other conclusions and quietly refuse it. Nor do they trouble much about disproving the assumptions on which it is based. Josephine argues, for instance, that the strain of working is bad for her voice, that the strain of working is of course nothing to the strain of singing, but it prevents her from being able to rest sufficiently after singing and to recuperate for more singing, she has to exhaust her strength completely and yet, in these circumstances, can never rise to the peak of her abilities. The people listen to her arguments and pay no attention. Our people, so easily moved, sometimes cannot be moved at all. Their refusal is sometimes so decided that even Josephine is taken aback, she appears to submit, does her proper share of work, sings as best she can, but all only for a time, then with renewed strength—for this purpose her strength seems inexhaustible—she takes up the fight again.

This is why, when Josephine disappears, narcissistically counting on the fact that her absence will cause the people to miss her, imagining how they will mourn her (like a child who, not feeling loved enough, runs away from home, hoping that his parents will miss him and desperately look for him), she totally miscalculates her position:

> She is a small episode in the eternal history of our people, and the people will get over the loss of her. Not that it will be easy for us; how can our

---

21   Ibid., p. 126.

gatherings take place in utter silence? Still, were they not silent even when Josephine was present? Was her actual piping notably louder and more alive than the memory of it will be? Was it even in her lifetime more than a simple memory? Was it not rather because Josephine's singing was already past losing in this way that our people in their wisdom prized it so highly? . . . So perhaps we shall not miss so very much after all, while Josephine, redeemed from the earthly sorrows which to her thinking lay in wait for all chosen spirits, will happily lose herself in the numberless throng of the heroes of our people, and soon, since we are no historians, will rise to the heights of redemption and be forgotten like all her brothers.

Fredric Jameson was right to read "Josephine" as Kafka's socio-political utopia, his vision of a radically egalitarian communist society—with the singular exception that Kafka, for whom humans are forever marked by superego guilt, was able to imagine a utopian society only among animals. One should resist the temptation to project any kind of tragedy onto Josephine's final disappearance and death: the text makes it clear that, after her death, Josephine "will *happily* lose herself in the numberless throng of the heroes of our people." As Jameson comments:

> It is perhaps the high point of Kafka's tale, and nowhere is the icy indiffer-ence of the Utopia of democracy more astonishingly revealed (but revealed by way of nothing and no reaction) than in the refusal of the people to grant her this form of individual difference. . . . Insofar as Josephine causes the essence of the people to appear, she also causes this essential indifference of the anonymous and the radically democratic equally to emerge. . . . Utopia is precisely the elevation from which this species forgetfulness and obliv-ion . . . takes place; it is anonymity as an intensely positive force, as the most fundamental fact of life of the democratic community; and it is this anonymity that in our non- or pre-Utopian world goes under the name and characterization of death.[22]

Note how Josephine is treated as a celebrity, but *not* fetishized—her admirers are well aware that there is nothing special about her, that she is just one of them. To paraphrase Marx, she thinks people admire her because she is an artist, but in reality she is an artist only because people treat her as such. Here we get an example of how, in a communist society, the Master-Signifier is still operative, but deprived of its fetish-istic effects—Josephine's belief in herself is perceived by the people as

---

22   Ibid., pp. 126–8.

harmless and rather ridiculous narcissism which should be gently, but ironically, tolerated and sustained. This is how artists should be treated in a communist society—they should be praised and flattered, but they should not be given any material privileges like exemption from work or special food rations. In a letter to Joseph Weydemeyer from 1852, Marx advised his friend on how to deal with Ferdinand Freiligrath, a poet who was politically a communist:

> Write Freiligrath a friendly letter. You do not have to be too sparing with compliments, for all poets, even the best ones, are *plus ou moins courtisanes* and *il faut les cajoler, pour les faire chanter.* Our F is the most amiable, unassuming man in private life, who beneath his real *bonhomie* conceals *un esprit très fin et très railleur;* his emotion is "truthful" and does not make him "uncritical" and "superstitious." He is a genuine revolutionary and an honest man through and through—and this can be said of few men. Nevertheless, whatever kind of *homme* he is, the poet needs praise and admiration. I believe that the genre itself requires this. I am telling you all this simply to point out that in your correspondence with Freiligrath, you should not forget the difference between the "poet" and the "critic."[23]

Does the same not hold for poor Josephine? Whatever kind of *femme* she is, the artist needs praise and admiration—the genre itself requires this. Indeed, to put it in good old Stalinist terms: *Josephine, the People's Artist of the Soviet Mouse Republic* . . .

So what would a communist culture look like?

The first lesson of Kafka's "Josephine" is that we have to endorse a shamelessly total form of immersion into the social body, a shared ritualistic social performance that would send all good liberals into shock with its "totalitarian" intensity—something Wagner was aiming at in his great ritualistic scenes at the end of Acts I and III of *Parsifal.* Like *Parsifal,* a concert by the rock band Rammstein (say, the one in the arena of Nîmes on July 23, 2005) should also be called *Bühnenweihfestspiel* ("a sacred festival performance"), which is the "vehicle for the collectivity's affirmation of itself."[24] All liberal-individualist prejudices need to be abandoned here—yes, each individual should be fully immersed in the crowd, joyfully abandoning his or her critical distance, passion should obliterate all reasoning, the public should follow the rhythm and orders of the leaders

---

23   Karl Marx and Friedrich Engels, *On Literature and Art,* Moscow: Progress Publishers 1976, p. 398.
24   Jameson, *The Seeds of Time,* p. 125.

on stage, the atmosphere should be fully "pagan," an inextricable mixture of the sacred and the obscene, and so on. In this way, the very act of over-identification with "totalitarian" *sinthomes* suspends their articulation into a properly "totalitarian" ideological space.

Let us make a detour through cinema once again. One reliable way to identify a half-educated pseudo-intellectual is through his or her reaction to the well-known scene from Bob Fosse's *Cabaret* in which, outside a country inn, the camera shows the face of a young blond man in close-up—he starts to sing about how nature is gradually awakening, how the birds have started to sing again and so on; the camera moves to two of his buddies, who join him in song; then, all the guests in the inn join in, the singing becoming more and more passionate, the lyrics describing how the fatherland should also awaken, until, finally, we notice on the singer's arm a swastika band. The pseudo-intellectual's reaction is something like: "Only now, on seeing this scene, do I understand what Nazism was, how it took possession of the Germans' souls!" The under-lying idea is that the raw emotional impact of the song accounts for the force of attraction of Nazism and thus tells us, more than any study of Nazi ideology, how it really functioned. Here, we should clearly disagree. Such a procedure, the very prototype of ideological liberalism, misses the point: not only are such mass performances not inherently fascist, they are not even "neutral," waiting to be appropriated by Left or Right—it was Nazism which stole them from the workers' movement, their original home. None of these "proto-fascist" elements is *per se* fascist, what makes them "fascist" is only their specific articulation—or, to put it in Stephen Jay Gould's terms, all such elements are "ex-apted" by fascism. In other words, there is no "fascism *avant la lettre*," because *it is the letter itself (the nomination) which makes fascism proper out of the bundle of elements.*

So, back to the song from *Cabaret* ("Tomorrow Belongs to Me"): there is nothing "inherently fascist" or "proto-fascist" about it—one can easily imagine the same song, with slightly changed words (celebrating the awakening of the working class from the slumber of its oppression), as a communist battle cry. The passion is what Badiou would call the nameless Real of the song, the neutral libidinal foundation which can be appropri-ated by different ideologies. (In a similar way, Sergei Eisenstein tried to isolate the libidinal economy of Ignatius Loyola's meditations, which can then be appropriated for communist propaganda—the sublime enthusi-asm for the Holy Grail and the enthusiasm of *kolkhoz* farmers for a new machine to produce butter from milk are sustained by exactly the same "passion.") Leftist libertarians see enjoyment as an emancipatory power: every oppressive power has to rely on libidinal repression, and the first act of liberation is to set the libido free. Puritan Leftists are, on the contrary, inherently suspicious of enjoyment: for them, it is a source of corruption and decadence, an instrument used by those in power to maintain their hold over us, so that the first act of liberation is to break its spell. The third position is that taken by Badiou: *jouissance* is the nameless "infinite," a neutral substance which can be instrumentalized in a number of ways.

To those who reject the notion of discipline, we should object that true poetry requires great discipline—no wonder three of the greatest poets of the twentieth century (more accurately, a writer and two poets) were bankers or insurance agents: Franz Kafka, T. S. Eliot, and Wallace Stevens. They needed the discipline of dealing with money not only as a counterpoint to poetic license, but as a means of installing order into the flow of poetic inspiration itself. The art of poetry is a constant struggle against its own source: the proper art of poetry consists in the way the poet dams up the free flow of poetic inspiration. This is why—in compliance with the banking metaphor—there is nothing liberating in getting the message of a poem; it is rather like getting a letter from the tax authorities, informing one of the state of one's debt to the big Other.

But here comes the surprise: the dissolution of "critical individuality" in the disciplined collective leads not to some Dionysian uniformity, but rather clears the slate and opens up the field for authentic idiosyncrasies. More precisely, what such passionate immersion suspends is not primarily the "rational Self" but the reign of the survival (self-preservation) instinct on which, as Adorno knew, the functioning of our "normal" rational egos is based:

> Speculations on the consequences of just such a general removal of the need for a survival instinct (such a removal being then in general what we call Utopia itself) leads us well beyond the bounds of Adorno's social lifeworld and class style (or our own), and into a Utopia of misfits and oddballs, in which the constraints for uniformization and conformity have been removed, and human beings grow wild like plants in a state of nature . . . no longer fettered by the constraints of a now oppressive sociality, they blossom into the neurotics, compulsives, obsessives, paranoids, and schizophrenics whom our society considers sick but who, in a world of true freedom, may make up the flora and fauna of "human nature" itself.[25]

---

25   Ibid., p. 99.

There is, of course, a third and crucial—structurally predominant— element of a communist culture: the cold universal space of rational thought (Badiou is quite right to emphasize that, at the most elementary level, thought as such, in contrast to mythic-poetic fabulation, is communist, its practice embodying the axiom of unconditional equality). Together, they form a Hegelian triad of universal thought, the Universal, Particular, and Individual (ritualistic immersion into particular social substance, individual idiosyncrasy) within which each element enables the other two to be kept apart: universal thought prevents idiosyncrasy from becoming trapped in the social substance (to each his or her own little fads: you can mix red wine with Coke, you can only make love leaning on a hot radiator, you can prefer Virginia Woolf over Daphne du Maurier [who, incidentally, is a much better writer than Woolf] . . . take your pick!); personal idiosyncrasies prevent the social substance from colonizing universal thought; the social substance prevents universal thought from turning into an abstract expression of the personal idiosyncrasy.

Jameson's example of such a utopian community is Andrei Platonov's *Chevengur*. The unique work of Platonov is indeed crucial for the proper understanding of the "obscure disaster" of Stalinism. His two great novels from the late 1920s (*Chevengur* and especially *The Foundation Pit*) are usually interpreted as critical depictions of the Stalinist utopia and its disastrous consequences; however, the utopia Platonov stages in these two works is not that of Stalinist Communism, but the Gnostic-materialist utopia against which "mature" Stalinism reacted in the early 1930s. Dualist-Gnostic motifs prevail here: sexuality and the entire bodily domain of generation/corruption are perceived as a hated prison, to be overcome by the scientific construction of a new, ethereal, and desexualized immortal body.[26] We should also bear in mind that Lenin was from the outset opposed to this Gnostic-utopian orientation (which attracted, amongst others, Trotsky and Gorky) with its dream of a short-cut to the new Proletarian Culture or the New Man. Nonetheless, one should see this Gnostic utopianism as a kind of "symptom" of Leninism, as a manifestation of what led the Revolution to fail, as the seed of its later "obscure disaster." To put it another way, the question to be raised here is whether

---

26   This is why Zamyatin's dystopia *We* is also not to be read as a critical portrayal of the totalitarian potential of Stalinism, but as an extrapolation of the Gnostic-utopian tendency of the revolutionary 1920s against which, precisely, Stalinism reacted. In this sense, Althusser was right and not peddling cheap paradoxes when he insisted that Stalinism was a form of humanism: its "cultural counter-revolution" was a humanist reaction against the "extremist" Gnostic-utopian post-humanist 1920s.

the utopian universe depicted by Platonov is an extrapolation of the immanent logic of a communist revolution, or, by contrast, an extrapolation of the logic underlying the behavior of those who precisely *fail* to follow the script for a "normal" communist revolution and instead opt for a millenarian short-cut, destined to end in dismal failure? How does the idea of a communist revolution stand with regard to the millenarian idea of the instant actualization of utopia? Furthermore, can these two options be clearly distinguished? Was there ever a "proper" communist revolution, undertaken when the time was "ripe"? And, if not, what does this mean for the very concept of such a revolution?

Platonov was in constant dialogue with this pre-Stalinist utopian core, which is why his last "intimate" love-hate engagement with Soviet reality related to the renewed utopianism of the first Five-Year Plan; after that, with the rise of high Stalinism and its cultural counter-revolution, the coordinates of the dialogue changed. Insofar as high Stalinism was anti-utopian, Platonov's turn towards a more "conformist" Socialist Realist writing in the 1930s cannot be dismissed as a mere external accommodation in response to heavy censorship and oppression: it was, rather, an immanent easing of tensions, up to a point even a sign of sincere proximity. High and late Stalinism had other immanent critics (Grossman, Chalamov, Solzhenitsyn, etc.) who were in "intimate" dialogue with it, sharing its underlying premises (Lukács noted that *One Day in the Life of Ivan Denisovich* meets all formal criteria of Socialist Realism).

This is why Platonov remains an ambiguous embarrassment for later dissidents. The key text of his "Socialist Realist" period is the short novel *The Soul* (1935), and although the typically Platonovian utopian group is still present—the "nation," a desert community of marginals who have lost the will to live—the reference points have totally changed. The hero is now a Stalinist educator, schooled in Moscow; he returns to the desert to introduce the "nation" to scientific and cultural progress and thus restore their will to live. (Platonov, of course, remained faithful to his ambiguity: at the novel's end, the hero has to accept that he cannot teach others anything.) This shift is signaled by the radically changed role of sexuality: for the Platonov of the 1920s, sexuality was the anti-utopian "dirty" power of inertia, while here it is rehabilitated as the privileged path to spiritual maturity—although he fails as an educator, the hero finds spiritual solace in sexual love, so that it is as if the "nation" were almost reduced to the status of a backdrop for the creation of a sexual couple.

However, do we not find, in popular contemporary TV series and films (*Heroes*, *X-Men*, and, at a much lower level, *The League of Extraordinary Gentlemen*) the same motif of the alternative community of freaks, where a group of outcasts forms a new collective—the difference being that, here, they stand out not on account of their psychic freakishness but of their uncommon psycho-physical abilities?[27] The unsurpassed origin and model of this topic remains Theodor Sturgeon's *More Than Human* (1953), which tells the story of the coming together of six extraordinary people with strange powers who are able to "blesh" (blend-mesh) their abilities and, in this way, act as one organism, reaching the *homo gestalt*, the next step in human evolution. In the novel's first section, "The Fabulous Idiot," the Gestalt is born, as its components come together for the first time: Lone, a mentally defective youth with a powerful telepathic gift; Janie, a stubborn child with telekinetic abilities; Bonnie and Beanie, twins who are incapable of speech and yet can teleport their bodies at will; and Baby, a profoundly retarded infant whose brain works like a computer. Each of these handicapped, misfit individuals is incapable of functioning on his or her own, but together they add up to a complete being: as Baby tells Janie, "the I is all of us." In the second section, "Baby is Three," the Gestalt grows up, emerging into the outside world and facing the challenges of survival. Several years have passed; Lone, the "head" of the Gestalt body, is dead, and his place has been taken by Gerry, an abused street urchin consumed by anger and hatred. Handicapped before because of Lone's limited mental capacity, the Gestalt is handicapped now by Gerry's moral emptiness. Gerry's ruthlessness serves the Gestalt, though, for he is willing to do anything to preserve it against separation. In the concluding section, "Morality," the Gestalt matures, completing its evolution into a fully realized being. Again, many years have passed; this time the narrative proceeds from the viewpoint of Hip, a young man who has been the subject of a cruel experiment of Gerry's, and whom Janie, rebelling, decides to rescue. Gerry attacks Hip mentally, driving him to mental breakdown and amnesia, but Hip confronts Gerry, and becomes the last part of the Gestalt, its conscience. Hip thus turns out to be the Gestalt's single missing element, without which it cannot take the next step in its development.

---

27   Chitral, a small community in northernmost Pakistan, has a separate "menstruation house" to which women withdraw in the time of their periods; oppressive as this measure is, one can also imagine it as a kind of small "liberated territory"—since men are forbidden to enter this house, women can organize their own space there and talk freely. Is this "menstruation home" not a model of a communist collective subtracted from the official public space? What if a playwright were to write a feminist theater piece on the conversations that take place in such a house?

The novel has a number of features which prevent a simplistic New Age reading of the plot. First, in contrast to the usual paranoid fear that "post-humans" will threaten ordinary humans, Sturgeon's Homo Gestalt acts on the basis of a moral duty to guide and protect Homo Sapiens, which is the Gestalt's own source material. Second, the individual members of the Gestalt are not reduced to caricatured, depersonalized, perfect beings whose identity is drowned in the Gestalt—no robotic ants blindly fulfilling their function, they display all the passion, aggressiveness, vulnerability, and weaknesses of actual individuals, and, if anything, are more freakish and "individualistic" than ordinary humans—their coming-together as a new One creates the conditions for their peculiarities to flourish. Does this weird collective not recall Marx's claim that, in a communist society, the freedom of all will be grounded in the freedom of every individual? (Sturgeon and his followers also provide a new figure of a properly communist Evil—the dissenter who wants to use his paranormal power for destructive goals.) However, one should always bear in mind that this unencumbered blossoming of idiosyncrasies can only thrive against the background of a shared ritual. This takes us back to Wagner's *Parsifal*, the central problem of which is that of a ceremony: how is it possible to perform a ritual in conditions where there is no transcendence to guarantee it? As an aesthetic spectacle? The enigma of *Parsifal* turns on determining the limits and contours of a ceremony. Is the ceremony only that which Amfortas is unable to perform, or is part of the ceremony also the spectacle of his complaint and resistance and final willingness to perform the ceremony? In other words, are Amfortas's two great complaints not highly ceremonial, ritualized? Is not even the "unexpected" arrival of Parsifal (who, nonetheless, arrives just in time, that is, just at the moment when the tension is at its highest) to replace him also part of a ritual? And do we not find a ritual also in *Tristan*, in the great duet that takes up most of Act II? The long introductory part consists of the emotional ramblings of the couple, and the ritual proper begins with "*So sterben wir um ungetrennt ...*" with its sudden shift to a declamatory/declaratory mode—from this point on, it is no longer the two individuals who sing/talk, it is a ceremonial Other which takes over. One should always bear in mind this feature which disturbs the opposition between the Day (symbolic obligations) and the Night (endless passion): the highest point of *Lust*, the immersion into the Night, is itself highly ritualized, it takes the form of its opposite, of a stylized ritual.

And is this problem of ceremony (liturgy) not also the problem of all revolutionary processes, from the French Revolution with its spectacles to the October Revolution? Why is this liturgy necessary? Precisely because of the precedence of non-sense over sense: the liturgy is the symbolic frame within which the zero-level of sense is articulated. The zero-experience of sense is not the experience of a determinate sense, but the absence of sense, more precisely: the frustrating experience of being sure that something has a sense, but not knowing what it is. *This vague presence of a non-specific sense is sense "as such," sense at its purest* — it is primary, not secondary; in other words, all determinate sense comes second, as an attempt to fill in the oppressive presence-absence of the that-ness of sense without its what-ness. This is how we should answer the reproach that "communism" is being used here as a magic word, an empty sign lacking any precise or positive vision of a new society, merely a ritualized token of belonging to a new initiatic community: there is no opposition between liturgy (ceremony) and historical opening; far from being an obstacle to change, liturgy keeps the space for radical change open, insofar as it sustains the signifying non-sense which calls for new inventions of (determinate) sense.

Along the same lines, one could interpret *Man with a Movie Camera*, by Dziga Vertov (Eisenstein's great opponent), as an exemplary case of cinematic communism: the affirmation of life in its multiplicity, enacted through a kind of cinematic parataxis, a setting side-by-side of a series of daily activities — washing hair, wrapping packages, playing piano, connecting phone wires, dancing ballet — which resonate with each other at a purely formal level, through the echoing of visual and other patterns. What makes this cinematic practice communist is the underlying assertion of the radical "univocity of being": the various phenomena are all equalized, all the usual hierarchies and oppositions among them, including the official communist opposition between the Old and the New, are magically suspended (recall that the alternative title of Eisenstein's *The General Line*, shot at the same time, was precisely *The Old and the New*). Communism is here presented less as the struggle for a goal (with all the pragmatic paradoxes this involves: the struggle for universal freedom in a new society means maintaining the harshest discipline, and so on), than as a fact, a present collective experience. In this utopian space of "communism now," the camera is again and again directly shown, not as a traumatic inscription of the gaze into the image, but as an unproblematic part of the picture — there is no tension between the eye and the gaze here, no suspicion or urge to penetrate the deceptive surface in search of the secret truth or essence, just the symphonic texture of life in all its positive diversity, like an ironic cinematic version of Stalin's first law of dialectics, "everything is connected with everything else."[28] This practice of Vertov culminates in his *Donbas Symphony* from 1931, his first sound film in which the harsh reality of building a gigantic hydroelectric plant is "sublated" into an intricate dance of formal (visual and audio) motifs. There is, of course, a price to be paid for this: the obverse of the symphonic texture—the *suspicious Stalinist gaze* always on the lookout for enemies and saboteurs—returns with a vengeance in Eisenstein's *Ivan the Terrible* (as a gigantic iconic eye painted on the crooked walls of the Kremlin, as the eye of Malyuta Skuratov, Ivan's faithful watchdog).

What accounts for this blindness is Vertov's participation in the techno-Gnostic version of communism popular in the Soviet Union in the 1920s: comparing man unfavorably to machines, he believed that his concept of "Kino Eye" would help humanity to evolve into a higher, post-human, form which would exclude sexuality. This limitation is, however, no reason to ignore echoes of Vertov's polyphonic texture in later great directors—maybe even Altman's *Short Cuts* can be read as a new version of Vertov's practice. Altman's universe is effectively one of contingent encounters between a multitude of series, a universe in which different series communicate and resonate at the level of what Altman himself refers to as "subliminal reality" (mechanical shocks, encounters, and impersonal intensities which precede the level of social meaning).[29] We should, then, avoid the temptation of reducing Altman to being a poet of American alienation, rendering palpable the silent despair of everyday lives: there is another side to Altman, his receptivity to contingent joyful encounters. Along the same lines as Deleuze and Guattari's reading of Kafka's universe—in which the Absence of the elusive transcendent Center (Castle, Court, God) betrays the Presence of multiple passages and transformations—one is tempted to read Altmanian "despair and anxiety" as the deceptive obverse of a more affirmative immersion into the multitude of subliminal intensities. The latter is Altman's communism, rendered by the cinematic form itself, counteracting the depressing social reality depicted.

Altman brings us to another key feature of communist culture: the properly communist form of *collective intimacy*, epitomized by Eric Satie's piano

---

28   I owe this reference to Vertov to Jacques Rancière, "Cinematographic Vertigo" (unpublished paper).
29   See Robert T. Self, *Robert Altman's Subliminal Reality*, Minneapolis: Minnesota University Press 2002.

pieces. Can one imagine a stronger contrast than that between Eric Satie's gently melancholic piano pieces and the universe of communism? The music usually associated with communism consists of propaganda songs and choruses or bombastic cantatas celebrating state events and leaders — and, from this standpoint, is Satie not the very embodiment of "bourgeois individualism"? The fact that in the early 1920s, during the last years of his life, Satie was not only a member of the newly constituted French Communist Party, but even served on its Central Committee, was then surely just a personal idiosyncrasy or provocation? The first surprise here is that another paragon of French "bourgeois" restraint, Maurice Ravel, rejected the invitation to join the *Académie Française* in protest against the way France was treating the Soviet Union; he furthermore set to music North African songs protesting against French colonial power. The music in which Ravel is close to Satie's musical communism is not "Bolero," but his chamber music, which is painfully beautiful in its restraint. What if, then, in order to get at the most elementary idea of communism, we need to forget all about Romantic explosions of passion and imagine instead the clarity of a minimalist order sustained by a gentle form of freely imposed discipline? Recall Brecht's "In Praise of Communism" from *The Mother*, set to music by Hans Eisler in a very Satiean mood: soft, gentle, and intimate, with no pomposity — and, indeed, do Brecht's words not almost sound like a description of Satie's music?

> It's quite straightforward, you'll understand it. It's not hard.
> Because you're not an exploiter, you'll easily grasp it.
> It's for your own good, so find out all about it.
> They're fools who describe it as foolish, and foul who describe it as
>   foulness.
> It's against all that's foul and against all that's foolish.
> The exploiters will tell you that it's criminal,
> But we know better:
> It puts an end to all that's criminal.
> It isn't madness, but puts
> An end to all madness.
> It doesn't mean chaos
> It just means order.
> It's just the simple thing
> That's hard, so hard to do.[30]

---

30   Bertolt Brecht, "In Praise of Communism," from *The Mother*, London: Methuen 1978, p. 28.

Satie used the term "furniture music (*musique d'ameublement*)," by way of implying that some of his pieces should function as mood-setting background music. Although this may seem to point forwards to commercialized ambient music (or "Muzak"), what Satie was aiming at was the exact opposite: a music which subverts the gap separating the figure from the background. When one truly listens to Satie, one "hears the background." This is egalitarian communism in music: a music which shifts the listener's attention from the great Theme to its inaudible background, in the same way that communist theory and politics refocus our attention away from heroic individuals to the immense work and suffering of the invisible ordinary people. Is this popular-democratic dimension not clearly discernible in Satie's own programmatic statements?

> Insist upon Furniture Music. Have no meetings, no get-togethers, no social affairs of any kind without Furniture Music ... Don't get married without Furniture Music. Stay out of houses that don't use Furniture Music. Anyone who hasn't heard Furniture Music has no idea what true happiness is.

> We must bring about a music which is like furniture, a music, that is, which will be part of the noises of the environment, will take them into consideration. I think of it as ... softening the noises of the knives and forks, not dominating them, not imposing itself. It would fill up those heavy silences that sometimes fall between friends dining together. It would spare them the trouble of paying attention to their own banal remarks. And at the same time it would neutralize the street noises which so indiscreetly enter into the play of conversation. To make such a noise would respond to need.[31]

No wonder, then, that John Cage — the key figure of the twentieth-century musical vanguard whose treatment of the minimalist dialectics of sound and silence can be compared only to Webern's — was a great admirer of Satie. For Cage, the most elementary aspect of music is duration: the only feature which both sound and silence share is duration. "Silence is important, as it is the opposite of sound" and, "therefore, a necessary partner of sound." It is here, at the level of musical structure, that Satie, together with Webern, introduced the only really new idea since Beethoven. As Cage writes, in his "Defense of Satie":

---

31   All following quotes from Satie and Cage are from Matthew Shlomowitz, "Cage's Place in the Reception of Satie," available online at www.af.lu.se.

With Beethoven the parts of a composition were defined by means of harmony. With Satie and Webern they were defined by means of time lengths. The question of structure is so basic, and it is so important to be in agreement about it, that one might ask: Was Beethoven right or are Webern and Satie right? I answer immediately and unequivocally, Beethoven was in error, and his influence, which has been as extensive as it is lamentable, has been deadening to the art of music.

Linked to this are two further innovations, identified by Constant Lambert. First, in an apparent paradox (but really a profound dialectical necessity), this very shift onto duration as the main structural principle enabled Satie to break out of temporality to atemporal eternity:

> By his abstention from the usual forms of development and by his unusual employment of what might be called interrupted and overlapping recapitulations, which causes the piece to fold in on itself, as it were, he completely abolishes the element of rhetorical argument and even succeeds in abolishing as far as possible our time sense. We do not feel that the emotional significance of a phrase is dependent on its being placed at the beginning or end of a particular section.

Is this structure not the one of *parataxis*, of atemporal constellation replacing linear temporal development? Where there is parataxis, the parallax, its dialectical counterpoint, is not far away:

> Satie's habit of writing his pieces in groups of three was not just a mannerism. It took place in his art of dramatic development, and was part of his peculiarly sculpturesque views of music. When we pass from the first to the second *Gymnopédie* . . . we do not feel that we are passing from one object to another. It is as though we were moving slowly round a piece of sculpture and examining it from a different point of view . . . It does not matter which way you walk around a statue and it does not matter in which order you play the three *Gymnopédies*.[32]

One should be very precise here: the point is not that the three versions (ultimately fail to) imitate the same transcendental object which resists being directly rendered in music. The parallactic gap is inscribed into the Thing itself: the multitude of "subjective" perceptions-impressions of the object bring about the inner fracture of the object. It is thus only a slight,

---

32   Constant Lambert, *Music Ho!*, Hogarth Press, London 1985, p. 119.

albeit crucial, displacement which separates Cage from Satie: for Satie, music should be a part of the sound environment, whereas for Cage, the noises of the environment *are* the music. Here is Cage's final judgment on Satie: "It's not a question of Satie's relevance. He's indispensable." As is communism.

Violence Between Discipline and Obscenity

This assertion of ritual as central to communist culture has consequences even for our innermost subjective attitudes. Let me recall "The Third Wave," the social experiment conducted by history teacher Ron Jones at Cubberley High School in Palo Alto during first week of April 1967. In order to explain to his students how the German populace could claim ignorance of the Holocaust, Jones started a movement called "The Third Wave" and convinced his students that its purpose was to eliminate democracy; he emphasized this in the movement's motto: "Strength through discipline, strength through community, strength through action, strength through pride." On the fourth day, however, Jones decided to terminate the experiment which was now slipping out of his control: the students had become increasingly involved in the process and their discipline and loyalty to the project were astounding—some of them even denounced their peers whom they suspected of not fully believing in the project. Jones ordered the students to attend a rally at noon next day, where, instead of the expected televised address from their leader, the students were presented with an empty screen. After a few minutes of waiting, Jones announced that they had been a part of an experiment in fascism and that they had all willingly created a sense of superiority similar to that of German citizens in the Nazi period.[33]

Predictably, liberals were fascinated by "The Third Wave," discerning in it the "deep" *Lord of the Flies*-style insight into how, beneath the civilized surface, we are all potential fascists—the barbarian-sadistic beast is lurking within all of us, just awaiting its opportunity. But what if we shift the perspective a little bit and view the "authoritarian personality" as the "repressed" obverse of the "open" liberal personality itself? The same ambiguity appears in the legendary study on the "authoritarian personality" in which Adorno participated.[34] The features of the "authoritarian personality" are clearly opposed to the standard figure of the "open"

33   For the basic data, see the Wikipedia entry for "The Third Wave."
34   T. W. Adorno et al., *The Authoritarian Personality*, New York: Harper and Row 1950.

democratic personality, and the underlying dilemma consists in determining whether the two types are simply opposites in a struggle, such that we have to choose to fight for one or the other. The question, in other words, concerns the status of those features which are held to be the opposite of those defining the "authoritarian personality." Are they simply to be endorsed as features of the "democratic personality" (ultimately the position taken by Habermas), or is the "authoritarian personality" to be conceived as the symptomal "truth" of the "democratic personality" (the view of, say, Agamben)? Along these lines, the shift between Adorno and Habermas apropos modernity can be formulated in these terms: the core thesis of Adorno and Horkheimer's *Dialectic of Enlightenment* is that phenomena such as fascism are "symptoms" of modernity, its necessary consequence (which is why, as Horkheimer put it in a memorable line, those who do not want to talk critically about capitalism should also keep quiet about fascism), while for Habermas the same phenomena indicate that modernity remains an "unfinished project," that it has not yet developed its full potential. This undecidability is ultimately a special case of the more general undecidability of the "dialectic of Enlightenment" itself, well-perceived by Habermas: if the "administered world" is the "truth" of the Enlightenment project, how, precisely, can it be criticized and counteracted by way of fidelity to that project itself?[35]

One is tempted to claim that, far from representing a simple failure on Adorno's part, this reluctance to take the step into positive normativity signals his fidelity to the Marxist revolutionary project. This is also how one should read the liberal enthusiasm for the Third Wave phenomenon: its function is to assert the struggle of liberal "openness" against totalitarian "closure" as our fundamental struggle, and thus to obliterate their mutual complicity, namely the fact that "totalitarianism" is the "return of the repressed" of liberalism itself. This obliteration also enables us to condense Fascism and Communism into one and the same anti-liberal "totalitarian" figure, and thus to block the search for a *third* option—the "personality structure" of a subject engaged in a radical emancipatory struggle, a subject who subscribes without any qualms to the motto "Strength through discipline, strength through community, strength through action, strength through pride," and yet remains engaged in the egalitarian emancipatory struggle. The liberal will either dismiss such a subject as another version of the "authoritarian personality," or claim that

35   See Jürgen Habermas, *The Philosophical Discourse of Modernity*, Cambridge, MA: MIT Press 1990.

it displays a "contradiction" between the goals of the struggle (equality and freedom) and the means employed (collective discipline, etc.) — in both cases, the specificity of the subject of the radical emancipatory struggle is obliterated, it remains "unseen," there is no place for it in the liberal's "cognitive map."[36]

There is another, apparently opposite, political strategy, involving the use of anti-semantic violence inherent to language. A couple of decades ago, in Carinthia, (*Kaernten*) Austria's southern province which borders on Slovenia, German nationalists organized a campaign against the alleged Slovene "threat" under the motto "*Kaernten bleibt deutsch!*", to which Austrian Leftists found the perfect answer. Instead of rational counter-arguments, they simply printed, in the main newspapers, an advertisement with obscene, disgusting-sounding variations of the nationalists' motto: "*Kaernten deibt bleutsch! Kaernten leibt beutsch! Kaernten beibt dleutsch!*" Is this procedure not worthy of the obscene, "anal," meaningless speech spoken by Hynkel, the Hitler figure in Chaplin's *The Great Dictator*? This is what Rammstein, the rock band which is part of *Neue Deutsche Haerte* (the "New German Hardness"),[37] does to totalitarian ideology: it de-semanticizes it and shows up its obscene babble in its intrusive materiality.

Rammstein's music exemplifies perfectly the distinction between sense and presence, the tension in a work of art between the hermeneutic dimension and the dimension of presence "this side of hermeneutics," a dimension which Lacan indicated by the term *sinthome* (formula-knot of *jouissance*) as opposed to symptom (bearer of meaning). What Lacan conceptualizes is the non-semantic dimensions in the symbolic itself. The direct identification with Rammstein is an over-identification with *sinthomes* which undermines ideological identification. We should not fear such direct over-identification, but rather the articulation of this chaotic

---

36   Consequently, in every political struggle, one should begin with avoiding false battles and locating the right enemy. In today's Zimbabwe, President Mugabe's destructive economic politics exploits the racial division in order to obfuscate the class division, i.e., the fact that a new black elite took the place of the old white elite. And the danger is that, confronted with the growing gap between rich and poor in South Africa, the ANC will succumb to the same temptation. That is to say, the main economic result of the fall of apartheid has been the rise of a new black ruling class which joined the old white elite, while the black majority lives in the same abject poverty; such a situation opens up the dangerous possibility that, in order to redirect the popular discontent, the new black elite will also play the race card and place all the blame on the old white colonialists. And the same goes for Latin-American anti-US populism: no wonder that, in November 2009, Chávez defended Carlos, Mugabe, etc., as authentic revolutionary heroes.

37   Although the name refers to Ramstein, the US military airbase in West Germany, it is written with an additional "m", as RaMMstein, making it readable as "ramming stones," a paraphrase of "rolling stones."

field of energy into a (fascist) universe of meaning. No wonder that Rammstein's music is violent, invasive and intrusive with its loud volume and deep vibrations—its materiality is in constant tension with its meaning, undermining it all the time. Alejandro Zaera Polo formulated the shift from classical rock with its "revolutionary individualism" to more "immersive" later developments:

> Another relevant case of how the politics of cultural production has evolved under the effect of globalization and digital technology can be found in the culture of contemporary electronic music: as opposed to rock'n'roll's revolutionary individualism, the culture of techno has neither an overt revolutionary aspiration nor a utopian formulation. It operates within the system. In order to do this techno music replaces more traditional musical figures—melody and harmony—with a texture of absorbing the multiplicity of positions and rhythm, as primary forms of expression. The image of the rave, a collective environment capable of mobilizing crowds of people into a single rhythm appears to be a perfect incarnation of associative democracy as a coexistence of heterogeneous populations and informal associations.[38]

One should nonetheless draw a clear line of distinction, within this field, between an appeasing techno (which clearly does "operate within the system") and the unleashed brutality of Rammstein which undermines the system not through some critical-utopian vision but through the obscene brutality of the immersion it enacts. One should therefore resist the Susan Sontagesque temptation to reject as ideologically suspect the music of Rammstein with its extensive use of "Nazi" images and motifs—what they do is the exact opposite: by pushing their listeners into a direct identification with the *sinthomes* used by the Nazis, by-passing their articulation in Nazi ideology, they render palpable a gap where ideology imposes the illusion of seamless organic unity. In short, Rammstein *liberates* these *sinthomes* from their Nazi-articulation: they are offered to be enjoyed in their pre-ideological status as "knots" of libidinal investment. One should thus not be afraid to draw a radical conclusion: enjoying Riefenstahl's pre-Nazi films or the music of bands like Rammstein is *not* ideological, while the struggle against racist intolerance in the name of tolerance *is*. So when (in response to a Rammstein video depicting a blonde girl in a cage,

---

38   See Alejandro Zaera Polo, "The Politics of the Envelope: A Political Critique of Materialism," *Volume*, 17, p. 103.

with characters in dark uniforms evoking Nordic warriors and so on) Leftist liberals fear that the uneducated public will miss the irony (if there is any) and directly identify with the proto-Fascist sensibility on display, we should counter with the good old motto: the only thing we have to fear here is fear itself. Rammstein undermine totalitarian ideology not with an ironic distance towards the rituals they imitate, but by directly confronting us with its obscene materiality and thereby suspending its efficacy.

The Infinite Judgment of Democracy

The only way to orient ourselves through the conundrum of violence is to focus on its parallax nature, noted long ago by Mark Twain in his *A Connecticut Yankee in King Arthur's Court*:

> There were two "Reigns of Terror" if we would remember it and consider it; the one wrought in hot passion, the other in heartless cold blood . . . our shudders are all for the "horrors" of the minor Terror, the momentary Terror, so to speak, whereas, what is the horror of swift death by the axe compared with lifelong death from hunger, cold, insult, cruelty, and heartbreak? A city cemetery could contain the coffins filled by that brief Terror which we have all been so diligently taught to shiver at and mourn over; but all France could hardly contain the coffins filled by that older and real Terror, that unspeakably bitter and awful Terror, which none of us have been taught to see in its vastness or pity as it deserves.[39]

In order to grasp this parallax nature of violence, one should focus on the short-circuits between different levels, between, say, power and social violence: an economic crisis which causes devastation is experienced as uncontrollable quasi-natural power, but it *should* be experienced as *violence*. The same goes for authority: the elementary form of the critique of ideology is precisely to unmask authority as violence. For feminism, male authority *is* violence. I am referring here to Hannah Arendt who, in her *On Violence*,[40] elaborated a series of distinctions between "power," "strength," "force," "violence," and "authority." *Force* should be reserved for the "forces of nature" or the "force of circumstances": it indicates the energy released by physical or social movements. It should never be used interchangeably with *power* in the study of politics: force refers to

---

39   Mark Twain, *A Connecticut Yankee in King Arthur's Court*, New York: Dover 2001, p. 64.
40   See Hannah Arendt, *On Violence*, New York: Harvest 1970.

movements in nature, or to other humanly uncontrollable circumstances, whereas power is a function of human relations. Power in social relations results from the human ability to act *in concert* to persuade or coerce others, while *strength* is the individual capacity to do the same. *Authority* is a specific *source* of power. It represents power vested in persons by virtue of their offices, or of their "authoritativeness" where relevant information and knowledge is concerned. There is such a thing as personal authority, such as, for instance, in the relation between parent and child, between teacher and pupil—or it can be vested in offices (a priest can grant valid absolution even though he is drunk). Its hallmark is unquestioning recognition by those who are asked to obey: neither coercion nor persuasion is needed. Authority thus does not stem merely from the attributes of the individual. Its exercise depends on a willingness *on the part of others* to grant respect and legitimacy, rather than on one's personal ability to persuade or coerce.

It is therefore crucial to distinguish between power and *violence*: power is psychological, a moral force that makes people want to obey, while violence enforces obedience through physical coercion. Those who use violence may manage to temporarily impose their will, but their command is always tenuous because when the violence ends, or the threat of it lessens, there is even less incentive to obey the authorities. Control through violence requires constant vigilance. Too little violence is ineffective; too much violence generates revolt. Violence can destroy the old power, but it can never create the authority that legitimizes the new. Violence is therefore the poorest possible basis on which to build a government. Violence is the weapon of choice for the impotent: those who have little power often attempt to control or influence others by using violence. Violence rarely creates power. On the contrary, groups or individuals who use violence often find that their actions diminish what little power they *do* have. Groups that oppose governments often try to compensate for their perceived lack of power by using violence. Such violence simply reinforces state power. A terrorist who blows up a building or assassinates a politician gives the government the excuse it wants to crack down on individual liberties and expand its sphere of control. When a government turns to violence, it is because it feels its power is slipping away. Governments that rule through violence are weak. Dictators have always had to rely on terror against their own populations to compensate for their powerlessness. Protracted violence results in diminished power, making more violence necessary.

Unsurprisingly, Arendt uses these distinctions to attack Marx for a confusion between violence and power which opens up the path to totalitarian rule. However, the point of Marxism is here precisely that there is a structurally necessary breakdown of the distinction in reality itself: not only is political power ultimately a (monopoly) power to apply violence, it is itself grounded on (a threat of) violence. One should link this weak point to Arendt's dismissal of the economy, of the sphere of production, from politics proper: what she misses is Marx's key insight into how the political struggle is a spectacle which, in order to be deciphered, has to be referred to the sphere of economics. To quote Wendy Brown: "if Marxism had any analytical value for *political* theory, was it not in the insistence that the problem of freedom was contained in the social relations implicitly declared 'unpolitical'—that is, naturalized—in liberal discourse."[41]

There is thus violence and violence, and the point is not to disqualify a priori any mode of violence, but to inquire into which mode we are dealing with. In his recent book, a true manifesto of the liberal counter-revolution, Bernard-Henri Lévy offers his explanation for why the terrifying experience of the four years of Khmer Rouge reign in Kampuchea (1975–79) was so important for the Left: it compels us to dismiss once and for all the standard notion that hitherto revolutions failed because they were not "radical enough," because they compromised with what they were trying to overcome and did not follow their logic to the end.[42] The one thing that can be said for the Khmer Rouge is that they went to the bitter end, to the extreme of a social transformation as thorough as could be imagined: cities were emptied, money and the market abolished, all education was brought to a standstill in order to create a New Man from zero-level, the family unit itself was suspended (children were soon taken from their parents)—and the result was a nightmare. Against this apparently convincing observation, one should nonetheless persist with the claim that the Khmer Rouge were, in a way, *not radical enough*: while they took the abstract negation of the past to the limit, they did not invent any new form of collectivity, they just replaced the old order with a primitive regime of egalitarian control and ruthless exploitation, in which social relations were reduced to the most elementary paradox of the obscenity of power—the Khmer Rouge effectively treated *itself* as an illegal obscenity: to inquire into the structure of state power was considered a crime.

---

41 Wendy Brown, *States of Injury*, Princeton: Princeton University Press 1995, p. 14.
42 Bernard-Henri Lévy, *Left in Dark Times: A Stand Against the New Barbarism*, New York: Random House 2009.

Its leaders were referred to anonymously as "Brother No. 1" (Pol Pot, of course), "Brother No. 2," etc., and the governing party was simply called "Angka," usually translated as "Organization"—the gangster connotations are here fully justified, not only with respect to the crimes committed, but in the sense of the organization treating *itself* as if it were a secret body, a Maoist Cosa Nostra.

Take, in contrast to the Khmer Rouge, the 2008 student protests in Greece which were threatening to spread all over Europe, from Croatia to France. Many observers have noted, as one of their key features, their *violent* character—not violent in the sense of killing people, but in the sense of disturbing public order and destroying (well-selected) objects of private and state property, with the goal of stopping state and capitalist machinery from functioning smoothly. The wager of Leftist political terrorism (the Red Army Faction in Germany, the Red Brigades in Italy, Action Directe in France, etc.) was that, in an epoch in which the masses are totally immersed in capitalist ideological torpor, so that the standard critique of ideology is no longer operative, only a resort to the raw Real of direct violence — "*l'action directe*" — can awaken them. While one should reject without ambiguity the murderous way in which this insight was enacted, one should not be afraid to endorse the insight itself. Today's post-political "silent majority" is not stupid, but it is cynical and resigned. The limitation of post-politics is best exemplified not only by the success of rightist populism, but by the aforementioned UK elections of 2005: in spite of the growing unpopularity of Tony Blair (regularly voted the most unpopular person in the UK), there was no way for this discontent to find a politically effective expression. Something is obviously very wrong here — it is not that people "do not know what they want," but rather that cynical resignation prevents them from acting upon it, with the result that a weird gap opens up between what people think and how they act (or vote). Such frustration can foment dangerous extra-parliamentary explosions, which the Left should not bemoan, but take the risk of relating to in order to "awaken" the people. In Berlusconi's Italy, where a self-proclaimed clown enjoys over 60 percent popularity ratings, some form of violence will clearly have to be rehabilitated.

It is easy to note how, from within the Kantian horizon, the "terroristic" aspect of democracy—the violent egalitarian imposition of those who are "surnumerary," the "part-of-no-part" — can only appear as its "totalitarian" distortion. Within this horizon, the line that separates the authentic democratic explosion of revolutionary terror from the "totalitarian" Party-State regime (or, to put it in reactionary terms, the line that separates the "mob rule of the dispossessed" from the Party-State's brutal oppression of the "mob") is obliterated. (One can, of course, argue that a direct "mob rule" is inherently unstable and that it necessarily turns into its opposite, a tyranny over the mob itself; however, this shift in no way changes the fact that, precisely, we are dealing with a shift, a radical turnaround.)

It was noted long ago that democracy can be justified by either of two opposed stances, one involving trust, the other a radical distrust: (1) the majority of people are ultimately good, just, and rational enough to make the right decisions; or (2) people are generally so corrupt that power can never be entrusted to individuals without keeping them under constant check. But rather than seeing these two positions as opposed, one should grasp this unique combination of trust and distrust as lying at the very heart of the democratic vision. It would be (all too) easy to apply Lacan's "formulae of sexuation" here, by claiming that the first stance obeys the masculine logic of the All and the second the feminine logic of the non-All: people are good as an All, but to be distrusted if taken individually. It would also be (all too) easy to claim that, while non-liberal-democratic regimes wanting to impose their Ideal of the best possible society function in a "masculine" way, always relying on a constitutive exception (the "enemy"), liberal democracy operates in the "feminine" way of the "non-all," not pretending to offer the Best, but merely the least bad relatively speaking—it is not even that *all* other political systems are worse, it is, more precisely, that *each* of them, taken one by one, is "worse" when compared with democracy. Applied in this way, however, the formulae of sexuation are too abstract-formal (in Hegel's meaning of the term): one might just as easily say that Stalinism was "masculine" (politicizing society through its exception: technology and language were seen as non-ideological, as neutral means, so that, in Stalinism, "everything is political"—but with exceptions) and Maoism "feminine."[43]

True, democracy is our last fetish—but a fetish which protects us against democracy itself, against its own "non-democratic" core, the violent "terroristic" excess which the complex democratic rules try to keep at

---

43   In Maoism, "there is nothing which is not political," which precisely prevents us from asserting that "everything is political": the political names the very principle of "non-All" of a society, its antagonism which cannot be totalized, a difference which cannot be reduced to a specific difference within a neutral genus—"class struggle" does not mean that "society is composed of classes which fight each other," but that, in the guise of class struggle, society confronts its own limitation (in class struggle, specific—intra-social—difference overlaps with the difference between society itself and the non-social).

bay. In his famous essay "Federalist No. 10," James Madison confronted the problem of how to prevent democracy from becoming involved in disputes about "the various and unequal distribution of property. Those who hold and those who are without property have ever formed distinct interests in society." In short, the problem is class struggle: how to prevent the poor majority from "discover[ing] their own strength" given to them in principle in a democracy. His solution is an "extensive" federalist republic, for then "it will be more difficult for all who feel it to discover their own strength, and to act in unison with each other. . . . The influence of factious leaders may kindle a flame within their particular States, but will be unable to spread a general conflagration through the other States."[44] Therein resided the much celebrated "wisdom of the founding fathers": how to contain the potentially radical dimension of democracy. One of the few who remained faithful to that potential was Jefferson, who famously wrote that "a little rebellion now and then is a good thing": "It is a medicine necessary for the sound health of government. God forbid that we should ever be twenty years without such a rebellion. The tree of liberty must be refreshed from time to time with the blood of patriots and tyrants. It is its natural manure."[45] This is why, unlike the French Revolution, the American Revolution was not a real revolution: it did not go to the end and fully develop its "terroristic" potential.

What gets lost in institutionalized democracy is precisely this overlapping which turns antagonism into something that perturbs the very universal notion of society: although, in democracy, there is no substantial big Other, no positive agent with a legitimate a priori claim to occupy the place of Power, and although the gap between this empty place and the positive bearer of power is irreducible, we still have a "big Other" in the guise of this empty form itself, of a neutral frame (minimally determined by democratic procedures) which guarantees the translation of antagonism into agonism—political struggles in a democracy never reach the level of radical antagonism, all antagonisms are transposed into agonisms regulated by the democratic form. Democracy is thus transcendental, in the precise sense of Kantian formalism: the big Other is deprived of its substance, but it survives as the empty form. And, again in Kantian terms, divine violence is the terrifying point of the *direct intervention of the noumenal into the phenomenal*. Divine violence

---

44   Quoted in Howard Zinn, *A People's History of the United States*, New York: HarperCollins 2001, pp. 96–7.
45   Quoted in ibid., p. 95.

is not a deplorable but inevitable use of violent means towards non-violent ends. Here, the "critique of instrumental reason" has done its job, demonstrating that means are never purely instrumental: the "means" we use to achieve emancipatory social ends have to display the character of these ends themselves, to act as their manifestation, otherwise we expose ourselves to the infamous Stalinist "dialectics" of violence and non-violence in which the state "withers away" by fortifying itself (especially its organs of control and oppression).

The problem for emancipatory politics is how to reintroduce into this democratic field the radical antagonism (the difference which cuts into the social itself in its universality, which admits no big Other, neither substantial nor formal) — and the solution is: the "dictatorship of the proletariat." "The time is out of joint; — O cursed spite, That ever I was born to set it right" — is this famous couplet from *Hamlet* (I, v) not a succinct description of the proletarian position? Are proletarians not the "out of joint" element in the social structure, "cursed" with the revolutionary task of setting things right? The "dictatorship of the proletariat" is ultimately indifferent towards formal democracy — what matters is not the mode of selection of the government, but the pressure exerted on it by the people's mobilization and self-organization. Does this notion of the "self-organization of the people" not surreptitiously imply a rehabilitation of populism? No, because the "people" referred to here are what one usually refers to as the *plebs*, the plebeian crowd, not the People of a populist project. What the plebs excludes is precisely the unity involved in the populist notion of the People.

One can see here how these intricacies of the notion of democracy directly involve philosophical premises: the Lefortian notion of democracy as relying on the empty place of power, on the logic of implying its own imperfection and endless self-correction, etc., is clearly Kantian (the Real is here simply impossible), while the passage from Kant to Hegel compels us to accept that the Real as impossible effectively takes place in the guise of democratic terror. In Hegelese: terror is the species of the genus of democracy in which democracy encounters itself, among its species, in its "oppositional determination," directly actualizing itself in its (abstract) universality. Pure democracy *has* to appear as its opposite: if it were to appear as democracy, we would effectively be in the "metaphysics of presence."

This identity of opposites does not mean that democracy is actual only inasmuch as it is "impure," in other words, that a fully-realized democracy cancels itself and turns into its opposite: democratic terror still *is* democracy. (Benjamin's name for this "democratic terror" is divine violence.) Where do we find it today? James Cameron's *Avatar*, an exemplary exercise in Hollywood Marxism, tells the story of a disabled ex-Marine sent from Earth to infiltrate a race of blue-skinned aborigines on a distant planet and persuade them to let his employer mine their homeland for natural resources; the aborigines live in harmony with nature and are simultaneously deeply spiritual. Predictably, the Marine falls in love with the beautiful aboriginal princess and eventually joins the aborigines in the final battle, helping them to throw out the human invaders and save their planet . . . It is easy to discern, beneath the obvious politically correct themes (the honest white guy siding with ecologically correct aborigines against the "military-industrial complex" of the imperialist invaders), a whole array of brutal racist motifs which circulate around the topic of "the man who would be king": a crippled outcast from Earth is good enough to win the hand of the local princess, and to help win the decisive battle. Furthermore, the idyllic portrait of the blue aborigines totally blinds us to their own oppressive hierarchies, which must surely be in place if they have a princess. The film's lesson is clear: the only choice the aborigines have is to be saved by the humans or destroyed by them, to be either the brutal victims of imperialist reality, or to play their allotted role in the white man's fantasy—in both cases, they become a plaything in human hands. The very hyper-reality of the film, with its combination of real actors and 3-D digital animation, renders palpable the fantasmatic status of life on the invaded planet.

At the same time this film was taking in money all around the world, reaching one billion dollars after less than three weeks on release, something strangely resembling its plot was taking place in the real world. The hills in the south of the Indian state of Orissa, inhabited by the Kondh tribe, were sold to mining companies who plan to exploit their immense reserves of bauxite (the deposits are considered to be worth at least 4 trillion dollars). In reaction, a Maoist (Naxalite) armed rebellion exploded, confirming the old saying that a natural resource can be a curse. The Maoists' guerrilla army

is made up almost entirely of desperately poor tribal people living in conditions of such chronic hunger that it verges on famine of the kind we only associate with sub-Saharan Africa. They are people who, even after sixty years of India's so-called Independence, have not had access to education, healthcare or legal redress. They are people who have been mercilessly exploited for decades, consistently cheated by small businessmen and money lenders, the women raped as a matter of right by police and forest department personnel. Their journey back to a semblance of dignity is due in large part to the Maoist cadres who have lived and worked and fought by their sides for decades. If the tribals have taken up arms, they have done so because a government which has given them nothing but violence and neglect now wants to snatch away the last thing they have — their land . . . They believe that if they do not fight for their land, they will be annihilated . . . their ragged, malnutritioned army, the bulk of whose soldiers have never seen a train or a bus or even a small town, are fighting only for survival.[46]

The Indian prime minister characterized this rebellion as the country's "single largest internal security threat"; the media, which present it as resistance to progress, are full of stories about "Red Terrorism," replacing stories about "Islamist Terrorism." No wonder that the Indian state is responding with a major military operation against "Maoist strongholds" in the jungles of central India. It is true that both sides have resorted to brutal violence, and that the Maoists' "people's justice" is harsh. However, no matter how unpalatable to our liberal tastes this may be, *we have no right to condemn it*. Why? Because the rebels' situation is precisely that of Hegel's rabble: the Naxalite in India are a starving tribal people to whom the minimum of a dignified life has been denied and who are fighting for their lives. But in contrast with Cameron's film, in Orissa there are no noble princesses waiting for the white hero to seduce them and help save their people; there are just the Maoists mobilizing the starving farmers. Perhaps the true avatar here is *Avatar* itself, the film substituting itself for reality.

The Agent

How, then, does the subject engaged in such divine violence function in his or her libidinal economy? As the exact opposite of the disengaged Hindu or Buddhist subject who, from a position of neutrality, exempt from all passion, observes the illusory "theater of shadows" into which he is thrown with his acts. An extreme case of the apocalyptic subject is provided by *The Grey Zone* (Tim Blake Nelson, 2001), set in

---

46   Arundhati Roy, "Mr Chidambaram's War," November 9, 2009, available at outlook.india.com.

Auschwitz-Birkenau in the Fall of 1944, among a *Sonderkommando* unit (prisoners selected to do the dirty job of taking victims to the gas chambers and then robbing and disposing of the bodies). These units were given much better conditions and more food, etc., though they knew they would all be liquidated after three or four months, in order to erase the traces of their work. In the middle of the film, there is an intriguing dialogue between two of these "privileged" Jewish prisoners — a top surgeon who does medical research on the corpses for the infamous Dr. Mengele, and an "ordinary" *Sonderkommando* who escorts the victims to the gas chambers, sorts out their bodies, and so on. The doctor (D) is a survivalist whose attitude is "I am just doing what I am told, I am not killing anyone," while the other (S) is more aware of the moral deadlock of his situation:

> D: "I never asked to be doing what I do."
> S: "You volunteered."
> D: "They wanted doctors for a hospital."
> S: "You knew the sort of work you'd be doing and you continue doing it."
> D: "I don't kill."
> S: "And we do?"
> D: "I didn't say that."
> S: "You give killing purpose."
> D: "We're just trying to make it to the next day, that's all any of us is doing."
> S: "You have no idea, do you?"
> D: "I don't know what you're talking about."
> S: "I do not wish to be alive when all of this is over."
> D: "I don't believe that."
> S: "I know you don't."

Twice the "ordinary" *Sonderkommando* makes the correct penetrating moral insight. First, he points out that, although his work is more "dirty" and comes closer to killing (he may not press the button to release the gas, but he does direct the victims to the chamber, convincing them it is just a shower room, sorts out the victims' clothing and packages, burns the corpses, etc.), the doctor's work (dissecting and analyzing selected corpses) is ethically much more problematic: the doctor "gives killing [a] purpose" by way of providing a medical justification. Second, the "ordinary" *Sonderkommando* outlines the extreme ethico-existential deadlock to which the doctor is blind on account of his survivalist stance, the deadlock of a subject aware that what he has done in order to survive has compromised him so much that there is now no way back to normality: given the obscenity of his actions, he has forfeited the right to normal life. If he is still alive "when all this is over," he will not be able to avoid committing suicide: what he has done can in no way be re-integrated into the "normal" coordinates of ethical decency. In the camp, he knows there is absolutely no hope for him; his situation is a nightmare, and once the nightmare is over, his life will have become impossible. A suicidal rebellion against the camp guards is thus not only the only ethical thing he can do, but also the only way out of an existential deadlock in which his sole choice is between the bad (the present nightmare) and the worse (normality).

There is, however, also an aspect of liberation in this radical deadlock — no wonder that a similar deadlock characterizes the subjective position of a radical revolutionary. Once I forfeit my right to a "normal life," I also, in a way, forfeit my right to "bare life," I cut off my link with mere survival, with clinging to life for life's sake, and join the "living dead," becoming someone who, in renouncing his right to life, thereby overcomes his fear of death. Imagine a revolutionary who, on account of his utter dedication to the political struggle, neglects his family and thereby loses his wife and children; his only justification for continuing to live remains his political struggle — were he no longer able to participate in it, there would be nothing left for him to do. One suspects that Brecht would have found such a position fascinating.

About an hour into Bernardo Bertolucci's film *1900*, there is a shockingly violent scene during a confrontation between the poor striking farmers and their landowner. The landowner explains that, due to catastrophic weather which has ruined the harvest, he has to cut the farmers' wages by half. Exasperated by their mute resistance to his "rational" arguments, he shouts at one of them: "Don't you have two big ears to hear me?" The farmer then takes a knife from his belt, and with one strike cuts off his left ear and offers it to the landowner who, terrified by this crazy gesture, runs away in a panic. This scene (structurally similar to the famous one from David Fincher's *Fight Club* where, during a confrontation with his boss, Edward Norton starts to beat his own face with his fist), with its logic of the realized metaphor ("Lend me your ears"), conveys in a harsh manner the price (the proverbial pound of flesh) one has to pay for liberation: the defiant offering of one's ear, with its implicit subversion: "Now I no longer have ears, I will not hear you, I am deaf to your arguments!"

Again, such a refusal, such a withdrawal or disconnection from the shared field of communication, is a condition sine qua non of freedom.

Is such a radical gesture of "striking at oneself" not constitutive of subjectivity as such? And does this not imply that the time of subjectivity is a priori the time of a state of emergency: being a subject means that things can never "return to normal"? In every "normal run of things," the subject who participates in it escapes the traumatic abyss that lies at the heart of subjectivity and "regresses" to a substantial mode of being, that is, reduces itself to a subordinated moment of a higher substantial order.

What, then, is to be done? How are we to choose between the three main options: (1) the "Bartleby politics" of doing nothing; (2) preparing for a radical violent Act, a total revolutionary upheaval; (3) engaging in local pragmatic interventions? Here we must insist first on the dialectical link between the particular and the universal, as a result of which the very focus on an apparently particular problem can trigger a global transformation. That is to say, the political effect of an intervention cannot be constrained by the tension between its enunciated content and the position of enunciation. In his propagandizing for *perestroika* and *glasnost*, Gorbachev undoubtedly spoke from the position of the ruling *nomenklatura*, with the aim only of rendering the Communist system more efficient. Nevertheless, by overestimating the amount of *perestroika* the system could integrate, he set in motion the system's disintegration—hence all those skeptics who warned that Gorbachev merely wanted to reform the system, to make it stronger, were proven wrong, although they had been in a sense correct. Sartre made a similar mistake when, in his belated but perspicuous analysis (written in 1970) of the vacuity of Khrushchev's 1956 "secret" report on Stalin's crimes to the twentieth Communist Party congress, he noted that

> it was *true* that Stalin had ordered massacres, transformed the land of the revolution into a police state; he was *truly* convinced that the USSR would not reach communism without passing through the socialism of concentration camps. But as one of the witnesses very rightly points out, when the authorities find it useful to tell the truth, it's because they can't find any better lie. Immediately this truth, coming from an official mouth, becomes a lie corroborated by the facts. Stalin was a wicked man? Fine. But how had Soviet society perched him on the throne and kept him there for a quarter of a century?[47]

---

47   Quoted in Ian H. Birchall, *Sartre Against Stalinism*, New York: Berghahn Books 2004, p. 166.

Indeed, was not Khrushchev's later fate (he was deposed in 1964) proof of Oscar Wilde's quip that, if one tells the truth, one will sooner or later be caught out? Sartre's analysis nonetheless falls short on one crucial point: Khrushchev's report *did* have a traumatic impact, even if he "was speaking in the name of the system: the machine was sound, but its chief operator was not; this saboteur had relieved the world of his presence, and everything was going to run smoothly again."[48] His intervention set in motion a process which ultimately brought down the system—a lesson worth remembering today. Our answer to the "What is to be done?" question raised above is thus simple: why impose a choice in the first place? A Leninist "concrete analysis of concrete circumstances" will make clear what the proper way to act in a given constellation might be—sometimes, pragmatic measures addressed to particular problems are appropriate; sometimes, as in a radical crisis, a transformation of the fundamental structure of society will be the only way to solve its particular problems; sometimes, in a situation where *plus ça change, plus ça reste la même chose*, it is better to do nothing than to contribute to the reproduction of the existing order.

We should always bear in mind the lesson first clearly elaborated by La Boétie in his treatise on *la servitude volontaire*: power (the subordination of many to one) is not an objective state of things which persists even if we ignore it, it is something that persists only with the participation of its subjects, only if it is actively assisted by them. What one should avoid here is the predicament of the Beautiful Soul described by Hegel: the subject who continually bemoans and protests his fate, all the while overlooking how he actively participates in the very state of things he deplores. We do not fear and obey power because it is in itself so powerful; on the contrary, power appears powerful because we treat it as such. This obscene collaboration with the oppressor is the topic of Ismail Kadare's *The Palace of Dreams*, a story of the Tabir Sarrail, the "palace of dreams" in the capital of an unnamed nineteenth-century Balkan empire (modeled on Turkey). In this gigantic building, thousands of palace bureaucrats assiduously sort, classify, and interpret the dreams of citizens systematically and continuously gathered from all parts of the empire. Their immense work of interpretation is Kafkaesque: intense yet a meaningless fake. The ultimate goal of their activity is to identify the Master-Dream that will provide clues to the destiny of the empire and of its sultan. This is why, although Tabir Sarrail is supposed to be a place of mystery exempt

---

48   Ibid.

from daily power struggles, what goes on there is inevitably caught up in such conflicts—which dream is to be selected (or perhaps even invented) as the Master-Dream becomes the subject of dark intrigues. The reasons for these struggles are nicely spelled out by Kadare:

> "In my opinion," Kurt went on, "it is the only organization in the State where the darker side of its subjects' consciousness enters into direct contact with the State itself."
>
> He looked around at everyone present, as if to assess the effect of his words.
>
> "The masses don't rule, of course," he continued, "but they do possess a mechanism through which they influence all the State's affairs, including its crimes. And that mechanism is the Tabir Sarrail."
>
> "Do you mean to say," asked the cousin, "that the masses are to a certain extent responsible for everything that happens, and so should to a certain extent feel guilty about it?"
>
> "Yes," said Kurt. Then, more firmly: "In a way, yes."[49]

In order properly to interpret these lines there is no need for any obscurantist thesis positing a "dark irrational link (or secret solidarity) between the crowd and its rulers." The question to be raised concerns *power (domination) and the unconscious*: how does power work, why do its subjects obey it? This brings us to the (misleadingly named) "erotics of power": subjects obey not only because of physical coercion (or the threat of it) and ideological mystification, but because they have a libidinal investment in power. The ultimate "cause" of power is the *objet a*, the object-cause of desire, the surplus-enjoyment by means of which power "bribes" those it holds in its sway. This *objet a* is given form in the (unconscious) fantasies of the subjects of power, and the function of Kadare's "Tabir Sarrail" is precisely to interpret those fantasies, to learn what kind of (libidinal) objects they are for their subjects. These obscure "feedback mechanisms"—between the subjects of power and its holders—regulate the subjects' subordination, such that if they are disturbed the power structure may lose its libidinal grip and dissolve.

The Palace of Dreams is, of course, itself an impossible fantasy: the fantasy of a power capable of directly managing its own fantasmatic support. And it is here that what we have called "Bartleby politics" enters: rather than actively resisting power, the Bartleby gesture of "preferring

---

49   Ismail Kadare, *The Palace of Dreams*, New York: Arcade Publishing 1998, p. 63.

not to" suspends the subject's libidinal investment in it—the subject stops dreaming about power. To put it in mockingly Stalinist terms, emancipatory struggle begins with the ruthless work of self-censorship and auto-critique—not of reality, but of one's own dreams.

The best way to grasp the core of the obsessive attitude is through the notion of *false activity*: you think you are active, but your true position, as embodied in the fetish, is passive. Do we not encounter something akin to this false activity in the typical strategy of the obsessive neurotic, who becomes frantically active in order to prevent the real thing from happening (in a tense group situation, the obsessive talks continually, cracks jokes, etc., in order to ward off that awkward moment of silence in which the underlying tension would become unbearable)? The "Bartleby act" is violent precisely insofar as it entails refusing this obsessive activity—in it, not only do violence and non-violence overlap (non-violence appears as the highest violence), so too do act and inactivity (here the most radical act is to do nothing). The "divine" dimension lies in this very overlapping of violence and non-violence.

If theology is again emerging as a point of reference for radical politics, it is so not by way of supplying a divine "big Other" who would guarantee the final success of our endeavors, but, on the contrary, as a token of our radical freedom in having no big Other to rely on. It was already Dostoevsky who showed how God gives us both freedom and responsibility—he is not a benevolent Master steering us to safety, but the one who reminds us that we are totally left to our own devices. This paradox lies at the very core of the Protestant notion of Predestination: Predestination does not mean that since everything is determined in advance we are not really free; rather, it involves an even more radical freedom than the ordinary one, the freedom to retroactively determine (that is, change) one's Destiny itself.[50]

The God we get here is rather like the one in the Bolshevik joke about a talented Communist propagandist who, after his death, finds himself sent to Hell. He quickly sets about convincing the guards to let him go to Heaven. When the Devil notices his absence, he pays a visit to God, to demand that the propagandist be returned to Hell. However, as soon

---

50   Catholicism is often seen as a compromise between "pure" Christianity and paganism—but what then is Christianity at the level of its notion? Protestantism? One should take a step further here: the only Christianity at the level of its notion, that is, which draws all the consequences from its basic event—the death of God—is atheism. Buenaventura Durutti, the famous Spanish anarchist, said: "*The only church that illuminates is a burning church.*" He was right, although not in the immediate anti-clerical sense in which his remark was intended: religion only arrives at its truth through its self-cancellation.

as the Devil begins his address, starting with "My Lord . . .," God interrupts him, saying: "First, I am not your Lord but a comrade. Second, are you crazy for talking to fictions—I don't even exist! And third, be quick, otherwise I'll miss my Party meeting!" This is the kind of God needed by the radical Left today: a God who has fully "become a man," a comrade amongst us, crucified together with two social outcasts, who not only "does not exist" but also *knows this himself*, accepts his own erasure, passing over entirely into the love that binds all members of the "Holy Ghost," that is, of the Party or emancipatory collective.

Index